BEST PRACTICES OF LITERACY LEADERS

BEST
PRACTICES
OF LITERACY
LEADERS

Keys to School Improvement

edited by
RITA M. BEAN
ALLISON SWAN DAGEN

THE GUILFORD PRESS
New York   London

© 2012 The Guilford Press
A Division of Guilford Publications, Inc.
72 Spring Street, New York, NY 10012
www.guilford.com

Printed in the United States of America

This book is printed on acid-free paper.

Last digit is print number: 9   8   7   6   5   4   3   2   1

Library of Congress Cataloging-in-Publication Data

Best practices of literacy leaders: keys to school improvement/
[edited by] Rita M. Bean, Allison Swan Dagen.
    p. cm.
  Includes bibliographical references and index.
  ISBN 978-1-60918-942-6 (hardback) — ISBN 978-1-60918-941-9 (paperback)
  1. School improvement programs.   2. Language arts.   3. Academic
achievement.   I. Bean, Rita M.   II. Swan Dagen, Allison.
  LB2822.82.B485 2012
  371.2′07—dc23

                                                        2011027910

About the Editors

Rita M. Bean, PhD, is Professor Emerita in the School of Education at the University of Pittsburgh. Her research focuses on the roles of the reading specialist and the literacy coach, professional development for teachers, and the evaluation of large-scale efforts to improve literacy instruction in the elementary school. Dr. Bean's book *The Reading Specialist: Leadership for the Classroom, School, and Community* (Second Edition, Guilford Press, 2009) addresses the leadership, instructional, and assessment roles of reading specialists.

Allison Swan Dagen, PhD, is Associate Professor in the College of Human Resources in Education at West Virginia University. Her research focuses on practices that affect literacy teacher/reading specialist preparation and ongoing professional development. In 2009, Dr. Swan Dagen received the Outstanding Researcher Award from the College of Human Resources in Education at West Virginia University.

Contributors

Patricia L. Anders, PhD, College of Education, University of Arizona, Tucson, Arizona

Rita M. Bean, PhD, School of Education, University of Pittsburgh, Pittsburgh, Pennsylvania

Jill Castek, PhD, Graduate School of Education, University of California, Berkeley, Berkeley, California

Lauren Catherwood, MST, Virginia Polytechnic Institute and State University, Blacksburg, Virginia

Renée T. Clift, PhD, College of Education, University of Arizona, Tucson, Arizona

Cynthia E. Coburn, PhD, Graduate School of Education, University of California, Berkeley, Berkeley, California

Janice A. Dole, PhD, Department of Educational Psychology, University of Utah, Salt Lake City, Utah

Susan Dougherty, EdD, Graduate School of Education, Rutgers, The State University of New Jersey, New Brunswick, New Jersey

Laurie Elish-Piper, PhD, Department of Literacy Education, Northern Illinois University, DeKalb, Illinois

Carolyn B. Gwinn, PhD, Anoka–Hennepin School District, Coon Rapids, Minnesota; Literacy Program, Bethel University, St. Paul, Minnesota

Afra Ahmed Hersi, PhD, Literacy Education Program, Teacher Education Department, Loyola University Maryland, Baltimore, Maryland

James V. Hoffman, PhD, Department of Curriculum and Instruction, The University of Texas at Austin, Austin, Texas

Jacy Ippolito, EdD, School of Education, Salem State University, Salem, Massachusetts

Jennifer Jones, PhD, College of Education and Human Development, Radford University, Radford, Virginia

Jennifer Jordan, PhD, Department of Theory and Practice in Teacher Education, College of Education, Health, and Human Sciences, University of Tennessee, Knoxville, Tennessee

Amanda Kloo, PhD, School of Education, University of Pittsburgh, Pittsburgh, Pennsylvania

Susan K. L'Allier, EdD, Department of Literacy Education, Northern Illinois University, DeKalb, Illinois

Suzanne Lane, PhD, School of Education, University of Pittsburgh, Pittsburgh, Pennsylvania

Laura M. Lester, MEd, Department of Curriculum and Instruction, Virginia Polytechnic Institute and State University, Blacksburg, Virginia

Joanna Lieberman, MEd, Cambridge Public Schools, Cambridge Massachusetts

Anne McGill-Franzen, PhD, Department of Theory and Practice in Teacher Education, College of Education, Health, and Human Sciences, University of Tennessee, Knoxville, Tennessee

Michael C. McKenna, PhD, Curry School of Education, University of Virginia, Charlottesville, Virginia

Heidi Anne E. Mesmer, PhD, Department of Teaching and Learning, School of Education, Virginia Polytechnic Institute and State University, Blacksburg, Virginia

Debra Moore, MA, Department of Psychology in Education, University of Pittsburgh, Pittsburgh, Pennsylvania

Kristin L. Nelson, PhD, Teacher Education Department, Weber State University, Ogden, Utah

Jodi Nichols, EdD, College of Education, Frostburg State University, Frostburg, Maryland

Jeanne R. Paratore, EdD, School of Education, Boston University, Boston, Massachusetts

Misty Sailors, PhD, College of Education and Human Development, The University of Texas at San Antonio, San Antonio, Texas

Allison Skerrett, PhD, Department of Curriculum and Instruction, The University of Texas at Austin, Austin, Texas

Lilly M. Steiner, EdD, School of Education, Monmouth University, West Long Branch, New Jersey

Allison Swan Dagen, PhD, College of Human Resources and Education, West Virginia University, Morgantown, West Virginia

MaryEllen Vogt, EdD, College of Education, California State University, Long Beach, Long Beach, California

Sharon Walpole, PhD, School of Education, University of Delaware, Newark, Delaware

Sarah L. Woulfin, MA, Graduate School of Education, University of California, Berkeley, Berkeley, California

Naomi Zigmond, PhD, School of Education, University of Pittsburgh, Pittsburgh, Pennsylvania

Preface

The challenges that schools face in the 21st century are many: the new and always changing technological tools available to students and teachers; the increasing diversity present in schools today; the ever-shifting policies of school districts, states, or the nation; and the demands for accountability from school districts, schools, and teachers through both value-added teacher evaluation and student achievement on mandated standardized tests. Such challenges have created pressures on schools and especially teachers, who must have the knowledge, skill sets, and dispositions that enable them, with support, to meet these challenges and to provide a high-quality education for every student.

Those who study schools, school reform, and school improvement highlight the importance of quality teachers and teaching and address issues of how to prepare and then support these personnel. Educators such as Fullan (2001) write about the importance of providing environments and opportunities that help teachers develop "habits of learning" (p. 253) that will prepare them to address the challenges that they face. These new demands and expectations are especially prevalent in the area of literacy, which permeates all curricular areas at all levels. As is often stated, students must not only learn literacy skills but they also must be able to use literacy to learn. In other words, literacy provides the foundation for learning.

There are two major themes that permeate all chapters of this book; these themes are supported by the research in the education field and reflect the beliefs and knowledge of the editors and authors of this text. Each theme is summarized below.

LITERACY LEADERSHIP IS EXEMPLIFIED
AND SHARED BY MANY IN SCHOOLS

In policy briefs, professional journals, and books, and at school board meetings of local school districts, there is an ever-growing awareness that these
new times call for new ways of functioning. An emerging message is that
leadership should be shared by many personnel in schools in ways that
reflect their expertise, unique knowledge, roles, and skills. In addition to
capable administrative leadership, there is also a need for leadership by all
those who educate students in schools: literacy coaches or facilitators, teachers, and specialized personnel, such as reading specialists, special educators,
speech and language teachers, and content teachers. Such leadership must
be seamless; it must flow top-down, bottom-up, and horizontally. Our belief
is that effective leadership, especially literacy leadership, can be the catalyst
for improving classroom practice and student learning. One of the essential
roles of the principal as a designated leader is to maximize opportunities
for others to assume leadership roles and to foster the capacity of others to
serve as leaders. Literacy personnel may have formal roles (e.g., the literacy
coach), or they may serve informally as leaders (e.g., the classroom teacher
who serves as chair of the curriculum committee). Special educators, psychologists, guidance counselors, and speech and language personnel all have
specialized knowledge that can enhance the literacy program in schools and,
as such, they also serve as literacy leaders.

LITERACY LEADERSHIP FUNCTIONS
MOST EFFECTIVELY IN A CULTURE
OF COLLABORATION

Our vision of shared leadership, described above, can only happen in a culture of collaboration, one that recognizes that each of us has the potential
to lead and that provides an opportunity for such leadership to flourish.
York-Barr and Duke (2004), in their review of research about teacher leadership, identify the following conditions as important for shared leadership
and collaboration: active support from both principal and colleagues, available time and resources, and opportunities to learn how to function as a
leader. When collaboration is encouraged—that is, when schools function
in ways in which staff members have opportunities to interact and talk
collegially about issues related to their own as well as student learning,
and are supported by administrators who recognize the importance of such
collaboration—then schools can become places of learning for both stu-

dents and teachers. The success of such collaborative initiatives requires that staff members serve as leaders as well as followers; that they share a vision, common goals, and a common language; and that they are involved in inquiry and reflection about how best to serve their students.

KEY FEATURES

In this book, our goal is to provide evidence-based information about literacy leadership in schools. In Part I, authors provide in-depth background and research about how specific role groups can contribute to student literacy learning. In Part II, authors with expertise in specific areas provide a summary of the key research about that aspect of literacy and then identify implications for those serving as literacy leaders in schools to consider. In Part III, authors address perspectives about special topics, such as technology, home–school partnerships, policy, and teacher learning. There are several key features in this book that lead to its usefulness and practicality.

- Each chapter begins with guiding questions that highlight the major concepts of the chapter and serve as an advanced organizer to promote thinking and understanding.
- The book addresses literacy leadership through the grades (kindergarten through grade 12), with specific chapters that address emergent literacy, as well as issues that affect elementary, middle, and high schools.
- There are two chapters that focus on the role of the literacy coach: one that addresses coaching in the elementary grades and another on coaching in middle and high schools.
- The authors are well-known authorities in the field, especially in the areas about which they are writing. Moreover, we have included experts from areas other than literacy, given that effective literacy instruction requires that we tap the expertise of those who can help us think about literacy from a different perspective or through a different lens.
- Each chapter includes a case example, specifically, a short problem that can be used by the individual reader to think about the concepts addressed in the chapter. These open-ended cases can also be used for small-group discussions.
- The end of each chapter features engagement activities, with the first activity always related to the case example presented in that chap-

ter. We also include, when appropriate, activities that ask readers to
think about connections between and among chapters in this book.

CONTENT

In Chapter 1, Bean provides the background and the conceptual framework
for the book, which is that literacy leaders in grades K–12 must be focused
on improving instruction for students and that all staff members in schools
have the responsibility to serve as leaders. Bean discusses leadership in general and then summarizes the literature and research that address the importance of literacy leadership. She concludes by suggesting practical ideas for
literacy leaders in schools.

In Chapter 2, Swan Dagen and Nichols discuss the critical roles
and responsibilities classroom teachers can assume in informal and formal leadership positions. These roles involve working with a variety of
stakeholders: other teachers, administrators, parents, community members, and students. The chapter also presents characteristics of teacher
leaders and concludes by exploring conditions and outcomes of teacher
leadership.

In Chapter 3, L'Allier and Elish-Piper describe the role of the literacy
coach in the elementary school, using evidence from their own as well
as others' research to identify the activities of coaching that make a difference in promoting teacher and student learning. They also discuss the
challenges that these coaches face and present a model of coaching that
can be used for reflecting on the approach to coaching in elementary
schools.

In Chapter 4, Ippolito and Lieberman describe the role of literacy
coaches in secondary schools and then address important questions about
how these coaches might organize their time to work effectively with principals and teachers of various content areas. They also describe the importance of collaboration and teacher leadership as a means of developing sus-
tainability.

Zigmond and Kloo, in Chapter 5, provide a brief historical description
of the evolution of special education in the United States and also discuss the
"balancing act" that special educators must address. They emphasize the
fact that special educators serve as literacy leaders and at the same time have
responsibilities for providing the "special" instruction needed by students
who have difficulties learning.

In Chapter 6, Walpole and McKenna discuss research about the leadership role of the principal and then illustrate how one middle school principal
applied his knowledge of the research findings to his work. The authors pro-

vide many references and resources for those wanting to learn more about how principals can function more effectively to build leadership capacity in the school.

In Chapter 7, McGill-Franzen and Jordan discuss emergent literacy and highlight the changes that have occurred in terms of expectations for young readers and writers. They focus on the importance of the reading and writing connection and suggest practical ideas for how to incorporate such instruction in classrooms.

In Chapter 8, Dole and Nelson describe the role of the literacy leader in the elementary school. They use the Standards for Reading Professionals (International Reading Association, 2010) as a framework for their chapter. They discuss the importance of Common Core State Standards for Language Arts and its implications for literacy leaders. Finally, they describe the importance of selecting appropriate materials for students and suggest sources that might be useful to literacy leaders responsible for selecting such materials.

Anders and Clift, in Chapter 9, discuss the ways that research about language, reading as a meaning-making and social activity, and the growth of technology (i.e., new literacies) have influenced secondary reading program development. They also describe specific examples of one secondary school's reading initiative and how that effort changed the ways that the school functioned and also influenced student learning.

In Chapter 10, Sailors and Hoffman discuss the role of a print-rich environment in student achievement. They also present a framework for evaluating a print-rich environment focusing on types of texts found in high-achieving classrooms as compared to low-achieving classrooms. Finally, they present implications for practice.

In Chapter 11, Mesmer, Jones, Catherwood, and Lester address the topic of differentiation, providing the research base that establishes its importance and discussing principles that are important for understanding it. They follow this discussion with explicit and pragmatic suggestions for helping teachers differentiate instruction in their classrooms.

In Chapter 12, Skerrett and Hersi provide in-depth information about the knowledge and understanding that literacy leaders must have if schools are to provide effective culturally responsive instruction that accommodates the linguistic and cultural diversity found in classrooms. They address issues related to materials, language diversity, social justice, technology, and assessment.

In Chapter 13, Vogt summarizes the research related to instruction for English learners and then discusses a specific framework, sheltered instruction observation protocol (SIOP), which describes what literacy leaders should see in classrooms where effective instruction for English learners occurs. She also addresses the specific needs of adolescents who are English learners.

Lane and Moore, in Chapter 14, discuss the ways that recent educational legislation has influenced assessment and then describe sources of validity evidence. They also describe recent modifications in assessment design that may positively affect literacy assessment. Finally, they discuss the strengths and weaknesses of specific assessment measures used for students who are beginning readers.

In Chapter 15, Castek and Gwinn discuss how the new technologies are transforming how reading and writing are taught in grades K–12. They also describe the ways in which standards create new opportunities for using technology. In a final section, they present specific examples of professional development that literacy leaders may find useful for their own and teacher learning.

In Chapter 16, Paratore, Steiner, and Dougherty provide a research base that establishes the importance of parental involvement in schools. They also discuss the challenges that might hinder parental involvement, as well as issues of parental role construction, self-efficacy, and access to resources. They conclude by providing specific ideas that literacy leaders might use in enhancing the role of parents as partners.

In Chapter 17, Woulfin and Coburn address the issues of reading policies and their effect on classroom practices. They discuss various factors, including prior knowledge, teacher beliefs, and context, that influence teachers' acceptance or rejection of specific policies. They conclude by discussing implications for how literacy leaders might work with teachers to ensure understanding and acceptance of new policy guidelines.

Finally, in Chapter 18, Bean and Swan Dagen summarize for readers the key themes of the book, highlight the research related to the school as a place of learning for teachers and students, and suggest specific ideas for how schools can implement effective job-embedded professional development in a culture that promotes shared leadership and collaboration.

For us, this book is the culmination of years of experience, first serving in the schools as teachers and reading specialists, and then as teacher educators working with teachers, administrators, and literacy personnel to help create learning environments that promote high-level student thinking and learning. It has been rewarding to collaborate with the authors of the chapters, whose views of literacy and literacy leadership have helped us formulate the themes that permeate this book. Educators must take collective responsibility for improving student learning in a school and such responsibility can be enhanced through shared leadership and collaboration.

REFERENCES

Fullan, M. (2001). *The new meaning of educational change* (3rd ed.). New York: Teachers College Press.

International Reading Association (2010). *Standards for reading professionals (revised).* Newark, DE: Author.

York-Barr, J., & Duke, K. (2004). What do we know about teacher leadership? Findings from two decades of scholarship. *Review of Educational Research, 74*(3), 255–316.

Contents

PART I

MULTIPLE ROLES IN SCHOOL LEADERSHIP

1

Literacy Leadership in a Culture of Collaboration

RITA M. BEAN

Guiding Questions

- How is leadership defined in this book, and why is such leadership essential in schools?
- Why is literacy leadership an essential ingredient in school improvement (K–12)?
- What are the research findings that support the importance of leadership as a distributed process?
- What does the research evidence suggest in terms of how to promote effective literacy leadership in schools?

During the past several decades, much has been written about the need for changes in how schools (K–12) function; phrases such as *school reform, school restructuring,* or *school improvement* are commonly used to describe such initiatives. The demand for such change comes from the recognition that too few schools provide a high-quality education for all the students they serve. There is a need to develop more schools that provide a first-class education for all students, an education that enables students to successfully compete in the highly technological world in which they live and to be college and career ready. In many of the materials written about school change, readers can find references to the importance of school leadership as a critical ingredient for school success. Much emphasis has been given, in fact, to the importance of the school principal who in his or her role as leader, is a leading agent of change and a major contributor to school success, especially student achievement (Murphy, 1988; Leithwood, Seashore-Louis, Anderson, & Wahlstrom, 2004; Marzano, Waters, & McNulty, 2005; Bryk, Sebring, Allensworth, Luppescu, & Easton, 2010). At the same time, as highlighted in this book, there is a need for leadership by others in the school (e.g., classroom teachers, reading specialists/literacy coaches, special educators) as a means of enhancing the educational program for students.

In the case example below, I describe the dilemma faced by Brenda, a reading specialist in an urban school whose position changed from working with students who were experiencing difficulty in reading, to one in which she was asked to support teachers in their efforts to improve literacy instruction and student achievement.

CASE EXAMPLE

Brenda had served as the reading specialist (K–5) in an urban elementary school for 6 years. She worked both in the classroom and in a pullout setting with students who had been identified as needing additional reading support. It had taken Brenda several years to develop a program that, in her view, was effective. Teachers were comfortable with her being in the classroom and they had established a routine where Brenda would work with identified students during the time that other students were involved in working independently in centers or with the classroom teacher. Brenda felt as though she knew the students and teachers; moreover, she felt as though students with whom she was working were making steady progress. However, district administrators, concerned about the lack of overall student progress, had applied for and received funding from a state grant that had several stipulations. First, each school would need to employ a literacy coach to work with teachers as a means of improving classroom instruction. Second, the school district had agreed that it would rethink its approach to reading instruction. There would be more emphasis on writing and more focus on reading in the content areas, especially in grades 3–5. Given Brenda's experience and her excellent rapport with teachers, she was asked to assume this role in the school. After her meeting with the principal and the assistant superintendent (who told Brenda that they saw great promise in this new initiative, especially with her involvement), Brenda begin to think about what this change in role meant. She sighed: What would the teachers who were her colleagues think about this? What did *she* think about this? What did it mean for her current students? How would she begin? And did she have the knowledge, leadership, communication, and interpersonal skills to effectively handle these new responsibilities?

Many reading specialists, teachers, principals, or other specialized personnel have faced similar dilemmas as expectations change for how personnel work to promote student learning. Teachers are expected to work with grade-level teams, to discuss their teaching with peers, and to participate as members of leadership teams. Such expectations are prevalent for those who are literacy leaders; literacy cuts across all subject lines and provides both the foundation for student learning and the means by which students at higher grade levels learn. In this chapter, I describe the notion of leadership promoted in this book and why such leadership is essential in schools. I also provide a summary of the research and literature that undergirds that definition and highlight some of the practical implications for literacy leaders in schools. I conclude by identifying ideas that may help literacy leaders such as Brenda work effectively with colleagues.

WHAT IS LEADERSHIP?

As I reflected on my own experiences as a teacher and reading specialist, many years ago, I realized that I was fortunate to work in a district that believed teachers had to be involved in setting goals for the various curricular areas and in making decisions about curriculum and instruction. I served as chair of the Elementary Reading Committee and with representatives from each different grade level, developed a proposal for an elementary reading curriculum that was then submitted to administration for their review. At the same time, teacher colleagues were doing the same in the areas of math, social studies, and science. The four of us who chaired these committees also met with principals of the four elementary schools and the assistant superintendent to discuss the relationships between what each of us was proposing and the more general goals for the school. In other words, we were leaders in our schools, working in what today might be called a "professional learning community." Although I didn't realize it at the time, those experiences were crucial in helping me learn how to work collegially while also building my understanding of what an effective reading program is, how it relates to the other academic subjects, and the need for helping teachers integrate all they do into meaningful learning experiences for students. Fast forward! We now have strong evidence that those schools in which leadership among professional personnel is encouraged and promoted, in which teachers collectively have a voice in what and how to teach, is an important ingredient in promoting student learning. (Bryk et al., 2010; Little, 2003; Louis, Leithwood, Wahlstrom, & Anderson, 2010; Marzano, 2003).

So, on to the question of leadership. Offering a definition of leadership is not easy because of the many different ways in which leadership is defined. Some view leadership as a function of *position* (the superintendent, the principal); individuals find themselves in positions of power that give them the authority to be leaders. Others describe leadership as *traits*: leaders are flexible, fair, and passionate about what they do; in other words, "leaders are born, not made." Some describe a *style* of leadership (democratic, laissez-faire, authoritative). However, leadership in this book is all of these and more. We recognize that there are many leaders in schools, both formal and informal, who lead by *influence,* that is, they encourage, nudge, and persuade colleagues in ways that effect change in practices and policies. The specific definition of individual leadership in this book is similar to one proposed by Kaser, Mundry, Stiles, and Loucks-Horsley (2002): "an individual's ability to work with others to accomplish some agreed-upon end" (p. 2). Leithwood and Jantzi (2008) describe four categories of leadership activities or functions: (1) setting goals or directions for the school; (2) developing people, that is, providing professional development that helps individuals grow as professionals; (3) redesigning the organization, that is, changing the school structure so that it facilitates the work of teachers and promotes student learning; and (4) managing the instructional program, that is, using data to monitor student and school progress, establishing routines and procedures that facilitate efforts to achieve school goals, and selecting approaches that meet the specific needs of students.

Leadership in this book then refers to more than traits, style, or position; rather it describes a set of actions. Teachers serve as leaders in many ways: mentoring colleagues; facilitating the work of tutors, volunteers, or student teachers; identifying student needs and possible instructional strategies for addressing those needs; working with parents; and so on. Reading specialists or literacy coaches, although they have a position that indicates they are leaders in the school, generally don't have the positional authority to "require" teachers to make changes, and so on, rather, they serve as leaders by providing insights and resources, and influencing others to consider ideas for change (Bean, 2010a). They also lead because of their specific knowledge or expertise, often working with the principal to make recommendations about the materials or instructional approaches being used in the classroom. Specialized personnel, such as special educators, psychologists, guidance counselors, and speech and language teachers, bring knowledge that can inform others about how to address various problems in the school; for example, what are some additional ways of promoting positive behavior in students? And principals, in addition to their traditional role as designated leader, facilitate the leadership of others in the school by helping to create the conditions that support such behavior. Such leadership, as Elmore (2000) states, is "the guidance and direction of instructional improvement" (p. 13).

As Lambert (1998) describes it, "leadership is about learning together, and constructing meaning and knowledge collectively and collaboratively" (p. 5). Such a definition highlights the importance of building capacity in schools and recognizes the importance of multiple leaders in schools, some with positional authority and others without. In schools with such a shared leadership model, there is the recognition that the adults as well as students are learners. Moreover, leadership will not look the same across individuals or schools; some leaders will work with other teachers to improve instruction (i.e., coaching); others will chair committees or serve on task forces; all will lead in their daily work with others by raising questions, identifying solutions to problems, suggesting alternatives, and so on. I'm reminded of a teacher who told me that in her early years as a teacher, she would go to the principal and "ask" if she could try a new approach or use alternative materials with her students. As she said, "now I go to the principal and present my rationale for why I want to use something different." In a sense, this experienced teacher felt a sense of self-efficacy and empowerment, recognizing that she had the responsibility and the right to make recommendations that would improve instruction for her students as long as she could present a sound rationale for her perspective. She also felt comfortable going to this principal, knowing that her views and perspectives would be heard; the climate in that school was one that promoted teacher risk taking and involvement in decision making.

The concept of leadership reflected in this book is that of a shared perspective of distributed leadership (Spillane, Halverson, & Diamond, 2001). In such a perspective, leadership does not refer to the actions of an individual, but what various individuals know and do together—in other words, their interactions with each other. Distributed perspective defines leadership as a "system of practice comprised of a collection of interacting components: leaders, followers, and situation" (Spillane, 2005, p. 150). As such, one must understand not only the actions of various individuals but also the interactions among them. For example, in one school, the principal, with little literacy background, might rely greatly on the expertise of the literacy coach in making decisions about instructional approaches, grouping, and scheduling. In another school, the principal, with a master's in reading, might work much more collaboratively with the literacy coach or reading specialist, taking on much more responsibility for decision making about instructional approaches, and so on. In both cases, leadership is shared, but the way in which that leadership is distributed is different. In other words, the issue is not that leadership is distributed, but rather *how* it is distributed.

So, as mentioned previously, leadership will not look the same in different schools; rather, leadership can be stretched over or distributed across individuals and situations (Spillane et al., 2001) depending on the expertise, experience, or preferences of individuals. Leadership "is not simply a function of an individual leader's ability, skill, charisma, and cognition" (p. 27). In fact, in an intriguing book about leadership in business organizations, *Good to Great,* Collins (2001), like other researchers, found that leadership was an important factor in companies identified as going from good to great. Unexpectedly, however, these leaders, rather than being charismatic and autocratic, were humble, determined, and modest. Their leadership emphases were on building leadership capacity in the organization and supporting the growth of leadership skills and abilities of others. Collins's findings have implications for schools and their leaders, and they support the notion of distributed and shared leadership as a means of improving the organization, teacher practices, and ultimately, the desired outcome, that of student learning.

Stoelinga (2008) presents examples of three schools to illustrate the relationships among principals, more formal teacher leaders such as literacy coaches or coordinators, and teachers who serve as informal leaders in the school. The findings illustrate the impact of the informal relationships that exist in an organization on the ways in which a formal teacher leader (i.e., the literacy coordinator) enacted his or her role. For example, in one school, where teachers valued autonomy, there were several strong, informal teacher leaders who were resistant to the literacy coordinator in the role of mentor or coach. This literacy coordinator, with only 4 years of teaching experience, had little influence on instructional practices in classrooms. In another school, the literacy coordinator had a well-defined and focused role for mentoring teachers; teachers identified this coordinator, the principal, and the bilingual coordinator as important resources about literacy. In the third school, the literacy coach, the principal, and a sixth-grade teacher, were all seen as key resources. However, the literacy coordinator's role was to tie together the many different programs in the school and spent little time mentoring individuals. These three cases illustrate the different ways by which informal networks can influence the work of colleagues in schools. Stoelinger concludes that informal teacher leaders in schools can have a powerful influence on school improvement or reform in a positive or negative way. Moreover, her work provides a clear illustration about the complexity of leadership as an influence on school change or reform. In discussing or studying leadership, attention must be given to the impact of factors such as school organization or culture, and the experiences, beliefs, and values of school personnel.

WHY LITERACY LEADERSHIP IS ESSENTIAL

Although much of the previous discussion addresses leadership in general, the focus of this text is on literacy leadership in schools. There are few who would dispute the notion that one of the critical keys to future success for students is their ability to read, write, think, and communicate, that is, to be proficient with language and literacy. For schools, the ultimate test of school effectiveness (agree or disagree) is often the school's ability to achieve Adequate Yearly Progress (AYP) on one or more standardized test of reading. Several important factors contribute to an even greater emphasis on literacy learning.

- *Common Core Standards for English Language Arts and Literacy in History/Social Studies, Science and Technical Subjects (2010)*. These standards, adopted by a majority of the states, call for an effort by schools to ensure that "all students are college and career ready in literacy by no later than the end of high school" (p. 1). What is significant is that the standards address literacy, not only in the English language arts, but also in the social and natural sciences. In other words, teachers in the various academic disciplines also need to assume responsibility for literacy learning as a means of helping students learn content. In order to accomplish the goals of these standards, schools will need to develop a comprehensive, coherent literacy program for a full range of learners, including gifted students, learners who need Title 1 or compensatory services, and learners requiring special education support. Likewise, such a program must have high expectations for all students, providing them with access to effective learning experiences. Literacy leaders will need to work with school personnel to address issues of both horizontal and vertical alignment. In other words, are the expectations in all third-grade classrooms in a specific school similar, that is, is there horizontal alignment, for example, in complexity of assignments and reading materials, and so on? Also, is there vertical alignment from grade to grade, and especially at important transition points when students may be asked to learn in new and different ways, for example, what are the expectations for kindergarten students when they come to school? For grade 3 students entering 4th grade? For students entering middle school? For students entering high school?

- *Technological demands of the 21st century*. Technology has affected both teaching and learning. Teachers must learn new ways of using technology, its limitations, and benefits. At the same time, students, because of their access to and familiarity with technology, often need instructional support as to how to judge the merit of various resources, and how to use various technological tools appropriately and effectively.

- *Diversity in the schools*. The population in our schools is changing and as it does, the challenge to meet the needs of all students, those who are culturally, ethnically, racially, or language different puts a great demand on literacy learning in the schools.

- *Differentiating instruction*. Teachers must be able to address the specific instructional needs of students effectively, using a variety of approaches, materials, and groupings. Many schools are using response to intervention

(RTI) as a framework for making decisions about assessing students' needs, planning, and implementing instructional programs. RTI, built into the reauthorization of the Individuals with Disabilities Education Act (IDEA) of 2004 calls for a focus on prevention for identifying and providing support for students who are not achieving.

These factors as well as others have created challenges for teachers, specialized personnel, and administrators in schools and have stimulated the need for new ways of functioning. Teachers are learning from each other, and often, there are support personnel (e.g., facilitators, coaches, resource teachers) available to help build teacher knowledge and promote effective instructional practice. As one of my colleagues often said, "Business as usual must give way to unusual business!" In the chapters in this text, authors address each of the factors mentioned above as well as others (e.g., parent involvement, assessment, curriculum) that often prove challenging to school leaders.

RESEARCH RELATED TO LITERACY LEADERSHIP IN SCHOOLS

In the following section, I describe and summarize key research studies that address school leadership, often literacy leadership, and highlight specific conclusions that we can draw from the research. The findings of these studies can be summarized as follows: a shared perspective of distributed leadership is a factor in school improvement; teachers learn from each other; and distributed leadership occurs in a culture of collaboration.

Distributed Leadership Is a Key Factor in School Improvement

Previously, I had cited the work of Bryk et al. (2010) in which they describe the cumulative body of research conducted over a 10-year period in the Chicago public schools. Bryk and colleagues collected and analyzed information from a large number of schools, including some that had substantially improved and others that had not. They identified a number of critical ingredients for school success, each of which is essential for student learning. Leadership, however, was identified as the "driving subsystem for improvement" (p. 61). Although they emphasized the importance of the principal as leader, they were clear that the principal cannot transform a school alone, and that there is a need to bring all partners—teachers, parents, and community members—into leadership roles as a means of building school capacity. They highlighted the importance of school leaders in engaging teachers and providing opportunities for them to lead as well. In other words, they acknowledged the importance of promoting the growth of a professional community that is guided by a shared vision and a coherent strategic plan. Bryk et al. use as their metaphor of school improvement, "baking a cake," indicating that just like baking a cake, all of the critical ingredients (flour, sugar, eggs, etc.) are important; if any is missing, the result suffers. Likewise, there is less possibility of student learning unless five core elements are in place. First, there must be *instructional guidance*, which refers to curricular alignment; in other words, there must be a coordinated set of goals, both vertically (across grades) and horizontally (within a grade). Second, efforts to build *professional capacity* are critical; teachers must be knowledgeable about the subjects they teach, and in addition, schools must provide the professional development essential for ongoing teacher learning. Such professional development includes building a community where teachers interact about their instructional practices and problems, and seek solutions for improving curriculum and instruction. Third, *parent–community–school ties* are essential for school success. Fourth, the *school learning climate* must be one in which students feel safe, there is a sense of order, and students value learning. Again, the fifth essential core, the catalyst for school change, is *school leadership*, and according to Bryk and colleagues, some form of distributed leadership is key.

Louis et al. (2010) conducted an extensive 6-year study of 180 schools in 43 districts across nine states, to investigate the influence of school, district, and state leadership on student learning. They found that school leadership was second only to classroom instruction as an influence on student learning and that many different people exercised formal or informal leadership in schools and districts. Specifically, they found that student achievement was linked to what they call *collective leadership,* in which educators, parents, and others have a voice in making school decisions. They found that such leadership can take many patterns, determined by the specific personnel and/or situation in the school. Louis et al. found that the principal not only played an important role as instructional leader but also established conditions that promoted effective instruction. Several key implications include the importance of focusing on specific goals and expectations for student learning by providing professional development for teachers and creating a structure in which teachers collaborate. They also indicated that less is known about leadership at the secondary level, but that most frequently, department chairs, or those who have special expertise in various content areas, provide important leadership for other teachers. Specifically, they highlight the fact that the principal in such a situation cannot possess the knowledge necessary to be an instructional leader for all subject areas, but again must set the conditions for collective leadership among teachers.

Teachers Learn from Each Other

Supovitz, Sirinides, and May (2010) investigated the influence of both principals and peers on teachers' instructional practice and student learning. Survey data to address questions about principal and teacher leadership were collected from teachers in a midsized urban district with a large number of schools. Although Supovitz et al. found that principal leadership was critical, they also found that peers had a great deal of influence on each other through collaborative discussions about teaching and learning, peer coaching, and instructional advice networks. These authors "found empirical evidence that principal leadership influences student learning indirectly through teachers' instructional practices" (p. 45); they also found that teacher peers influenced each others' classroom practices. The influence of both principals and peers was also significantly related to literacy learning. Supovitz et al. also highlighted the fact that principals had the greatest impact on learning when they fostered a climate of instructional collaboration and communication; in other words, principals "work through other leaders in schools to influence what goes on inside of classrooms" (p. 47).

Marzano (2003) synthesized 35 years of research in his book, *What Works in Schools: Translating Research into Action*. One of the school factors that he identifies as critical for improving schools is that of collegiality and professionalism defined as "the manner in which staff members in the school interact and the extent to which they approach their work as professionals" (p. 60). He suggests three action steps to foster such collegiality. First, schools must establish norms of conduct and behavior (i.e., identifying how staff members will address and solve professional issues). Second, Marzano promotes teacher involvement in making decisions and setting policies; and third, teachers must participate in meaningful professional development activities. Such professional activities need to be focused on content, include active learning opportunities, and be perceived as a coherent whole with a sequence of learning activities that build on previous ones. In other words, Marzano's work highlights the need for shared leadership in schools with opportunities for teachers, as well as students, to be ongoing learners.

One of the approaches in schools that can lead to a shared concept of distributed leadership and teacher collaboration is that of the notion of professional learning communities. Vescio, Ross, and Adams (2008) provide a review of 11 studies that contain empirical evidence about the impact of professional learning communities (PLCs) on both teaching practice and student learning, most frequently, literacy learning. Their findings include (1) teachers in these studies appreciated and valued PLCs, (2) PLCs had an impact on practice as "teachers became more student centered" (p. 88), and (3) there were improvements in student achievement. The notion of learning communities is discussed in more depth in Chapter 18.

Distributed Leadership Occurs in a Culture of Collaboration

Distributed leadership cannot occur in isolation; rather, it requires "creating a common culture, a set of values, symbols, and rituals" (Elmore, 2000, p. 15). Elmore discusses Rosenheltz's (1986) work in which she describes two types of cultures: collegial or teacher autonomy. In a collegial culture, teachers have an agreed upon and coherent set of goals. In cultures where there is teacher autonomy, the focus is on individual goals and teachers are accountable to no one; rather, they work in isolation. Leana and Pil (2006), in a study of schools in a large urban district, found that the interactions and relationships among teachers and administrators, what they termed *social capital,* were essential for improved student achievement. Some of the dimensions of social capital included a shared vision or common goals for student outcomes, sense of responsibility for all students, high expectations for student learning, and a belief that all students can learn. Creating a collaborative culture is not easy; it requires excellent leadership on the part of the principal and a recognition that the adaptive challenges in schools today require a new style of leadership. Heifetz and Laurie (2002) identify a number of principles related to this new style of leadership; they include:

- View the situation from a distance or as they state it, "get on the balcony and off the dance floor" (p. 1). In other words, try to see the situation from a different perspective, or step away from the conflict or controversy, thinking about it from an outsider's point of view. What are the beliefs or thoughts of students, parents, or perhaps a small group of teachers that have been identified as resistant or negative?
- Identify the specific challenges and the conflicts that might exist about values and norms.
- Regulate distress by maintaining a balance between pressure and support. Consider the demands that are placed on teachers (i.e., multiple and perhaps conflicting initiatives, overemphasis on test scores). Be deliberate in setting the rate of change. Aim high but at the same time provide the support needed to achieve the set goals.
- Value the diversity and different perspectives of colleagues. There will always be differences among individuals; effective leaders recognize and value those differences. Moreover, individuals differ in the time they need to adjust to change.
- Instill a sense of self-confidence in the staff as a whole; they can address the challenges. Individuals within the school have different areas of expertise that they can bring to the table.
- Protect those who lead from those who might be negative. Encourage

a sense of risk taking among the staff so that they feel comfortable raising issues.

Vescio et al. (2008), in their study, found that PLCs had an impact on the culture in schools because of the collaboration among teachers, the focus on student learning, and the increased decision-making opportunities for teachers; what Vescio et al. call "teacher authority" (p. 88). These decisions were made based on student data and teachers' knowledge of effective instructional approaches and materials. Likewise, Saunders, Goldenberg, and Gallimore (2009), who were interested in PLCs, conducted a 5-year, quasi-experimental study comparing achievement gains between nine experimental and six matched elementary schools. In the experimental schools, grade-level teams were given time to meet, support for their efforts, and explicit protocols that focused on how to meet students' needs. The authors concluded that teachers need to be provided with structural opportunities and skills to focus on improving their practices. They also highlight the fact that just providing time and support is not enough; collaborative work must take place under the right conditions with appropriate leadership.

Just recently, I had the opportunity to observe in schools in which I saw distributed leadership in action. I was asked by the Pennsylvania Technical Training and Technical Assistance Network (PaTTAN) to visit schools as a means of getting a better sense of how the role of specialized personnel had changed because of the schools' involvement in the response to instruction and intervention (RTII) initiative in the state. I observed in five elementary schools involved in the RTII initiative (Bean, 2010b). Given the goals of RTII, which highlight the importance of providing effective core, supplemental, and intensive instruction for students, the purpose of the observations and interviews was to get a more in-depth picture of how personnel in the school were working together and what skill sets they needed to function effectively. One of the key findings that relate to the topic of this chapter was that these schools functioned effectively because of the shared leadership and collaboration among staff. Figure 1.1 describes visually the interactions that occurred at all of the schools. It identifies the ways in which various personnel influenced and were influenced by others. All personnel were involved and represented in instructional goal setting and decision making; although principals served as the central figures for promoting a positive school climate and establishing norms for collaboration, district understanding and support were essential. Moreover, in each school, there was a leadership team that included reading specialists or coaches, special educators, the principal, and often the psychologist or teacher of English Language Learners; this team reviewed schoolwide data, discussed successes and challenges, and made suggestions about ways to support teachers in their efforts to improve student learning. Each school also had teacher

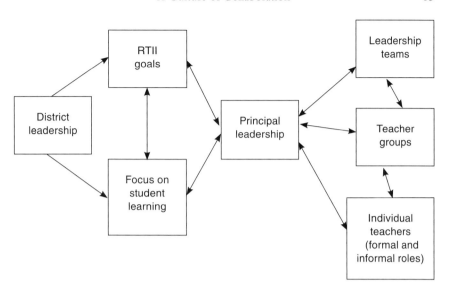

FIGURE 1.1. Shared leadership. Adapted from Bean, 2010b, p. 2, with permission of the Pennsylvania Department of Education.

groups, generally grade level teams, that met to discuss student learning and how they might modify instruction to meet student needs. At times, reading specialists or coaches met with these teams to facilitate the meetings or simply to gain a better understanding of how they, the specialists, might better support teachers' work. Finally, individual teachers also served as literacy leaders in the schools. Teachers with formal roles, that is, reading specialists and coaches, special educators, speech and language teachers, often met with classroom teachers on an individual basis to problem solve or provide guidance. Likewise, classroom teachers with experience or special expertise often functioned informally and were sought out by their peers as a source of information or reassurance. In other words, the culture in these schools was such that collaboration was the norm. What was also evident was the importance of district guidelines and support.

This finding is similar to those of Leithwood and Jantzi (2008), who in their study addressed several questions about the importance of leadership. They were interested in the extent to which district leadership and district organizational conditions influenced school leader efficacy and found that the effects of this leadership were largely indirect; that is, district leaders created conditions that were important for enhancing and supporting the work of schools leaders. They also found that building a collaborative culture was important. Likewise, Camburn, Kimball, and Lowenhaupt (2008), in a case study of a literacy coach initiative, identified the ways that district guidelines and support can serve to either promote or dilute the potential effectiveness of such an initiative. They highlight the need for both district guidance and acknowledgment of the specific needs of individual schools. In other words, district guidelines must allow for the individual differences and needs of specific schools in the district.

In the following section, I describe an example of a specific school reform effort that provides an excellent example of the notion of a shared perceptive of distributed leadership and the importance of a culture of collaboration.

EXAMPLE OF A SCHOOL REFORM EFFORT

Taylor, Pearson, Peterson, and Rodriguez (2005) studied both school-level programming and classroom-level practices on reading achievement in 13 schools involved in a school reform effort. A well-developed, research-based framework for literacy instruction was implemented and studied over a 2-year period. Several of their findings have relevance to the notion of literacy leadership in this book. First, in those schools identified as high implementers of reform, teachers met regularly to share successes and deal with schoolwide issues, and there were effective internal leadership teams. Further, the more elements of the school reform model implemented, the greater the growth in students' reading comprehension and fluency, especially after 2 years. Taylor et al. concluded that sustained collaborative work with colleagues was important as was shared leadership and job-embedded professional development. In fact, in higher-implementing schools, there was typically "one strong and respected teacher leader who was persistent in helping teachers examine the data linking students' growth to classroom practices" (p. 65). Moreover, this teacher leader was supported by a teacher leadership team and by the school principal. This is similar to the findings of Camburn, Rowan, and Taylor (2003) who found in their research of 100 elementary schools involved in reform efforts that responsibility for leadership was typically distributed among three to seven people. Often, one of these individuals was an individual responsible for coordinating the literacy program (e.g., reading or literacy coach, literacy specialist, or reading coordinator).

CONCLUSION

The evidence that a shared perspective of distributed leadership promotes improved teacher practices and enhanced student learning is strong and suggests the following:

- The principal of the school serves as an important literacy leader, and at the same time, cannot do it alone. There is no place for the "heroic" or superman (or superwoman) view of leadership. Principals are more effective when they establish conditions for success and involve others in both formal and informal ways to promote literacy instruction in the school.

- Teacher leaders can be both formal (e.g., literacy coaches, facilitators) or informal (teacher peers), and it is critical to help teachers understand what leadership means, how they can develop such skills, and how they might function as leaders.

- Literacy leaders must have an in-depth understanding of leadership, that is, how to lead, which includes working with other adults, possessing the interpersonal and communication skills necessary for interacting effectively with others and understanding how to improve a school's literacy program. Specifically, literacy leaders must be knowledgeable about how to establish a community of learning and to set into motion the leadership of others.

- Literacy leaders must also possess an in-depth knowledge of literacy that helps them think about goals for the program, appropriate materials and resources, ways to evaluate the effectiveness of the program, and the professional development that will enable staff members to improve instruction for all students.

- Because literacy instruction is important across all subject areas, there is often a need for a designated individual or several individuals (literacy coaches, specialists) with content expertise and excellent leadership skills to work with principals in maintaining a focus on how literacy instruction is taught, not only for students learning how to read and write, but as a tool for learning in the various academic disciplines. In other words, literacy leadership that enables a school to set a focused, coherent vision and agenda for literacy instruction is critical for school success regardless of level or subject.

- Effective literacy leadership can be promoted through the development of a culture in which teachers and administrators work collectively to set goals and establish a vision and common expectations for students. Such a culture can promote the development of staff members as decision makers, professionals, and leaders.

The message is clear! There is evidence that student achievement in schools is enhanced when leadership is shared. Such leadership leads to the setting of common goals and a shared vision for improved student learning. Such leadership is based on the belief that all students can learn and that as educators we have a responsibility to do our best to facilitate their learning.

Such leadership changes schools so that they are places in which collaboration, interdependence, and professionalism exists—and there is a deemphasis on the isolation and independence that too often is seen in schools. This is the message that is conveyed throughout this book. Authors address the following questions in this text: How can various role groups function so that they are involved in meaningful literacy leadership? What is the content knowledge that they must have about each of the components of literacy? And finally, what might professional development look like in a school in which such shared literacy leadership exists?

ENGAGEMENT ACTIVITIES

1. Reread the case example. Talk with others about the issues that Brenda has identified and address the questions raised by Brenda. What do you think are the key issues that Brenda will face and what suggestions would you make to her about how to begin this new work?

2. Talk with others and identify the specific interpersonal, communication, and leadership skills that Brenda might need to be successful in her position. Then, individually analyze your own experiences and education: How ready would you be to assume such a position? What are the skills and abilities that you would bring to the position? What types of professional development would you need or want?

3. Interview a principal at a school and obtain his or her responses to the following questions. Then ask a teacher and a reading specialist or literacy coach to respond to the same questions. Finally, analyze the results to determine similarities or differences in responses across the role groups.

    a. In what ways are teachers (literacy coaches, special educators, etc.) involved in setting goals for the schools? (Question for teacher/literacy coach or reading specialist: In what ways have you been involved in setting goals for the school?)

    b. In what ways are teachers (literacy coaches, reading specialists, etc.) involved in making decisions about curriculum and instruction? Professional development?

    c. What are the structures that are in place that enable teachers and others to participate in shared decision making (common planning time, etc.)?

4. Think about the four categories of leadership functions described on p. 6 of this chapter. In what ways are you, in your current role, involved in any of these functions?

Example: Reading coach	
Function	Identify your role
Setting goals	As facilitator of grade-level team, I help teachers set goals for the year for their students. I also work with the leadership team to set schoolwide goals. This year, we are focusing on the vocabulary of our students.

REFERENCES

Bean, R. M. (2010a). *The reading specialist: Leadership in the classroom, school, and community* (2nd ed.). New York: Guilford Press.

Bean, R. M. (2010b). *Making response to instruction and intervention (RTII) work: What school personnel need to know and be able to do.* Retrieved December 29, 2010, from *www.pattan.net/files/RTI/RtII-Rolefunction.pdf.*

Bryk, A. S., Sebring, P. B., Allensworth, E., Luppescu, S., & Easton, J. Q. (2010). *Organizing schools for improvement: Lessons from Chicago.* Chicago: University of Chicago Press.

Camburn, E. M., Kimball, S. M., & Lowenhaupt, R. (2008). Going to scale with teacher leadership: Lessons learned from a districtwide literacy coach initiative. In M. M. Mangin & S. R. Stoelinga (Eds.), *Effective teacher leadership: Using research to inform and reform* (pp. 120–143). New York: Teachers College Press.

Camburn, E., Rowan, B., & Taylor, J. (2003). Distributed leadership in schools: The case of elementary schools adopting comprehensive school reform models. *Educational Evaluation and Policy Analysis, 25*(4), 347–373.

Collins, J. (2001). *Good to great: Why some companies make the leap ... and others don't.* New York: Harper Collins.

Common Core State Standards for English Language Arts and Literacy in History/ Social Studies, Science and Technical Subjects. (2010). Retrieved January 5, 2011, from *www.corestandards.org/the-standards/english-language-arts-standards.*

Elmore, R. F. (2000, Winter). *Building a new structure for school leadership.* The Albert Shanker Institute. Retrieved November 15, 2010, from *www.ashankerinst.org/Downloads/building.pdf.*

Heifetz, R. A., & Laurie, D. L. (2002, December). *The work of leadership.* Harvard Business Review on Point. Retrieved December 20, 2010, from *www.hbr.org.*

Individuals with Disabilities Education Act. (2004). 20 U.S.C. §1415 et seq.

Kaser, J., Mundry, S., Stiles, K. E., & Loucks-Horsley, S. (2002). *Leading every day: 124 actions for effective leadership.* Thousand Oaks, CA: Corwin.

Lambert, L. (1998). *Building leadership capacity in schools.* Alexandria, VA: Association for Supervision and Curriculum Development.

Leana, C. R., & Pil, F. K. (2006). Social capital and organizational performance: Evidence from urban public schools. *Organization Science, 17*(3), 353–366.

Leithwood, K., & Jantzi, D. (2008). Linking leadership to student learning: The contributions of leader efficacy. *Educational Administration Quarterly, 44*(4), 496–528.

Leithwood, K., Seashore-Louis, K. S., Anderson, S., & Wahlstrom, K. (2004). *How leadership influences student learning.* Minneapolis, MN, University of Minnesota: Center for Applied Research and Educational Improvement.

Little, J. W. (2003). Inside teacher community: Representations of classroom practice. *Teachers College Record, 105*(6) 913–945.

Louis, K. S., Leithwood, K., Wahlstrom, K. L., & Anderson S. E. (2010). *Investigating the links to improved student learning: Final report of research findings.* Unpublished document, University of Minnesota.

Marzano, R. J. (2003). *What works in schools: Translating research into action.* Alexandria, VA: Association for Supervision and Curriculum Development.

Marzano, R. J., Waters, T., & McNulty, B. A. (2005). *School leadership that works: From research to results.* Alexandria, VA: Association for Supervision and Curriculum Development.

Murphy, J. (1988). The characteristics of instructionally effective school districts. *Journal of Educational Research, 81*(3), 176–181.

Saunders, W., Goldenberg, C. N., & Gallimore, R. (2009, December). Increasing achievement by focusing grade-level teams on improving classroom learning: A prospective, quasi-experimental study of title 1 schools. *American Educational Research Journal, 46*(4), 1006–1033.

Spillane, J. P. (2005, Winter). Distributed leadership. *Educational Forum, 69,* 143–150.

Spillane, J. P., Halverson, R., & Diamond, J. B. (2001). Investigating school leadership practice: A distributed perspective. *Educational Researcher, 30*(23), 23–28.

Stoelinga, S. R. (2008). Leading from above and below: Formal and informal teacher leadership. In M. M. Mangin & S. R. Stoelinga (Eds.), *Effective teacher leadership: Using research to inform and reform* (pp. 99–119). New York: Teachers College Press.

Supovitz, J., Sirinides, P., & May, H. (2010). How principals and peers influence teaching and learning. *Educational Administration Quarterly, 46*(1), 31–56.

Taylor, B. M., Pearson, P. D., Peterson, D. S., & Rodriguez, M. C. (2005, January/February/March). The CIERA school change framework: An evidence-based approach to professional development and school reading improvement. *Reading Research Quarterly, 40*(1), 40–69.

Vescio, V., Ross, D., & Adams, A. (2008). A review of research on the impact of professional learning communities on teaching practice and student learning. *Teaching and Teacher Education, 24,* 80–91.

2

Teachers as Literacy Leaders

ALLISON SWAN DAGEN
JODI NICHOLS

> Within every school there is a sleeping giant of teacher
> leadership that can be a strong catalyst for making changes to
> improve student learning.
> —KATZENMEYER AND MOLLER (2009, p. 2)

Guiding Questions

- How is teacher leadership defined?
- What are the roles and responsibilities of teacher leaders?
- What characteristics do teacher leaders possess?
- What conditions support teacher leadership in schools?
- What are known outcomes of teacher leadership initiatives?

Almost a decade ago, the Institute for Educational Leadership (IEL) published a fundamental report titled *Leadership for Student Learning: Redefining the Teacher as Leader* (Institute for Educational Leadership [IEL], 2001). The task force, formed as an extension of IEL's School Leadership for the 21st Century Initiative, explored two critical principles: the role of teachers as instructional leaders and the central role these highly prepared professionals can play in school reform. It is imperative, the report asserts, for teachers to be part of policy shaping, decision making, and collaborative leadership in schools where they work. Teacher leaders can have an impact on students, colleagues, and themselves (Lambert, 2003) with the ultimate end goal being improved student achievement (York-Barr & Duke, 2004; Wynne, 2001).

In the past, teachers have assumed leadership roles through one of three tracks: school administration, activist-type teacher movements, or union representation (IEL, 2001). More recently however, teachers are taking on formal and informal leadership roles as literacy coaches, instructional leaders, mentors, data analysts, curriculum developers, and school and parent advocates (Danielson, 2007; Harrison & Killion, 2007; York-Barr & Duke, 2004). For some teachers, the need to lead and exercise influence on the day-to-day realities of the job is satisfying, empowering, and provides incentive and motivation to remain in the teaching profession. We present a case example of a literacy leader who fits this model.

CASE EXAMPLE ⟿

Marcella has always been considered a natural leader. As a novice teacher, she eagerly joined several committees within her school and often found herself taking the lead within these committees. After teaching for just a few years, she was presented with opportunities to travel to national conferences and was then asked to conduct professional development sessions for her school staff. When she earned her master's degree in educational leadership, she became the teacher in charge when her principal was not available. Currently, grant funding has allowed her to continue teaching middle school reading for part of the day and participate in leadership activities for the remainder of the day. Her principal wants her to be involved in peer coaching, data analysis, and mentoring new teachers, as well as instructing students. Marcella is very happy to be part of the school's leadership team, informally, without having to leave the classroom to assume a full-time administrative position.

After 15 years of successful teaching, Marcella is highly respected by her colleagues. However, some are not convinced that an instructional leader is needed in the school. The teachers argue that instead of cutting Marcella's teaching load, she should be teaching a full day so that class sizes can be smaller. Some of her colleagues do not realize the additional responsibilities that the school's administration has placed upon Marcella. On a typical school day, in additional to preparing and teaching her reading classes, Marcella may be writing grants, mentoring novice teachers, preparing for an evening parent meeting, analyzing data from formative assessments, and/or conducting classroom observations. Since all of these tasks cannot be completed within the scope of the school day, Marcella regularly works for 1 to 2 hours at home each evening. The teachers who resent her course releases have little sense of the time it takes to effectively fulfill her informal leadership job responsibilities.

Recently, some of Marcella's colleagues have also begun speaking out against the reading initiative that she is spearheading. Because the school did not make Adequate Yearly Progress (AYP) in reading, Marcella and her principal are encouraging the content-area teachers to participate in a semester-long graduate-level reading course offered through the regional land grant university—at no cost to the teachers. Marcella has even arranged to have the class sessions held in the school's library starting 30 minutes after the students' dismissal. The cost of the teachers' textbooks would be covered by the principal's budget, and the teachers would receive graduate credit, which they are required to get to maintain state teaching certification. Some teachers have reacted negatively and do not see themselves as "reading teachers" and believe that Marcella should teach these reading strategies in her reading classes and that the graduate course work is "not for them." Marcella tries to convince the teachers that not making AYP is not a problem for reading teachers only, but is instead a school problem. As such, she advocates for everyone to take ownership and be a part of the solution.

Teachers like Marcella, who fulfill the role of informal teacher leader, those with leadership responsibilities without a formal title, are in a unique position to influence their peers and their schools without the constraints of formal authority. In some cases, teachers with informal leadership roles are widely accepted by their peers and are able to develop more trusting relationships in their nonsupervisory leadership role than teachers who have been assigned formal leadership roles (e.g., literacy coaches, special educators).

The *Redefining the Teacher as Leader* report suggests that opportunities for leadership need to come from within and that school decision makers must recognize that the time is right to explore "a potentially splendid resource for leadership and reform that is now being squandered" (IEL, 2001, p. 2) and that is the experience, skills, knowledge, and leadership capacity of classroom teachers. Additionally, providing willing teachers with opportunities to lead can result in an increase in job satisfaction, renewed enthusiasm for daily work, and even encourage highly qualified teachers (HQT) to remain in the profession (Gordon, 2004; Katzenmeyer & Moller, 2009).

Unfortunately though, most schools simply are not designed around a teacher as leader model and the cliché—principals lead and teachers follow—is alive, well, and thriving in most of today's high- and low-performing schools. Top-down hierarchical models of principal as leader and teachers as workers serve to marginalize teachers from the hub of meaningful, democratic participation in the day-to-day operations of educating students. Current calls for universal programmatic fidelity further remove the teacher from the instructional decision-making process. Instead of turning to teachers for input and to help improve the system, the system is telling teachers what to do and then pointing the finger of blame their way if student achievement goals are not met. Rather than being encouraged to pursue collaborative opportunities, teachers have been socialized to be private "door closers" and tend to avoid taking on responsibilities outside of their classrooms (Lieberman & Miller, 1999).

In this chapter, we explore the possibilities of classroom teachers as leaders, focusing on research defining teacher leadership, elaborating on roles and responsibilities, and important professional and personal characteristics, and exploring conditions and outcomes of teacher leadership. Additionally, throughout the chapter, we revisit and share some of the experiences of Marcella, our teacher leader.

DEFINITION OF TEACHER LEADERSHIP

In order to understand how teacher leadership initiatives influence school culture, teachers, and students, it is imperative to first understand how teacher leadership is defined and why it is important within the current educational landscape. First, much of the positive shift in focus on teacher leadership is situated within the educational reforms of the last three decades calling for teacher professionalism, performance-based compensation, site-based management, and professional development schools (York-Barr & Duke, 2004). Both the No Child Left Behind Act of 2001 (2002) and the reauthorization of the Individuals with Disabilities Education Act of 2004 (IDEA) recognize teacher quality and expertise and call for HQTs to ensure students' success. Additionally, President Obama's Race to the Top Fund reform initiative espouses four crucial objectives for improving schools: elevating the profession by rewarding teachers, focusing on teacher effectiveness, increasing the number of effective teachers and leaders, and strengthening pathways into teaching and school leadership (United States Department of Education, 2010).

Although there is not one standard characterization of school-based teacher leadership, several top researchers in the field have crafted definitions of the term *teacher leader*. Commonalities among these descriptions of teacher leaders include educators who influence their peers and school community through collegial interactions (Danielson, 1998; Fullan & Hargreaves, 1996; Lambert, 2003; York-Barr & Duke, 2004); work both within the classroom and the overall school system (Fullan & Hargreaves, 1996; Katzenmeyer & Moller, 2009); and focus their efforts on improving schools, specifically focusing on student growth and achievement (Crowther, Ferguson, & Hann, 2009; Danielson, 1998; Donaldson, 2006; York-Barr & Duke, 2004; Wasley, 1991).

The concept of teachers as leaders is distinctly different from administrative or managerial concepts of leadership that use a top-down approach focusing on oversight and supervision. Those who write about teacher leaders tend not to subscribe to traditional definitions of leadership as exclusive or elevated positions within a hierarchy, especially for those with informal leadership responsibilities who function in a nonsupervisory capacity. They tend to view leadership as a more collaborative effort among teachers to promote and improve professional development and educational services. Teacher leaders recognize that with the ever-increasing demands on today's schools, administrators cannot perform the entire scope of leadership tasks alone, thus amplifying the need for teacher leaders to oversee some of the curricular, instructional, and supervisory tasks within the school. Literacy coaches and special educators are examples of teacher leaders who have more formal responsibilities with students and other school professionals, but yet are still not part of the formal administrative structure. The roles and responsibilities of these two specialized professionals are addressed in detail in Chapters 3, 4, and 5 of this text. Whether the roles are formal or informal, they foster the school's capacity to improve (Harrison & Killion, 2007). Teacher leadership, however, is not for everyone, and in fact, some highly qualified, experienced teachers may choose to pursue other challenging venues in education to improve their teaching, their schools, or their students' success by pursuing content-area specialization, research opportunities, or advanced graduate work (Crowther et al., 2009).

ROLES OF TEACHER LEADERS

More prevalent in the literature than definitions of teacher leadership is an inventory of the variety of roles and responsibilities teacher leaders may have. Nanus (1992) contends that effective leaders juggle four broad roles: direction setters, change agents, spokespeople, and coaches and team builders. First, teacher leaders act as direction setters who see the future and draw others to it. They have a vision and are able to articulate this vision and garner enthusiasm from their colleagues. Next, they are change agents who create a sense of urgency that encourages risk taking, while providing a safety net. In addition, they also act as spokespeople, elevating the voices of accomplished teachers, while at the same time being skillful listeners. Last, they act as coaches and team builders, leading teachers to increased collaboration and collegiality, while moving away from the isolation that is far too common in many schools.

Furthermore, within the range of the various roles teacher leaders play, they are provided opportunities to interact with an array of school stakeholders: teachers, administrators, students, and parents and community members. Through their work with these groups, teacher leaders are able to build bridges and make connections, with the ultimate goal being student success and achievement (York-Barr & Duke, 2004; Wynne, 2001). In this section we describe teacher leaders' responsibilities with four groups of stakeholders: peer teachers, administrators, students, and parents and communities.

Working with Teachers

Current research trends indicate that 40–50% of all new teachers will leave their jobs after the first 5–7 years (Ingersoll & Smith, 2003; Gordon & Maxey, 2000). The sobering statistic in urban schools, where student need is the highest, is that 50% of new teachers leave within the first 3 years of their career. Moreover, those who stay in at-risk, urban schools typically lack access to highly qualified mentor teachers or teacher leaders, given the high teacher turnover (International Reading Association's Literacy Leadership for Urban Teacher Education Commission, 2010). The National Commission for Teaching and America's Future (2007) asserts that it is not a teacher shortage that we are facing, but instead one of retention. Schools must be proactive in maintaining and nurturing talented educators, and this is where teacher leaders can play an important role.

Because of their knowledge and expertise, it is common for teacher leaders to mentor novice teachers. This style of mentoring may take the form of modeling lessons, observing teachers teaching and providing constructive feedback, offering suggestions for using research-based strategies, sharing resources and assisting with curricular mapping and lesson/unit plan development. By carrying out these responsibilities, teacher leaders are assisting their schools with the enculturation of novice teachers (Lambert, 2003) who must receive the support, encouragement, and expert mentoring from their seasoned colleagues if there is any hope of them remaining in the field long term.

As a learning facilitator, working with practicing teachers, reading specialists, or special educators, a teacher leader may craft and implement professional development opportunities for all colleagues (e.g., recruiting fellow teachers for an after-school professional reading group) as well as opportunities for collaboration by establishing professional learning communities (PLC). In these circumstances, teacher leaders are at an advantage since they very likely have established social or professional relationships with the teachers with whom they work—sometimes these preexisting relationships create favorable situations and other times, they do not (see Box 2.1).

In her book titled *Becoming a Literacy Leader,* Allen (2006) describes the experiences of her first year as a literacy leader. Her strategy for recruit-

---

Box 2.1. Working with Teachers

For 13 of her 15 years of teaching, Marcella has served as the organizer and facilitator of the Sunshine Club, arranging small birthday celebrations in the faculty lounge, ordering fruit baskets to congratulate colleagues on personal accomplishments, and sending flowers to a hospitalized peer. Marcella even took care of making arrangements for out-of-school functions like bus trips to New York, wine-and-cheese parties, and a welcome-back-to-school party at her home each August. The teachers Marcella works with not only count on her for this work, they also greatly appreciate her efforts. Marcella is well liked by all of her peers. However, after being appointed to serve as instructional leader, she noticed that the same teachers she worked and socialized with seem uncomfortable around her, both in and out of school.

---

ing peers for active participation in their in-house professional development meetings included identifying those she felt were most confident in their teaching abilities. She then tailored these meetings to meet their needs. Additionally, at one school, she was able to garner veteran teacher interest by scheduling the meetings at 7 A.M. since most of the teachers arrived at school early. On the flip side, at a second school, she scheduled after-school meetings for the newer teachers, most of who had young children and were willing to stay an hour after school but not come in as early. Even if teachers were somewhat reluctant, her strategic approach in giving them ownership was wise; their participation was important, especially when they were respected teachers in the school, as this sent a message to the remaining teaching staff.

Through needs assessments, teacher leaders can gain an understanding of the interests and needs of their peers and then provide them with necessary resources such as books, articles, or lesson plans. As a curriculum specialist, teacher leaders may communicate their understanding of content standards and curriculum and demonstrate that understanding by planning instruction with teachers. As a data coach, they might assist teachers in analyzing classroom assessment data and propose suggestions on how to use these data to drive instructional decision making. Also, the teacher leader acts as a cheerleader, providing colleagues with much-needed support and encouragement. Overall, the role teacher leaders play with their peers needs to be based on collegiality and mutual respect.

Working with Administrators

Principals play a critical role in the development of teacher leaders (York-Barr & Duke, 2004). As such, teacher leaders must work closely with site-based administrators. Teacher leaders must have the support of the administration if this working relationship is to be successful (Box 2.2). Ongoing communication between the principal and teachers, and among the teachers themselves, sets the stage for advancement.

Studies suggest that problems often result when teacher leadership roles are not well defined (Hart, 1990). Consequently, school administrators need to clearly define the expectations for the teacher leader or allow the leader to participate in shaping the job description or the roles and responsibilities of this new position. Examples of a principal's actions to support teacher leadership initiative include encouraging teachers to serve on and lead meaningful committees, providing teachers with the opportunity to visit other classrooms, purchasing materials for book talks, or extending resources for a schoolwide action research project. In fact, one principal we know sometimes steps in and teaches the teacher leader's students when the teacher leader is in other classrooms modeling strategies or conducting observations. See Chapter 18 for additional examples of how principals can develop leadership opportunities for their schools.

Working with Students

All efforts to cultivate teacher leadership capabilities must be done with the goal of increasing student achievement (York-Barr & Duke, 2004). Because of a commitment to students, most teacher leaders remain in the classroom for all or a part of the school day, dividing their time between teaching and their teacher leader role. When teachers sense that reform initiatives are directly connected to meeting the needs of students, they are more likely to take on leadership roles (Lattimer, 2007). Teacher leaders might be asked to create student engagement activities (Box 2.3), pilot a new reading series, or chair the committee in charge of selecting a computer-based supplemen-

---

Box 2.2. Working with Administrators

Marcella and her principal have an excellent relationship, both inside and outside of school. Mrs. Sterling respects Marcella's knowledge and leadership, and knows she can rely on Marcella to step in at a moment's notice. In fact, when Mrs. Sterling needs to leave the building, it is common knowledge that Marcella is the new "go to" for all school issues. Last winter, Marcella was responsible for making a decision regarding a note found in the girl's bathroom warning of the potential for school violence, which she felt unqualified for and uncomfortable in handling.

Box 2.3. Working with Students

Marcella has been a member of the local chapter of the state reading council since her semester of student teaching as an undergraduate. She tries to attend at least two meetings a year and is especially excited about the group's community and school-based outreach program. This year, she arranged to have her district's fifth-grade students participate in the local reading council's Children's Choice book selection process. Each classroom would receive five copies of each of the eight trade books under consideration. The students would be required to rank their selections and provide feedback for reading council decision makers. She knows some of the students are not proficient readers but she feels by giving them a voice in this selection process, they would gain confidence in and ownership for their reading abilities. Additionally, since the teachers are able to keep the trade books, Marcella thought they could be added to the classroom libraries or the teachers would be able to use the multiple copies of the high-quality books in their class literature circle meetings.

---

tal phonics program. By spending time in their classrooms, as well as the classrooms of their peers, teacher leaders have firsthand knowledge of the challenges and struggles faced by their colleagues, and they tend to be more empathetic. They are more likely to garner the support and respect of their colleagues and be accepted by their peers as *one of them.*

Despite the additional roles and responsibilities that occur as the result of serving as a teacher leader, these professionals are consistently seeking to stay abreast of the latest research findings and trends as to what works best for students in the school. In a sense, they are on the front lines of ongoing professional development. They may observe in other teachers' classrooms, model the administration of informal reading inventories, or lead a discussion of an article about literacy instruction at a faculty meeting. All of these experiences may contribute to the evolution of their own teaching and impact student learning.

Working with Parents and Community

Teacher leaders may also work with parents and community members (York-Barr & Duke, 2004). Accordingly, teacher leaders often act as liaisons between the home and school. At the elementary school level, most teachers become involved in their school's parent–teacher association or organization. Exemplary classroom teachers, Paratore (2005) contends, should "help parents to learn about and engage their children in literacy practices that are closely related to success in school" (p. 394). School-based teacher leaders can be called upon to create school-based parent involvement opportunities (Box 2.4) and/or assist families in getting necessary resources from the school, as well as from outside agencies such as literacy councils, health departments, or social service agencies.

Involvement with parents is as important in middle and high schools as it is in the elementary school. The Harvard Family Research Project (2006) indicates that "adolescents whose parents monitor their academic and social activities have lower rates of delinquency and higher rates of social competence and academic growth" (p. 2). To address the specific needs of adolescents, teacher leaders may initiate evening programs at the school, inviting parents to the school to discuss a variety of topics that are relevant to the population the school serves. As a teacher leader in a mid-Atlantic school, one of us (Jodi Nichols) created a successful program called "Connextions." The goal of the initiative was to strengthen the home–school–community connection and the school hosted monthly evening meetings and encouraged parents and teachers to attend. This locally designed, grant-funded program was able to bring in national presenters and other experts to share their knowledge with the students, their families, and teachers. Topics included Internet safety, bullying, reading with your child(ren), helping children develop study skills, and preparing for high-stakes state assessments.

CHARACTERISTICS OF TEACHER LEADERS

Who are these teacher leaders, and what are the qualities and competencies that teacher leaders must possess? Teacher leaders should possess a combi-

---

Box 2.4. Working with Parents and Community

Marcella settles easily into her new role as teacher leader. One of the first initiatives Marcella is put in charge of is a Family Literacy Night, a monthly event held in the middle school library. After 3 years of trying to increase attendance and participation, the previous teacher in charge decided to give up the task. After an extensive literature search on pitfalls to parent involvement efforts, Marcella decided to "go right to the sources" and survey parents and teachers on what they wanted from these Friday evening school events. By surveying parents before planning, Marcella has increased attendance at these meeting. Parent participation numbers are up, and some of the schools' teachers are now volunteering to participate in the evening meetings. Given Marcella's and the other teachers' hard work and success, two other school principals in the district decided to hold Family Literacy Nights at their schools.

nation of educational experiences, expertise, and personal qualities (Figure 2.1). Researchers (Boyd-Dimock & McGree, 1995; Crowther et al., 2009; Danielson, 2007; Katzenmeyer & Moller, 2009; Wynne, 2001; York-Barr & Duke, 2004) agree that teacher leaders must have significant teaching experience, deep pedagogical knowledge, and a well-developed personal philosophy of education. In a recent study of reading specialist program graduates, Nilsson (2010) found that novice educators perceived full-time teaching experiences as important to obtain first before taking on the responsibility of a literacy leader. Literacy leaders should be lifelong learners, staying abreast of the latest research and incorporating best practices into their daily instruction. They must also have extensive knowledge about the curriculum and content to be covered. They have the ability and vision to see the big picture, allowing them to assess, interpret, and prioritize needs within a school.

Furthermore, in addition to assuming school-based leadership responsibilities, Katzenmeyer and Moller (2009) suggest these teachers often choose to pursue advanced degrees, seek National Board certification (Box 2.5), join professional networks, attend workshops and conferences, engage in action research, or become more involved at the university level in the preparation of preservice teachers. They are constantly seeking to grow as professionals. These leaders are often at a stage where they feel confident in their teaching ability, which allows them to effectively fulfill such leadership positions.

Equally important to professional knowledge and experience, teacher leaders must have the ability and desire to form solid relationships with their colleagues (Boyd-Dimock & McGree, 1995). They understand that they need to have the support of their peers if trusted relationships are to form. They should have the ability to communicate effectively with their colleagues, and most importantly, engage in active listening. Additionally,

Educational Experience/Expertise	Personal Qualities
• Significant teaching experience • Deep pedagogical knowledge • Extensive knowledge of curriculum • Knowledge of best practices • Well-developed philosophy of education • Ability to translate ideas into action • Ability to analyze and make improvements and adjustments as necessary	• Gains trust and support of others • Hardworking • Takes initiative • Effective communication skills • Action-oriented/initiative • Reflective • Strong sense of self • Takes risks • Handles conflict • Lifelong learner

FIGURE 2.1. Academic and personal traits of teacher leaders.

Box 2.5. Teachers as Lifelong Learners

Marcella has been working on obtaining National Board for Professional Teaching Standards (NBPTS) certification. She was inspired to pursue this certification because she believed that it would help her to be more reflective about her teaching, which would directly benefit her students. Through this rigorous process, she enjoyed evaluating her small-group activity, as well as her large-group discussion in her classroom. Marcella captured the instructional scenarios with a small FLIP camera she won at the reading council meeting last year. After viewing her own teaching, she reflects on how she can improve her questioning techniques. As she is putting together her portfolio, she feels confident that her artifacts will help to demonstrate her expertise in providing constructive feedback to her students.

---

they may be put into situations where they are expected to address and/or mediate conflicts that may arise.

Personally, teacher leaders are often risk takers who are both goal oriented and action oriented. They often tend to be inquisitive and reflective with a strong sense of self. They stand up for what they believe to be right and are not easily silenced by others. They are often flexible and hardworking, with a desire to make a strong impact on others in both their professional and personal lives. Katzenmeyer and Moller assert that teacher leaders are not born, instead they grow (2009) and by using self-assessment tools, teachers can gauge their own propensity for teacher leadership. Their framework for leadership development focuses attention to four lines of inquiry: personal assessment (Who am I?), changing schools (Where am I?), influencing strategy (How do I lead?), and planning for action (What can I do?) (p. 58). From their years of work with teacher leadership, Katzenmeyer and Moller created the Teacher Leader Self Assessment to help teachers assess their individual readiness to take on the challenge of teacher leadership. This instrument, a useful tool for personal goal setting, focuses on seven scales vital to teachers as they embark on the early stages of assuming teacher leadership roles. The scales include understanding of:

- self-awareness and reflective practice (e.g., I reflect on what I do well and also on how I can improve as a classroom teacher);
- elements of the change process (e.g., I understand the importance of school and district culture to improving student outcomes);
- effective communication (e.g., I seek perspectives of others and can reflect others' thoughts and feelings with accuracy);
- recognition of diversity and acceptance of others' ideas (e.g., I make special efforts to understand the beliefs and values of others);

- instructional proficiency (e.g., I use research-based instructional practices);
- continuous improvement and decision making (e.g., I analyze and use assessment information when planning); and
- self-organization (e.g., I work effectively as a team member). (Katzenmeyer & Moller, 2009, pp. 52–55)

IMPLICATIONS FOR TEACHERS AS LITERACY LEADERS

In their synthesis of research on teacher leadership, York-Barr and Duke (2004) identify three conditions for teacher leadership to flourish or flounder: school culture and context, roles and relationships, and structural systems of the school (e.g., site-based management). Current research also supports the assertion that the environment of school is one of the most critical variables in the success, or failure, of teacher leadership initiatives (Crowther et al., 2009; Danielson, 2007; Ingersoll, 2007; Lattimer, 2007). School stakeholders need to support conditions conducive for teacher learning, risk taking, collaboration, shared decision making, and critical reflection. Cultivating this type of climate should be a priority of those who wish to develop teacher leaders. Simply, without an accepting school culture, teacher leadership initiatives are likely to fail. Katzenmeyer and Moller (2009) identify seven strategies necessary to cultivate a culture of collaborative leadership in schools. These include supporting teachers' learning by providing guidance and coaching; recognizing teachers' contributions; bestowing increased autonomy to encourage initiative; increasing participation in decision making; maintaining ongoing and open communication within the school; fostering a positive environment among teachers, parents, students, and administrators; and creating opportunities for teacher collaboration (see Box 2.6).

As described above, a receptive culture is a necessary component for teacher leadership opportunities. Equally important are the relationships that exist among key stakeholders who work in the schools. In the best situation, these relationships are respectful, productive, and collaborative. However, any negative relationships teacher leaders have with school administrators or fellow teachers may also serve as an obstacle for teacher leadership.

Lack of support and encouragement from school administration and the relationship with the particular administrator in charge (e.g., principal, curriculum supervisor) often pose a hurdle for teacher leaders, whether they have a formal or informal leadership role (Danielson, 1998; IEL, 2001). The school administrators must believe that teachers, because of their daily

---

Box 2.6. School-Based Collaborative Opportunities

Marcella's district administrator asked if she would be interested in facilitating an after-school study group of teachers in the district's elementary school. This school, made up of mainly minority students, has just replaced its retiring principal, has been awarded a $40,000 foundation grant for teacher development, and recently completed small-scale renovations to the school's library and multimedia classroom. This group of teachers is struggling with the changes that have taken place over the last few years in their school and would like to focus on two issues: English-language learners (ELLs) and technology and New Literacies. There has been some talk of providing teachers with a small stipend from the development grant for their participation. Eleven of the 61 teachers, four paraprofessionals, and the new principal have expressed interest in participating, especially if Marcella is involved, as most in the district know and respect Marcella. Marcella knows she will rely on the groups to set the content of the session, whereas she will facilitate the direction and process.

---

interaction with students, are in the best position to make critical decisions about curriculum and instruction. Consequently, they must be willing to relinquish some of their control and allow teacher leaders to assume additional responsibilities. Barth (2001) asserts lack of support by a school principal may be an indication that he or she wants to keep a strong hold on the decision-making process, may prefer top-down hierarchical model of leadership, or feels teacher leadership is time consuming and creates division among teachers.

Relationships among fellow teachers are also a critical dimension of teacher leadership initiatives. Issues of perceived equity within the ranks of teachers crop up when the responsibilities of the teacher leaders shift (Lambert, 2003; Katzenmeyer & Moller, 2009; Wynne, 2001; York-Barr & Duke, 2004). The egalitarian view, which espouses the notion that all teachers are equal, stands to take a direct hit when one of their own is promoted or granted leadership roles and responsibilities. Danielson (2007) refers to this as the "tall poppy syndrome" where "those who stick their heads up risk being cut down to size" (p. 18). Equally unflattering is the notion of the *crab bucket mentality* likening teachers' behavior to crabs in a bucket that will work to pull the others back in, if and when they try to get out. These views are not only ugly; sadly, they are sometimes quite accurate. Whereas informal leadership assignments might not confuse the existing hierarchy, as Marcella experienced, formal leadership role designations almost certainly create a division that can result in conflict among teachers (Darling-Hammond, 2003) or create an imbalance of hierarchy (York-Barr & Duke, 2004).

In addition to the relationship issues that impede leadership, the structures or organization of a school can also be roadblocks for teacher leadership. As cited previously in this chapter, new demands on a teacher's time, both in and outside of school, are required of the teacher leader. Many teachers already lament "our plate is full" (Barth, 2001, p. 445) so taking on any additional school-based responsibilities does not seem sensible. Moreover, for teacher leaders like Marcella, who do take on the additional responsibilities and still stay in the classroom, full or even part time, the demands on time are even more greatly exaggerated. In addition to writing lesson plans, grading papers, and dealing with student issues, teacher leaders are also dealing with teacher issues and a wide array of other responsibilities, many requiring extensive amounts of time, usually tacked onto the end of the school day or in the evening at home.

Last, lack of preparation for leadership is another issue facing teachers who might consider pursuing leadership opportunities. Simply, most teachers are not prepared for such roles (IEL, 2001). Efforts in higher-education institutions to prepare novice teachers might include a range of course work and assignments focusing on reading and discussing articles, completing reflective writing, or attending a series of seminars. At West Virginia University, preservice teachers enrolled in the Five-Year Teacher Education Program (certification and master's) are required to take a three-credit graduate-level course titled "The Teacher as Leader" during their final semester immediately following their student teaching internship. In this semester-long course, students are taught the significance of assuming a leadership role and are also provided the tools to engage in leadership. One assignment requires the "intern" candidates to return to the school where they completed their teaching placement and develop a plan for job-embedded professional development. To successfully complete the assignment, the interns are required to conduct a needs assessment, craft a plan, and implement a professional development activity that encourages best practices. One group of interns, who taught at the same elementary school, teamed up and focused their plan on explicitly incorporating science into the literacy and mathematics curriculum. The interns demonstrated integrated lessons in many of the teachers' classrooms, hosted a guest speaker from the National Aeronautics Space Administration, developed a Family Science Literacy night, and also scheduled debriefing, discussion, and goal-setting sessions with some of the teachers at the school. These novice teacher interns were passionate about their topic and enthusiastic about the possibilities of becoming teacher leaders. In a written reflection on this assignment, one intern said, "Our love and passion for reaching all of our students drives us to join PLCs, and take a first-hand role in school practices and policy" (Student M, personal communication, April 15, 2010).

Even while efforts by higher education are respectable, novice teachers often assume jobs in schools where teacher leader roles can be nurtured at the inservice level. These schools must address the teachers' needs through high-quality, ongoing professional learning opportunities. For example, as reported in the IEL report titled *Teacher Leadership in High Schools: How Principals Encourage It, How Teachers Practice It* (Institute for Education Leadership [IEL], 2008), one principal asked prospective teacher leaders to participate in a reading/study group. He asked them to read *Results Now: How We Can Achieve Unprecedented Improvements in Teaching and Learning* by Michael Schmoker (2006). The focus in this text is teacher leadership initiatives. The group scheduled meetings where they were encouraged to think about and plan for how they could implement some of the ideas presented in the book in their own schools.

OUTCOMES OF TEACHER LEADERSHIP

After completing an extensive review of research pertaining to teacher leaders, York-Barr and Duke (2004) concluded the clearest effect of teacher leadership is growth and learning among teachers themselves. Teachers who partake in leadership roles report the following positive results: a break from the routine of the classroom in order to engage with colleagues and administrators, increased satisfaction and retention, a chance to learn more about the *big picture* of the school and schooling, and the ability to exercise creativity through collegial and administrative work. Given the exposure to new information and increased collaboration among peers, improved teaching practice is also a positive outcome of teacher leadership. Barth (1999) supports this notion and indicates that teachers who choose the path of teacher leadership experience some of the best learning opportunities (Box 2.7) of their careers, renewed enthusiasm and hope, a greater sense of school community, and a reduction in isolation. These teachers, Barth asserts, "become owners and investors in their schools, rather than mere tenants" (Barth as cited in Lambert, 2003, p. 41).

For example, by participating in the National Writing Project (NWP), an exemplary model of leadership-centered professional development, teachers are provided a context for collaboration with peers, both through workshops and conferences. Since the project itself is a network of linked sites working in collaboration with colleges and universities, participants may become connected with the culture of the anchoring institutions and may have additional access to resources, consultants, and educators affiliated with the NWP. Moreover, participating in an external school endeavor like NWP is an example of teacher leadership and most teachers, but not all, who complete the process are expected to serve as teacher leaders (Wade & Ferriter, 2007). The intrinsic rewards experienced through participation

---

Box 2.7. Professional Learning and Opportunities

Marcella was delighted to learn her proposal, Literacy Strategies for English Language Learners (ELLs), was accepted for presentation at the International Reading Association conference. She has worked hard over the past 6 years learning about strategies for ELLs, as the number of ELL students at her school has increased and a large number of them score below basic on the state tests. Marcella has presented at regional and state conferences before, but this will be her first national presentation. She is nervous about presenting but is also excited about attending sessions at the 4-day conference. Additionally, Marcella hopes to see some of the teachers around the county with whom she has been communicating through a blog focusing on school-based literacy initiatives like response to intervention (RTI).

---

in high-quality professional development opportunities such as NWP come from reflection, inquiry, and dialogue (Lambert, 2003). On the contrary, Lambert (1998) cautions that the use of external rewards or incentives to coax teachers into participating in professional development or taking on responsibilities that come along with teacher leadership roles, is not an effective motivational tool and in fact can be detrimental.

Unfortunately, the impact of teacher leadership on student learning has not been well documented or reported. York-Barr and Duke (2004) reported finding less than half a dozen studies, over a two-decade span, that focused specifically on the effect of teacher leadership on students. Across the small sample reported, there appeared to be a causal relationship between variables of school culture, principal leadership, and teachers' shared decision making with a positive impact on student achievement. This finding is consistent with other reviews of research in the area (Hallinger & Heck, 1996) as well as a recent Organisation for Economic Co-operation and Development (OECD) report (Mulford, 2003), which concluded that the relationship between leadership and student achievement is mainly indirect and that "Good leadership helps foster the kind of school climate in which learning flourishes, rather than directly inspiring students to achieve" (p. 3). Consequently, given what is known and not known about the impact of teacher leadership on students, perhaps the best and most hopeful way to summarize what we know, based on research findings, is that when changes are observed in teachers' behavior, learning, and practice, there is a subsequent increase in student achievement (National Reading Panel, 2000).

Finally, the work of teacher leaders in directing various initiatives and projects can create positive outcomes on the entire school. For example, as a teacher leader in a middle school in Maryland, one of us (Jodi Nichols) spearheaded two key initiatives over the past 2 years. First, as a teacher leader, she played a primary role in the selection, adoption, and implementation of the Voyager reading intervention program. Voyager, a computer-based program designed for struggling readers, focuses on comprehension skills and strategies for middle school students. Jodi's dissertation study completed during the following school year found that the general-level students, most of whom were struggling readers, showed significant gains in reading ability after 1 year in this intervention program (Nichols, 2009). The second initiative developed at the school was a schoolwide effort to address students' reading comprehension. As part of this successful initiative, content-area teachers were provided with professional development and were asked to reinforce one designated reading skill per month using a variety of strategies, as directed by the teacher leader. Although hesitant initially, many of these content-area teachers became more confident in their abilities to teach reading and began intentionally integrating additional skills and strategies into their daily plans. Students were also noticing that reading skills are used in all content subjects, and not just in reading class. According to the principal of this school, both of these initiatives likely played a role in student achievement, as well as with the school's AYP status.

CONCLUSION

A decade ago, in their discussion of exceptional schools, the IEL (2001) noted that there was a "growing number of glittering exceptions" (p. 2) where teacher leaders were successfully executing leadership roles and responsibilities. However, they quickly followed up with the fact that the majority of the 100,000 plus number of schools operating in the United States today remain mainly "unexploited" for teacher leadership opportunities. Providing educators—teachers, reading specialists, special educators, and so on—with opportunities for leadership may break some of the unflattering stereotypical views of teaching: (teaching as) a flat profession where the job remains the same from induction to retirement (Danielson, 2007, p. 14); (teaching as) an isolating career choice (Fullan, 1993); (teachers') notions of *my students* (Katzenmeyer & Moller, 2009); I am *just a teacher* mentality (Crowther et al., 2009); and school as a place where teachers behave similar to preschoolers, who engage in parallel play (Barth, 2006).

In this era of increased accountability, in order to retain highly qualified teachers, we need to rethink the role and responsibilities of classroom teachers—both operationally and conceptually—and focus on initiatives that will make teacher leaders the norm rather than the exception. The role of teacher leader is an evolving one whose description and responsibilities need to be regularly revisited or reshaped by the changing context of the school and educational reform initiatives. The traditional school-based governance structure needs to evolve, embrace the notion of teachers as equal partners in leadership (Wynne, 2001), and resemble a horizontal contour rather than a vertical one (IEL, 2001)—one where all school professionals have the potential to impact leadership. Ongoing communication among key stakeholders: policymakers, researchers, university educators, school administrators, principals, and the teachers themselves is necessary in order to advance the notion of teachers as leaders.

To close, in summarizing the efforts of three teacher leaders, Danielson (1998) so simply yet powerfully synthesized their actions and said, "They saw a need; they recognized an opportunity to do something differently for the direct benefit of students; they pulled it off" (p. 10). As straightforward and encouraging as this quote seems, not all teachers have been fully awakened to the possibilities of teacher leadership and its impact on their students. The difference then between those who "stir" and those who remain "dormant" is determined by the belief, or lack thereof, that teacher leadership capacity resides in all to improve the education of the students they teach.

ENGAGEMENT ACTIVITIES

1. Reread the case example of Marcella, a teacher with informal leadership responsibilities. Discuss with peers the following questions: How can Marcella convince her colleagues of the importance of the *reading* initiative in the school? How should she and the principal address the concern that she stay in the classroom to reduce class sizes? Is there an effective and positive way to inform her colleagues about what she is accomplishing behind the scenes?

2. Identify, observe, and interview a teacher leader in a school. These questions may be used as a guide or you may develop your own. What is his or her roles and responsibilities? Is his or her position an informal or formal role? What aspects of his or her position seems most rewarding? What professional and personal traits does he or she demonstrate?

3. Using the framework provided in this chapter (working with teachers, administrators, students, and parents and community), what would be the benefits and challenges of working with each group? Which group of stakeholders might pose the greatest challenge to work with, and what strategies can be implemented to address these?

4. Review the seven scales of the Teacher Leader Self Assessment presented on pp. 32–33. Think about where you are in your teaching career and on your professional experiences, as well as your personal attributes,

and ask yourself whether you are ready to take on the role of teacher leader in your school. Reflect on the traits represented in the six scales. What can you do to nurture these traits in yourself and fellow teachers at your school?

REFERENCES

Allen, J. (2006). *Becoming a literacy leader.* Portland, ME: Stenhouse.

Barth, R. (1999). *The teacher leader.* Providence: Rhode Island Foundation.

Barth, R. (2001). Teacher leader. *Phil Delta Kappan, 82,* 443–449.

Barth, R. (2006). Improving relationships within the schoolhouse. *Educational Leadership, 63*(6), 8–13.

Boyd-Dimock, V., & McGree, K. (1995). *Leading change from the classroom: Teachers as leaders issues ... about change. 2*(2). Austin, TX: Southwest Educational Development Laboratory.

Crowther, F., Ferguson, M., & Hann, L. (2009). *Developing teacher leaders: How teacher leadership enhances school success* (2nd ed.). Thousand Oaks, CA: Corwin Press.

Danielson, C. (1998). *Teacher leadership that strengthens professional practice.* Alexandria, VA: Association for Supervision and Curriculum Development

Danielson, C. (2007). The many faces of leadership. *Educational Leadership, 65*(1), 14–19.

Darling-Hammond, L. (2003). Keeping good teachers: Why it matters, what leaders can do. *Educational Leadership, 60*(8), 6–13.

Donaldson, G. (2006). *Cultivating leadership in schools: Connecting people, purpose, and practice.* New York: Teachers College Press.

Fullan, M. (1993). *Change forces: Probing the depth of educational reform.* Levittown, PA: Falmer Press–Taylor and Francis.

Fullan, M., & Hargreaves, A. (1996). *What's worth fighting for in your school* (2nd ed.). New York: Teachers College Press.

Gordon, S., & Maxey, S. (2000). *How to help beginning teachers succeed* (2nd ed.). Alexandria, VA: Association for Supervision and Curriculum Development.

Gordon, S. P. (2004). *Professional development for school improvement: Empowering learning communities.* Boston: Allyn & Bacon.

Hallinger, P., & Heck, R. (1996). The principal's role in school effectiveness: A review of methodological issues. In K. Leithwood, J. Chapman, D. Corson, P. Hallinger, & A. Weaver-Hart (Eds.), *The international handbook of educational leadership and administration.* Dordrecht, Netherlands: Kluwer.

Harrison, C., & Killion, J. (2007). Ten roles for teacher leaders. *Educational Leadership, 65*(1), 74–77.

Hart, A. (1990). Impacts of the school social unit on teacher authority during work redesign. *American Educational Research Journal, 27*(3), 503–532.

Harvard Family Research Project. (2006). *Family involvement makes a difference in school success.* Retrieved August 13, 2010, from *www.hfrp.org/publications.*

Individuals with Disabilities Education Act of 2004, 20 U.S.C. 1415 et seq. (2004).

Ingersoll, R. (2007). Short on power, long on responsibility. *Educational Leadership,* 65(1), 20–25.

Ingersoll, R. M., & Smith, T. M. (2003). The wrong solution to the teacher shortage. *Educational Leadership, 60*(8), 30–33.

Institute for Educational Leadership. (2001). *Leadership for student learning: Redefining the teacher as leader.* Washington, DC: Author.

Institute for Educational Leadership. (2008). *Teacher leadership in high schools: How principals encourage it, how teachers practice it.* Washington, DC: Author.

International Reading Association's Literacy Leadership for Urban Teacher Education Commission (2010). *Improving teacher preparation and development for promoting literacy achievement in high poverty urban schools: A systemic approach.* Newark, DE: Author.

Katzenmeyer, M., & Moller, G. (2009). *Awaking the sleeping giant: Helping teachers develop as leaders* (3rd ed.). Thousand Oaks, CA: Corwin.

Lambert, L. (1998). *Building leadership capacity in schools.* Alexandria, VA: Association for Supervision and Curriculum Development.

Lambert, L. (2003). *Leadership capacity for lasting school improvement.* Alexandria, VA: Association for Supervision and Curriculum Development.

Lattimer, H. (2007). To help and not hinder. *Educational Leadership, 65*(1), 70–73.

Lieberman, A., & Miller, L. (1999). *Teacher leadership.* San Francisco: Jossey-Bass.

Mulford, B. (2003). *School leaders: Changing roles and impact on teacher and school effectiveness.* Tasmania: Organisation for Economic Co-operaton and Development.

Nilsson, N. (November, 2010). Examining the initial career paths of graduates of a maters program in reading designed to prepare candidates as literacy leaders. Paper presented at the meeting of Association of Literacy Educators and Researchers (ALER), Omaha, NE.

Nanus, B. (1992). *Visionary leadership: Creating a compelling sense of direction for our organization.* San Francisco: Jossey-Bass.

National Commission for Teaching and America's Future. (2007). *The high cost of teacher turn over.* Washington, DC: Author.

National Reading Panel. (2000). *Teaching children to read: An evidence-based assessment of the scientific research literature on reading and its implications for reading instruction.* Washington, DC: National Institute of Child Health and Human Development.

Nichols, J. (2009). *Text format, text comprehension, and related reader variables.* Retrieved August 30, 2010,from ProQuest Dissertations and Thesis database (*www.proquest.com*).

Nilsson, N. (2010, November). *Examining the initial career paths of graduates of a master's program in reading designed to prepare candidates as literacy leaders.* Paper presented at the meeting of the Association of Literacy Educators and Researchers, Omaha, NE.

No Child Left Behind Act of 2001, Pub. L. No. 107–110, § 115, Stat. 1425 (2002).

Paratore, J. (2005). Approaches to family literacy: Exploring the possibilities. *Reading Teacher, 59*(4), 394–396.

Schmoker, M. (2006). *Results now: How we can achieve unprecedented improvements in teaching and learning.* Alexandria, VA: Association for Supervision and Curriculum Development.

United States Department of Education. (2010). *A blueprint for reform: The reauthorization of the elementary and secondary education act.* Washington, DC: Author.

Wade, C., & Ferriter, B. (2007). Will you help me lead? *Educational Leadership, 65*(1), 65–68.

Wasley, P. A. (1991). *Teachers who lead: The rhetoric of reform and the realities of practice.* New York: Teachers College Press.

Wynne, J. (2001). *Teachers as leaders in education reform.* New York: ERIC Clearinghouse on Teaching and Teacher Education (No. ED462376).

York-Barr, J., & Duke, K. (2004). What do we know about teacher leadership? Findings from two decades of scholarship. *Review of Educational Research, 74*(3), 255–316.

3

Literacy Coaches in Elementary Schools

SUSAN K. L'ALLIER
LAURIE ELISH-PIPER

> I think that teaching literacy is a craft. And, very much like any fine craftsman, I feel like I'm in the apprentice stage. I'm still learning how to use all the tools, and having a coach like Naomi has been outstanding. She's a great teacher, of course, and beyond that she has a wealth of knowledge and a variety of books, children's books, that she's read over the years and recommendations that she can make.
> —ELISH-PIPER AND L'ALLIER (2010b)

Guiding Questions

- What are the roles and responsibilities of elementary literacy coaches?
- How can elementary literacy coaches establish and maintain collaborative relationships with teachers?
- How can elementary literacy coaches promote students' reading and writing achievement?
- How can elementary literacy coaches support teachers' professional development?
- How can elementary literacy coaches address systemwide challenges?

The heartfelt comments from a second-year teacher presented above reveal just a few of the ways that elementary literacy coaches provide job-embedded professional development for teachers. The focus of their work is to help teachers enhance their instruction in order to support students' reading and writing development. They are literacy leaders who contribute in many ways to the effectiveness of teaching and learning in their schools. Because literacy coaching is a relatively new role for reading professionals, there are many questions that need to be answered. In this chapter, we address the guiding questions identified above by sharing current research from the professional literature and our own experiences working with literacy coaches.

As you read this chapter, think about the case described below and how you might address the challenges that Alicia Nuñez faces as a literacy coach in an elementary school.

Case Example

Alicia Nuñez is starting her third year as a literacy coach at Warren Elementary School, a large, inner-city school with range of diversity. Warren Elementary School's longtime principal just retired, so the school will have a new principal who has never worked with a literacy coach before. In addition, the school district is experiencing a budget shortfall so no funds will be available for new instructional materials or outside professional development support. This means that Alicia will have to "make do" with the resources currently available in her school and district. Additionally, class sizes have increased and many teachers have been talking about feeling overwhelmed and undersupported. As Alicia prepares for the coming year, she plans to focus on three goals. First, she must clarify her roles and responsibilities as a literacy coach with her new principal so that he understands her contributions as a literacy leader in the school. Second, Alicia wants to strengthen collaborative relationships with teachers so they can "lean on" her more as they work through the tough times at Warren Elementary School. And, third, she needs to consider how to provide meaningful professional development support for teachers without relying on outside funds or resources. If you were Alicia, what would you do to address these three goals?

WHAT ARE THE ROLES
AND RESPONSIBILITIES
OF ELEMENTARY LITERACY COACHES?

As we work with literacy coaches from different school districts and read the professional literature about literacy coaches across the country, it is clear that there is not a consistent description of the roles and responsibilities of literacy coaches in elementary schools. The differences in coaching roles and responsibilities appear to fall into three categories: (1) time allocated for coaching in the school, (2) the specific responsibilities of the literacy coach, and (3) the time coaches spend working directly with teachers.

Time Allocated for Coaching in the School

The recent focus on literacy coaching appears to be a direct result of the Reading First Initiative (United States Department of Education, 2002). Schools that received Reading First grants were expected to hire literacy coaches to provide ongoing professional development for classroom teachers in order to improve student reading performance (Gamse, Jacob, Horst, Boulay, & Unlu, 2008). Most often these were full-time literacy coaches who were not expected to spend any of their time providing direct instruction to students.

While more than 5,200 schools hired literacy coaches through the Reading First grant program (Moss, Jacob, Boulay, Horst, & Poulos, 2006), districts that did not receive Reading First grants also recognized the potential benefits of literacy coaching and hired literacy coaches (Russo, 2004). These school districts had more freedom in determining the roles of their literacy coaches. When working with non-Reading First districts, we saw that the time allocated for literacy coaching varied considerably. One district asked reading specialists who had been working only with students to become full-time literacy coaches, working only with teachers. This change was motivated by a district initiative to strengthen the core instruction by having literacy coaches provide ongoing professional development for teachers. In another district the reading specialists spent half of their time working with students and the other half coaching teachers. The district's philosophy was that this dual-role position would allow the most struggling readers to continue receiving services from highly qualified reading specialists while also strengthening core instruction by providing coaching to classroom teachers. Third, we worked in a district that, as a first step in developing its literacy coaching program, asked reading specialists to allocate some time in their weekly schedules (e.g., an hour each day or a block of 3 hours per week) to work with teachers. Regardless of the amount of time allocated for literacy coaching within a school district, it is important to consider the primary emphases of that literacy coaching.

Designated Responsibilities of the Literacy Coach

In examining the literature that describes the major responsibilities of literacy coaching, the focus is frequently placed on the interactions between coaches and teachers (Dole, 2004; International Reading Association [IRA], 2004). For example, the International Reading Association [IRA] Position Statement entitled *The Role and Qualifications of the Reading Coach in the United States* (IRA, 2004) delineates teacher-related coaching activities into three levels of literacy coaching (Bean, 2004). These levels are based on the degree of formality of the coaching activities and whether teachers perceive them as intrusive or threatening. The most informal and least intrusive activities are designed to help literacy coaches build relationships with teachers (e.g., conversing with colleagues, developing and providing materials). When working with teachers with whom literacy coaches have already established relationships, coaches frequently engage in more formal activities to support student learning (e.g., leading professional development sessions, analyzing student work). The third level of literacy coaching activities is the most formal and focuses on supporting individual teachers by modeling, observing, and conferencing.

While the literature describing the key responsibilities of literacy coaches focuses on teacher-related activities, research indicates that coaches often have additional responsibilities (Bean, Swan, & Knaub, 2003; Elish-Piper & L'Allier, 2007, 2010a). When two groups of literacy coaches with whom we have worked independently developed lists of the activities in which they frequently engaged, each list consisted of more than 25 activities, including several that did not involve working directly with teachers. Some of these additional responsibilities included assessing students, analyzing assessment data, ordering materials, organizing book rooms, and serving as the literacy representative on school and district-level committees. A combination of teacher-related and other activities were also reported by Reading First literacy coaches working in five western states (Deussen, Coskie, Robinson, & Autio, 2007). In fact, although the literacy coaches in these five states were supposed to be spending the majority of their time working with teachers, results indicated that only 32% of the literacy coaches actually had a teacher-oriented focus. The others coaches were classified—in terms of the way they spent the majority of their time—as data-oriented coaches (15%) who focused on the collection, analysis, and use of student data; student-oriented coaches (24%) who focused on providing ongoing, direct instructional services to students; or managerial coaches (29%) who focused on administrative tasks such as finding and ordering resources for teachers and maintaining required paperwork.

Coaching Time Spent with Teachers

Given the breadth of responsibilities reported by literacy coaches, you may wonder how much time literacy coaches actually spend working with teachers. In our studies with Reading First coaches (Elish-Piper & L'Allier, 2010a,

2011), the literacy coaches' logs indicated that literacy coaches in one Reading First school district spent an average of 53% of their time working with teachers whereas coaches in another Reading First district spent an average of 49%. These results are somewhat higher than the results from the Deussen et al. study (2007) where coaches who had been asked to spend between 60 and 80% of their time working with teachers reported that they actually spent an average of only 29% of their time coaching teachers. Furthermore, two studies of Reading First literacy coaches in Pennsylvania (Bean et al., 2007, 2008) also indicated that literacy coaches, on average, spent about a third of their time working directly with teachers.

Cognizant of the many managerial/administrative tasks required of literacy coaches working in districts that received Reading First grants, we also investigated the amount of time literacy coaches spent with teachers in a district that had not received a Reading First grant. The results of our study of K–8 literacy coaches in a non-Reading First district indicated that these coaches spent an average of 65% of their time working with teachers (L'Allier & Elish-Piper, 2009). It may be that literacy coaches who are not required to engage in administrative duties, such as those related to Reading First grants, have more time to spend working directly with teachers.

Years of experience as a literacy coach may be another factor that influences the amount of time a coach spends working with teachers. An examination of the first- and third-year logs of literacy coaches working in Pennsylvania (Bean & Zigmond, 2007) revealed that literacy coaches increased the percentage of time spent on teacher-related activities in the third year and decreased the percentage of time spent on administrative tasks. In terms of time spent with teachers, coaches in their third year engaged in significantly more conferencing, observing, and co-teaching than they had during their first year, indicating that as coaches became more experienced, they provided individual teachers with more intensive support.

In other words, given that there is no universal description of literacy coaches who work in elementary schools, the ways in which coaches work and the amount of time that they allocate to coaching may differ considerably. Coaches may be full-time, half-time, or part-time, and they may or may not be spending the majority of their coaching time on what the literature considers their most important task—working with teachers.

HOW CAN ELEMENTARY LITERACY COACHES ESTABLISH AND MAINTAIN COLLABORATIVE RELATIONSHIPS WITH TEACHERS?

As we work with current and aspiring literacy coaches, a question we are commonly asked is "How can I build relationships with the teachers in my school?" Like any relationship, the literacy coach–teacher relationship takes time to build and effort to maintain. However, the hard work needed for building productive relationships is essential for effective literacy coaching. While each literacy coach–teacher relationship may have its own nuances, we identify three guidelines from the professional literature and from our work in the field that we believe can be helpful for establishing and maintaining collaborative relationships with teachers. These three guidelines are based on the premise that coaches and teachers are peers. Their primary responsibilities differ; teachers' primary focus is teaching children whereas literacy coaches spend a significant amount of their time working with teachers. Nevertheless, acknowledging the fact that they are peers provides a key foundation to establishing collaborative relationships. To situate themselves as peers with their teacher colleagues, literacy coaches must clarify their roles, build trust, and communicate effectively.

Clarifying Roles

Because literacy coaches observe instruction in classrooms, meet with administrators frequently, and coordinate aspects of the literacy program, teachers may assume that coaches are administrators. That assumption is false and can be the greatest hurdle for a literacy coach to overcome when trying to establish collaborative relationships with teachers (Casey, 2006; Toll, 2005). Literacy coaches can help to ensure that their roles and responsibilities are clear to teachers (and to administrators) by describing and discussing their position at an initial faculty meeting and following up at grade-level meetings. These discussions can focus on three key topics to ensure that teachers understand that their literacy coach is a peer, not a supervisor or evaluator: (1) job description of the literacy coach, (2) teacher–coach–administrator relationship model, and (3) services and support the literacy coach can provide for teachers.

If literacy coaches do not have a job description, we recommend that they draft one and share it with their supervisor and peers for input (Elish-Piper, L'Allier, & Zwart, 2008/2009). We worked with school-based educators to develop the model shown in Figure 3.1 to clarify the fact that the literacy coach is not a supervisor or evaluator (Elish-Piper et al.). In this model, the literacy coach does not report to the principal after observations or consultations with the teacher; rather the literacy coach is a support for teachers to think and problem solve with—not a supervisor or evaluator.

The most successful literacy coaches with whom we have worked begin each new school year by distributing a survey that lists what they can do to help support teachers (e.g., reviewing student work, locating resource materials, co-planning lessons, and co-teaching lessons). The survey also includes

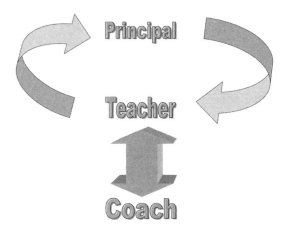

FIGURE 3.1. Model of the principal–teacher–coach relationship. From Elish-Piper et al. (2008/2009). Reprinted with permission.

a section for teachers to return, specifying their requests for support from the literacy coach. By reminding teachers through words and actions that they are "partners and peers" (L'Allier & Elish-Piper, 2009), literacy coaches can clarify their roles and responsibilities.

Building Trust

Trust is a key foundation to any productive relationship, including the literacy coach–teacher relationship. Literacy coaches can begin to build trust by openly and honestly valuing teachers' professional expertise and experiences (Knight, 2009). Furthermore, by focusing their discussions with teachers on how to collaboratively address the needs of students— rather than change teachers' instruction—literacy coaches can continue to develop trusting relationships with teachers (McCombs & Marsh, 2009).

By consistently following up on the promises and commitments they make to teachers, literacy coaches can build trusting relationships wherein teachers know they can depend on their coaches. Additionally, because literacy coaches visit many classrooms, discuss challenges that teachers experience, and work with school administrators, confidentiality must be a key consideration so that teachers know that their conversations with the literacy coach will not be reported to others or judged (Rainville & Jones, 2008). This important issue was explained by a classroom teacher in a study of literacy coaching when she stated, "I know my literacy coach is there to help me and not to judge me. She is professional, and she will keep my questions, no matter how silly I think they may be, private" (L'Allier, Elish-Piper, & Bean, 2010, p. 548).

Communicating Effectively

As in any relationship, the way things are said can promote or hinder effective working relationships (Rainville & Jones, 2008). For example, if a literacy coach asks, "Why did you teach that strategy?" the teacher may interpret it as questioning his or her professional judgment. If, on the other hand, the literacy coach had said, "Tell me about your goal for the strategy lesson," the teacher would more clearly understand that the literacy coach was interested in how that strategy was related to the students' learning. From our work with literacy coaches, we've learned that listening to what teachers say closely, choosing words carefully, and providing invitations for discussion are effective strategies for promoting teacher–coach communication (L'Allier & Elish-Piper, 2009).

If literacy coaches listen carefully to what teachers say, they are able to adjust their coaching stance and language to communicate effectively with that teacher (Lipton & Wellman, 2007). Literacy coaches use three stances (i.e., facilitating, collaborating, and consulting), which vary in terms of whether the teacher or the literacy coach takes the lead in providing information and problem solving.

When teachers have a great deal of experience and pose specific questions to the literacy coach such as "I have been looking at my students' reading responses, and I have noticed some interesting things. Can we discuss what I've noticed?" the literacy coach can then take a *facilitating stance* (adapted from Lipton & Wellman, 2007) by asking the teacher an open-ended question to promote discussion. For example, the coach might say, "I'd love to talk about the students' reading responses. What were some of the things you noticed?" In this stance, the teacher provides most of the information, and the coach mainly paraphrases and asks open-ended questions to promote clarification.

Teachers often bring some specific experiences and ideas to the coaching conversation by making statements such as "I have noticed some growth in my students' abilities to make inferences. What I've taught so far has worked well. I have some ideas about what additional instruction I can provide, but I'm not sure what I should try next." The literacy coach can take the *collaborating stance* (Lipton & Wellman, 2007) to work with the teacher to review what he or she has already done, how the students have grown, and possible options for further instruction. When taking the collaborating stance in these types of situations, the literacy coach frequently uses inclusive pronouns such as *us, our,* and *we* to clarify the collaborative nature of the conversation. For example, the literacy coach can use statements such as "Let's look at the types of inferences they made so we can figure out what types they are not yet making. Once we figure that out, we can consider which option for instruction makes the most sense to try next."

Sometimes teachers are frustrated or overwhelmed when they converse with the literacy coach. In these situations, the coach can take the *consulting stance* (Lipton & Wellman, 2007) where the coach provides some information for the teacher to consider. For example, Miss Jackson told her literacy coach, "My students need to develop their higher-level comprehension skills, but I've taught all of the lessons related to higher-level comprehension from our reading program. I just don't know what else to do now!" In response, the literacy coach, taking the consulting stance, might respond, "Higher-level comprehension is difficult to learn so some students might need more scaffolding and practice. Let's look through the strategy lessons you've taught and talk about what the students understood and what they still seem to need to work on. Then perhaps I can give you a few suggestions about what you could do next to help the students build their higher-level comprehension."

While we have presented the three coaching stances separately, it is important to note that many literacy coaching conversations with teachers include more than one stance because as the conversation develops and teachers share their ideas, questions, and concerns, the literacy coach adjusts stances to allow for the most effective communication with the teacher.

HOW CAN ELEMENTARY LITERACY COACHES PROMOTE STUDENTS' READING AND WRITING ACHIEVEMENT?

As literacy coaches establish trusting, collaborative relationships and begin working with teachers, they may find themselves a bit overwhelmed with the many ways they can spend their time and wonder how they can best use their time to support student reading and writing achievement. Using the findings from our studies, we developed the Research-Based Model of Literacy Coaching Focused on Promoting Student Reading and Writing Gains (see Figure 3.2). This evidence-based model can assist literacy coaches in planning their work and help principals and teachers understand the rationale for the priorities established by their literacy coaches.

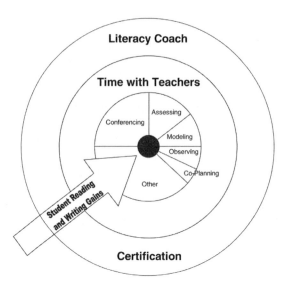

FIGURE 3.2. Research-based model of literacy coaching focused on promoting student reading and writing gains.

The Research-Based Model of Literacy Coaching Focused on Promoting Student Reading and Writing Gains (hereafter referred to as the Model) is depicted as a three-ring target with the bull's-eye representing student reading and writing gains. Literacy Coach Certification, which occupies the outer ring of the Model, is considered to be a foundational component. In studies involving Reading First (Elish-Piper & L'Allier, 2010a, 2011) and non-Reading First (Elish-Piper & L'Allier, 2010b) districts, students in classrooms supported by literacy coaches who held either a Reading Teacher Endorsement (24 graduate credit hours in Reading) or a Reading Specialist Certificate (32 graduate credit hours in Reading) made greater gains in reading than students in classrooms supported by literacy coaches who did not hold a reading endorsement or certificate. These results suggest that the graduate reading course work completed by those who hold either type of reading certification fosters the development of the "in-depth knowledge of reading processes, acquisition, assessment, and instruction" that the IRA (2004, p. 3) purports to be an essential requirement for effective literacy coaching.

The second ring of the Model indicates that the amount of time the literacy coach spends with classroom teachers is important. In one study of Reading First coaches (Elish-Piper & L'Allier, 2007), the highest average student gains were produced in classrooms served by the literacy coaches who had the highest number of teacher interactions. The lowest average student gains were tied to classrooms served by the literacy coaches who spent the smallest percentage of time with teachers. In two other studies (Elish-Piper & L'Allier, 2010a, 2011), students made significant progress when literacy coaches spent at least 30% of their time working with teachers. It appears that when literacy coaches spend at least a third of their time working with teachers, it can be predicted that, on average, students in those teachers' classrooms will make significant gains in reading and writing.

The inner ring of the Model more specifically answers the question of how literacy coaches can allocate their time. The subdivision of this ring into pieces suggests that, when spending time with teachers, coaches should focus on specific coaching activities rather than engaging in "random acts of coaching." In our research, five coaching activities were identified as significant predictors of student reading and/or writing gains: conferencing with teachers, administering and discussing assessments, modeling, observing, and co-planning. The sections in the inner ring of Figure 3.2 vary in size based on the number of grade levels at which the coaching activity was a significant predictor of student reading and writing gains. For example, the conferencing section is the largest because that literacy coaching activity was a strong predictor at multiple grade levels. On the other hand, co-planning is represented by a smaller section because it was only a significant predictor at one grade level. Additionally, the section of the inner ring of the Model labeled "Other," illustrates that these five activities do not account for all of the important literacy coaching activities that may influence students' reading and writing gains.

In addition to providing literacy coaches with specific research-based suggestions about how they might prioritize their work, the Model can provide guidelines for administrators as well. After studying the Model, administrators might be encouraged to hire literacy coaches who hold some type of reading certification, to help literacy coaches establish a schedule that allows them to spend a great deal of time working with teachers, and to communicate to teachers that working with literacy coaches in specific ways can have a positive impact on students' reading and writing achievement.

HOW CAN ELEMENTARY LITERACY COACHES SUPPORT TEACHERS' PROFESSIONAL DEVELOPMENT?

When implementing many of the literacy coaching activities described in the Model, literacy coaches are providing ongoing, job-embedded professional development for individual or small groups of teachers. In addition, literacy coaches typically provide professional development on a broader scale. As literacy coaches plan to provide professional development for the teachers in their schools, they are charged with making many important decisions. For example, they must determine the topic and format for professional development activities. They also need to provide choice for teachers regarding what and how they will learn (Knight, 2009). In our work with literacy coaches and reading professionals, we've successfully used a planning approach that focuses on topic selection, grouping options, and choice to help balance the many decisions and considerations associated with planning for professional development.

Topic Selection

 Meaningful professional development connects directly with school goals, student assessment data, and teacher needs (L'Allier & Elish-Piper, 2006/2007). When determining the focus for a year- or semester-long professional development initiative, literacy coaches need to work with a committee comprised of the principal and other teachers in the school to examine school goals (e.g., school improvement plan, building leadership team goals, learning standards, implementation of a new reading or writing program, or mission statement), review student assessment data, and survey teachers about their professional learning goals and needs. Using all of the available information, the committee can then select a topic for the professional development initiative. For example, in one school where we recently worked, many of the teachers noted a lack of progress in reading-level growth when reviewing quarterly student assessment data. The teachers expressed a desire to increase the amount of daily guided reading instruction and individual reading practice in order to build students' reading skills. The Building Leadership Team (composed of the principal, literacy coach, ESL teacher, special education teacher, and one teacher from each grade level) studied several options and identified the Daily Five (Boushey & Moser, 2006) as an organizational approach to help teachers address their concerns and meet their goal of increasing reading instruction and practice. Because assessment data, teacher concerns, and goals were the basis for the selected topic, the teachers "bought into" the topic and participated enthusiastically in the professional development activities facilitated by the literacy coach.

Grouping Options

When literacy coaches plan professional development, we recommend providing a balance of whole-group sessions to help to build a sense of community, small-group sessions to allow for focused work and direct application of new ideas in a team setting, and one-on-one coaching to provide differentiated support to meet individual teachers' needs and goals (L'Allier & Elish-Piper, 2006/2007). When implemented in tandem, a balance of whole-group, small-group, and individual coaching provides a well-rounded professional development program.

In the Daily Five example mentioned previously, the literacy coach provided an overview of the Daily Five (Boushey & Moser, 2006) at a staff meeting to build a shared understanding of the model and its benefits. She followed this by meeting with each grade-level team to discuss their specific questions and concerns. Next, she provided voluntary small-group sessions for primary teachers to view videos of the Daily Five in action, and she then provided similar sessions for intermediate-grade teachers. The literacy coach also invited volunteers to participate in a book study about the Daily Five. Additionally, she offered to work with individual teachers who wished to implement the Daily Five model in their classrooms. She also volunteered to cover teachers' classrooms so they could visit each other's classrooms or other classrooms in the district where teachers were implementing the Daily Five. Near the end of the first semester, the literacy coach facilitated a whole-group session where she invited teachers to share their successes, frustrations, and questions associated with the Daily Five. After that whole-group session, many teachers who had not participated in the previous small group or individual sessions expressed an interest in learning more about the Daily Five, so the literacy coach invited those teachers to participate in the various formats of professional development planned for the spring semester.

Choice

Adult learners are highly motivated by choice (Knowles, Holton, & Swanson, 2005), and as mentioned in the two previous sections, choice must be a central consideration for meaningful professional development. In terms of topic selection, teachers must have input in order to have a sense of ownership and engagement with the topic. In addition, by providing various formats and options for professional development, teachers can choose those that match their learning preferences and professional goals. For example, some teachers prefer to work with their colleagues in grade-level teams to learn to implement a new model, approach, or strategy. Other teachers may prefer to participate in book study groups and make applications in their classrooms on their own. Still other teachers may find that individual coaching is the most effective way for them to build their professional knowledge and expertise. By providing choices in topic, format, and participation, teachers can take ownership of their own professional learning (Knowles et al.).

HOW CAN ELEMENTARY LITERACY COACHES ADDRESS SYSTEMWIDE CHALLENGES?

No matter how well prepared, enthusiastic, and motivated a literacy coach may be, challenges are simply part of the job. Several practical resources (Bean, 2010; Elish-Piper et al., 2008/2009; Toll, 2005, 2008) are available to help literacy coaches deal with common challenges associated with the day-to-day work of literacy coaches such as establishing credibility as a coach, working with hesitant teachers, and efficiently handling administrative tasks. Additionally, literacy coaches often encounter system-level challenges that can hinder their effectiveness. Based on our ongoing work with literacy coaches, we have identified three system-level challenges that can be addressed in a proactive manner before they become serious obstacles to literacy coaching. These challenges address the need for a system in which coaches have support from peers and principals and the importance of a school climate that fosters professional development and collaboration.

Establishing Support for Literacy Coaches

Literacy coaches often find themselves "caught in the middle between the clearly defined roles of teachers and administrators" (Elish-Piper et al., 2008/2009, p. 18). Additionally, a literacy coach may feel like an "island" because he or she is likely to be the only person in his or her school with coaching responsibilities. Furthermore, opportunities to connect with other literacy coaches in the school district or local area may be limited, resulting in feelings of isolation for some literacy coaches. Finally, because literacy coaches' work with teachers often deals with issues of change or frustration, coaches may find themselves depleted of energy, enthusiasm, or excitement about their work (Toll, 2005). Two effective strategies for establishing support systems for literacy coaches are mentors and building a support system of other professionals.

Mentors for Literacy Coaches

We have worked as mentors for literacy coaches for several years in multiple school districts. As literacy coaching mentors, we hold regular meetings to provide professional development for literacy coaches, conduct book study groups related to their coaching work, and conduct school-based visits with each literacy coach to address issues and challenges that are specific to that coach's situation and school. Since most literacy coaches are relatively new to the specific work of coaching, having a mentor can be an important key to successful coaching. A school district administrator such as the director of literacy programs can serve as a mentor for literacy coaches. Also, local college or university faculty members, as well as staff from regional offices of education or other countywide or statewide educational service providers can serve as mentors.

Support System of Other Professionals

Some literacy coaches may not be able to secure a mentor; therefore, they may need to "take matters into their own hands" to seek other sources of support (Toll, 2005). In larger districts, it may be possible to network with literacy coaches in other buildings to create an informal support system. If a literacy coach is enrolled in graduate courses, classmates and professors can become an excellent support system. In addition, local councils and chapters of professional organizations such as the IRA and National Council of Teachers of English (NCTE) offer networking opportunities for members to share their experiences and learn from each other. In addition, online resources such as the websites listed below provide opportunities to network with other literacy coaches around the country and world to share questions, solutions, and resources.

- Literacy Coaching Clearinghouse: *www.literacycoachingonline.org*
- K–12 Literacy Coach: *literacycoachonline.wordpress.com*
- Choice Literacy (free and subscription options): *www.choiceliteracy. com*

Securing Principal Support

When school administrators are supportive of literacy coaching, teachers are more likely to confer with the coach and participate in other literacy coaching activities (Matsumura, Sartoris, Bickel, & Garnier, 2009). Administrator support can be structural such as providing a clear job description for the literacy coach or common planning times for grade-level teams (Ippolito, 2009). It can also be relational, that is, the administrator can model collaboration, professionalism, and collegiality (Kral, 2007). Literacy coaches can build positive, supportive relationships with their principals by having regular meetings, engaging in open communication, and discussing and confirming their visions for the literacy coaching program. Furthermore, when literacy coaches are proactive and take on the role of literacy leaders in their buildings, their principals are more likely to invite them to assist in making decisions that affect their schools' literacy teaching and learning (Bean et al., 2008).

Developing a Climate for Professional Development

Literacy coaching puts ongoing professional development at the heart of teachers', administrators', and literacy coaches' work. This view of professional development requires a climate that promotes learning, collegiality, and conversations (Duncan, 2006). When literacy coaches work with their principals to develop schedules so grade-level teams have common planning times that align with the literacy coaches' schedules, coaches and teachers can use those times to discuss student work, curriculum, and professional development topics (Kral, 2007). In addition, literacy coaches can work with their principals to transform staff meetings so they focus on professional development rather than on logistical or procedural matters. For example, in one of the schools where we have worked, the principal sends a list of routine announcements via e-mail prior to the meeting so that the majority of staff meeting time can be devoted to professional development with teachers or teams sharing strategies, student work, or other classroom-related applications. In addition, teachers often read and discuss professional articles or book chapters in their staff meetings. These practices can lead to teachers being more open and interested in collaborating with literacy coaches to improve teaching and learning (Cornett & Knight, 2009).

CONCLUSION

Alicia, the elementary literacy coach introduced at the beginning of this chapter, ascribes to the belief that "Every decision a coach makes and every action a coach takes aims at improving the quality of teaching in order to improve the quality of student learning" (Casey, 2006, p. 22). Using ideas from this chapter, elementary literacy coaches like Alicia can work toward improving teaching and learning by establishing collaborative relationships, using evidence-based practices to prioritize their coaching, and delivering carefully designed professional development.

However, there is still much to learn about what constitutes effective literacy coaching at the elementary level. For example, what coaching activities in addition to conferencing, assessing, modeling, observing, and co-planning may positively influence student learning? How can we assess and improve the quality of literacy coaching? What are the strengths and limitations of the various allocations of time for coaching; does it matter if a coach is full-time, half-time, or serves as an "informal" coach? The answers to these questions could be instrumental in helping us move from discussing the "promise" of literacy coaching to confirming the "value" of literacy coaching.

ENGAGEMENT ACTIVITIES

1. Imagine that you are Alicia, the elementary literacy coach introduced in this chapter. As you prepare to meet with your principal to clarify the focus of your literacy coaching work for the school year, what key roles and responsibilities would you propose and why?

2. Rate your expertise from 1 to 5 (with 1 being low and 5 being high) on the following aspects of literacy: administering assessments, analyzing assessment data, and evidence-based instructional practices related to comprehension, vocabulary, fluency, word identification, phonemic awareness, differentiation, and motivation. If you are a literacy coach, what could you do to increase your expertise in any aspect you rated as a 3 or below? If you are a classroom teacher or administrator, how could you work with the literacy coach to increase your expertise in one or more of these areas?

3. If you are a literacy coach, record a coaching conversation with a teacher. As you listen to that recorded conversation, focus on the different stances (i.e., facilitating, collaborating, consulting) you took. In retrospect, did the stances you took match the teacher's expertise and needs? If not, what stances might have been more appropriate and why? How can your reflections about this conversation help you take appropriate stances in future coaching conversations?

4. Record all of your coaching-related activities for a 2-week period; include the teacher-related activities (e.g., modeling, co-planning, observing) as well as other coaching responsibilities (e.g., analyzing assessment data, planning professional development, attending meetings). As you analyze your work, ask the following questions: How much of my time was spent working directly with teachers? Is this consistent with the amount of time I want to be spending with teachers? If not, what changes could I make to focus more on teacher-related coaching activities? When working with teachers, how much of my time was spent on the activities included in the research-based Model discussed in this chapter? Are there opportunities that would enable me to concentrate more on these aspects of coaching?

5. Think about the description of the teacher literacy leader in Chapter 2. Compare those responsibilities with the ones described in this chapter for the elementary literacy coach. Are there any similarities? Any differences?

REFERENCES

Bean, R. M. (2004). Promoting effective literacy instruction: The challenge for literacy coaches. *California Reader, 37*(3), 58–63.

Bean, R. M. (2010). *The reading specialist: Leadership in the classroom, school, and community* (2nd ed.). New York: Guilford Press.

Bean, R. M., Belcastro, B., Draper, J., Jackson, V., Jenkins, K., Vandermolen, J., et al. (2008, December). *Literacy coaching in reading first schools: The blind men and the elephant.* Paper presented at the annual meeting of the National Reading Conference, Orlando, FL.

Bean, R. M., Jenkins, K., Belcastro, B., Wilson, R., Turner, G., & Zigmond, N. (2007, December). *What reading coaches do and why they do it: A diary study.* Paper presented at the annual meeting of the National Reading Conference, Austin, TX.

Bean, R. M., Swan, A. L., & Knaub, R. (2003). Reading specialists in schools with exemplary reading programs: Functional, versatile, and prepared. *Reading Teacher, 56,* 446–455.

Bean, R. M., & Zigmond, N. (2007, March). *A three year journey: The evolution of coaches and coaching in reading first schools.* Paper presented at the annual meeting of the American Educational Research Association Conference, Chicago, IL.

Boushey, G., & Moser, J. (2006). *The daily five: Fostering independence in the elementary grades.* Portland, ME: Stenhouse.

Casey, K. (2006). *Literacy coaching: The essentials.* Portsmouth, NH: Heinemann.

Cornett, J., & Knight, J. (2009). Research on coaching. In J. Knight (Ed.), *Coaching approaches and perspectives* (pp. 192–216). Thousand Oaks, CA: Corwin.

Deussen, T., Coskie, T., Robinson, L., & Autio, E. (2007). *"Coach" can mean many things: Five categories of literacy coaches in reading first* (Issues and Answers Report, REL 7007-No. 005). Washington, DC: U.S. Department of Education, Institute of Education Sciences, National Center for Education Evaluation and Regional Assistance, Regional Educational Laboratory Northwest. Retrieved July 5, 2007, from *ies.ed.gov/ncee/edlabs*.

Dole, J. A. (2004). The changing role of the reading specialist in school reform. *Reading Teacher, 57,* 462–471.

Duncan, M. (2006). *Literacy coaching: Developing effective teachers through instructional dialogue.* Katonah, NY: Owens.

Elish-Piper, L., & L'Allier, S. (2007). *Does literacy coaching make a difference? The effects of literacy coaching on reading achievement in grades K–3 in a reading first district.* Paper presented at the annual meeting of the National Reading Conference, Austin, TX.

Elish-Piper, L., & L'Allier, S. (2010a). Exploring the relationship between literacy coaching and student reading achievement in grades K–1. *Literacy Research and Instruction, 49,* 162–174.

Elish-Piper, L., & L'Allier, S. (2010b). *Literacy coaching and student reading and writing achievement in grades 1–7: Is there a relationship?* Research poster presented at the Annual Conference of the International Reading Association, Chicago, IL.

Elish-Piper, L., & L'Allier, S. K. (2011). Examining the relationship between literacy coaching and student reading gains in grades K–3. *Elementary School Journal, 112*(1).

Elish-Piper, L., L'Allier, S. K., & Zwart, M. (2008/2009). Literacy coaching: Challenges and promising practices for success. *Illinois Reading Council Journal, 37*(1), 10–21.

Gamse, B. C., Jacob, R. T., Horst, M., Boulay, B., & Unlu, F. (2008). *Reading first impact study final report* (NCEE 2009-4038). Washington, DC: National Center for Education Evaluation and Regional Assistance, Institute of Education Sciences, U.S. Department of Education.

International Reading Association. (2004). *The role and qualifications of the reading coach in the United States. A position statement of the International Reading Association.* Newark, DE: Author.

Ippolito, J. (2009). *Principals as partners with literacy coaches: Striking a balance between neglect and interference.* Literacy Coaching Clearinghouse Brief. Retrieved August 1, 2010, from *www.literacycoachingonline.org/briefs/Principals_as_Partners.pdf.*

Knight, J. (2009). Instructional coaching. In J. Knight (Ed.), *Coaching approaches and perspectives* (pp. 29–55). Thousand Oaks, CA: Corwin.

Knowles, M. S., Holton, E. F., & Swanson, R. A. (2005). *The adult learner* (6th ed.). Burlington, MA: Elsevier.

Kral, C. C. (2007). *Principal support for literacy coaches.* Literacy Coaching Clearinghouse Brief. Retrieved August 1, 2010, from *www.literacycoachingonline. org/briefs/PrincipalSupportFinal3-22-07.pdf.*

L'Allier, S. K., & Elish-Piper, L. (2006/2007). Ten best practices for professional development in reading. *Illinois Reading Council Journal, 35*(1), 22–27.

L'Allier, S. K., & Elish-Piper, L. (2009, May). *Literacy coaching in three school districts: Examining the effects of literacy coaching on student reading achievement.* Research poster presented at the Annual Conference of the International Reading Association, Minneapolis, MN.

L'Allier, S. K., Elish-Piper, L., & Bean, R. M. (2010). What matters for elementary literacy coaching? Guiding principles for instructional improvement and student achievement. *Reading Teacher, 63*(7), 544–554.

Lipton, L., & Wellman, B. (2007). How to talk so teachers listen. *Educational Leadership, 65*(1), 30–34.

Matsumura, L. C., Sartoris, M., Bickel, D. D., & Garnier, H. E. (2009). Leadership for literacy coaching: The principal's role in launching a new coaching program. *Educational Administration Quarterly, 45*(5), 655–693.

McCombs, J. S., & Marsh, J. A. (2009). Lessons for boosting the effectiveness of reading coaches. *Phi Delta Kappan, 90*(7), 501–507.

Moss, M., Jacob, R., Boulay, B., Horst, M., & Poulos, J. (2006). *Reading first implementation evaluation: Interim report.* Washington, DC: U.S. Department of Education. Retrieved July 5, 2007, from *www.ed.gov/rschstat/eval/other/readingfirst-interim/readingfirst/pdf.*

Rainville, K. N., & Jones, S. (2008). Situated identities: Power and positioning in the work of a literacy coach. *Reading Teacher, 61*(6), 440–448.

Russo, A. (2004). School-based coaching: A revolution in professional develop-ment—or just the latest fad? *Harvard Education Letter, 20*(4), 1–4.

Toll, C. A. (2005). *The literacy coach's survival guide: Essential questions and prac-tical answers.* Newark, DE: International Reading Association.

Toll, C. A. (2008). *Surviving but not yet thriving: Essential questions and practical answers for experienced literacy coaches.* Newark, DE: International Reading Association.

United States Department of Education. (2002). *Guidance for the reading first pro-gram.* Retrieved October 27, 2008, from *www.ed.gov/programs/readingfirst/guidance.pdf.*

4

Reading Specialists and Literacy Coaches in Secondary Schools

JACY IPPOLITO
JOANNA LIEBERMAN

Guiding Questions

How can secondary reading specialists and literacy coaches:

- Organize their time to work with both a large number of teachers across multiple content areas and a smaller number of literacy teacher leaders?
- Work with the principal and other literacy leaders in the building to create and implement a coherent plan for change?
- Encourage reluctant content-area teachers to invest deeply in disciplinary literacy practices?
- Gradually release responsibility for instructional improvement so that other stakeholders in the school are invested in the literacy growth of their colleagues and students?

Over the last decade, there has been a growing interest in the roles, responsibilities, and opportunities provided by literacy professionals working in secondary school settings (DeVries & Pratt-Fartro, 2010; Mason & Ippolito, 2009; Sturtevant & Calo, 2007). Literacy specialists and literacy coaches who are trying to create systematic instructional change at middle and high school levels face many challenges as they work with teachers to strengthen instructional practices and ultimately transform the culture of their buildings. Research suggests that it is not enough to introduce these roles into schools with few support systems established (Biancarosa, Bryk, & Dexter, 2010; Blachowicz, Obrochta, & Fogelberg, 2005; Brown et al., 2007; Kral, 2007; Ippolito, 2009, 2010a; Marsh, McCombs, Lockwood, Martorell, Gershwin, Naftel et al., 2008; Steckel, 2009; Resnick, 2009). Without appropriate supports or adequate attention to factors that encourage buildingwide growth, secondary literacy professionals may struggle to be successful. For instance, consider the wide range of factors that might determine the success of the middle school literacy coach in the case[1] below.

CASE EXAMPLE

Jessica, a successful eighth-grade English language arts (ELA) teacher in an urban middle school, was encouraged by her principal to enroll in a university-directed literacy coaching program sponsored by her district. After completing the program, Jessica became a coach in her own building and worked with colleagues one on one and in small groups on a regular basis. Inspired by the reading/writing workshop model, Jessica worked diligently to share her knowledge with both teachers and school leaders. She began coaching in all middle school ELA classrooms and modeled lessons. She helped teachers plan units of study in reading and writing. She also partnered with content-area teachers to improve reading, writing, and content-area thinking in science, social studies, and math classrooms. Jessica set up occasional meetings with her principal to report on progress in the building, and, at the urging of district administrators, she taught her colleagues how to incorporate assessment data into their instructional decision making. After 4 years of coaching, Jessica believed that differentiated workshop instruction had taken root, replacing the more traditional pedagogy that had dominated classrooms in previous years. Then a medical issue forced Jessica to vacate her position for 6 months. When she returned, Jessica was dismayed to discover that many of her colleagues had abandoned workshop teaching during her absence. Jessica worried about the impact of this instructional shift on student achievement since the school had been making steady progress on state tests since she began coaching. She was also deeply troubled that without her daily presence none of the work seemed to "stick." Jessica questioned her abilities as a coach and worried that no one else in the building seemed to share responsibility for the success of the workshop model. What are the issues Jessica is facing? What are some actions Jessica might consider and the pros and cons of each?

---

[1]This case is a composite of several middle and high school literacy professionals, with personal details obscured to protect anonymity.

Jessica's dilemma is all too common for secondary literacy professionals. In the early stages of her coaching, she met with teachers, discussed their pedagogy, and saw student achievement increase. However, despite several years on the job, Jessica remains the sole change agent in her building. Without her presence, literacy practice can and will regress. Jessica and those around her clearly need to examine approaches that encourage others to own the work as well.

To support secondary literacy professionals such as Jessica, we use the four guiding questions outlined at the beginning of this chapter to explore perennial challenges faced by literacy leaders and suggest several ways to spur instructional change. Throughout this chapter we argue that secondary literacy professionals must scrutinize how they use time, relate to the principal, attend to content-area literacy, and empower colleagues. We assert that literacy professionals who answer these questions collaboratively with teachers and school leaders are well positioned to make lasting changes in their buildings. Before exploring these challenges and making suggestions, however, it is first important to define terms and situate this chapter within a few historic debates.

DEFINING TERMS AND DEFUSING DEBATES

One of Jessica's questions early in her career may well have been "What does it mean for me to be a literacy *coach*?" This is an excellent question, as the roles, responsibilities, and terminology surrounding coaching are not only context specific, but also have shifted over the past 20 years. During the mid-20th century, reading specialists worked almost exclusively with students; however, in the 1970s and 1980s, these specialists slowly took on professional development roles working with teachers (Dole, 2004; International Reading Association [IRA], 2004; Sturtevant, 2003). As professional development and coaching roles expanded for literacy specialists in the 1990s and early 21st century, partly as a result of the reauthorization of the Elementary and Secondary Education Act (ESEA) and Title I, researchers and school leaders began considering the potential and predicaments of specialists working as coaches in secondary settings (Shanklin, 2010a, 2010b; Sturtevant, 2003; IRA, 2006; Mason & Ippolito, 2009). Although reading specialists have worked with younger students and elementary school teachers for over 100 years, it was not until the end of the 20th century that coaching at secondary levels became a more widely adopted form of ongoing professional development (for a history of reading specialists and literacy coaches in the United States, see Bean, 2010; Cassidy, Garrett, Maxfield, & Patchett, 2010; DeVries & Pratt-Fartro, 2010; Dole, 2004; Hall, 2004; Sturtevant, 2003). Secondary schools eagerly hired literacy professionals in response to No Child Left Behind pressures, but lack of agreement about roles and responsibilities created several sprawling debates (Bean, 2010; Cassidy et al., 2010; Mason & Ippolito, 2009; Sturtevant, 2003).

One major ongoing debate pertains to what we call literacy professionals who are neither classroom teachers (content area or reading specific), nor administrators, and yet who sometimes perform roles traditionally associated with each of these. In this chapter, while we acknowledge that literacy professionals at the secondary level often shift between working with adults and working with students, we have adopted the term *literacy coach* as used by Rita Bean (2010) and in the International Reading Association's revised role definitions (2010). We assume that *reading specialists* are first and foremost reading teachers with advanced educational degrees and preparation who spend the majority of their time working directly with students to improve reading and writing achievement. On the other hand, *literacy coaches* are professionals who ideally hold the "gold standard" credentials of the reading specialist (i.e., an advanced degree in reading, specialized preparation in reading instruction; Frost & Bean, 2006) but who spend the majority of their time working directly with teachers to improve instructional practices. We appreciate Bean's (2010) distinction between "coach*ing*" and "coach*es*" (p. 108), as this acknowledges that many professionals in schools take on coaching roles when they collaboratively work on adult learning. This distinction allows for the term *reading specialist* to remain intact as a label for those who have specialized preparation and knowledge of literacy instructional practices, while signaling that *coaching* is a constellation of activities that specialists and teachers might engage in on a regular basis. Given these distinctions, this chapter focuses mainly on best practices for those reading specialists (such as Jessica) who spend a large portion of their time coaching ELA and content-area teachers at the middle and high school levels. We use *coach* throughout the chapter as a blanket term for these professionals. For in-depth reviews of the role of reading specialists working primarily with students at the secondary level, see DeVries and Pratt-Fartro (2010) and Mason and Ippolito (2009).

Although debates about coaching roles, responsibilities, and terminology are important and will surely continue as schools nationwide employ and deploy coaches in various ways, a larger debate deserves attention when considering best practices for secondary literacy professionals. Educators looking at coaching in secondary settings must consider differences between elementary and secondary school organizational structures and cultural norms. Are the differences between elementary and secondary organizational structures and norms *different enough* to require fundamentally different ways of working? This debate must be carefully considered so that coaches and literacy leadership teams can decide which evidence to rely upon as they begin to address challenges and opportunities at the secondary level.

Elementary versus Secondary Coaching: Which Differences Are Just a Matter of Degree?

As a coach working at the middle school level in a K–8 school, Jessica has often considered both the supposed and real differences between working in the elementary grades and working in the middle grades. Of course, she is not alone in thinking about this dichotomy. Differences between the roles, responsibilities, and challenges of coaches at elementary versus secondary levels have been noted across sources (Bean, 2010; DeVries & Pratt-Fartro, 2010; IRA, 2006; McKenna & Walpole, 2008; Shanklin, 2010b; Smith, 2007; Snow, Ippolito, & Schwartz, 2006; Sturtevant, 2003). Building on distinctions made in the *Standards for Middle and High School Literacy Coaches* (IRA, 2006; Snow et al., 2006), McKenna and Walpole recently provided a succinct table for comparing key differences between coaching activities and challenges in elementary versus middle school settings (McKenna & Walpole, p. 150, 2010). Most of the key differences concentrate on organizational and cultural differences between schooling in elementary versus secondary levels—differences such as the larger number of teachers at the secondary level, shorter blocks of instructional time, departmentalization and increasing teacher specialization by discipline, lack of teacher preparation and lack of focus on literacy issues embedded in content-area demands, and general teacher resistance to literacy professional development (McKenna & Walpole, 2008, p. 150; McKenna & Walpole, 2010). Beyond organizational and cultural differences, differences in students' skills and needs are also noted, with students beyond elementary school possessing a wider array of literacy skills and abilities, less motivation to read, increasingly complex social pressures, and increasingly difficult content-area texts (2008, p. 150). These hypothesized differences between coaching contexts at the elementary versus secondary levels are certainly important, and few would argue that these differences do not exist to some extent in all school districts. Yet it is critical for researchers to examine which organizational and cultural differences matter most, and which differences are simply differences of degree.

Take for instance the widely held notion that secondary reading specialists and coaches have less time than their elementary counterparts to work with teachers. This notion makes intuitive sense considering the long literacy blocks (e.g., 90 minutes) present in many high-functioning elementary schools as compared to the short instructional blocks (e.g., 50 minutes) in many middle and high schools. However, recent research indicates that coaches across all grade levels struggle to find time to work with teachers. One example comes from a prominent multistate study of elementary literacy coaches working in the northwest United States (Deussen, Coskie, Robinson, & Autio, 2007). Deussen et al. found that the 190 Reading First coaches who participated in their study spent, on average, less than a third of their professional time (28%) working directly with teachers. Compare this statistic to the recent RAND study of 124 middle school literacy coaches working in 113 middle schools across eight districts in the state of Florida (McCombs & Marsh, 2009; Marsh et al., 2008). Only 15% of the 124 coaches reported spending 30% or more of their time working one on one with teachers within a given 2-week period (Marsh et al., p. 85). This was well below the state's expectation that middle school coaches would spend half of their time working in teachers' classrooms. Lest we think that the coaches were spending all of their time working with groups of teachers, the researchers shared that more than half of the 124 coaches "reported spending five hours or less during a typical two-week period" on coaching groups of teachers or leading professional development sessions (Marsh et al., p. 86).

The finding that coaches across all levels are struggling to find time to work directly with teachers is important because it suggests a slight shift in the conversation about differences between elementary and secondary coaching work. It very well may be the case that many perceived differences between elementary and secondary coaching are not differences in *kind,* but more accurately differences in *degree.* When considering roles and respon-sibilities of coaches at the elementary level (Deussen et al., 2007; Walpole & Blamey, 2008) or at the middle and high school levels (Blamey, Meyer, & Walpole, 2008; Calo, 2008; IRA, 2006; Smith, 2007), we find coaches struggling to manage the large number and diversity of roles expected. When considering how coaches spend their time at the elementary level (Deussen et al., 2007; Atteberry, Bryk, Walker, & Biancarosa, 2008) and at the sec-ondary levels (Blamey et al., 2008; Calo, 2008; Marsh et al., 2008; Smith, 2007), we find similar struggles to find time to work directly with teach-ers, avoid noninstructional administrative tasks, and provide more than a "listening ear" to teachers (Marsh et al., p. 84). While there are many ways in which we can contrast the demographics, roles, and responsibilities of coaches working in elementary versus secondary settings, we believe that there may be more gained by considering the similar challenges faced by coaches across grade levels.

Another difference in degree comes from the *Standards for Middle and High School Literacy Coaches* (IRA, 2006), which set a high bar for coaches working at the secondary level. The 2006 standards challenged secondary coaches to operate as skillful collaborators, job-embedded coaches, evalu-ators of literacy needs, and instructional strategists. However, these same standards may apply generally to coaches working across all grade levels.

Perhaps elementary coaches may not need to invest *as deeply* in content-specific disciplinary knowledge and instructional strategies as high school coaches. Perhaps elementary coaches may need greater mastery of early reading assessments than high school coaches. However, these fine-grained differences in professional knowledge may be ultimately eclipsed by broad similarities in how coaches are underutilized, isolated, misunderstood, and generally susceptible to the norms of egalitarianism, autonomy, and seniority that prevent teachers from working productively with colleagues in coaching roles (Donaldson et al., 2008).

The debate about differences between elementary and secondary coaching work is important, and certainly there are differences between elementary and secondary reading specialist and coaching roles that matter (McKenna & Walpole, 2008; Mason & Ippolito, 2009; Shanklin, 2010b; Snow et al., 2006). Nevertheless, differences must no longer be presumed without further research confirming them. By highlighting the debate about grade-level differences, we hope to temporarily diffuse it and instead focus attention on recent research on coaching efficacy and related methods for spurring instructional change across levels.

CONSIDERING AND APPLYING OUR FOUR GUIDING QUESTIONS

Accepting the premise that many differences between elementary and secondary school coaching may be more a matter of *degree* than of fundamental difference, we now turn to valuable lessons from recent research across grades to provide immediate advice to professionals working specifically in middle and high schools. Although much of the emerging research on secondary literacy leaders is still unpublished, in the form of doctoral dissertations and unpublished manuscripts from ongoing studies (Shanklin, 2010b), educators in schools need concrete recommendations now for how to align administrator, coach, and teacher goals in order to promote collaborative reflective practice. Therefore, in the following section we survey a subset of the available literature on literacy leadership to make a brief case for why organizing time, cultivating relationships with principals, working across content areas, and distributing leadership are four areas that literacy leaders such as Jessica must consider to achieve success.

Finding Time: Research and Recommendations

How coaches spend their time is of utmost importance. Recent studies have repeatedly shown that coaches across levels (and perhaps particularly in middle and high schools) find it difficult to spend time working directly with teachers—arguably the primary role for any literacy professional hired as a *coach*. In the RAND study of literacy coaching in Florida middle schools (Marsh et al., 2008), the 124 coaches reported, on average, spending less than half their time in coaching sessions and cited the lack of meeting time as a major impediment to greater success with teachers and students. This concern about lack of time, and how time is utilized, is echoed across studies at both elementary and secondary levels (Bean, Draper, Hall, Vandermolen, & Zigmond, 2010; Calo, 2008; Deussen et al., 2007; L'Allier, Elish-Piper, & Bean, 2010; Marsh et al., 2008; Smith, 2007).

When asked about how their time was being spent other than in coaching teachers, participants in both elementary and middle school studies reported spending their time working with student data—an average of 25% of the 190 elementary coaches' time (Deussen et al., 2007), while more than two-thirds of the Florida middle school coaches "reported spending six hours or more every two-week period administering or coordinating student assessments" (Marsh et al., 2008, p. 89). Other prominent activities across studies included listening to teachers' concerns, planning and providing interventions, managing reading resources, and performing noncoaching-related duties (e.g., lunch duty, bus duty). Almost half of the coaches surveyed in Florida (47%) reported that other activities and responsibilities made it difficult for them to "spend time in classrooms working with teachers" (Marsh et al., p. 86). That coaches find it difficult to spend time *coaching* is further supported by detailed qualitative case study data (Smith, 2007).

These gaps are noteworthy because connections have been found between the amount of time coaches and teachers spend together, shifts in teacher practice, and gains in student achievement. L'Allier et al. (2010) review two studies that found significant correlations between the amount of time teachers spent with a literacy coach and gains in student achievement. Furthermore, members of the research team studying literacy collaborative (LC) coaching efforts found that the amount of coaching that teachers received predicted growth in how often teachers' implemented LC instructional practices and how expert the teachers became in those practices (Hough & Bryk, 2010).

Although several of these studies were conducted in elementary school settings, the general lessons apply to secondary schools as well. In secondary schools, coaches are regularly asked to work with a large number of teachers both in the language arts department and across other content-area departments (Marsh et al., 2008). If middle and high school coaches and principals do not find ways for coaches to spend more time with teachers (and not always in large-group settings), then changes in practice and gains in achievement may not be realized.

Thinking about how Jessica might have spent her time differently in order to build capacity among teachers and sustain literacy instructional work in her absence, several recommendations emerge. One promising approach to organizing time has been outlined by Saphier and West (2009/2010), who describe a teacher leader model of coaching. In this format, the coach works within the building to identify teachers willing to open up their practice to colleagues in the role of a teacher leader. This teacher leader is willing to share both his or her instruction and reflections on those practices with colleagues, thereby forging a building culture that values collaborative work and promotes a shared understanding of strong classroom literacy practices. To promote the success of the model, the coach spends a significant amount of his or her time working with the lead teacher(s). Together they build an environment that is both welcoming to colleagues and open to pedagogical inquiry. The lead teacher's classroom becomes a place where colleagues study and learn from one another. While some may question the need for the coach to devote so much time to accomplished teachers, one need only remember Jessica's dilemma. As Saphier and West write:

> If the coach focuses on teachers whose practice is close to where the district is heading and brings these teachers into collaboration, as well as deepens their capacity to articulate their pedagogical moves and strengthens their lesson designing habits, then this first round of lead teachers can be partnered with other faculty members, and the coaching strategy becomes one of "peer coaching." (p. 47)

This model ensures that community members, other than just a coach like Jessica, have a stake in the success of the literacy program. And, it offers a framework for organizing a coach's time. Rather than having the coach serve all teachers equally, he or she can invest his or her time thoughtfully for the greatest yield. Similarly, Moran (2007) proposes a framework for considering coaching activities along a continuum of intrusiveness (from less intrusive practices such as collaboratively managing resources, to more intrusive practices such as co-teaching and co-planning). Differentiating among types of coaching activities with teachers in a large middle or high school may prove to be the key to balancing time and meeting specific teachers' needs.

These models may prove especially useful at the secondary level where coaches are working with content-area teachers (Clary, Oglan, & Styslinger, 2008). If the literacy coach can build on successful relationships with lead math, science, or social studies teachers (or department heads), they can work in concert to lure other discipline-based colleagues into the literacy conversation gradually, with lead teachers taking charge and utilizing a variety of less, and then more, intrusive coaching activities.

Working with Principals: Research and Recommendations

A solid relationship between the principal and literacy coach is a critical component of successful literacy leadership (Matsumura, Sartoris, Bickel, & Garnier, 2009). Current research on coaching at all levels points to the need for three key elements in this relationship: a clear vision or plan for literacy learning in the school, time for the principal and coach to spend together, and the principal's support for the coach's work (Ippolito, 2009; Kral, 2007; Matsumura et al., 2009; Shanklin, 2007).

For coaching to take root and flourish in a school, the principal and coach must proceed with purpose. Shanklin (2007) outlines several facets of this plan. She argues that having a clear description of the coach's roles, responsibilities, and expectations is an important starting point. If a principal and coach can agree on and outline the position, they can clearly communicate expectations to community members, thereby reducing confusion and avoiding loss of work time. Shanklin states that coaches need time to analyze data, meet with teachers in various configurations, run study groups, coach individual teachers, and attend professional development sessions. Co-constructing a "vision for literacy learning" is another shared job for the coach, principal, and literacy team in general (p. 2). Kral (2007) agrees, writing, "It is imperative that the principal, together with teachers, develop a viable plan that supports and accounts for the coaching work at the school" (p. 3). If a principal lacks a coherent literacy plan, the omission seriously jeopardizes a coach's chances for success.

Practice-based suggestions about principals' roles are bolstered by findings from a recent research study demonstrating that principals' actions and beliefs influence teachers' participation in coaching efforts as well as how school communities view a coach, presumably important factors in ultimate coaching success (Matsumura et al., 2009). Matsumura et al. outline multiple ways in which the 15 principals in their study supported their coaches: "publicly identifying the coach as a source of literacy expertise" (p. 685), "actively participat[ing] in literacy reform activities" (p. 685), and conceptualizing coaches as professionals who "helped teachers improve their instruction" (p. 686). Each of these identified principal behaviors could be encouraged not only among principals, but also among department heads and other administrators and teacher leaders in larger middle and high school settings.

Another factor to consider in building principal–coach rapport is finding time to spend together. From his portrayal of three principal prototypes, Ippolito (2009) highlights behaviors that contributed to success in a recent study of coach–teacher relationships (2010a, 2010b). One such behavior is establishing a regular meeting time between principal and coach. If they are able to do so, they may more easily engage in "collaboration and collective decision-making," factors that may support a successful coaching program (p. 4). Ippolito (2009) also argues: "Literacy coaches and principals who want to form productive partnerships must find ways to talk with one another about their shared vision for literacy instruction and professional development" (pp. 4–5).

Finally, principal support of literacy leadership work can take a myriad of forms. Ippolito (2009) and Matsumura et al. (2009) encourage principals to participate in ongoing literacy professional development to bolster systemic efforts and to stay current in their own understandings of best practices. Kral (2007) exhorts school leaders to participate in professional development to model the importance of lifelong learning. Shanklin (2007) describes regular feedback from administrators as another form of support. Coaching can be isolating, and principals can provide a much-needed sounding board both to celebrate progress and to plan for the next phase of the work. While the connection between administrative support and literacy coaching will need further exploration in future studies, these areas of planning, time, and support are powerful starting places. In Jessica's case, had she and her principal regularly shared goals and reflected on progress, her principal might have been better equipped to support and promote the work while she was away.

There are several ways to nurture shared leadership directly with a principal. The first way is to institute learning walks or instructional rounds. Fink and Resnick (2001) describe this procedure as a systematic tour of the school with attention tuned to teaching and learning. In their model, the superintendent and the principal visit every classroom and examine the teaching and learning through a particular lens. Since the publication of their work, others have built upon and described similar walk-through models (Lemons & Helsing, 2009; Rissman, Miller, & Torgesen, 2009). City, Elmore, Fiarman, and Teitel (2009) have recently written about instructional rounds, in which stakeholders in a school develop a problem of practice and use their regulated classroom observations to gather data about this issue and ultimately make informed decisions about needed change. For secondary coaches, regular walkthroughs with the principal and teacher leaders provide an opportunity for principals, coaches, and teachers to study the instructional profile of the building and fine-tune the professional learning necessary for improvement. Importantly, instructional rounds and learning walks can be easily misconstrued by teachers as evaluative; therefore, principals and coaches must make it clear through actions and words that the walkthroughs are about leadership teams learning more about instruction— not about evaluating teachers.

Were Jessica and her principal able to conduct learning walks during her previous 4 years of coaching, the principal and literacy leadership team may have been able to play a greater role in sustaining the work during Jessica's leave. They might have been able to support practices such as literacy-focused content-area meetings even though Jessica was not there to lead them. Armed with data from learning walks, they might have been able to ask other teachers to take on leadership roles in team meetings. Finally, the principal's presence during past learning walks would have emphasized that workshop literacy practices were a building priority, not just Jessica's preference. Such involvement by a principal has been described in case studies of coaches who successfully distribute literacy leadership in their buildings (Ippolito, 2009, 2010a). Although we are not suggesting that such strong collaborative relationships are easily or quickly built, we would argue that the time it takes to establish shared ownership of instructional improvement is worth the initial investment.

Related to learning walks and the collective ownership of the improvement process is the collaborative use of tools for reflecting on the relationship among leadership, coaching, teaching, and learning. One tool used in LC schools that might be adopted across grade levels to strengthen coach–principal relationships is the *Affirmation Document*.[2] As part of the annual review of progress in LC schools, literacy coaches complete an affirmation document that encourages them (with their principal and literacy leadership team) to reflect on the implementation and efficacy of the model. By examining elements of the model both individually and in concert with one another, the coach and principal (as well as the literacy leadership team as a whole) can support what is working and plan for adjustments.

Irvin, Meltzer, Mickler, Phillips, and Dean (2009) offer another rubric to help literacy leaders: "*The teacher literacy leader selection tool*" (pp. 210–211). This tool allows the principal and coach to identify the "potential roles and responsibilities of teacher leaders," to measure the feasibility of fulfilling these responsibilities in the building, and to target teachers who demonstrate strength in these areas and may be able to assume a leadership role. Again, by adopting this tool of reflection, the principal must actively seek ways to involve others in the building's literacy learning progress.

Using an affirmation document or a teacher literacy leader selection tool not only make literacy improvement efforts public, but also directly involve school principals. Because these tools demand honest reflection on implementation and progress, more community members feel a sense of responsibility. For example, if a coach is only able to fulfill a portion of his or her coaching schedule, then the coach and principal could collaboratively use these guides to explore and remedy the situation. In Jessica's case, completing an affirmation document at the end of the school year with her

---

[2]To view the *Affirmation Document*, see *www.lcosu.org/documents/lcforms/AffirmationDocument2010.pdf*.

colleagues and principal might have clarified areas of need for the principal and literacy leadership team to nurture in her stead.

Working across Content Areas: Research and Recommendations

It is a daunting task for secondary coaches to become experts not only in reading and writing research and instructional strategies, but also in the four major content areas and their canonical texts and methodologies (IRA, 2006; Snow et al., 2006; Sturtevant, 2003). In the United States we have a long national history of encouraging all content-area teachers to focus on literacy, including arguably failed efforts such as "the national Right to Read campaign, whose slogan was 'Every teacher a teacher of reading,'" which many content-area teachers viewed as a call to " 'stop' and teach the 'content' of reading in addition to that of their discipline" (Jacobs, 2008, p. 19). While numerous books filled with content-area literacy strategies have been published, many middle and high school literacy professionals such as Jessica struggle when it comes to supporting literacy work in math, social studies, and science classrooms (Jacobs). A new focus on *disciplinary literacy* might provide some answers.

Recently, research on content-area literacy has changed course. In the last few years, the focus has shifted to examining *disciplinary literacy*, or the notion that disciplinary experts (i.e., applied mathematicians, bench scientists, social historians) each rely on unique ways of thinking, reading, and writing. Shanahan and Shanahan (2008) describe a multiyear project examining how content experts approached the literacy demands of their discipline. They emerged from the study recommending that teachers model strategies that disciplinary experts use themselves (e.g., mathematicians rereading proofs again and again until they can define every term; historians reading for bias in primary documents). Although there may be certain fundamental similarities in reading a historical document and a new mathematical treatise (e.g., high-frequency English words might appear in both), the specialized vocabulary along with the particular purposes for reading each could very well dictate qualitatively different strategies needed to comprehend the two pieces. Shanahan and Shanahan (2008) and Moje (2008) argue that while the earliest grades should rightly focus on "basic" and "intermediate" literacy skills (Shanahan & Shanahan, pp. 43–46) such as decoding words and building fluency, respectively, middle and high school content-area teachers need support in teaching the particular disciplinary ways of thinking, reading, and writing that occupations demand. The need for disciplinary literacy support provides a window of opportunity for many secondary coaches.

Beyond a focus on disciplinary literacy, successfully working across content areas also requires higher degrees of collaboration and administrative support. Clary et al. (2008) suggest a number of important factors when focusing on content-area professional development: fostering "teachers' understanding of themselves as change agents" (p. 3), "involving teacher-leaders" from the content areas who are deeply invested in school reform efforts (p. 3), and building sustainable structures for professional development that connect school and district efforts. Similarly, the Pennsylvania High School Coaching Initiative (PAHSCI) coaching project in Pennsylvania (Brown et al., 2007) demonstrated great success with coaching content-area teachers when efforts were tailored toward content-area teachers' instructional goals and supported by building and district administrators. This study showed that principals, coaches, and teachers must all see how the professional development work will enrich classroom instruction in each content area to sustain investment in coaching efforts.

Thinking of how Jessica might apply these notions, we would recommend that she shift the nature of the conversation by working alongside content-area lead teachers, tailoring general literacy strategies to meet specific disciplinary goals, and collaboratively designing curricula that bolster students' content knowledge and literacy skills. In many ways, this recommendation echoes changes Jessica is already seeking. Not only can Jessica no longer be the lone expert, but also she must encourage her content-area colleagues to analyze the literacy demands of their content areas and develop disciplinary literacy expertise alongside her. She would be well advised to keep the content front and center, and then help colleagues to decide which instructional and cognitive strategies best serve content goals.

Jessica might also focus on vocabulary and classroom discussions. The collaborative study and instruction of academic language and use of classroom discussion are two specific areas that may be seen as important to both secondary coaches and content-area teachers. The Word Generation[3] project, begun by the Strategic Education Research Partnership, has found that when groups of content-area teachers collectively teach the same academic vocabulary words (i.e., words found across content-area texts), and explicitly focus on generating vocabulary-rich classroom discussions, literacy achievement can be influenced (Snow, Lawrence, & White 2009; Lawrence, White, & Snow, 2010; White & Kim, 2009). Findings are preliminary, but the project has wide implications for how vocabulary instruction and classroom discussions might be a way for coaches to begin more disciplinary-specific conversations with content-area teachers.

Related findings from the Reading Assistance Initiative for Secondary School Educators (RAISSE) project, another initiative looking at literacy

---

[3]For more information about Word Generation, see *wg.serpmedia.org*.

learning in secondary schools, suggest other directions for professional development (Clary et al., 2008). In this study, a content-area teacher prepared as a literacy teacher leader attended professional development and led site-based study groups over the course of 2 years. Factors that influenced the successful transformation of classroom practice included allowing teacher leader candidates to influence the agenda of their own professional development and encouraging collaboration of experts among and between content areas. In Jessica's school, findings from these studies may prove especially helpful as she seeks to recruit the next wave of literacy leaders. She may need to identify future teacher leaders who come from the content areas and invest deeply in disciplinary literacy learning to capture the attention of and create investment for all her colleagues.

Gradually Releasing Responsibility: Research and Recommendations

Although the gradual release of responsibility model of instruction (Pearson & Gallagher, 1983) is now well known by many teachers working with students, it is a model that is less often discussed by those working with adults in professional development settings. However, in considering the effect coaches have on transforming literacy, it may well be the essential element in creating lasting change. For literacy coaches to permanently and effectively change teacher practice in a building, they must seek to share the responsibility for transformation with others.

Part of the work of releasing responsibility to teachers is carefully considering if and when a middle or high school faculty is ready to engage in coaching work. City (2007) studied two small urban high schools with new coaching programs. In both cases, she determined that employing coaches may not have been the best use of resources because neither school was philosophically nor organizationally prepared to make good use of the coach. She argues that many schools need to "cultivate the conditions for coaching first before deploying this potentially rich resource" (p. 7). Principals, coaches, and literacy leadership teams need to carefully consider if and when coaching is the right format for literacy learning for a school at a particular time. Once having determined that there is a cadre of teachers open to the prospect, then other factors might be considered. In her review of 60 dissertations on coaching written in the last decade, Shanklin (2010b) found promising reports of coaching and literacy learning in secondary schools where data were examined and instructional improvement was valued by the various stakeholders. Ensuring that teachers regularly reflect on their practice in small-group settings before introducing coaching might increase the ripple effect of literacy learning and instructional change once a coach is introduced.

In addition to fostering a receptive climate for change, research on how teachers talk about instructional practice within their buildings (to whom, how often, etc.) within professional networks is emerging as another important way for thinking about spreading change (Atteberry & Bryk, 2010). Changing teachers' instructional practices can be a long and difficult enterprise (Guskey, 2002; Guskey & Yoon, 2009; Huberman, 1995). Recently, complex networks describing how adult professional learning in schools affects student learning have been hypothesized and preliminarily tested (Atteberry & Bryk, 2010; Atteberry et al., 2008; Biancarosa et al., 2010; Resnick, 2009). Increasingly, organizational researchers are studying how teacher leaders affect adult learning and improvements in student achievement, including how professionals such as coaches can influence social networks in schools over time (Atteberry & Bryk). As part of a recent study of LC coaching,[4] researchers determined that with a coaching program in place not only did teacher expertise and student achievement increase, but professional interactions increased as well (Atteberry & Bryk). Over the course of the 4-year study, on average, more teachers participated in professional conversations about literacy practice, and they began speaking with colleagues in new configurations: both across and within grade levels. It seems that the schools witnessing the greatest student achievement also witnessed greater adult communication (Atteberry & Bryk, p. 3). All of this points to the need for literacy coaches to urge colleagues to share ownership for collective instructional improvement. The coach cannot remain at the center of all professional conversations if systemic improvement is the goal.

While many of our suggestions assume a shared responsibility for change, there are several documented ways to promote stronger communities. The first is the literacy leadership team. Every LC coach knows that he or she must convene and participate in a literacy leadership team in his or her building. The team meets regularly to raise buildingwide literacy issues, think through possible responses to those issues, and devise buildingwide policies that strengthen teaching and learning. While the coach is an integral member of the team, it is not *his or her* team alone. Voices of teachers, including content-area teachers, the coach, and the administrator carry equal weight.

Lent (2007) outlines another vision for how adults in a school community work together to sustain a meaningful dialogue about their students' learning and their role in teaching them. Lent envisions school communities crafting a 3-year plan, moving from exploration of literacy learning to "embedded professional development" to sustained literacy learning, that

---

[4]For an online summary, see *literacycollaborative.org/docs/TQ-summary-for-website-new.pdf*.

reaches out to all the faculty and eventually the students as well (p. 53). In this model, willing and interested faculty members (including the principal) meet regularly to define a literacy challenge that is informed by data. A requirement of Lent's model is a "commitment to deep understanding" on the part of the members (p. 52). Members of this professional learning community make a promise to work collaboratively to uncover better literacy understandings with the goal of transforming students' learning experiences. Had Jessica's school established a vibrant literacy leadership team or a literacy learning community in the earlier years of her coaching, others might have recognized the need to carry on the planning and policy making in her absence.

Finally, the use of formal or informal discussion protocols for observing instruction, discussing best practices, and conducting learning walks has been identified as a key factor in helping coaches balance the competing pressures of instituting particular practices while simultaneously helping teachers develop skills and practices of their own choosing (Ippolito, 2010a). For our purposes, protocols are any agreed upon set of discussion or observation rules that guide coach/teacher/student work, discussion, and interactions (Ippolito & Lieberman, 2010). Protocols for guiding group observations of instruction, debriefing observations, and planning have recently been posted by literacy coaches and teacher leaders on the Literacy Coaching Clearinghouse (LCC).[5] While the protocols posted on the LCC are literacy-specific, discussion guides that might be used among middle and high school content-area teachers, department heads, and administrators are offered by the School Reform Initiative[6] and in *The Power of Protocols* (McDonald, Mohr, Dichter, & McDonald, 2007). McDonald et al. (2007) assert that protocols "force transparency by segmenting elements of a conversation whose boundaries otherwise blur: talking and listening, describing and judging, proposing and giving feedback" (p. 7). Using discussion protocols can help teachers and administrators respectfully share ownership of the improvement effort, reflect on their own practices, and closely examine the many factors in schools that perpetuate poor achievement (Fahey, 2011; McDonald et al.). Whether exploring a professional text, examining samples of student work, or scrutinizing a lesson plan gone awry, all participants, not just the coach, must contribute. With effective facilitators of protocol-based discussions (initially the literacy coaches themselves, and then eventually all participating teachers), participants do not feel judged. In fact, they often come to view themselves as critical stakeholders in their own progress as well as that of their colleagues. By engaging in protocol-

---

[5]For sample coaching-related protocols, see *www.literacycoachingonline.org/tools.html*.

[6]See *www.schoolreforminitiative.org/protocol/sitemap.html*.

based discussions early in her coaching work, Jessica could have established structures for teachers to use in her absence.

CONCLUSION

As we consider the next generation of literacy coaching at the secondary level, we need to develop practices that enable us to build capacity at the district and building levels. In many ways, the next wave of work runs parallel to the gradual release of responsibility we see in our strongest literacy classrooms. As the teacher models, scaffolds, and supports his or her students' learning, he or she gradually releases that support to determine the extent to which students can navigate on their own. Literacy coaches must do the same. The coach cannot be the sole purveyor of literacy expertise; that expertise must be shared among the building leader, department heads, other teachers, and specialists.

Jessica's case arises at an interesting time in the history of literacy coaching. As we have noted, coaching is no longer a novel phenomenon, and research is beginning to offer valuable insights. We now know that secondary literacy professionals struggle to find enough coaching time, strive to develop better relationships with administrators, seek to integrate content learning into their practice, and yearn to share their expertise and leadership with others. Yet, professionals like Jessica are still facing uncharted waters. They do not always know or cannot always put into action the steps that will transform teacher practice, build community, and raise student achievement. By highlighting research and best practices related to our four guiding questions, we offer secondary literacy professionals a means of analyzing their practice and experimenting with new ideas—first steps to help make coaching "stick."

ENGAGEMENT ACTIVITIES

1. Reread the opening case example. How might you respond to the following questions based on information presented in the chapter?
   a. *Time.* Jessica has decided to alter her coaching schedule. She has opted to coach in cycles, working with a few teachers at a time, several periods a week, rather than every teacher once in a while. How might Jessica plan her coaching cycles to maximize efficacy? Who might Jessica's allies be in collaboratively designing such a plan?
   b. *Relationship with principal.* Jessica has managed to set up a weekly time to meet with her principal. What might she discuss in those

meetings? Who else might she invite to work on a literacy leadership team together? What actions might be taken as a result of these meetings?

    c. *Content-area literacy.* Jessica would like to see more attention paid to literacy learning across content areas. How might her coaching work with content-area teachers differ from her work with English teachers? How might it overlap?

    d. *Gradual release of responsibility.* Jessica would like other teachers in her building to take on more leadership roles related to literacy instruction. How might Jessica start to plan for a teacher–leader program in her building?

2. After reading Chapters 3 and 4, discuss with peers the following questions: What are your thoughts about the similarities and differences in roles and responsibilities of the elementary versus secondary literacy coach? At which level would you feel more comfortable working—and why?

REFERENCES

Atteberry, A., & Bryk, A. S. (2010). *The effects of literacy coaching on school professional networks.* Paper presented at the annual conference of the American Educational Research Association, Denver, CO.

Atteberry, A., Bryk, A. S., Walker, L., & Biancarosa, G. (2008). *Variations in the amount of coaching in literacy collaborative schools.* Paper presented at the annual conference of the American Educational Research Association, New York, NY.

Bean, R. M. (2010). *The reading specialist: Leadership in the classroom, school, and community* (2nd ed.). New York: Guilford Press.

Bean, R. M., Draper, J. A., Hall, V., Vandermolen, J., & Zigmond, N. (2010). Coaches and coaching in reading first schools. *Elementary School Journal, 111*(1), 87–114.

Biancarosa, G., Bryk, A. S., & Dexter, E. R. (2010). Assessing the value-added effects of literacy collaborative professional development on student learning. *Elementary School Journal, 111*(1), 7–34.

Blachowicz, C. L. Z., Obrochta, C., & Fogelberg, E. (2005). Literacy coaching for change. *Educational Leadership, 62*(6), 55–58.

Blamey, K. L., Meyer, C. K., & Walpole, S. (2008). Middle and high school literacy coaches: A national survey. *Journal of Adolescent and Adult Literacy, 52*(4), 310–323.

Brown, D., Reumann-Moore, R., Roseann, H., Jolley, B. C., Riffer, M., du Plessis, P., et al. (2007, October). *Making a difference: Year two report of the Pennsylvania high school coaching initiative: Executive summary.* Philadelphia: Research for Action. Retrieved April 22, 2008, from *www.researchforaction.org/search2.*

Calo, K. M. (2008). *An exploration of middle school literacy coaching across the United States.* Doctoral dissertation, George Mason University. Retrieved June 15, 2010, from *digilib.gmu.edu:8080/bitstream/1920/3086/1/Calo_Kristine. pdf.*

Cassidy, J., Garrett, S. D., Maxfield, P., & Patchett, C. (2010). Literacy coaching: Yesterday, today, and tomorrow. In J. Cassidy, S. D. Garrett, & M. Sailors (Eds.), *Literacy coaching: Research & practice: 2009 CEDER yearbook* (pp. 15–28). Corpus Christi, TX: Center for Educational Development, Evaluation, and Research; Texas A&M University–Corpus Christi College of Education.

City, E. A. (2007). Is coaching the best use of resources? For some schools, other investments should come first. *Harvard Education Letter, 23*(5), 8, 6–7.

City, E. A., Elmore, R. F., Fiarman, S. E., & Teitel, L. (2009). *Instructional rounds in education: A network approach to improving teaching and learning.* Cambridge, MA: Harvard Education Press.

Clary, D., Oglan, V., & Styslinger, M. (2008). It is not just about content: Preparing content area teachers to be literacy leaders. *Literacy Coaching Clearinghouse.* Retrieved August 8, 2010, from *www.literacycoachingonline.org/briefs/Preparing_Content_Area.pdf.*

Deussen, T., Coskie, T., Robinson, L., & Autio, E. (2007). *"Coach" can mean many things: Five categories of literacy coaches in reading first* (Issues & Answers Report, REL 2007-No. 005). Washington, DC: United States Department of Education, Institute of Education Sciences, National Center for Education Evaluation and Regional Assistance, Regional Educational Laboratory Northwest.

DeVries, N., & Pratt-Fartro, T. (2010). *Literacy coaching to build adolescent learning: 5 pillars of practice.* Thousand Oaks, CA: Corwin.

Dole, J. A. (2004). The changing role of the reading specialist in school reform. *Reading Teacher, 57*(5), 462–471.

Donaldson, M. L., Johnson, S. M., Kirkpatrick, C. L., Marinell, W. H., Steele, J. L., & Szczesiul, S. A. (2008). Angling for access, bartering for change: How second-stage teachers experience differentiated roles in schools. *Teachers College Record, 110*(5), 1088–1114.

Fahey, K. M. (2011). Still learning about leading: A leadership critical friends group. *Journal of Research in Leadership Education, 6*(1), 1–35.

Fink, E., & Resnick, L. B. (2001). Developing principals as instructional leaders. *Phi Delta Kappan, 82*(8), 598–606.

Frost, S., & Bean, R. (2006). Qualifications for literacy coaches: Achieving the gold standard. *Literacy Coaching Clearinghouse.* Retrieved June 15, 2010, from *www.literacycoachingonline.org/briefs/LiteracyCoaching.pdf.*

Guskey, T. R. (2002). Professional development and teacher change. *Teachers and Teaching: Theory and Practice, 8*(3/4), 381–391.

Guskey, T. R., & Yoon, K. S. (2009). What works in professional development? *Phi Delta Kappan, 90*(7), 495–500.

Hall, B. (2004). Literacy coaches: An evolving role. *Carnegie Reporter, Carnegie Corporation of New York, 3*(1). Retrieved June 15, 2010, from *www.carnegie. org/reporter/09/literacy/index.html.*

Hough, H. J., & Bryk, A. S. (2010). *The effects of literacy coaching on teacher practice.* Paper presented at the annual conference of the American Educational Research Association, Denver, CO.

Huberman, M. (1995). Networks that alter teaching: Conceptualizations, exchanges, and experiments. *Teachers and Teaching: Theory and Practice, 1*(2), 193–211.

International Reading Association. (2004). *The role and qualifications of the reading coach in the United States* [Position statement]. Newark, DE: Author. Retrieved June 15, 2010, from *www.reading.org/Libraries/Position_Statements_and_Resolutions/ps1065_reading_coach.sflb.ashx.*

International Reading Association. (2006). *Standards for middle and high school literacy coaches.* Newark, DE: Author. Retrieved June 15, 2010, from *www.reading.org/downloads/resources/597coaching_standards.pdf.*

International Reading Association. (2010). *Standards for reading professionals— Revised 2010.* Newark, DE: Author.

Ippolito, J. (2009). Principals as partners with literacy coaches: Striking a balance between neglect and interference. *Literacy Coaching Clearinghouse.* Retrieved June 15, 2010, from *www.literacycoachingonline.org/briefs/Principals_as_Partners.pdf.*

Ippolito, J. (2010a). Three ways that literacy coaches balance responsive and directive relationships with teachers. *Elementary School Journal, 111*(1), 164–190.

Ippolito, J. (2010b). Investigating how literacy coaches understand and balance responsive and directive relationships with teachers. In J. Cassidy, S. D. Garrett, & M. Sailors (Eds.), *Literacy coaching: Research & practice: 2009 CEDER yearbook* (pp. 45–66). Corpus Christi, TX: Center for Educational Development, Evaluation, and Research; Texas A&M University–Corpus Christi College of Education.

Ippolito, J., & Lieberman, J. (2010). *Coaches as critical friends: A sustainable model for coach support.* Presentation at the 2nd Annual International Literacy Coaching Summit, Texas A&M University–Corpus Christi, TX.

Irvin, J. I., Meltzer, J., Mickler, M. J., Phillips, M., & Dean, N. (2009). *Meeting the challenge of adolescent literacy: Practical ideas for literacy leaders.* Newark, DE: International Reading Association.

Jacobs, V. A. (2008). Adolescent literacy: Putting the crisis in context. *Harvard Educational Review, 78*(1), 7–39.

Kral, C. (2007). Principal support for literacy coaches. *Literacy Coaching Clearinghouse.* Retrieved June 15, 2010, from *www.literacycoachingonline.org/briefs/PrincipalSupportFinal3-22-07.pdf.*

L'Allier, S., Elish-Piper, L., & Bean, R. M. (2010). What matters for elementary literacy coaching? Guiding principles for instructional improvement and student achievement. *Reading Teacher, 63*(7), 544–554.

Lawrence, J. F., White, C., & Snow, C. E. (2010). The words students need. *Educational Leadership, 68*(2), 23–26.

Lemons, R. W., & Helsing, D. (2009). Learning to walk, walking to learn: Reconsidering the walkthrough as an improvement strategy. *Phi Delta Kappan, 90*(7), 478–484.

Lent, R. C. (2007). *Literacy learning communities: A guide for creating sustainable change in secondary schools.* Portsmouth, NH: Heinemann.

Marsh, J. A., McCombs, J. S., Lockwood, J. R., Martorell, F., Gershwin, D., Naftel, S., et al. (2008). *Supporting literacy across the sunshine state: A study of Florida middle school reading coaches.* Prepared for Carnegie Corporation of New York. Santa Monica, CA: RAND Corporation.

Mason, P. A., & Ippolito, J. (2009). What is the role of the reading specialist in promoting adolescent literacy? In J. Lewis (Ed.), *Essential questions in adolescent literacy: Teachers and researchers describe what works in classrooms* (pp. 312–336). New York: Guilford Press.

Matsumura, L. C., Sartoris, M., Bickel, D. D., & Garnier, H. (2009). Leadership for literacy coaching: The principal's role in launching a new coaching program. *Educational Administration Quarterly, 45*(5), 655–693.

McCombs, J. S., & Marsh, J. A. (2009). Lessons for boosting the effectiveness of reading coaches. *Phi Delta Kappan, 90*(7), 501–507.

McDonald, J. P., Mohr, N., Dichter, A., & McDonald, E. C. (2007). *The power of protocols: An educator's guide to better practice* (2nd ed.). New York: Teachers College Press.

McKenna, M. C., & Walpole, S. (2008). *The literacy coaching challenge: Models and methods for grades K–8.* New York: Guilford Press.

McKenna, M. C., & Walpole, S. (2010). *Literacy coaching in the middle grades.* Retrieved June 15, 2010, from *www.adlit.org/article/36143.*

Moje, E. B. (2008). Foregrounding the disciplines in secondary literacy teaching and learning: A call for change. *Journal of Adolescent and Adult Literacy, 52*(2), 96–107.

Moran, M. C. (2007). *Differentiated literacy coaching: Scaffolding for student and teacher success.* Alexandria, VA: Association for Supervision and Curriculum Development.

Pearson, P. D., & Gallagher, M. C. (1983). The instruction of reading comprehension. *Contemporary Educational Psychology, 8,* 317–344.

Resnick, L. B. (2009). Nested learning systems for the thinking curriculum. *Educational Researcher, 39*(3), 183–197.

Rissman, L. M., Miller, D. H., & Torgesen, J. K. (2009). *Adolescent literacy walkthrough for principals: A guide for instructional leaders.* Portsmouth, NH: RMC Research Corporation, Center on Instruction.

Saphier, J., & West, L. (2009/2010). How coaches can maximize student learning. *Phi Delta Kappan, 91*(4), 46–50.

Shanahan, T., & Shanahan, C. (2008). Teaching disciplinary literacy to adolescents: Rethinking content-area literacy. *Harvard Educational Review, 78*(1), 40–59.

Shanklin, N. (2007). What supports do literacy coaches need from administrators in order to succeed? *Literacy Coaching Clearinghouse.* Retrieved June 15, 2010, from *www.literacycoachingonline.org/briefs/LCSupportsNSBrief.pdf.*

Shanklin, N. (2010a). Literacy coaching: What are we learning? In J. Cassidy, S. D. Garrett, & M. Sailors (Eds.), *Literacy coaching: Research & practice: 2009 CEDER yearbook* (pp. 31–44). Corpus Christi, TX: Center for Educational Development, Evaluation, and Research, Texas A&M University–Corpus Christi College of Education.

Shanklin, N. (2010b). *Middle school & high school coaching: What can we learn from the current research?* Presentation at the 2nd Annual International Literacy Coaching Summit, Texas A&M University–Corpus Christi, TX.

Smith, A. T. (2007). The middle school literacy coach: Considering roles in context. In D. W. Rowe, R. T. Jiménez, D. L. Compton, D. K. Dickinson, Y. Kim, K. M. Leander, & V. J. Risko (Eds.), *56th yearbook of the national reading conference* (pp. 53–67). Oak Creek, WI: National Reading Conference.

Snow, C., Ippolito, J., & Schwartz, R. (2006). What we know and what we need to know about literacy coaches in middle and high schools: A research synthesis and proposed research agenda. In International Reading Association *Standards for Middle and High School Literacy Coaches* (pp. 35–49). Newark, DE: Author. Retrieved June 15, 2010, from *www.reading.org/downloads/resources/597coaching_standards.pdf.*

Snow, C. E., Lawrence, J. F., & White, C. (2009). Generating knowledge of academic language among urban middle school students. *Journal of Research on Educational Effectiveness, 2*(4), 325–344.

Steckel, B. (2009). Fulfilling the promise of literacy coaches in urban schools: What does it take to make an impact? *Reading Teacher, 63*(1), 14–23.

Sturtevant, E. G. (2003). *The literacy coach: A key to improving teaching and learning in secondary schools.* Washington, DC: Alliance for Excellent Education. Retrieved June 15, 2010, from *www.all4ed.org/publications/LiteracyCoach.pdf.*

Sturtevant, E. G., & Calo, K. M. (2007). Crafting successful roles for literacy coaches in secondary schools (remember chocolate). In J. Lewis & G. Moorman (Eds.), *Adolescent literacy instruction: Policies and promising practices* (pp. 110–123). Newark, DE: International Reading Association.

Walpole, S., & Blamey, K. L. (2008). Elementary literacy coaches: The reality of dual roles. *Reading Teacher, 62*(3), 222–231.

White, C., & Kim, J. (2009). *Putting the pieces of the puzzle together: How systematic vocabulary instruction and expanded learning time can address the literacy gap.* Center for American Progress. Retrieved June 15, 2010, from *www.americanprogress.org/issues/2009/05/pdf/elt_may09.pdf.*

5

—

The Role
of the Special Educator
A Balancing Act

Naomi Zigmond
Amanda Kloo

Guiding Questions

- In what ways has the role of the special educator changed over the last 10 years?
- What are some of the issues and challenges confronting the special education teacher today?

Special education is in place to provide the additional services, support, programs, and/or specialized placements or environments to ensure that *qualifying* students' educational needs are provided for. Qualifying students have a disability *and* educational needs that require support that goes beyond what is normally offered or received in the general education school/classroom setting.

Special education teachers provide this unequal support to students with disabilities in a variety of settings. Some have their own classrooms of only special education students. Others work as special education resource teachers and offer individualized help to students included in general education classrooms. Still others teach together with general education teachers in classes that include both general and special education students. Considerably fewer special education teachers work in residential facilities or tutor students in homebound or hospital environments.

Special educators teach children and youth whose learning is affected by autism, emotional disturbance, learning disabilities, mental retardation, multiple disabilities, orthopedic impairments, other health impairments, sensory impairments, speech and language impairments, and traumatic brain injury. Typically, special educators at the elementary level provide early learning skills, behavioral strategies, reading instruction, and content knowledge. Special educators at the secondary level focus on subject-specific information, practical life skills, career counseling, and the transition from school to the workforce. Special education teachers use various techniques to promote learning. Depending on the student, teaching methods can include intensive individualized instruction, problem-solving assignments, and small-group work.

Most special education teachers do more than teach; they also assume leadership roles in their school. They work closely with parents to inform them of their children's progress and suggest techniques to promote learning outside of school. They help general educators adapt curriculum materials and teaching and testing techniques to meet the needs of students with disabilities. They coordinate the work of teachers, teacher assistants, and related service personnel, such as therapists and social workers, to meet the individualized needs of the student within inclusive special education programs. They communicate and coordinate with others involved in the child's well-being, including parents, social workers, school psychologists, occupational and physical therapists, school administrators, reading specialists, and teachers. These leadership roles often cause considerable stress; they require a substantial amount of paperwork documenting each student's progress and carry with them the threat of litigation by parents against the school or district if correct procedures are not followed or if the parents feel that their child is not receiving an adequate education. As leaders, special educators must skillfully balance pedagogy and methodology, advocacy and collaboration, and policy and practicality to provide a comprehensive yet individualized and appropriate education to students with disabilities.

The following case study illustrates the pressures and pitfalls of this balancing act as one special educator grapples with the multiple facets of his leadership role.

CASE EXAMPLE

Stephen had been teaching third grade for 5 years. He had an excellent teaching record, and positive relationships with colleagues and parents. Each year, about 17 or 18 of his 25 students scored proficient or above in reading and math on the state accountability test. But although most of his students were doing well, Stephen was frustrated about being unable to address the needs of his lowest-performing students, especially those students with disabilities who were fully included in his classroom. Fueled by this frustration, Stephen took a 1-year leave of absence to earn special education certification. When he returned to the district as a special education teacher, Stephen was assigned to provide learning support to grades K–3 at the very school at which he had been teaching. He was excited about his new role in that school. He now had a fresh arsenal of specialized skills for diagnostic teaching, direct instruction, positive behavior support, reading and math intervention, instructional accommodations, and curricular modifications. He was sure he could make a real difference in the academic achievement of the very students he had not helped before.

There were 16 primary grade (K–3) students eligible for special education on Stephen's student roster. Stephen was responsible for developing and revising the 16 individualized education plans (IEPs), for completing reevaluations for some of these students, for devising behavior intervention plans for others, and for completing a variety of paperwork. His students all began the school year fully included at their grade level, and Stephen began the year co-teaching in reading and/or math in multiple kindergartens through third-grade classrooms. Additionally, he was scheduled to provide 30 minutes daily of small-group, Tier 3 instruction as part of the school's response-to-intervention (RTI) framework. His intervention group consisted of five kindergarten and five first-grade students considered at serious risk for failure, only four of whom had IEPs, were eligible for special education, and on his case roster. On top of that, Stephen was expected to provide professional support to fellow primary teachers in progress-monitoring methodologies, RTI decision making, and differentiated instruction for students with IEPs as well as students at risk. Of course, he also had to adapt materials for his 16 students to promote their access to grade-level content, to consult with their general education teachers about each students' learning and behavior needs, to consult with teachers and related service personnel about new students being referred for a special education evaluation, to plan for and proctor accommodated testing experiences for eligible students, and to communicate progress and problems to his students' parents.

Stephen enjoyed being part of the primary grades RTI team and was skilled in implementing the scripted intervention program that had been adopted for Tier 3 intervention but there were at least 12 students on his case roster to whom he never provided direct instruction. He saw value in being with his students in their general education classrooms and he liked being able to help them complete their in-class assignments, but he knew his students had deficits in prerequisite skills that Stephen did not have time to deal with. He felt empowered and appreciated for the support and guidance he provided to his colleagues. But he had become a special education teacher to provide direct and special instruction to struggling students, not to teachers. Furthermore, Stephen worried about being held responsible for his students' meeting their IEP goals as well as for the success of the school's "IEP subgroup" on the annual state test. Ultimately, Stephen sacrificed his lunch period and made himself available before school and after school to help students with schoolwork on a catch-as-catch-can basis. What are the issues facing Stephen? Why can't he just take his 16 students to a special education classroom and teach them what he thinks they need to learn? How might he find a more satisfying balance of responsibilities and roles?

A BRIEF HISTORY OF SPECIAL EDUCATION

To understand the contemporary pressures experienced by the special education teacher in today's schools, it is useful to review, briefly, the evolution of special education in modern times. Compared to general education, mandated special education in the United States is relatively new. At the beginning of the 19th century, and for about a century afterward, there was no special education in public schools; nearly all special education was reserved for persons who were blind or deaf, or persons with severe mental retardation or severe emotional disturbance and services were provided in residential treatment programs or institutions that "protect[ed] ... the handicapped from society and society from the handicapped" (Lilly, 1979, p. 4).

Milder forms of disability became apparent in the schools only after states changed their public education laws from permissive to mandatory and students attended school because it was required, not because they wanted to. Teachers found these students bothersome and the curriculum not appropriate for them. A new and heightened interest in the use of intelligence tests defined many of them as *morons* (the unfortunate term used to describe students with mild mental retardation; Lilly, 1979, p. 4). To accommodate teacher complaints, these "unsuitable students" were expelled, excluded, or segregated to special education classes or schools. Public schools were not *required* to educate students with disabilities, and, "as recently as 1958 and 1969, the courts upheld legislation permitting the exclusion of students whom school officials judged would not benefit from public education or who might be disruptive to other students" (Yell, 1998, p. 54).

During the last half of the 20th century, great strides were made through litigation, legislation, and public policy to bring the right to a free, public education to all citizens on an equal basis. The 1954 *Brown v. Board of Education* Supreme Court decision and subsequent civil rights legislation guaranteed equal access to educational opportunities for students from minority groups (Elementary and Secondary Education Act of 1965, especially Title I), students whose primary language was not English (Title VI of the Civil Rights Act of 1964), and girls (Title IX of the Education Amendments of 1972). A natural extension of this push for civil rights and equal educational opportunity (though it was largely ignored until many years later) was Section 504 of the Rehabilitation Act of 1973, "the civil rights declaration of the handicapped" (Humphrey in Yell, 1998, p. 95). Section 504 called for structural alterations, redesign of equipment, reassignment to classes, assignment of aides, regular classroom interventions, and *reasonable accommodations and modifications* of classroom methods, materials, and procedures to make them accessible and allow the student with a disability an *equal* opportunity to benefit from the educational program being provided to others (Zirkel & Kincaid, 1993). The focus was on accessibility and equivalence. Section 504 was a civil rights law, not a *special education* law.

Modern special education was born 2 years later with the passage of Public Law 94-142 (Education of All Handicapped Children, 1975). The law was a natural, though hard-fought, extension of the civil rights legislation that preceded it, but Public Law 94-142 went further than the promise of *equal* educational opportunity. It promised *un*equal educational opportunities for those students with disabilities who needed a *special* education. Public Law 94-142 (henceforth Individuals with Disabilities Education Act [IDEA]) addressed the procedural responsibilities, identification and evaluation, placement, reevaluation, and procedural safeguards outlined in Section 504. However, IDEA was unique in that it focused on ensuring educational benefit, not equivalency, for those students whose disabilities adversely impacted their educational performance. It implied that for some students with disabilities, the equal access and equal opportunity guaranteed to traditionally marginalized minorities through civil rights legislation was not sufficient to produce educational benefit. It called for identification of students with disabilities in need of a *special* education and defined the free appropriate public education to be provided to them. Congress estimated that up to 12% of school-age children in public schools would fall under this "protected provision" and be entitled to a *special* education. This 30-year-old estimate was not far off: recent data suggest that "the percentage of all students covered under IDEA rose to a high of 13.8% in the 2004–05 school year and dropped to about 13.4% beginning in 2007–08" (Samuels, 2010).

THE SPECIAL EDUCATOR'S BALANCING ACT

Balancing Individualized Instruction and Instructional Accommodations

In the years immediately following the passage of IDEA, the most common service delivery models for special education in elementary, middle, and high schools were the self-contained class and the resource room. In these models the special education teacher took over responsibility for instruction in basic skill subjects and, sometimes, content subjects for a "class list" of 12–25 qualifying special education students. The instruction delivered by the special education teacher supplanted instruction that would otherwise have been delivered in a general education classroom by a general education teacher. At the elementary level, the primary focus in both self-contained and resource room settings was on teaching literacy and numeracy skills. Using small-group and one-to-one instruction, and instructional materials and texts not usually used in general education classrooms, the special education teacher's literacy curriculum included prereading, decoding, and comprehension skills as a developmental or remedial program of studies depending on the needs of his or her special education students. The special education teacher also included content not usually taught in the general education curriculum such as social skills needed by students with emotional or behavior disorders; or self-help and communication skills needed by students with more severe disabilities; or vocational and self-advocacy skills needed by students with disabilities transitioning from school to adult life; or foundational academic skills like beginning or functional reading skills needed by high school students with disabilities who still had not learned to read. In this model of service delivery, special education tended to be disconnected from general education and the special education teacher(s) in a school tended to feel isolated from the mainstream of the school's mission and practice. But the role of special educators was clear: they were responsible for teaching whatever needed to be taught to the eligible students assigned to them.

But about 10 years after the passage of the landmark special education entitlement, criticisms of special education programs developed along two separate but related spheres. First, critics (see Will, 1986; Lipsky & Gartner, 1987) asserted that pullout special education instruction was, for the most part, ineffective. While these arguments were eventually shown to be fallacious, their impact was still far reaching (Kavale & Forness, 2000; Zigmond, 2003). Second, critics focused their attention on the organization and structure of *general* education. Citing the increasing numbers of diverse, exceptional, and at-risk learners in mainstream classrooms, reformers contended that the traditional practices of *general* education were no longer viable. Regular classroom instruction needed to be reconceptualized such that the diverse educational needs of general education learners could be met more effectively (Wang, Reynolds, & Walberg, 1994/1995). Special education teachers were considered to be central to this reconceptualization. Given their pedagogical training and expertise, special education teachers could be reassigned to regular education classrooms to help general educators implement "individualized, cooperative, and adaptive learning environments" (Stainback, Stainback, Courtnage, & Jaben, 1985, p. 148) for *all* students, even students not eligible to receive a special education. The role of special educators would shift from providing direct instruction to planning and helping to implement instructional accommodations. For students with disabilities, this meant a phasing out of pullout programs in favor of inclusion with other students into the diverse general education classroom. Full inclusion and co-teaching became the preferred mechanisms for delivering special education. This trend was reinforced by provisions of the No Child Left Behind Act of 2001 (No Child Left Behind Act [NCLB], 2001) and the 2004 reauthorization of the IDEA (Individuals with Disabilities Education Act [IDEA], 2004) that mandated not only access to the general education curriculum for students eligible for special education services, but also full participation in the state accountability assessments. Full inclusion and co-teaching were embraced as the way to enhance instruction and facilitate learning for *all* students, including the students with disabilities in general education classrooms.

In today's schools, pressures for inclusion and anxieties over participation in state accountability assessments have forced special educators to choose between small-group, pull-out, instructional interventions (favored by researchers as necessary to improving academic achievement), and inclusive, on-grade-level co-teaching (favored by parents and school practitioners) in which the learning needs of students with disabilities are accommodated but not "remediated." In choosing inclusion and co-teaching, the special educator often assumes a leadership role in developing and helping to implement accommodations for the broad array of diverse learners in today's classrooms. But at the same time, the special educator forgoes the opportunity to provide intensive, relentless academic instruction to students eligible for special education and to teach them the extracurricular content (social skills, study skills, organizational skills, transition skills) that is not taught explicitly in the general education curriculum. In many schools, the special education teacher knows what needs to be taught, but does not have the time or the administrative support to teach it.

Balancing Intervention and Prevention

Historically, special education services have been provided only to students who qualify. Eligibility is established through a referral and assessment process that often includes a time-consuming and expensive multidisciplinary evaluation. A team consisting of school personnel and the child's parents review referral and assessment data and determine whether the student has one of the 13 disabilities listed in IDEA and is in need of a *special* education.

Using these procedures, the number of children identified as learning disabled and in need of special education increased dramatically over the years and by 2005 represented more than half of the 6.2 million school children identified for special education, or about 6% of all children in public schools (Fletcher, 2006). Reports indicate that 80–90% of the students identified as learning disabled have reading disabilities and about 40% of all special education students have problems acquiring and using reading skills (National Research Council, 1998).

Special education research has demonstrated that intensive, small-group or one-to-one instruction delivered by a certified special education teacher can dramatically improve the reading capacity of these students (see Elbaum, Vaughn, Hughes, & Moody, 2000; Torgesen et al., 2001; Vaughn et al., 2003). But the research has also demonstrated that the reading problems of students with disabilities are not unique. Learning/reading problems are common in schools and, too often, can be traced to instructional inadequacies. Because the skills that prevent reading failure can be taught, many believe that a substantial number of students found eligible for special education may be simply instructional casualties who did not get adequate literacy instruction early in their school careers.

According to Torgesen (2004), early intervention is not only possible, it is a better, more effective solution to rampant reading failure than special education remediation. Teaching reading more effectively the first time around could not only benefit all students but also reduce the number of students designated as learning disabled. That would reserve special education for those students with disabilities—students who are the most difficult to teach (National Institute of Child Health and Human Development, 2000; National Research Council, 1998; Torgeson et al., 2001). So the reasoning went as Congress debated and passed the reading initiatives in No Child Left Behind (NCLB, 2001). And, in the reauthorization of IDEA (2004) shortly thereafter, the shift to prevention was again underscored. The core idea was that special education can't "fix" reading problems; not only is it available too late, but by the time students with reading failures are placed in special education, there are simply too many of them to implement the needed intensive, small-group remediation. In response, both laws proposed a system in which all children are assessed regularly to identify early those in need of extra help. Those students would be provided with interventions in the classroom first and then through supplemental instruction, as required. This approach was dubbed "Response to Intervention" and defined as "the provision of early intervention when students first experience academic difficulties, with the goal of improving the achievement of all students, including those who may have LD" (National Joint Committee on Learning Disabilities, 2005, p. 1). All students start within the general curriculum and move through the curriculum receiving adapted and individualized interventions of increasing intensity depending on a student's earlier responses. Typically,

RTI models include three tiers: classwide group instruction in the general education setting (Tier 1, or primary intervention); targeted or remedial intervention (Tier 2, or secondary intervention); and intensive individual intervention (Tier 3, or tertiary intervention).

Within IDEA, these tiered interventions, delivered within the general education classroom to students who have not yet qualified for special education, are part of a system of "early intervening services (EIS)," and could be paid for, at least in part, with special education/IDEA funds. The expectation was that EIS would reduce the need to label children as disabled in order to address the learning and behavioral needs of children who were falling behind academically. Generally speaking, only once a child had received all tiers of intervention and was still not progressing at a typically developing rate, would he or she be referred for the evaluation to determine whether special education and related services were warranted.

RTI introduced a new role for the special education teacher—the provider of "EIS" to students who have not yet been found eligible for special education services. Services might include educational and behavioral screening evaluations, scientifically based literacy instruction generally in Tier 2 or Tier 3, and other preventive services and supports in the general education classroom, as needed. This role fit well with the pressures for special education personnel to be present and visible in general education classrooms and to extend the special education teacher's expertise to students who were at risk for failure but had not been referred for an eligibility determination for special education services.

Of course, one person cannot do everything, and time spent on prevention is time taken away from intervention. Again, special education teachers must balance their commitment to direct, intensive remedial instruction to students already qualified for special education services (an often difficult and thankless task where success is judged in very small increments of progress), and their usefulness in providing the tiered interventions in a preventive, RTI model (a more stimulating and potentially rewarding task because of the high likelihood of substantial progress in students at risk).

Balancing Leadership and Partnership

Advocacy has always been considered an integral part of the role of the special education teacher. The special education teacher in a school is expected to look out for his or her students, to ensure access and inclusion in curricular and extracurricular activities, to educate the other adults and students in the school and community about disability, and to facilitate the use of needed accommodations and modifications in assignments, assessments, and even architecture. The special education teacher serves as the liaison between the students with disabilities and the rest of the school population.

And, as general education classrooms become increasingly populated with diverse learners, this liaison role has been expanded and formalized as a way to enhance instruction and facilitate learning for all students. Special education teachers often find themselves in the role of coach, consultant, or collaborator; they work with their general education colleagues to design and implement appropriate instructional programs; and are sought after to teach about, demonstrate, and encourage differentiated instruction.

Skills in consultation and collaboration have long been part of the special educators' expertise. They are the key ingredient in the school-based problem-solving teams designed to reduce inappropriate referrals to special education and enhance the teaching repertoire of general education teachers such that students' needs could be met more effectively and efficiently within general education (Fuchs, Mock, Morgan, & Young, 2003). Problem-solving teams led by the special educator proliferated during the late 1980s and 1990s under the names of mainstream assistance teams (Fuchs, Fuchs, Bahr, Fernstrom, & Stecker, 1990), intervention assistance teams (Whitten & Dieker, 1995), instructional support teams (Kovaleski, Gicking, Morrow, & Swank, 1999), prereferral intervention teams (Graden, Casey, & Christenson, 1985), and instructional consultation teams (Rosenfield & Gravois, 1996). They have gained in popularity in the last several years, bolstered at least in part by the introduction of a literacy or reading coach in the Reading First initiative embedded in No Child Left Behind (NCLB, 2002), and the use of problem-solving teams or data decision-making teams as part of the RTI initiative (Bahr & Kovaleski, 2006). In a 2003 survey of the 50 directors of special education including the District of Columbia, 43% of the state special education directors reported that the use of prereferral intervention teams was required, whereas another 29% reported that their use was recommended (Truscott, Cohen, Sams, Sanborn, & Frank, 2005). A 2005 national telephone survey by the same researchers 2 years later produced comparable results: 41% of the states reported mandated prereferral intervention teams and 44% recommended them. With the widespread acceptance of RTI, there is every reason to believe that a more current survey would indicate even higher rates of implementation of this form of consultation.

Despite a wide array of terminology, most teams employ the eight-step problem-solving model described by Bahr and Kovaleski (2006):

1. Request for assistance from a teacher.
2. Analysis of the presenting problem.
3. Precise statement of the problem.
4. Setting of a performance goal.
5. Identification and selection of an intervention.
6. Support of the strategy in the classroom.

7. Monitoring of the student's progress during the intervention.
8. Evaluation of the outcomes of said intervention/s (p. 3).

Within this process, the special education teacher is often the person expected to model differentiated instruction, recommend appropriate instructional accommodations, and provide examples of instructional modifications. As a coach, or a member of a teacher assistance team, the special educator has to choose whether to assume the role of an expert giving advice, or of a fellow teacher with different, but not greater, expertise, working collaboratively to find a solution to an instructional problem. Whether suggestions are accepted and implemented will often depend on the delicate balance struck by the special educator.

STRIKING A BALANCE, FINDING THE PATH

Recent educational reform initiatives have focused on preventing students from falling behind in the first place. Through NCLB and IDEA 2004, schools have been charged with the daunting task of developing schoolwide reading programs that begin in the early grades and prevent reading failure from taking hold. They have been encouraged to use progress-monitoring tools like oral reading fluency measures to ensure the success of these prevention models. They have promoted the use of differentiated instruction, based on the idea that "all learners do not necessarily learn in the same way, and ... each learner receives the methods and materials most suitable for that particular learner at that particular place in the curriculum" (Mastropieri & Scruggs, 2007, p. 126). Differentiated instruction is viewed as the keystone to effective and successful general education curricular instruction for *all* students, including those with disabilities. Special educators are schooled in how to accomplish differentiated instruction, but is prevention the role of the special education teacher?

Throughout the history of special education, attention to the unique needs of the individual has been paramount. Since 1975, students with disabilities have been entitled to a special education of explicit, intensive, and prolonged instruction delivered by instructional experts. A student's IEP is the road map to this specialized instruction. Historically, the job of the special educator was clearly defined as direct service to the student, whether that meant working on phonemic awareness and phonics skills typical of first grade with a fifth grader who significantly struggles with decoding and encoding, or, providing explicit instruction in comprehension strategies using second-grade-level controlled text with a dysfluent fourth grader. But public concerns over rampant underachievement in the nation's schools, and social policy favoring equity and inclusion have placed new demands on the special education teacher. As a pedagogical expert (rather than a subject matter specialist) the special educator can play a major role in redesigning how students are taught the general education curriculum. Special educators understand about adaptations and modifications to the general education learning environment and curriculum that accommodate the unique needs of students (Gartin, Murdick, Imbeau, & Perner, 2002; Mastropieri & Scruggs, 2007; Tomlinson, 2001). But is assuming a leadership role with general education teachers the job of the special education teacher?

In a perfect world (or in a perfect school) the special education teacher would assume primary responsibility as the remediation/intervention specialist for improving the literacy skills of students with disabilities. He or she would teach students in small groups of no more than four or five students, providing daily, intensive, individually tailored instruction in reading *and* in all the other skill areas in which a student with disabilities needs explicit instruction. In fact, specifying the specialized individualized curriculum that a student with disabilities needs and teaching that unique curriculum to each individual student with a disability could easily be a full-time job for the special education teacher. However, an equally important role is to provide consultative services to classroom teachers to support the grade-level reading instruction into which most students with disabilities would be included, perhaps even co-teaching all or some of the general education classroom reading lessons. The special education teacher as coach would work with fellow teachers to change their attitudes, expectations, and teaching and testing styles. He or she would provide the job-embedded staff development that would help general education teachers learn how to appropriately modify learning environments and instructional strategies to effectively provide differentiated instruction for the individuals with exceptional learning needs in their classrooms (Deshler, Ellis, & Lenz, 1996; Mastropieri & Scruggs, 2007). But special education teacher as coach or co-teacher is also a full-time job. And, of course, the special education teacher must also serve on prereferral intervention teams, attend IEP meetings, communicate with parents, complete all the required compliance paperwork, and advocate for access and inclusion for students with disabilities. Is this too much for one person? Perhaps as Zigmond (2007) has suggested, delivering the highest-quality special education in a school building is (at least) a two-person job.

Being a special educator is a balancing act (see Figure 5.1). Priorities are often dictated by forces over which the teacher has little control: a principal concerned about his or her school "making Adequate Yearly Progress (AYP)" and focusing all school personnel on reading instruction for students at risk; a district concerned about overrepresentation of minorities in special education and focusing all school personnel on prereferral interventions; a decision by the director of special education that pull-out programs must

Individualized instruction vs. **Instructional accommodations**

• Daily, small group or individual, direct   • Consultation or co-teaching in general
  instruction   education classroom

Intervention vs. **Prevention**

• Intensive instruction on deficient skills   • Helping with tiered reading instruction for
  for qualifying students   any student

Leadership vs. **Partnership**

• Expert in differentiated classroom   • Helpful colleague in exploring
  instruction   accommodations and modifications

FIGURE 5.1. The balancing act of a special education teacher.

end and co-teaching will be the only service delivery model; a school team that calls for more direct, small-group, reading instruction for students with disabilities impeding AYP achievement. The list is endless! How to choose what to do?

We believe that a deliberate focus on student instruction helps special educators to strike the needed balance. A special educator's number one priority should be to develop and implement sound instructional plans that support and enhance students' learning; figuring out what students need and hoping that they will get it in the general education classroom is not enough. Active teaching and assessment of students' learning not only ensures direct provision of a special education to the student, but also creates the pathway for leadership and professional collaboration. Focusing first on teaching students equips the special educator with the data upon which to design accommodations and modifications with the general education teacher. These data are the foundation for intervention and remediation planning with related service personnel such as the reading specialist. These data are the evidence for achievement and accountability discussions with administrators. These data reveal what types of professional development might help teachers better meet students' needs. These data are the substance on which to build effective communication with parents. To be an instructional leader, the special educator must have the time, resources, and support to *teach* his or her students. Only then can he or she adequately work with colleagues to satisfy other professional and leadership responsibilities.

CONCLUSION

The field of special education has contributed significantly to the research on understanding, preventing, and correcting reading disabilities. Researchers, scholars, and teacher educators in special education and reading education have collaborated extensively to improve literacy instruction for students who are hard to teach. That collaboration should certainly extend into everyday practice in the schools. Special educators have much to offer all the teachers and students in their schools, but their first and foremost commitment and concern must be for students who qualify for special education services. Special education must involve individually planned and systematically monitored arrangements of teaching procedures, adapted equipment and materials, accessible settings, and other interventions designed to help learners with disabilities and special learning needs achieve a higher level of personal self-sufficiency and success in school and community than would be available if these students were only given access to a typical classroom education. Special education is mandated for students who are the hardest to teach, and ensuring an appropriate and productive school career for them is what special education must be all about.

ENGAGEMENT ACTIVITIES

1. Revisit the case example and reflect on Stephen's professional dilemma. What aspects of his professional concerns resonate most with you? Do you see these hurdles as being contextually mediated (i.e., they are unique to his school setting) or are they byproducts of the current educational system? Do you think it is possible for Stephen to change his situation?

2. Find a school that is implementing RTI. Interview a special education teacher and a reading specialist in that school. What do they each feel is their role in implementing RTI? Do they have separate, or overlapping, responsibilities?

3. What experiences or educational preparation do you think equips the special education teacher to assume a leadership role in a school?

REFERENCES

Bahr, M. W., & Kovaleski, J. F. (2006). Need for problem-solving teams: Introduction to the special issue. *Remedial and Special Education. 27*(1), 2–5.

Brown v. Board of Education of Topeka, Kansas, 347 U.S. 483 (1954), 74 S.Ct. 686, 98 L.Ed. 873, 38 A.L.R.2d 1180.

Civil Rights Act, 42 U.S.C. § 1983 (1964).

Deshler, D. D., Ellis, E. S., & Lenz, B. K. (1996). *Teaching adolescents with learning disabilities: Strategies and methods.* Denver, CO: Love.

Education of All Handicapped Children Act, 20 U.S.C. § 1400 *et seq*(1975).

Elbaum, B., Vaughn, S., Hughes, M. T., & Moody, S. M. (2000). How effective are one-to-one tutoring programs in reading for elementary school students at risk for reading failure? A meta-analysis of the intervention research. *Journal of Educational Psychology, 92*(4), 605–619.

Elementary and Secondary Education Act, 20 U.S.C. § 2701 *et seq.* (1965).

Fletcher, J. (2006, April). *Why RTI? Some research findings.* PowerPoint presentation given at the Response to Intervention Symposium in Austin, TX. Retrieved October 1, 2010, from *www.centeroninstruction.org/files/RtIResearchAndPolicyFoundations.pdf.*

Fuchs, D., Fuchs, L., Bahr, M., Fernstrom, P., & Stecker, P. (1990). Prereferral intervention: A prescriptive approach. *Exceptional Children, 56,* 493–513.

Fuchs, D., Mock, D., Morgan, P. L., & Young, C. L. (2003). Responsiveness-to-intervention for the learning disabilities construct. *Learning Disabilities Research and Practice, 18*(3), 157–171.

Gartin, B. C., Murdick, N. L., Imbeau, M., & Perner, D. E. (2002). *How to use differentiated instruction with students with developmental disabilities in the general education classroom.* Arlington, VA: Council for Exceptional Children.

Graden, J. L., Casey, A., & Christenson, S. L. (1985). Implementing a prereferral intervention system: Part I. The model. *Exceptional Children, 51,* 377–384.

Individuals with Disabilities Education Act, 20 U.S.C. § 1415 *et seq* (2004).

Kavale, K. A., & Forness, S. R. (2000). Policy decisions in special education: The role of meta-analysis. In R. Gersten, E. P. Schiller, & S. Vaughn (Eds.), *Contemporary special education research syntheses of the knowledge base on critical instructional issues* (pp. 137–178). Mahwah, NJ: Erlbaum.

Kovaleski, J. F., Gickling, E. E., Morrow, H., & Swank, P. R. (1999). High versus low implementation of instructional support teams: A case for mainstreaming program fidelity. *Remedial and Special Education, 20,* 170–183.

Lilly, M. S. (1979). *Children with exceptional needs: A survey of special education.* New York: Holt, Reinhart & Winston.

Lipsky, D. K., & Gartner, A. (1987). *Beyond separate education: Quality education for all.* Baltimore: Brookes.

Mastropieri, M., & Scruggs, T. (2007) *The inclusive classroom: Strategies for effective instruction* (3rd ed.). Upper Saddle River, NJ: Pearson.

National Institute of Child Health and Human Development. (2000). Report of the National Reading Panel. *Teaching children to read: AR evidence-based assess-*

ment of the scientific research literature on reading and its implications for reading instruction (NIH Publication No. 00-4769). Washington. DC: U.S. Government Printing Office.

National Joint Committee on Learning Disabilities. (2005). *Responsiveness to intervention and learning disabilities.* Retrieved October 1, 2010, from *www.ldonline.org/about/partners/njcld.*

National Research Council. (1998). *Preventing reading difficulties in young children.* Washington, DC: National Academy Press.

No Child Left Behind Act, Public Law No. 107-110, 115 Stat. § 1425 *et seq.* (2001).

Rosenfield, S. A., & Gravois, T. A. (1996). *Instructional consultation teams: Collaborating for change.* New York: Guilford Press.

Samuels, C. (2010, September 15). Boom in learning disabled enrollment ends. *Education Week, 30*(3), 1, 14–15.

Section 504 of the Rehabilitation Act, 29 U.S.C. § 794 *et seq.* (1973).

Stainback, W., Stainback, S., Courtnage, L., & Jaben, T. (1985). Facilitating mainstreaming by modifying the mainstream. *Exceptional Children, 52,* 144–152.

Title IX of the Education Amendments, 20 U.S.C. § 1680 *et seq.* (1972).

Tomlinson, C. A. (2001). *How to differentiate in mixed-ability classrooms* (2nd ed.). Alexandria, VA: Association for Supervision and Curriculum Development.

Torgesen, J. K. (2004, Fall). Avoiding the devastating downward spiral: The evidence that early intervention prevents reading failure. *American Educator.* Retrieved October 1, 2010, from *www.aft.org/newspubs/periodicals/ae/fall2004/index.cfm.*

Torgesen, J. K., Alexander, A. W., Wagner, R. K., Rashotte, C. A., Voeller, K. K. S., & Conway, T. (2001). Intensive remedial instruction for children with severe reading disabilities: Immediate and long-term outcomes from two instructional approaches. *Journal of Learning Disabilities, 34,* 33–58, 78.

Truscott, S. D., Cohen, C. E., Sams, D. P., Sanborn, K. J., & Frank, A. J. (2005). The current state(s) of pre-referral intervention teams: A report from two national surveys. *Remedial and Special Education, 26,* 130–140.

Vaughn, S., Linan-Thompson, S., Kouzekanani, D., Bryant, P., Dickson, S., & Blozis, S. (2003). Reading instruction grouping for students with reading difficulties. *Remedial and Special Education, 24*(5), 301–315.

Wang, M. C., Reynolds, M. C., & Walberg, H. J. (1994/1995). Serving students at the margins. *Educational Leadership, 52,* 12–17.

Whitten, E., & Dieker, L. (1995). Intervention assistance teams: A broader vision. *Preventing School Failure, 50,* 41–45.

Will, Madeleine C. (1986) Educating children with learning problems: A shared responsibility. *Exceptional Children, 53,* 411–415.

Yell, M. (1998). *The law and special education.* Upper Saddle River, NJ: Merrill Prentice Hall.

Zigmond, N. (2003). Where should SWDs receive special education services? Is one place better than another? *Journal of Special Education, 37,* 193–199.

Zigmond, N. (2007). Delivering special education is a two-person job: A call for unconventional thinking. In J. Crockett, M. Gerber, & T. Landrum (Eds.), *Radical reform of special education:* Essays in honor of James M. Kauffman. (pp. 115–142). Mahwah, NJ: Erlbaum.

Zirkel, P. A., & Kincaid, J. M. (1993). *Section 504, the ADA, and the schools.* Horsham, PA: LRP Publications.

6

Principals as Literacy Leaders

SHARON WALPOLE
MICHAEL C. MCKENNA

Guiding Questions

- What do recent research results suggest about the role of principals as instructional leaders?
- How do those results apply to principals at the elementary and middle school levels as illustrated in the case examples?
- What are some of the challenges that principals face in their efforts to provide leadership for literacy?
- Which of the suggested readings are best suited to building your own knowledge and skills as a literacy leader?

No one who works in a school is likely to argue that the principal does not influence student achievement; no one who has spent even 1 day with a principal will argue that this influence is simple to exert. In this chapter we summarize recent research about the influence of principals on teaching and learning, and from that research identify specific actions that principals can take as leaders in literacy. We close the chapter with a list of resources that can help potential or acting principals to build their own knowledge and skills in the important work of instructional leadership. These resources can also help other educators better understand the role of the principal as a literacy leader. As you read, consider the case of Barbara, a new elementary principal.

After teaching fifth grade for 5 years, Barbara earned her certificate as a building administrator and accepted a position as principal at Hamilton Elementary. Hamilton has a history of poor achievement as measured by the state's criterion-referenced test. Its faculty serve a challenging population characterized by high poverty and limited parental education. On the bright side, Hamilton has an excellent literacy coach, who has worked successfully as both a classroom teacher and a reading specialist. It is early August, and Barbara knows she must quickly develop a plan of action. Although her experience teaching fifth grade was successful, she is now responsible for reading on a K–5 basis, and she knows her expertise is limited. She has an abundance of data available to her but she recognizes that she may have difficulty interpreting these data properly. She has a faculty that includes seasoned veterans and new hires, and she suspects that some of the former are weak and that most of the latter will need mentoring. In short, Barbara has her work cut out for her, but she has at least framed the problem and is not without resources. What should she do to get started?

INSTRUCTIONAL LEADERSHIP: RESEARCH AND PRACTICE

Research on instructional leadership typically focuses on the principal's role in an *organization* rather than in a school. This subtle word choice, we think, is important to unpack. Principals actually operate within a larger organization, where policies and goals are first shaped by interpretations at the level of the state and the district. They are then reshaped by the principal before they are again reshaped and implemented by teachers. We might offer a corporate analogy and say that principals are like middle managers, who must function between higher levels of management and those they supervise. Even principals in schools where achievement is high or improving are not bound by the status quo—they problem solve around space and resources, they forge connections among objectives, and they are proactive about their planning for professional development (PD). Principals who are instructional leaders know (or learn) how to restructure the ways that they use their resources to deliver services to children and to teachers (Burch, Theoharis, & Rauscher, 2010).

The work that principals do, although it has some direct effect on student achievement (Nettles & Herrington, 2007), has larger indirect influences through the ways that their leadership influences teachers. Teacher instruction, of course, has the largest and most direct influence on student

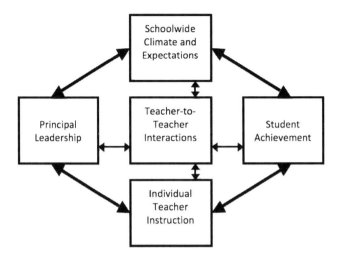

FIGURE 6.1. Possible routes from principal leadership to achievement.

achievement. Figure 6.1 represents some of the possible routes for the indirect effects of principal leadership, each of which, we think, has implications for the roles of principals as instructional leaders. In addition to these routes, the principal also manages another one—the route between the school and the community it serves. Leadership actions can build, rebuild, or damage those relationships.

The pathways from leadership to achievement are obviously complicated. To take advantage of some and minimize the effects of others, a principal must take specific actions that are likely to affect learning. In a test of the effects of elementary school principals on student achievement in reading, Hallinger, Bickman, and Davis (1996) defined instructional leadership to include formal classroom observations, time spent reviewing student achievement data with faculty, use of faculty meeting time to discuss instructional issues, emphasis on collective teacher work to coordinate instruction within and across grade levels, success in providing resources and opportunities for staff development, and visibility. Instructional leadership defined this way was not directly related to student achievement. However, it was directly related to the setting of a clear school mission. The mission included a focus on schoolwide instruction, coordinated and monitored through the grades, and associated with clear grade-level expectations. Mission was related to student opportunities to learn. These opportunities included few interruptions of student work or teacher instruction. Student opportunities to learn were related to high teacher expectations. High expectations included clear communication to parents and students about what was expected of them, teacher expectations that children would pass standardized tests, and an emphasis on student strengths and potential. It was high teacher expectations—influenced by the principal's instructional leadership in helping to clarify the school's instructional mission and maximize student opportunities to learn—that had a direct effect on student achievement in reading (Hallinger et al., 1996).

One of the main reasons why the road from a principal's leadership actions to the individual instruction of a teacher and subsequently to increases in student achievement is not simple is the fact that teachers learn socially, through formal and informal peer interactions, and such learning can be either positive or negative. As Figure 6.1 illustrates, a principal's influence on the instructional practice of an individual teacher may compete with that teacher's interaction with peers. For example, the social community and learning norms of a school may make it very difficult to introduce new ideas or practices because informally powerful veteran teachers actively or passively resist new ideas and alienate those who suggest or try them (Printy, 2008).

Principal leadership, then, affects individual teachers not only directly but also indirectly, through its effects on their peers. Supovitz, Sirinides, and May (2010) argue that there are three important categories of principal actions that have an indirect influence on student achievement: setting the mission and goals of the school, developing a culture of trust and collabo-

TABLE 6.1. Principal Action Categories with Examples from Supovitz, Sirinides, and May (2010)

Principal action category	Sample actions
Setting the mission and goals of the school	• Communicates expected standards. • Encourages raised test scores. • Expects teachers to meet instructional goals. • Expects teachers to continually grow.
Developing a culture of trust and collaboration	• Treats teachers with respect. • Makes teachers feel comfortable. • Is trustworthy. • Allows teachers to discuss feelings and frustrations. • Takes a personal interest in teachers.
Focusing on instruction	• Visits classrooms often. • Monitors instructional quality. • Links teachers with PD resources. • Encourages sharing of ideas. • Helps struggling teachers.

ration, and actively focusing on instruction. These principal actions affect the ways that teachers learn together and influence one another. Table 6.1 summarizes the definitions of these categories of action.

For a principal, at once charged with managing a building and all of its resources, answering to multiple stakeholders, and taking ultimate responsibility for student safety and for student achievement, this constellation of actions is much easier listed than accomplished. One of the most promising practices in recent research is the establishment of formal professional learning communities (PLCs). While PLCs do not automatically function as intended (e.g., Fisher, Frey, & Lapp, 2009; Saunders, Goldenberg, & Gallimore, 2009), they can become places where teachers take on new leadership roles with respect to one another (as mentors, coaches, specialists, advisors, or facilitators). They can likewise become places where, working from a set of shared values, teachers focus on student learning, collaborate to design instruction, and reflect on its effects. The principal's role in fostering PLCs, particularly with respect to allocating time and setting goals and norms, is crucial. (See Chapter 18 for a more in-depth discussion of learning communities.)

We imagine that few principals would quarrel with the goals of establishing their school's mission, developing their school's culture, and focusing their work on instructional improvement. However, we also know that many principals fail to accomplish these goals. One reason may be that the goals themselves may seem lofty and vague. Another may be that principals who are not actively reflecting on the extent to which they are meeting these goals may become complacent. Finally, the management responsibilities of principals may be so overwhelming that they are unable to fill their instructional leadership role. In the section that follows, we illustrate these goals in terms of a principal's roles and responsibilities. We use an extended case study to describe the journey of a hypothetical principal we will call James. James is a composite drawn from the principals we work with. In presenting his history, we will also draw on additional research as we describe his evolving definitions of his roles and responsibilities.

A PRINCIPAL'S ROLES AND RESPONSIBILITIES

James came to Jefferson Middle School from out of state after 3 years as an assistant principal (AP) with relatively few instructional responsibilities. He left his AP job because he wanted to be an instructional leader rather than a disciplinarian. His EdD in Educational Leadership had emphasized the principal's instructional role and focused on strategies for viewing and building schools as learning organizations. This vision was inconsistent with the organizational norms that defined his previous job.

James joined an experienced AP and a new AP at Jefferson. They had their work cut out for them—only 60% of their fifth-grade students had met the state standards in English language arts (ELA) the previous year, and their school status was under Academic Watch in the state's rating system—meaning that the need to improve reading achievement was real if the administration and staff wanted to maintain their autonomy, and keep their jobs.

The school served just over 1,000 middle school students, 48% of whom qualified for federal lunch subsidies. Schoolwide Title I status provided some additional funds and flexibility for PD, as did School Improvement Grant moneys. As a new hire, new to the community, James began by meeting with department chairs in ELA, math, science, and social studies—to listen. He learned that there were serious student behavior problems to address and that teacher morale was low. He also learned that there was significant resistance to inclusion for students with disabilities and for a growing population of English language learners. He learned that the staff was relatively inexperienced, but that department chairs were among the most seasoned teachers on the staff. When he asked the department chairs about instruction and PD, they told him that they took responsibility for that within their own program areas. They did this through two-hour-long PD meetings each month that were already built into the teachers' schedules.

Setting a Mission and Goals

As James thought about a mission and goals for the school, he realized that to engage his teachers in collaborative dialogue he first had to *set direction*. He needed to prompt a shared vision and purpose that would inspire and motivate others to view and contribute to the school as an organic organization capable of positive change. This direction setting also would motivate specific checks on the school's performance, clarify and focus communications, and set the stage for collaboration (Leithwood & Jantzi, 2008). James met with his APs and began a series of more interactive discussions about the mission of the school. He invited the APs to help him select among three slogans for the school:

Jefferson Middle School—Where Improvement Is Our Goal.
Jefferson Middle School—Read! Think! Write!
Jefferson Middle School—Where Everyone Succeeds. No Exceptions.

Together they chose the third slogan, as it reflected the real need to improve achievement and implied the only route to that end—improving instruction, including instruction for students most at risk for academic failure.

James knew already that to enact any changes he had to face the fact that teachers' beliefs were inconsistent with the idea that all students could succeed. He saw the changing of teacher beliefs as essential to his leadership agenda (Ross & Gray, 2006). In order to begin that work, he asked one of his APs to review test data for the previous 3 years and identify 10 eighth-grade students who had improved their reading achievement for 3 years running and then to identify their teachers. He sent a formal letter, through regular mail, to each of these teachers, identifying the student, summarizing his or her test scores, and asking them to share with James their insights about how they had personally contributed to this student's success. He received quick responses that he shared at the opening of faculty meetings—masking teacher names. He then introduced his plans to make sure that all teachers had the tools and knowledge they needed to make every student more successful.

James realized that he had to focus the school's mission to improve the school's culture, but that an improved culture without differences in curriculum and instruction would not be likely to yield any effects on student achievement (Dumay, 2009). With relatively little understanding of the strengths and weaknesses of his staff, James had to learn more. He could not do that alone. To facilitate widespread success would require the talents of more than one leader. He decided to enact a distributed leadership plan, by which he would provide teachers with leadership opportunities and champion their development as leaders. This plan would also protect the school from mistakes he might make, given his limited information or perspectives. While distributing leadership, in and of itself, would not improve achievement, it would likely build support for decisions through faculty involvement and input and through transparency in the processes used to make them (Leithwood & Mascall, 2008).

Building and Distributing Leadership

James wanted to be sure that he could rely on his APs as part of his leadership team; he knew that principal-led initiatives that did not include other administrators could disenfranchise them (e.g., Fisher et al., 2009). He also knew that, like himself, these APs had not had much experience actually working in an instructional leadership role. He called the team together and asked them to help him get a snapshot of instruction. From an alphabetized list of the faculty, each member of the team was assigned a group of faculty members. Team members would spend 10 minutes observing in each of their assigned classrooms and then make a list of what they saw the teacher and students actually doing during that time.

When the leadership team met to share their findings, the results were sobering. Dominant teacher activities included sitting at a desk doing paperwork, reading aloud from the textbook, and lecturing. Dominant student activities included listening, copying, and working independently. In order to change this dominant instructional climate, James knew that he had to begin a process of distributing leadership to teachers, but that he would also have to provide support for teachers to build their own leadership knowledge and skills. He and the APs decided that they first should visit the existing PD sessions, led by the department chairs. These visits indicated what the team feared—the time was used for routine paperwork and communication that could be accomplished in other ways. There was little mention of instruction and no focus on the actions teachers could take to improve literacy achievement.

James established a larger instructional leadership team (ILT), which included the APs, department chairs, grade-level representatives, special educators, the counselor, and the school psychologist. The ILT would meet monthly after school. He introduced the ILT members to their collective charge: Together they would lead the faculty to significantly improve literacy instruction. They would translate state standards into actual instructional guidance, choose school-level formative assessments, interpret the results of those assessments, identify teacher PD needs, and plan the 2 hours of PD formerly led by the department chairs (Saunders et al., 2009). Those PD meetings would work toward becoming true PLCs, with teams of five teachers from the same content area led by one member of the ILT. Either James or one of the APs would serve as an ex officio member, taking meeting notes. During the PLC meetings, teachers would build their content knowledge, work on lesson planning, and interpret assessment data. Although the members of the ILT were supportive of this plan, they were also skeptical. In effect, James was *redesigning the organization* by deliberately facilitating and structuring collaboration (Leithwood & Jantzi, 2008). This was a major step, one that involved clear risks and an uncertain outcome.

In order for the ILT to do its important work, James had to focus on *developing people,* especially in the areas of knowledge and skills related to improving instruction. This would mean more than providing or supporting PD. Developing people also includes individualizing support, creating an intellectually stimulating environment, and providing encouragement and feedback (Leithwood & Jantzi, 2008). In forming the ILT, James had created an enabling structure that would allow teacher leaders to emerge by affording many opportunities to develop leadership skills (Copland, 2004). James began to focus on developing his ILT members by buying each of

them two books: one about literacy achievement and one about either organizational change or professional learning. He personalized the delivery of
the books, taking them to the ILT members in their classrooms or offices,
and taking the time to tell each one why he thought that they would benefit
from reading those particular books. While this gesture may have increased
their buy-in slightly, the real challenge was building their content knowledge
in the area of literacy instruction.

Guiding Curriculum Selection and Adaptation

Now that James had a strategy for distributing leadership, he could focus
on collective efforts to *manage the instructional program* (Leithwood &
Jantzi, 2008). In order to provide an initial focus for the PD work of the
ILT members, James had to guide them to select particular instructional
strategies that would be appropriate across content areas and that were
known to be associated with literacy achievement (Fisher et al., 2009). He
also knew that he would have to abide by their decisions. James decided
that he would actually deliver PD to his ILT, and, after that PD, engage
them in choosing instructional strategies that would be used schoolwide.
From his own graduate work, James knew that the Center on Instruction
(*www.centeroninstruction.org*) disseminated research and PD resources
related to literacy.

James selected a set of aligned PD materials from the Center on Instruction. They included a practice brief for him to read (Boardman et al., 2008),
a facilitator's guide to help him plan (Murray et al., 2010), and even a fully
developed PowerPoint presentation to deliver. The materials identified a
specific set of vocabulary strategies, comprehension strategies, and motivation strategies with evidence for their effectiveness in improving adolescent
literacy achievement. Since James had not prepared the materials himself, he
was free to focus on preparing to deliver the PD, and he would not have any
emotional investment in the ILT's ultimate choices of strategies from among
the small set identified in the presentation. The materials were organized for
a 1- or 2-day delivery format. James chose the 1-day format and scheduled
it for a Saturday, when all members of the ILT would be paid for their extra
time and free from school-day interruptions. His goal was to give them the
available information, allow them to decide which strategies to target, and
then create a master calendar to guide presentation of those strategies to the
rest of the faculty through the PLCs.

Preparing for the Saturday session gave James empathy for the difficulty that his ILT members faced when they prepared to run their own
PLCs. Preparation for teacher PD was totally different from preparation for
teaching students. However, James's willingness to take such a risk paid off.
ILT members were engaged and supportive during the session and decided

that, rather than choosing among the strategies, they would use the entire set, staggering their introduction across the rest of the current school year and the first half of the next one. Given the research base included in the PD materials, ILT members were convinced that building teacher capacity to teach a small set of vocabulary, comprehension, word study, and motivation strategies was essential to improving student literacy achievement across the content areas. They also saw the fact that these strategies were selected by a set of reading experts (rather than them) as a strength; together they could explore this externally-identified plan without offending their colleagues by rejecting their ideas.

Planning Effective PD

James had to caution the ILT members to plan their PD initiative carefully. He knew that PD generally had to include a cycle of theory, demonstration, practice, and feedback (Joyce & Showers, 1988). With only 1 PLC hour every 2 weeks, the ILT members had to chunk the presentation content into 1-hour segments. Those chunks would constitute theory-building sessions. After each one, teachers could choose to read the relevant sections of the practice guide to deepen their understanding, but all would have to identify an upcoming text for which they would plan to implement the strategy. During the second PLC meeting of the month, teachers would prepare to implement the strategy, using a simple protocol that had been used success-fully in teacher PLCs elsewhere (Saunders et al., 2009). This protocol is represented in Figure 6.2.

Building a Climate of Reflection

Although the focus on literacy strategies validated with adolescents and the scheduling of a cyclical PD initiative integrated into the workday made good sense, success was a long way off. Because James and the APs served on each of the PLCs, they knew that the teams actually met and that teach-ers had the opportunity to share reflections on their successes (and fail-ures). Individual PLCs functioned differently, partially because of their members and partially because of the talents of the ILT member leading the PD effort. As a result of these differences, this initial focus on literacy schoolwide, although successful at building a shared vocabulary, was not building shared practice.

    James considered ways of making teachers aware of how differently their colleagues were implementing the instructional approaches. He decided to devote his next after-school faculty meeting time to a standards-based walkthrough (Roberts & Pruitt, 2003). He created a chart that listed all of the instructional strategies that had been discussed in the PLCs and

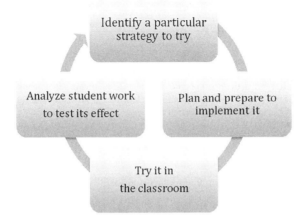

FIGURE 6.2. PLC structure.

his own ideas about what evidence might exist in a classroom—after the students were gone—that the strategy had been in use that day. His chart is presented in Table 6.2. Each of the PLCs was presented with the names (and classroom numbers) of two other PLCs. They were directed to visit those classrooms in search of evidence that the strategies had been used that day. Then they would return to discuss their findings. Not surprisingly, evidence was scant. Teachers claimed, however, that their empty classrooms were not good representations of their actual work. For some teachers, this was surely the case. For others, it was not.

The standards-based walkthrough raised some hackles among teachers who were not accustomed to having their classroom "invaded" by others. It also brought to the fore the fact that teachers outside of ELA really did not have the materials they needed to diversify student experience with texts in content-area learning. James considered it a "win" for his structural reorganization that this fact came through loud and clear through the ILT members. Apparently, the faculty was beginning to understand that ILT members did have decision- and policy-making influence. Together, James and the ILT crafted a procedure to have PLC members request additional reading materials that were related to content-area standards and that students would likely find engaging.

As James and the ILT debriefed about the results of the standards-based walkthough, it occurred to him that the focus on theory building had not resulted in some teachers actually implementing the strategies about which they were learning. He recalled that the PD model of Joyce and Showers

TABLE 6.2. Strategy Chart for a Standards–Based Walkthrough

Instructional goal	Possible evidence
Vocabulary focus	
• Provide daily direct instruction for specific words in all content areas • Provide repeated exposures to specific words and meanings • Supplement with additional exposures in reading and writing	• Words with definitions, contrasts, and examples • Pictures and maps to represent meanings • Content-area trade books and magazines
• Teach word-learning strategies	• Charts of word parts (prefixes, suffixes, roots) Webs of related words
Comprehension focus	
• Teach comprehension strategies: main idea and summarization, asking and answering questions	• Lists of strategy procedures • Summarization steps • Question types
• Use graphic organizers	• Blank graphic organizers • Filled, displayed organizers
Motivation focus	
• Use content-learning goals • Use engaging texts • Foster group work	• Goals and questions listed • Organized classroom libraries • Rooms set up for group work

(1988) called for theory building to be followed by demonstrations of how a particular strategy might be used in classroom settings. One way to provide such demonstrations was to arrange for teachers to model strategies for one another. James decided to build an extra hour of PD into the daily schedule each month to implement peer coaching. He used matched pairs of PLCs and initiated a monthly peer coaching requirement. Each member of the faculty would spend 45 minutes a month being coached in the use of the literacy strategies. The coaching would take the form of modeling only (Showers & Joyce, 1996). A teacher visiting a classroom would be coached by the teacher who was teaching. The coach would demonstrate the use of the literacy strategies through his or her actions, not through advice or critique. ILT members voiced concerns that not all teachers would complete the requirement, so together they crafted a procedure. As evidence that teachers were making their required visits, they would send their schedule to the administrator serving on their PLC and also complete a brief response after the visit. The visiting teacher was not to report compliance of their peer coach with the literacy strategies; the visitor would document only that he or she had completed a coaching session by visiting a colleague. This documentation would include a brief description of the content he or she observed his or her colleague teaching.

While the ILT hoped that the standards-based walkthrough and the cycles of peer coaching would increase implementation of the target literacy strategies, many teachers still did not make the strategies part of their daily routines. More important, perhaps, it was clear to James and the APs, whose jobs included walkthroughs, that even those who were routinely using the strategies were not doing so with high levels of quality or student engagement. James brought this matter to the ILT, and they considered possible causes and solutions. Some members candidly admitted that they thought their own PD and modeling could be the reason that the members of their PLCs did not use the strategies to their maximum potential—ILT members had neither the content-area expertise nor the literacy expertise to make a judgment of real quality for all members of the faculty. ILT members were doing their PD jobs, but they really needed more contact with experts (Fisher et al., 2009).

James realized that distributing instructional leadership meant that he had to include experts outside the building. Given his Title I funding and his school improvement funds, he could offer substantive PD. He decided to contract for a series of two one-semester content-area reading courses through the local university. The courses would be offered at Jefferson, and tuition would be paid by the school. The courses would be voluntary, of course, since the school could not pay for both faculty time and tuition. He would offer priority in the first semester to the ILT members, and then open up seats for any faculty member in the second semester. He hoped that a broader look at content-area reading would help faculty members put the school's focus on strategies into perspective. To underscore the importance of the courses, he made time to attend them himself (Murphy, 2004).

At the same time, James began to recognize that one element was still missing from the PD cycle of Joyce and Showers (1988). He had initiated theory building by arranging for teachers to study evidence-based strategies. He had provided for demonstration by asking teachers to observe their peers as they implemented these strategies. What he had not yet done was to find a means of providing teachers with feedback on the quality of their implementations. In peer coaching, teachers do not provide such feedback to one another, and James believed that more skillful coaching was required. Such coaching would need to be provided by a teacher knowledgeable about reading. He decided to restructure his unit count so that he could use one of his ELA teachers as a literacy coach. He chose a teacher who had a strong background in reading education and demonstrated strong practices in her classroom. The result was a trade-off. While he knew that he would lose the positive impact her instruction had on the achievement of her own students, he was counting on the potential impact on far more students if she taught the faculty how to be more effective.

Planning Effective Formative and Summative Observation

The role of the newly minted coach was very specific, and James described it to the faculty. The literacy coach would be a faculty resource to increase instructional quality through formative feedback. She would answer to James for her schedule, but she would not discuss teachers' work with him. He knew that if she were to succeed, teachers would have to know they could confide in her (Walpole & McKenna, 2004). James showed the faculty the coach's schedule. She was responsible for moving through two PLCs each month. During that month she would observe each PLC member three times, targeting strategies that the PLC member selected, and meeting with that PLC member once during a planning period to debrief. James charged the coach with creating observation protocols for each of the strategies on the school's list. Her observations would target only those strategies. She provided each faculty member a set of the observation protocols, so that her observation targets were transparent and clearly linked both to the PD that had been provided and to the school's literacy mission. James explained that a formative observation system, used regularly and universally, would help each faculty member get the support needed to enhance his or her use of the school's target strategies.

James also needed to change the way that he and the APs did their summative evaluations. These were vague and based on rubrics that were required by the state but that were not clearly related to the school's mission or strategies. James decided that he would work with the ILT to redesign the summative evaluation system. During visits, he and the APs would use forms that targeted the school's mission more directly—including attention to management, differentiation, and use of the literacy strategies. Then, in meetings with the faculty members to review the summative evaluations, administrators would help faculty members see how implementation of their school's instructional mission translated into the state evaluation rubric.

Using Data to Make Decisions

After 2 years of setting direction, developing people, redesigning the organization, and managing the instructional program, what did the data say? There were improvements overall, but disaggregating told a different tale. Students with federal lunch subsidies, students of color, students learning English, and students with disabilities were not faring as well as their white and/or more economically advantaged peers.

Although there were instructional changes and achievement gains to celebrate, a new set of problems emerged. Implementing research-based content-area reading strategies was having some impact, to be sure, but it was not targeting the skills deficits that some of the students faced. The key, James believed, was to complement the content-area strategies that teachers were now implementing with the targeted skills instruction that some students needed.

When James set out to plan for low-achieving students, he realized that he knew that they were struggling, but he did not know why. The state's required testing yielded standards-based data, but not diagnostic data. The school needed a data protocol to better reveal the needs of those students struggling to meet state literacy standards. With the help of the literacy coach and the district's director of special education, James decided to use the spring state test as a screening tool. For all students scoring below grade level, they would administer a fluency measure. If students scored poorly on the state test but well on the fluency measure, the team would assume they needed more support in the areas of comprehension and vocabulary. For students who scored poorly on the fluency measure, the team would give a decoding measure. If students scored poorly on the fluency measure but well on the decoding measure, the team would assume that they needed more support in fluency and comprehension. And finally, for those students who scored poorly on a decoding measure, intensive decoding intervention would be necessary (Walpole, McKenna, & Philippakos, 2011). Figure 6.3 outlines these steps as a series of key questions.

In order to implement targeted instruction for those students for whom data revealed specific needs, James had to reconsider the instructional schedule. He decided to implement an enrichment period for all students three times per week. During that time, students would either work in book clubs, with fairly minimal faculty support, or in targeted instruction matched to their needs. Essentially, James and the ILT would have to go back to the drawing board, guiding a new set of curriculum choices, reflecting on their implementation, planning PD, and linking formative and summative evaluation. And once they had accomplished that, data were likely to reveal the next set of challenges.

CHALLENGES FACING PRINCIPALS

It may be tempting to blame failed schools on failed principals, but the reality is more complex than that. The role of principal as instructional leader is only one of the complex roles principals must assume, and, for many, it is inconsistent with their preparation as managers. Institutions of higher education are charged with preparing principals to standards produced by

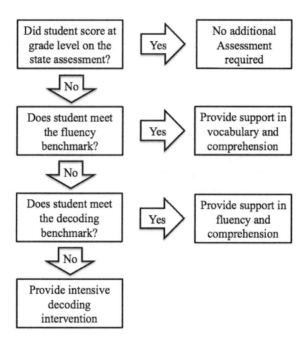

FIGURE 6.3. Decision sequence for determining the appropriate focus.

the National Policy Board for Educational Administration, the most recent of which (2002) highlights the complexities of the principalship, even for those whose preparation did target instructional leadership. The six standards read as follows: Candidates who complete the program are educational leaders who have the knowledge and ability to promote the success of all students by:

- Facilitating the development, articulation, implementation, and stewardship of a school or district vision of learning supported by the school community. (p. 2)
- Promoting a positive school culture, providing an effective instructional program, applying best practice to student learning, and designing comprehensive professional growth plans for staff. (p. 4)
- Managing the organization, operations, and resources in a way that promotes a safe, efficient, and effective learning environment. (p. 7)
- Collaborating with families and other community members, responding to diverse community interests and needs, and mobilizing community resources. (p. 9)
- Acting with integrity, fairly, and in an ethical manner. (p. 13)

- Understanding, responding to, and influencing the larger political, social, economic, legal, and cultural context. (p. 14)

Consider the principal's role as instructional leader within the larger context presented by the standards. Also consider the complexity of the role of instructional leader. In Table 6.3 we review the many facets of instructional leadership that were presented in our case study.

TABLE 6.3. Potential Actions for Fulfilling the Various Roles of Principal

Principal role	Potential actions
Setting a mission and goals	• Interpret federal, state, and district mandates • Bring stakeholders (administrators, teachers, parents, students) together for discussion • Summarize and communicate the results of achievement tests • Embrace a commitment to all students
Building and distributing leadership	• Identify current and future leaders • Create time for extended collaboration • Set protocols for decision making • Create systems for clear communication • Provide opportunities for individual growth
Guiding curriculum selection and adaptation	• Identify school needs, based on data and local conditions • Locate external research to guide selections • Set protocols for curriculum review • Schedule time for curriculum review
Planning for effective PD	• Locate, fund, and nurture coaches • Set roles and responsibilities of coaches • Identify targets for PD • Promote coherent PD for all faculty members • Select PD providers • Allocate adequate resources (time, money, materials) • Schedule classroom follow-up
Building a climate of reflection	• Facilitate classroom visits • Enable peer coaching • Gather and summarize data from observations and walkthroughs • Provide time for discussion
Planning formative and summative evaluation	• Monitor coaches' work • Distinguish between formative and summative evaluation • Link both types of evaluation to PD efforts
Using data to make decisions	• Summarize assessment data quickly and appropriately • Design assessment systems • Allocate resources based on student needs

JAMES: AN AFTERWORD

The systematic approach that James adopted toward improving reading instruction in his school was laudable. He did his best to translate theory into practice, and he transformed a culture of low expectations into one of professionalism. He helped to create teacher leaders and garner widespread buy in. His efforts to instill content-area reading strategies bore fruit, and his plan to use assessments to provide targeted skills instruction to students at risk (the point at which we left him) shows promise. Clearly, he has taken many of the actions needed to effect change. The measure of his success cannot be reduced to a single number, such as the percentage of students passing the state test. It must also be gauged in terms of the community he built, the leaders he created, and the minds he changed. His effectiveness as a leader, like that of any principal, is multidimensional. We believe that the most important step he took was to become aware of what those dimensions are.

STUDY GROUP MATERIALS

Principals (K–12), like all professionals, need continuous PD. In Figure 6.4, we provide a bibliography of resources that we have found especially helpful for principals. We suggest that you review the study group materials that we have presented and think about how a principal might actually use them. Note that documents from the Center on Instruction are downloadable from *www.centeroninstruction.org*.

ENGAGEMENT ACTIVITIES

1. Think about the case examples in this chapter.
    a. How would you advise Barbara, the elementary principal described in this chapter, to improve her expertise in reading? What steps should she take to build a productive relationship with her coach?
    b. Critique the strategies that James enacted as instructional leader. In each area, what could he have done differently? What lessons might Barbara learn from James's experiences at the middle level?

2. Consider ways that a principal can distribute leadership to include literacy professionals described in other chapters: reading specialists, literacy coaches, and special educators.

3. Tables 6.1 and 6.3 begin by indicating that it is important for a principal to set the mission and goals of the school. Table 6.1 lists actions suggested by Supovitz et al. (2010) that principals can take to realize this aim. Table 6.3 presents a second list of actions, recommended

by the National Policy Board for Educational Administration (2002). Compare and contrast these lists. Are they consistent? Can they be combined into a single list of actions an effective principal should take?

4. How does instructional leadership differ for principals at the elementary level, middle school level, and high school level? What special challenges does each face? How might they address them?

Boardman, A. G., Roberts, G., Vaughn, S., Wexler, J., Murray, C. S., & Kosanovich, M. (2008). *Effective instruction for adolescent struggling readers: A practice brief.* Portsmouth, NH: RMC Research Corporation, Center on Instruction.

Center on Instruction. (2006). *Designing high quality professional development: Building a community of reading experts in elementary schools.* Portsmouth, NH: RMC Research Corporation, Center on Instruction.

Kosanovich, M. L., Reed, D. K., & Miller, D. H. (2010). *Bringing literacy strategies into content instruction: Professional learning for secondary-level teachers.* Portsmouth, NH: RMC Research Corporation, Center on Instruction.

Moughamian, A. C., Rivera, M. O., & Francis, D. J. (2009). *Instructional models and strategies for teaching English language learners.* Portsmouth, NH: RMC Research Corporation, Center on Instruction.

Rissman, L. M., Miller, D. H., & Torgesen, J. K. (2009). *Adolescent literacy walk-through for principals: A guide for instructional leaders.* Portsmouth, NH: RMC Research Corporation, Center on Instruction.

Rivera, M. O., Moughamian, A. C., Lesaux, N. K., & Francis, D. J. (2008). *Language and reading interventions for English language learners and English language learners with disabilities.* Portsmouth, NH: RMC Research Corporation, Center on Instruction.

Scammacca, N., Vaughn, S., Roberts, G., Wanzek, J., & Torgesen, J. K. (2007). *Extensive reading interventions in grades K–3: From research to practice.* Portsmouth, NH: RMC Research Corporation, Center on Instruction.

Torgesen, J. K. (2006). *A comprehensive K–3 reading assessment plan: Guidance for school leaders.* Portsmouth, NH. RMC Research Corporation, Center on Instruction.

Torgesen, J. K. (2006). *Intensive reading interventions for struggling readers in early elementary school: A principal's guide.* Portsmouth, NH: RMC Research Corporation, Center on Instruction.

Torgesen, J. K., Houston, D., & Rissman, L. (2007). *Improving literacy instruction in middle and high schools: A guide for principals.* Portsmouth, NH: RMC Research Corporation, Center on Instruction.

Torgesen, J. K., Houston D., Rissman, L., & Kosanovich, K. (2007). *Teaching all students to read in elementary school: A guide for principals.* Portsmouth, NH: RMC Research Corporation, Center on Instruction.

Torgesen, J. K., & Miller, D. H. (2009). *Assessments to guide adolescent literacy instruction.* Portsmouth, NH: RMC Research Corporation, Center on Instruction.

FIGURE 6.4. Bibliography for study group materials.

REFERENCES

Boardman, A. G., Roberts, G., Vaughn, S., Wexler, J., Murray, C. S., & Kosanovich, M. (2008). *Effective instruction for adolescent struggling readers: A practice brief*. Portsmouth, NH: RMC Research Corporation, Center on Instruction.

Burch, P., Theoharis, G., & Rauscher, E. (2010). Class size reduction in practice: Investigating the influence of the elementary school principal. *Educational Policy, 24*, 330–358.

Copland, M. A. (2004). Distributed leadership for instructional improvement: The principal's role. In D. S. Strickland & M. L. Kamil (Eds.), *Improving reading achievement through professional development* (pp. 213–231). Norwood, MA: Christopher-Gordon.

Dumay, X. (2009). Origins and consequences of schools' organizational culture for student achievement. *Educational Administration Quarterly, 45*, 523–555.

Fisher, D., Frey, N., & Lapp, D. (2009). Meeting AYP in a high-need school: A formative experiment. *Journal of Adolescent and Adult Literacy, 52*, 386–396.

Hallinger, P., Bickman, L., & Davis, K. (1996). School context, principal leadership, and student reading achievement. *Elementary School Journal, 96*, 527–549.

Joyce, B. R., & Showers, B. (1988). *Student achievement through staff development: Fundamentals of school renewal*. White Plains, NY: Longman.

Leithwood, K., & Jantzi, D. (2008). Linking leadership to student learning: The contributions of leader efficacy. *Educational Administration Quarterly, 44*, 496–528.

Leithwood, K., & Mascall, B. (2008). Collective leadership effects on student achievement. *Educational Administration Quarterly, 44*, 529–561.

Murphy, J. (2004). *Leadership for literacy: Research-based practice, PreK–3*. Thousand Oaks, CA: Corwin Press.

Murray, C. S., Wexler, J., Vaughn, S., Boardman, A. G., Roberts, G., Tackett, K. K., et al. (2010). *Effective instruction for adolescent struggling readers: Professional development module facilitator's guide* (2nd ed.). Portsmouth, NH: RMC Research Corporation, Center on Instruction.

National Policy Board for Educational Administration. (2002). *Standards for advanced programs in educational leadership for principals, superintendents, curriculum directors, and supervisors*. Austin, TX: Author.

Nettles, S., & Herrington, C. (2007). Revisiting the importance of the direct effects of school leadership on student achievement: The implications for school improvement policy. *Peabody Journal of Education, 82*, 724–736.

Printy, S. (2008). Leadership for teacher learning: A community of practice perspective. *Educational Administration Quarterly, 44*, 187–226.

Roberts, S. M., & Pruitt, E. Z. (2003). *Schools as professional learning communities: Collaborative activities and strategies for professional development*. Thousand Oaks, CA: Corwin Press.

Ross, J., & Gray, P. (2006). School leadership and student achievement: The mediating effects of teacher beliefs. *Canadian Journal of Education, 29*, 798–822.

Saunders, W., Goldenberg, C., & Gallimore, R. (2009). Increasing achievement by focusing grade-level teams on improving classroom learning: A prospective, quasi-experimental study of Title I schools. *American Educational Research Journal, 46,* 1006–1033.

Showers, B., & Joyce, B. (1996). The evolution of peer coaching. *Educational Leadership, 53*(6), 12–16.

Supovitz, J., Sirinides, P., & May, H. (2010). How principals and peers influence teaching and learning. *Educational Administration Quarterly, 46,* 31–56.

Walpole, S., & McKenna, M. C. (2004). *The literacy coach's handbook.* New York: Guilford Press.

Walpole, S., McKenna, M. C., & Philippakos, Z. A. (2011). *Differentiated reading instruction in grades 4 and 5: Strategies and resources.* New York: Guilford Press.

PART II

WHAT LITERACY LEADERS NEED TO KNOW ABOUT LITERACY

7

Emergent Literacy

Anne McGill-Franzen
Jennifer Jordan

Guiding Questions

- What does developmentally appropriate instruction look like?
- What skills embedded into national standards are precursors to reading achievement?
- How does the activity of interactive writing bring both language modeling and literacy strategies into sharp focus for emergent readers?

Concern about the literacy achievement gap between poor, ethnic, and language-minority children and their more advantaged peers has intensified over the past decade, leading to unprecedented scrutiny of teachers and teaching, and this scrutiny has extended even to teaching our youngest children. In this chapter we discuss first the various iterations of developmentally appropriate instruction, a theoretical construct that is central to any examination of what literacy leaders need to know about emergent literacy. Next we describe the constellation of skills, embedded in national standards, that researchers have identified as precursors to later reading achievement. We examine in detail interactive writing—an undervalued context for high-quality language modeling and focused literacy instruction—and classroom talk. We conclude our chapter with recommendations for personalized professional development that enables teachers to observe good examples of high-quality interactions and obtain feedback on their own discourse with students. Below is a case study example of Caroline who is attempting to incorporate these new views about how young children become immersed in literacy and language in her classroom.

Caroline has been teaching kindergarten for 2 years and during this time she has been taking graduate-level literacy classes at her local university. During this time, she has learned a great deal about which skills and strategies are developmentally appropriate for emergent readers. Caroline was especially interested in interactive writing, an activity in which she and her students "share the pen" to compose text. She learned that interactive writing can support early reading skills such as phonemic awareness and sight-word recognition. Her grade level is getting prepared to teach a unit on beginning blends such as -sh, -th, and -wh and Caroline feels that these skills could be taught authentically through interactive writing lessons. She brought this new knowledge back to her classroom and tried to share what she had learned with her colleagues. Unfortunately, the other teachers, who have been teaching for several years, do not believe that their students are developmentally ready to learn the writing skills and strategies that Caroline is so excited about sharing. She now feels unsure about what to do. She thought about talking with one of the literacy leaders at her school or her principal, but she is concerned that this will compromise her job security. She does not have tenure, and is worried that she will be viewed as complaining or trying to buck the system if she does not teach in the more traditional manner that the other teachers are accustomed to. What are the issues that Caroline is facing? What are some of the alternative actions that she might consider and the pros and cons of each?

WHAT IS "DEVELOPMENTALLY APPROPRIATE PRACTICE"?

In 2009, the National Association for the Education of Young Children (NAEYC) revised the position statement, Developmentally Appropriate Practice (DAP) in Early Childhood Programs, defined by the organization as birth through 8 years old. In the Obama administration, as in the previous one, concerns for achievement and accountability have encompassed younger and younger grade levels. As a long-standing and highly influential professional organization that deals with accreditation and curriculum development issues for early childhood and kindergarten programs, the NAEYC recently has become a voice to be reckoned with in K–12 policy.

According to the National Institute for Early Education Research (NIEER), over 30% of 4-year-olds and 7% of 3-year-olds are enrolled in preschool programs, when both general education and special education are counted (National Institute for Early Education Research [NIEER], 2009), and another 500,000 or so in Head Start (United States Department of Health & Human Services, Administration on Children, Youth, & Families, & Head Start Bureau, 2003), making it critical that early childhood programs be philosophically aligned with the early grades in school so that teachers of children at varying developmental levels can build on what children know and are able to do.

The NAEYC has come a long way in its thinking about literacy and the young child since the first formal DAP position paper appeared in 1987, which listed "singing the alphabet song" and holding pencils to write as inappropriate, among other literacy activities (NAEYC, 1987). Taken to task for disadvantaging poor children, or second-language learners, who depend on early childhood programs to level the playing field and provide a "head start" for success in school, the NAEYC revised the DAP position in 1996 in response to equity concerns.

In its 1996 revision, the association welcomed the conversation with educators outside the early childhood domain and developed language that reflected sensitivity toward poverty and cultural and linguistic diversity. Along the way, the International Reading Association (IRA) joined the conversation with NAEYC, and together created a statement of developmentally appropriate practice that spanned the continuum of literacy development from preschool through third grade (International Reading Association and National Association for the Education of Young Children [IRA/NAEYC], 1998). Like the National Reading Conference monograph, Preventing Reading Difficulties in Young Children (Snow, Burns, & Griffin, 1998), which was released at about the same time, the IRA/NAEYC joint statement identified not only specific teaching activities to promote phonemic awareness, but also invented spelling as a way for children to develop an understanding of the way sound maps onto print. The joint statement marked a stunning departure in philosophy and practice on the part of NAEYC that, in the past, had held to a maturational view of literacy acquisition, that is, when "ready," children will discover the conventions of print and learn to read. Rather than eschew explicit teaching as "didactic" and hence inappropriate, the joint position statement acknowledged that adults can and should scaffold development:

> IRA and NAEYC believe that goals and expectations for young children's achievement in reading and writing should be developmentally appropriate, that is, challenging but achievable, with sufficient adult support. (1998, p. 15)

Several trends prompted the 2009 revision of DAP—the standards and accountability movement, increasing linguistic and cultural diversity, growing consensus on the importance of early schooling to mediate the deleterious effects of poverty on achievement, and the knowledge gained over the past decade about early cognitive development. Embedded within the 2009 position statement are specific recommendations for language and literacy practice. Vocabulary development within storybook reading and other contexts for extended discourse are emphasized, as is alphabet knowledge and phonological awareness. In an explicit reference to past prohibitions about literacy instruction, the position statement acknowledged the following:

> A decade ago, many preschool teachers did not perceive it as their role—or even see it as appropriate—to launch young children on early steps toward literacy, including familiarizing them with the world of print and the sounds of language. The early childhood profession now recognizes that gaining literacy foundations is an important facet of children's experience before kindergarten, although the early literacy component still needs substantial improvement in many classrooms. (p. 7)

Indeed, the work of the National Institute of Child Health and Human Development Early Childhood Research Network (2000, 2002, 2005; see also Pianta et al., 2005, and Justice, Mashburn, Hamre, & Pianta, 2008) suggested that the quality of teachers' interactions with children is highly variable, and unlikely to meet the emergent literacy and language needs of high-risk children in particular. The heart of developmentally appropriate practice, according to the NAEYC, lies in the quality of teachers' interactions—the ways that teachers implement activities and respond to individual children moment by moment. NAEYC refers to this quality as intentionality that is embedded in the "knowledge that practitioners consider when they are making decisions, and in always aiming for goals that are both challenging and achievable for children" (2009, p. 9).

WHAT EARLY LITERACY EDUCATORS SHOULD KNOW ABOUT THE DEVELOPMENT OF READING AND WRITING

One way to answer this question is to consult the standards for early literacy, either those developed by states themselves, such as early learning standards, or nationally. Presumably, the standards are aligned not only with our best research and thinking about early literacy development but also with the way students and more recently, teachers, are evaluated. The 2010 Common Core State Standards Initiative, developed by the Council of Chief

State Schools Officers and the National Governors' Association, presents a developmental progression of skills in essential literacy domains (Common Core State Standards for English Language Arts and Literacy in History/ Social Studies, Science and Technical Subjects, 2010). Adopted by over 40 states so far, the Core Standards are organized by grade with one section devoted to grades K–5. The standards emphasize key features of the English language arts curriculum across the grades and provide particular focus on the connections between reading and writing and language development.

Aspects of text complexity and the growth of comprehension jointly comprise the reading standards, from beginning reading to proficient levels. At all levels, the expectation holds that students "make fuller use of text," demonstrating increasing ability to make inferences within and across texts and read texts with a discerning and critical stance. The writing standards consider not only the process of writing, that is, the ability to plan, draft, revise, and edit, but also the specific kinds of writing required within different text types. Also expected is the ability to develop written responses to literary and informational texts and draw upon these texts to study topics of interest. The language standards frame speaking and listening in terms of peer collaboration and effective communication that may include drawing and digital media depending on the nature of the task and levels of the children. The language standards include the ability to learn the meanings of new words as well as the conventions of oral and written language.

Central to our discussion on emergent literacy are the foundational skills that are not an "end" in themselves but necessary elements in a comprehensive early literacy program that ultimately enables understanding and composition of text. Among these foundational skills are understanding the organization and basic features of print (alphabet knowledge, directionality and linearity, concept of word in text); understanding of spoken words, syllables, and sounds (rhyme, segmentation, and blending); knowing and applying grade-level phonics and word-analysis skills in decoding words; and ability to read grade-appropriate texts with fluency (*www.corestandards.org/the-standards/english-language-arts-standards*).

Although preschool is not included in the Common Core State Standards, the NIEER (2009) reported that last year that 47 states and Head Start had developed early learning standards for children before kindergarten age. Early standards typically include the domains of social, emotional, and motor development but recently have included early literacy domains similar to those articulated for the Common Core State Standards (Scott-Little, Kagan, & Frelow, 2006). For example, the state of Wisconsin expects that preschool children will show "an appreciation of books and understand[ing of] how print works"; develop alphabetic awareness, phonological awareness, and phonemic awareness; demonstrate "the use of strategies to read words"; and use "writing to represent thoughts or ideas" (Wisconsin Model

Early Learning Standards, 2008, p. 42). Likewise, the first two of eight domains in the Head Start Outcomes Framework are language and literacy standards. In this document language is broadly construed as listening and understanding, and speaking and communicating, whereas the literacy outcomes are more specific and reflective of the core standards of foundational knowledge: phonological awareness, book knowledge and appreciation, print awareness and concepts, early writing, and alphabet knowledge.

Besides the recently promulgated standards described above, the National Early Literacy Panel (2009) released the results of a number of research syntheses of approximately 500 empirical studies on early literacy development. Although the content of the report, *Developing Early Literacy*, is less accessible to the practitioner than either state early learning standards or the Core Standards, the report affirms the centrality of emergent literacy skills in later academic achievement. Among the questions posed by the panel and elaborated in the report were two of interest to readers of this chapter: What are the precursor or emergent literacy abilities that are linked to later reading, writing, and spelling achievement? and Which interventions support the development of these precursor abilities?

The panel identified several strong or moderate correlates of later reading achievement from these analyses, among them alphabet knowledge, phonological awareness, name writing, oral language, and print knowledge. (Note: Other variables were identified, but for the purposes of this chapter are not elaborated here, e.g., automaticity in letter, digit, and object naming). Oral language emerged as a potentially important variable in later reading comprehension, particularly if the researchers employed complex or composite measures of oral language in the studies. In fact, studies that used the most complex measures of oral language (such as listening comprehension, the ability to define words or understand grammatical constructions) obtained the highest correlation with reading comprehension of any measure (Shanahan & Lonigan, 2010). Not surprisingly, the panel also found that children learned what they were taught: instruction that focused on shared reading improved children's oral language abilities; those that focused on the alphabetic code improved children's letter knowledge, phonological awareness, and spelling.

"IT'S THE TEACHER THAT MATTERS!": WHAT COUNTS AS QUALITY IN CLASSROOM INTERACTIONS?

Unfortunately, teachers of our youngest learners all too often have an inadequate knowledge base on which to make instructional decisions. Some teachers still hold to a maturational view of literacy development, that is, children will discover the alphabetic code when they are "ready" (Powell, Diamond, Bojczyk, & Gerde, 2008; Teale, Hoffman, & Paciga, 2010). Even teachers who believe that they can and should teach early literacy skills to preschool and kindergarten children struggle to do so in the most challenging high-poverty school environments. Early literacy programs that emphasize fidelity of implementation basically require teachers to follow a set of procedures rather than engage in the "moment-by-moment" decision making that is essential for high-quality interactions with children. In fact, several recent research studies have demonstrated that teachers can implement most well-sequenced programs with near perfect fidelity after minimal training, yet these highly faithful implementations may make no difference whatsoever in the achievement of children (Justice & Ezell, 2002; Justice et al., 2008). Clearly, it is not the use of materials or implementation of a script per se that constitutes quality instruction; it is instead the moment-by-moment interactions during which teachers respond to cues by children and adjust their teaching accordingly (Henry & Pianta, 2010; Clay, 1998).

Recently, researchers involved with the National Center for Research on Early Childhood Education developed a rubric to scale the quality of teachers' interactions with children (Henry & Pianta, 2011; Justice et al., 2008). Based on extensive research into the kinds of instructional interactions that have been associated with children's growth in language and literacy, these researchers have added substantially to classroom observation protocols that attempt to document quality. The rubric emphasizes language modeling and literacy focus so that observers may identify the kinds of instruction that enhances children's development in these areas (Justice et al., 2008), and where lacking, initiate professional development to support teachers' development of these interactional and knowledge repertoires.

Language modeling is conceptualized as the frequency of talk initiated by children, teachers' engagement of children in extensive conversation, open-ended questions, teachers' repetition and extension of children's responses (also known as "uptake"), teachers' use of language to describe or "map" actions by him- or herself and students, and teachers' use of complex language. Literacy focus is conceptualized as "explicit, purposeful, and systematic" (Justice et al., 2008, p. 59) in that teachers use terms that "make clear the relation between oral and written language" (p. 59); define abstract terms such as sound, letter, word, sentence; relate code-based instruction to purposeful and authentic reading and writing; and organize instruction according to developmental progressions of skills (p. 59).

Traditional classroom activities like reading storybooks aloud or using materials such as informational texts leveled for difficulty and focused on a single topic, or writing a shared text can become the context for high-quality instructional interactions that enable children to achieve language and literacy competence. By elaborating the meanings of unfamiliar words during read-alouds (see Justice & Ezell, 2002, for example); engaging children in extended conversation about the motivation of characters, or similarity of events across stories (see McGill-Franzen, Lanford, & Adams, 2002; McGill-Franzen, Allington, Brooks, & Yokoi, 1999); or "sharing the pen" with children to jointly compose and write a text (Jordan, 2009), teachers can mediate children's understandings of the way reading and writing work and model for them meaning making from text. Interactive writing is poorly understood and underutilized, yet is a powerful instructional context for language modeling and explicit, purposeful, and systematic literacy focus.

BRINGING TOGETHER LANGUAGE AND LITERACY

Interactive Writing Instruction

"Interactive writing is a dynamic, collaborative literacy event in which children actively compose together, considering appropriate words, phrases, organization of the text, and layout" (McCarrier, Pinnell, & Fountas, 2000, p. xv). Children are viewed as apprentices to an expert writer, the teacher or their peers, as they construct meaningful texts together that are beyond what the students could have composed on their own. "At the core of effective instructional interaction there is a shared exchange of ideas between teacher and student—and a more balanced role for all participants" (Langer & Applebee, 1984, p. 175).

Writing in an interactive format is designed to instruct students from preschool through second or third grade in the emergent, early, transitional, and self-extending stages of reading and writing. The texts that are created by teachers and students can be considered instructional materials, because students can later revisit these texts to read, copy strategies used, and gather ideas for future writing (Button, Johnson, & Furgerson, 1996). Through revisiting the written texts, students may increasingly take up writing skills and become more independent writers.

Interactive writing can be viewed as a transitional tool that strives to move children toward individual writing. Through modeling of skills and strategies, students may begin to transfer these strategies and skills learned in interactive writing into their independent text construction. "For beginning writers, putting together and talking about ideas, negotiating the text with others, and sharing the pen to write it, propel them toward grasping the power of the written word" (McCarrier et al., 2000, p. xix). Once students begin to understand that writing is oral language written down and how and why people write, they may begin to write purposeful texts on their own and possess the strategies to do so.

According to McCarrier et al. (2000) there are eight steps to the inter-active writing process:

1. Provide a base of active learning experiences.
2. Talk to establish purpose.
3. Compose the text.
4. Construct the text.
5. Reread, revise, and proofread the text.
6. Revisit the text to support word solving.
7. Summarize the learning.
8. Extend the learning. (p. 73)

These steps usually occur in a recursive manner, rather than a lockstep format. An interactive writing lesson usually begins with exploring shared experiences. These experiences can be from home or school, and may include literature previously read aloud (Lancia, 1997). Literature read-alouds are opportunities to draw children's attention to concepts of print, literary syntax, style and genre, story structure, and connections between reading and writing.

Dialogue between teacher and students to establish an authentic purpose is also a key aspect of interactive writing (Gundlach, 1982; Wiley, 1999). Having a purpose to write is highly engaging and meaningful and therefore motivating (Pajares & Valiante, 2005). Writing a morning message, extending or summarizing a read-aloud, recording new information, writing letters, and writing labels are all purposeful activities. Through meaningful discussion, students draw on their teacher, peers, and literature as models of how to discuss what to write and how to write.

Once students form a foundation based on experience and purpose, composition occurs. Composition refers to the process of discussing what will be written. Children are engaged in, and take ownership of, the writing process through the dialogue between teacher and student as well as through the actual writing of letters and words. Children must think about, and discuss, the message they want to convey, the audience they are targeting, and what words are most suitable to convey that message. They also draw from their knowledge of previously read or written texts to decide on how to structure the text and which conventions of writing will be required depending on the genre. Through these discussions, students generate different ways of conveying the same message and build upon others' ideas. They also may expand their own speaking and listening vocabularies through these discussions.

In one classroom lesson observed by Jordan (2009), Caroline, the teacher featured in our case study, read *Knuffle Bunny* by Mo Willems (2004) to provide a base of active learning experiences. She then led a discussion about the main idea of the story:

CAROLINE: So what is the main idea of the story?

SARAH: She lost Knuffle Bunny.

CAROLINE: What was the main character's name?

ALLISON: Trixie.

CAROLINE: So Trixie lost Knuffle Bunny. Then what happens?

PAUL: They look for Knuffle Bunny.

KEVIN: She forgot Knuffle Bunny.

LILY: She helped her daddy put the laundry.

CAROLINE: Is that what it is mostly about?

LILY: No.

CAROLINE: Should we say we lost or forgot Knuffle Bunny?

(Students vote for forgot.)

CAROLINE: Where?

MATT: At the laundry mat.

SAM: And she was looking for him.

CAROLINE: So Trixie forgot Knuffle Bunny and was looking for him at the laundry mat?

After discussion of what to write, the class jointly constructed the text. The construction of the text involved writing down the previously agreed upon message by the teacher and students.

Deciding on topics and choosing students to participate in sharing the pen depends on the instructional needs of the students and will shift throughout the year. Focusing on too many concepts can be confusing. Therefore, children do not need to write every word; rather the teaching points should be selected carefully and be focused on the needs of the individual students. The teacher should have learning outcomes for each student in mind during the interactive writing lesson. When constructing texts, standard conventions of written language should not be ignored. Some skills to focus on may include phonics, phonemic awareness, vocabulary, fluency, reading comprehension, capitalization rules, and punctuation. In this particular lesson Caroline drew the children's attention to the *kn* and *th* sounds:

CAROLINE: Come up and find a word that has a *sh, th,* or *kn* sound.

(Will underlines *they.*)

CAROLINE: What did you find?

Will: *th.*

CAROLINE: *th* in the word *they.*

JESSIE: (Underlines *Knuffle Bunny*.)

JESSIE: The *kn* in *Knuffle Bunny*.

CAROLINE: Are there any others?

ALL: No.

CAROLINE: We didn't find a *sh* this time, but maybe we will next time.

Discussion during interactive writing revolves around making letter to sound connections for emergent writers. Connections should also be made to reinforce the fact that words they use in conversations can be written down and that the spelling of those words is consistent: "They are learning how to learn about print. They are learning how to look, where to look, and what to look at, and they are connecting that knowledge to what they hear and what their fingers do" (McCarrier et al., 2000, p. 75). Higher-order writing skills, such as sequencing of events and how to vary word choice, may also be appropriate for some learners. These interactive writing texts may be reread many times by the children and when "displayed in the classroom, they provide a permanent demonstration and reminder to the children of how to go about writing" (p. 27).

Composing texts may require students to engage in certain processes during construction, as well as after it, in order to be effective. While composing the text, the class rereads, revises, and proofreads the text. Rereading the text serves as a means of remembering the text and anticipating what will come next. Revising sometimes occurs when students want to clarify the meaning of the text. Students constantly proofread as they write, revise, and edit to ensure intended meaning and conventional grammar.

After proofreading, teachers may revisit the text to harvest words for word study. During word study teachers direct children's attention to the orthography—the patterns and principles of spelling and morphology. In addition to gains in spelling skills, Jordan (2009) found that students who reread texts multiple times for authentic purposes during composition increased their rate of reading and fluency.

Interactive writing is designed to be an integral part of any writing curriculum that encompasses explicit teaching of written language conventions within a framework of authentic student writing. Assessment of students' progress and needs may be accomplished through conversation and observation. Systematic anecdotal records may be used to track children's ongoing literacy development and help guide instructional focus in subsequent small-group teaching. Students may take up or appropriate the language that teachers model for them in interactive writing. If that happens—if students carry these types of dialogic interactions over into their own individual work and into other subject areas, teachers and literacy leaders can assume that learning has occurred.

Reading and Writing: Reciprocal Processes

Reading and writing "depend on identical or similar knowledge representations, cognitive processes, and contexts and contextual restraints. Therefore, we should expect reading and writing to be quite similar, their development should parallel each other closely, and some type of pedagogical combination may be useful in making learning more efficient" (Fitzgerald & Shanahan, 2000, p. 40). This view departs from the traditional belief that children should learn to read before they learn to write (Shanahan & Lomax, 1986; Fitzgerald & Shanahan, 2000). Although not all processes of reading and writing are related, research has shown a positive relationship between spelling and reading, writing and reading vocabulary, reading comprehension and complexity of writing, and reading comprehension and writing structure or organization (Jordan, 2009; Shanahan, 1984). Not only do reading and writing bear a reciprocal relationship to each other in terms of the processes employed, but by integrating reading and writing instruction we enable children to examine literacy from different cognitive perspectives, thereby deepening their learning (Shanahan, 2005).

As Caroline learned from her professional study, reading and writing are reciprocal language processes. Teachers can support vocabulary development, print and genre knowledge, and the conventions of writing by integrating reading and language arts instruction. To illustrate, we use an example from Kindergarten Literacy (McGill-Franzen, 2006)—the text set. Teachers can develop text sets by gathering a number of books about the same story character, say, Biscuit or Clifford, or they can gather informational books by different authors and publishers organized around the same topic. Figure 7.1 shows a display of 16 books on the topic of "animal babies"—several read-aloud big books, and some leveled books for guided reading that Knox County, Tennessee, reading specialists Susanne Worth, Ruth Lindsey, and Theresa Wishart gathered for professional development. The purpose of the professional development was to illustrate how a text set can be used for conceptual development of science vocabulary, guided and independent reading, and as a springboard for shared and interactive writing. Figure 7.2 illustrates how one teacher used the information from the animal babies text set to construct shared writing and interactive writing experiences that helped consolidate content vocabulary as well as print conventions and more fluent word recognition.

"It's Not Just What You Say but How You Say It!": Classroom Talk

As we pointed out in an earlier section of the chapter, the quality of classroom discourse is an important factor in determining what type of learning

FIGURE 7.1. A text set of 16 books on the topic of "animal babies."

will occur in any given classroom. Typical classrooms are organized so that the teacher is the giver of knowledge and the students are viewed as empty vessels. In these classrooms, the teacher usually participates in dialogue described as initiate, respond, and evaluate, where the student is prompted by a question to which the teacher already knows the answer (Cazden, 1988). The teacher then evaluates the students' response to that question. Usually, this type of dialogue is disjointed from students' own experiences. This means "instead of the knowledge-in-action that both allows and develops through participation in culturally significant traditions of discourse, we have emphasized the knowledge-out-of-context" (Applebee, 1996, p. 26).

Nystrand (1997) studied classroom discourse and found that it was primarily one sided or teacher directed with the teachers lecturing and then asking questions. These questions tended to be unauthentic and teachers rarely followed up on student responses. Through this type of interaction, children implicitly learned what topics were appropriate for discussion in school as well as how these topics were to be addressed (Applebee, 1996).

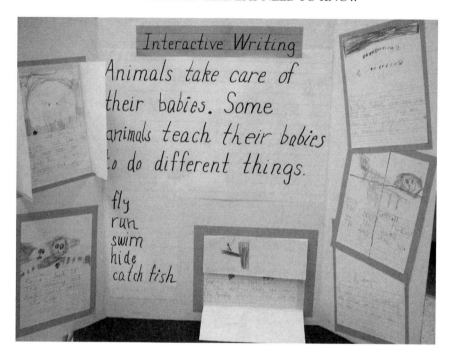

FIGURE 7.2. An example of interactive writing developed by a kindergarten teacher and her class using information from the animal babies text set. Alongside the class composition are examples of individual students' independent writing on that topic. For example, the top right student writing "A baby cheetahs mom and dad tak food to his baby vere fast so the baby wot cri for his mom and dad.") and left bottom writing ("The mommy and dad [lion] will prtet the cub.") suggest parental responsibilities.

This format provides no option for negotiating meaning, risk taking, or for students to discuss their own personal connections and experiences.

In contrast to this more traditional classroom setting, is a dialogic environment that encourages conversation between the teacher and students as would be observed in dialogic storybook read-alouds and an interactive writing setting. The teacher engages in uptake where he or she expands on students' prior discussions and experiences. Under this model, school provides children a place to learn language as well as learn through language (Applebee, 1996; Johnston, 2004; Wells, 1999). "The roles we establish as teachers and the interactions we undertake with our students, through our questions, responses, and assignments, inexorably set out the possibilities for meaning in our classes, and, in this way, the context of learning" (Nystrand,

1997, p. 9). This type of discourse requires negotiation among participants that leads to better student understanding and knowledge (Nystrand, 1986). "Whereas monologically organized instruction seeks to transmit information, dialogic instruction works by cultivating knowledge—transforming understandings through reflection and talk" (Nystrand, 1997, p. 26).

Caroline encouraged uptake in her classroom during interactive writing lessons by validating what her students were saying and encouraging them to expand on their ideas. Her students were writing about their favorite sports after watching a short segment of the Olympics on the TV earlier in the day. She used repetition and uptake to expand her students' ideas during the following conversation:

CAROLINE: We like golf because. … What did you say? It is fun to hit the ball? What did you say, Nathan?

NATHAN: Because you get to hit the ball.

SUZY: It is fun to hit the ball.

CAROLINE: Because it is fun.

NATHAN: It is fun to hit the ball in the tube.

CAROLINE: In the tube. Are you talking about miniature golf?

NATHAN: Yeah, miniature golf.

CAROLINE: We like to play miniature golf because it is fun to hit the ball. Is that what you want to write?

SUZY: Yeah.

Christoph and Nystrand (2001) followed a teacher as she tried to transition to more dialogic teaching strategies by integrating dialogic bids such as asking authentic questions, practicing uptake, and using high-level evaluation. In the beginning of the study the teacher asked 99% of the questions, of which 7% were authentic and 9% were marked by uptake in which the teacher built on previous student talk to build an authentic conversation. Through gradual change this teacher began her journey toward a more dialogic classroom. She realized, "some of these interruptions and off-topic comments actually made learning possible because they bridged the lives of the students to the coursework in ways that were meaningful to the students" (p. 276). The teacher's knowledge of her students and consideration of their suggestions gradually created an environment of involvement and respect, thereby transforming the students' role to one of active engagement (Maloch, 2002; McIntyre, Kyle, & Moore, 2006).

During activities such as interactive writing students benefit from peer to peer interaction as well as that of the teacher—peers are able to complete tasks together that they might not have been able to finish on their own, build a relationship with an audience, and build knowledge through exploratory talk (Jordan, 2009). As children communicate with each other they begin to understand concepts more fully. Thus, "by contributing to the joint meaning making with and for others, one also makes meaning for oneself and in the process, extends one's own understanding" (Wells, 1999, p. 108).

Again, according to Wells (1999), "in this sort of accepting climate, speech allows all participants to enter the dialogue at the level of which they are capable; it also enables the teacher or tutor to offer immediate support and assistance that is tailored to the needs of the individual student" (p. 115).

CONCLUSION

Early literacy educators and those who provide leadership for early literacy programs should emphasize the quality of the interactions between children and those who teach them. To emphasize a strict implementation of commercial programs, no matter the research base, or the use of particular materials, no matter how attractive, would be misguided. Professional development should target the early literacy skills that are related to reading achievement and most important, the kinds of instructional interactions that enable children to learn these skills.

Teachers need to observe firsthand effective language modeling and focused literacy instruction with children of diverse developmental levels; they need to receive feedback from colleagues and literacy leaders on the quality of their own instructional interactions. Given the advances in technology and digital media, such personalized approaches may not be out of reach for literacy leaders and the practitioners whose professional development they support. Finally, even though we provided a detailed description of interactive writing and its concomitant research and theoretical base, most of the traditional activities of the reading and writing block can become the context for high-quality language and literacy interactions. Of utmost importance, however, is that a "cultural shift" may be required of teachers who are wedded to child-directed instruction at the expense of learners who need explicit, authentic, and systematic teaching.

ENGAGEMENT ACTIVITIES

1. Discuss the case example of Caroline. What are the issues she faces? What are some of the alternate actions that she might consider and the pros and cons of each?

2. Observe in an early childhood setting or kindergarten classroom to describe the nature of children's writing. What were children asked to do? How much time did they spend writing?

3. Interview the teacher. What did he or she hope to accomplish in the instructional activity you observed?

4. How would you define developmentally appropriate instruction for emergent readers and writers? What are the skills and strategies that emergent readers and writers should possess?

REFERENCES

Applebee, A. N. (1996). *Curriculum as conversation: Transforming traditions of teaching and learning.* Chicago: University of Chicago Press.

Button, K., Johnson, M. J., & Furgerson, P. (1996). Interactive writing in a primary classroom. *Reading Teacher, 49*(6), 446–454.

Cazden, C. B. (1988). *Classroom discourse: The language of teaching and learning.* Portsmouth, NH: Heinemann.

Christoph, J. N., & Nystrand, M. (2001). Taking risks, negotiating relationships: One teacher's transition toward a dialogic classroom. *Research in the Teaching of English, 36,* 249–286.

Clay, M. (1998). *By different paths to common outcomes.* York, ME: Stenhouse.

Common Core State Standards for English Language Arts and Literacy in History/Social Studies, Science and Technical Subjects. (2010). Retrieved November 23, 2010, from *www.corestandards.org/the-standards/english-language-arts-standards.*

Fitzgerald, J., & Shanahan, T. (2000). Reading and writing relations and their development. *Educational Psychologist, 35*(1), 39–50.

Gundlach, R. A. (1982). Children as writers: The beginnings of learning to write. In M. Nystrand (Ed.), *What writers know: The language, process, and structure of written discourse* (pp. 129–147). New York: Academic Press.

Henry, A. E., & Pianta, R. C. (2011). Effective teacher–child interactions and children's literacy: Evidence for scalable, aligned approaches to professional development. In S. D. Neuman and D. K. Dickinson (Eds.), *Handbook of early literacy research* (Vol. 3, pp.308–321). New York: Guilford Press.

International Reading Association and National Association for the Education of Young Children. (1998). *Learning to read and write: Developmentally appropriate practices for young children.* Retrieved November 23, 2010, from *www.reading.org/General/AboutIRA/PositionStatements/Developmentally ApropriatePosition.*

Johnston, P. H. (2004). *Choice words: How our language affects children's learning.* Portland, ME: Stenhouse.

Jordan, J. (2009). *Beyond sharing the pen: Dialogue in the context of interactive writing.* Unpublished doctoral dissertation, University of Tennessee at Knoxville.

Justice, L., & Ezell, H. K. (2002). Use of storybook reading to increase print awareness in at-risk children. *American Journal of Speech–Language Pathology, 11*(1), 17–32.

Justice, L., Mashburn, A. J., Hamre, B. K., & Pianta, R. C. (2008). Quality of language and literacy instruction in preschool classrooms serving at-risk pupils. *Early Childhood Research Quarterly, 23*(1), 51–68.

Lancia, P. J. (1997). Literary borrowing: The effects of literature on children's writing. *Reading Teacher, 50*(6), 470–475.

Langer, J. A., & Applebee, A. N. (1984). Language, learning, and interaction: A framework for improving the teaching of writing. In A. N. Applebee (Ed.), *Contexts for learning to write: Studies of secondary school instruction* (pp. 169–182). Norwood, NJ: Ablex.

Maloch, B. (2002). Scaffolding student talk: One teacher's role in literature discussion groups. *Reading Research Quarterly, 37*(1), 94–112.

McCarrier, A., Pinnell, G. S., & Fountas, I. C. (2000). *Interactive writing: How language and literacy come together, K–2.* Portsmouth, NH: Heinemann.

McGill-Franzen, A. (2006). *Kindergarten literacy: Matching assessment and instruction.* New York: Scholastic.

McGill-Franzen, A., Allington, R. L., Brooks, G., & Yokoi, L. (1999). Putting books in their hands is necessary but not sufficient. *Journal of Educational Research, 93*(2), 67–74.

McGill-Franzen, A., Lanford, C., & Adams, E. (2002). Learning to be literate: A comparison of five early childhood programs. *Journal of Educational Psychology, 94*(3), 443–464.

McIntyre, E., Kyle, D. W., & Moore, G. H. (2006). A primary-grade teacher's guidance toward small-group dialogue. *Reading Research Quarterly, 41*(1), 36–66.

National Association for the Education of Young Children. (1987). *NAEYC position statement on licensing and other forms of regulation of early childhood programs in centers and family day care.* Washington, DC: Author.

National Association for the Education of Young Children. (1996). NAEYC position statement: Responding to linguistic and cultural diversity recommendations for effective early childhood education. *Young Children, 51*(2), 4–12.

National Association for the Education of Young Children. (2009). *Developmentally appropriate practice in early childhood programs serving children from birth through age 8.* Retrieved November 23, 2010, from *www.naeyc.org/files/naeyc/file/positions/PSDAP.*

National Early Literacy Panel. (2009). *Developing early literacy: Report of the National Early Literacy Panel.* Jessup, MD: National Institute for Literacy.

National Institute of Child Health and Human Development, Early Child Care Research Network. (2000). The relation of child care to cognitive and language development. *Child Development, 71*(4), 960–980.

National Institute of Child Health and Human Development, Early Child Care Research Network. (2002). Child care structure process outcome: Direct and indirect effects of child care quality on young children's development. *Psychological Science, 13*(3), 199–206.

National Institute of Child Health and Human Development, Early Child Care Research Network. (2005). Early child care and children's development in the pimary grades. Follow-up results from the NICHD study of early child care. *American Educational Research Journal, 42*(3), 537–570.

National Institute for Early Education Research. (2009). *The state of preschool 2009: State preschool yearbook.* New Brunswick, NJ: Rutgers University, Graduate School of Education. Retrieved November 23, 2010, from *www.nieer.org/yearbook/pdf/yearbook.pdf.*

Nystrand, M. (1986). *The structure of written communication: Studies in reciprocity between writers and readers.* Orlando, FL: Academic Press.

Nystrand, M. (1997). *Opening dialogue: Understanding the dynamics of language and learning in the English classroom.* New York: Teachers College Press.

Pajares, F., & Valiante, G. (2005). Self-efficacy beliefs and motivation in writing development. In C. A. MacArthur, S. Graham, & J. Fitzgerald (Eds.), *Handbook of writing research* (pp. 158–170). New York: Guilford Press.

Pianta, R. C., Howes, C., Burchinal, M., Bryant, D., Clifford, R., & Early, D. (2005). Features of pre-kindergarten programs, classrooms, and teachers: Do they predict observed classroom quality and child–teacher interactions? *Applied Developmental Science, 9*(3), 144–159.

Powell, D. R., Diamond, K. E., Bojczyk, K. E., & Gerde, H. K. (2008). Head Start teachers' perspectives on early literacy. *Journal of Literacy Research, 40,* 442–460.

Scott-Little, C., Kagan, S. L., & Frelow, V. S. (2006). Conceptualization of readiness and the content of early learning standards: The intersection of policy and research? *Early Childhood Research Quarterly, 21,* 153.

Shanahan, T. (1984). Nature of the reading–writing relation: An exploratory multivariate analysis. *Journal of Educational Psychology, 76*(3), 466–477.

Shanahan, T. (2005). Relations among oral language, reading, and writing development. In C. A. MacArthur, S. Graham, & J. Fitzgerald (Eds.), *Handbook of writing research* (pp. 171–183). New York: Guilford Press.

Shanahan, T., & Lomax, R. G. (1986). An analysis and comparison of theoretical models of the reading–writing relationship. *Journal of Educational Psychology, 78*(2), 116–123.

Shanahan, T., & Lonigan, C. (2010). The National Early Literacy Panel: A summary of the process and the report. *Educational Researcher, 39*(4), 279–285.

Snow, C. E., Burns, M. S., & Griffin, P. (1998). *Preventing reading difficulties in young children.* Washington, DC: National Academy Press.

Teale, W., Hoffman, J. L., & Paciga, K. A. (2010). Where is NELP leading preschool literacy instruction? Potential positives and pitfalls. *Educational Researcher, 39*(4), 311–315.

United States Department of Health and Human Services, Administration on Children, Youth, and Families, and Head Start Bureau. (2003). *The Head Start path to positive child outcomes.* Washington, DC: Authors. Retrieved November 23, 2010, *www.hsnrc.org/CDI/pdfs/hsoutcomespath28ppREV.pdf.*

Wells, G. (1999). *Dialogic inquiry: Toward a sociocultural practice and theory of education.* Cambridge, UK: Cambridge University Press.

Wiley, B. J. (1999). Interactive writing: The how and why of teaching and learning letters, sounds, and words. In I. C. Fountas & G. S. Pinnell (Eds.), *Voices on word matters: Learning about phonics and spelling in the literacy classroom* (pp. 25–36). Portsmouth, NH: Heinemann.

Willems, M. (2004). *Knuffle bunny.* New York: Hyperion Books.

Wisconsin Model Early Learning Standards, 2nd Ed. (2008). Available from Wisconsin Child Care Information Center, 2109 South Stoughton Road, Madison, WI 53716. Retrieved May 17, 2011, from *www.collaboratingpartners.com/ docs/ec-wmels-bk.pdf.*

8

Literacy Leadership in the Elementary School Reading Program

JANICE A. DOLE
KRISTIN L. NELSON

Guiding Questions

- What do literacy leaders need to know and be able to do to assist teachers in designing and implementing an integrated, comprehensive, and balanced curriculum?

- What do literacy leaders need to know and be able to do to assist teachers in the use of appropriate and varied instructional approaches?

- What do literacy leaders need to know and be able to do to assist teachers in using a wide range of texts from traditional print, digital, and online resources?

This chapter describes and explains the curriculum and instruction of literacy and the actions and behaviors literacy leaders need to take to support effective literacy instruction for elementary-age students. We organize this chapter around three important concepts: (1) curriculum, or what to teach; (2) instruction, or how to teach; and (3) materials. The chapter uses as the foundation for its content the International Reading Association's (IRA) *Standards for Reading Professionals—revised 2010* (International Reading Association [IRA], 2010). The *Standards for Reading Professionals* arose from a significant body of research, summarized in seminal publications such as *Handbook of Reading Research* (Pearson, Barr, Kamil, & Mosenthal, 1984; Barr, Kamil, Mosenthal, & Pearson, 1991; Kamil, Mosenthal, Pearson, & Barr, 2000), *Preventing Reading Difficulties in Young Children* (Snow, Burns, & Griffin, 1998), *Developing Literacy in Second-Language Learners* (August & Shanahan, 2006), and the *Report of the National Reading Panel* (National Institute of Child Health and Human Development [NICHD], 2000). In this paper we use several elements taken from Standard 2: Curriculum and Instruction, to delineate critical knowledge about curriculum, instruction, and materials for effective leadership in literacy. Throughout, we supplement our discussion of the standards with our colleagues' knowledge and expertise as well as our own as we have worked in leadership capacities. We begin our discussion with a case example of a fairly typical elementary school and the conundrums faced by many literacy leaders.

CASE EXAMPLE

Susan Metcalf, a college professor, was asked to evaluate the reading program at one Title I elementary school in an urban district. This school's population was changing rapidly, with more and more second-language learners coming into the district and this particular school. What had been a largely white, working class neighborhood was being transformed into a more diverse neighborhood with a large population of Hispanic families moving in. Reading scores were never good in the school, but over the last 5 years, they have been consistently declining further.

Dr. Metcalf examined the test scores of the students over the last 10 years and then began the important process of looking into classrooms and talking to teachers. She found that although the district had adopted a research-based reading program a few years ago, there was great variability among the teachers as they used the program. Some teachers followed the program quite closely, others more sparingly. One teacher used a special education phonics program to teach phonics to her young charges. Some teachers refused to use the program at all and had their own selection of novels or picture books for children to read. Teachers who did use the program used whole-group instruction only. Teachers who selected novels had literature circles where students worked in small groups discussing the novels. Teachers reported various and sundry reasons for their use or non-use of the core program and trade books and many reasons as well for the particular instructional strategies they used.

This case illustrates a common occurrence in elementary schools. Teachers often "do their own thing," with little understanding or even knowledge of what other teachers are doing and how the literacy curriculum, instruction, and materials need to align both horizontally—across classrooms in the same grade, and vertically—from one grade to the next. The big question for this chapter is How can literacy leaders assist in helping an elementary school staff collaborate in terms of the literacy curriculum, instruction, and materials?

A DISTRIBUTED LEADERSHIP PERSPECTIVE

In this paper we work from a distributed leadership perspective on instructional leadership. A distributed leadership perspective acknowledges that the knowledge and expertise needed for literacy leadership often extends well beyond what any one principal or administrator could be expected to know and be able to do. Educators and researchers alike have begun to argue that instructional leadership can be shared or distributed across a number of educators, including principals, assistant principals, teachers, curriculum coordinators, and policymakers (Elmore, 2002; Spillane, Halverson, & Diamond, 2001). Such leadership involves a group of educators who have different levels of expertise in literacy, but who together can lead a school and/or district in the improvement of instruction and student achievement. More about the theory and research behind distributed leadership is explained in other chapters of this book (see, e.g., Chapters 1 and 6).

COMPETENCE IN LEADING
THE LITERACY CURRICULUM

Literacy leaders need to be effective leaders in assisting teachers to monitor carefully what is taught in literacy. We use IRA's *Standards for Reading Professionals* (2010) Standard 2, Element 2.1 (Use foundational knowledge to design or implement an integrated, comprehensive, and balanced curriculum; IRA, 2010, p. 20) to discuss effective leadership with regard to the literacy curriculum.

Assisting Teachers in Designing and Implementing
an Integrated, Comprehensive, and Balanced Curriculum

Knowledge of the literacy curriculum—what is important to teach when teaching literacy—has benefited greatly over the last decade by the compilation of research that points in a clear direction. The *Report of the National Reading Panel* (NICHD, 2000) established five areas in reading—phonemic awareness, phonics, fluency, vocabulary, and comprehension—that are critical to teach when teaching reading. In addition, effective literacy leaders understand that literacy does not consist *simply* of these five areas. For example, the development of oral language is critically important, especially at the K–3 grade levels. Most important, writing is essential at all grade levels. Further, schools must think about how they assist students in developing a love of reading, that is, to motivate students to read. Understanding that a solid literacy curriculum must be comprehensive—including all the important components of literacy—and balanced in nature is important for the kind of student achievement gains that all literacy leaders would like to see. IRA (2010), in its Standards document, indicates that the following areas must be included in a reading curriculum: concepts of print, phonemic awareness, phonics, vocabulary, comprehension, fluency, critical thinking, motivation, and writing (p. 21).

Common Core State Standards

While the Report of the National Reading Panel (NICHD, 2000) led the way to a consensus-driven and research-based reading curriculum, literacy leaders now have a cogent, agreed-upon set of standards to follow as to what should be taught in literacy at the different grade levels. The Common Core State Standards for English Language Arts and Literacy in History/ Social Studies, Science and Technical Subjects (2010) is a new set of standards recently developed as a joint project of the Council of Chief State School Officers and the National Governors' Association. Both groups are independent, nonprofit entities consisting, respectively, of the 50 state superintendents of schools as well as the 50 governors of the states.

> The Common Core State Standards provide a consistent, clear understanding of what students are expected to learn, so teachers and parents know what they need to do to help them. The standards are designed to be robust and relevant to the real world, reflecting the knowledge and skills that our young people need for success in college and careers. (Common Core State Standards, 2010)

The Common Core State Standards (2010) have been developed in the areas of the English language arts as well as literacy in history/social studies/ science/and technical subjects and mathematics. The English language arts are broken down into reading, writing, listening and speaking, and language for the elementary grades. The reading standards are set up according to texts and grades: (1) Reading Standards for Literature, K–5, which includes both fiction and poetry; (2) Reading Standards for Informational Text, K–5; and (3) Reading Foundational Skills, K–5, which includes phonics and decoding skills. The reading standards for literature and informational text are further broken down into reading for *key ideas and details, craft and structure,* and *integration of knowledge and ideas.* In addition, there is a special standard at all the grade levels on *Range of Reading and Level of Text Complexity.* The focus of this standard is on students reading increasingly complex texts within their grade range (e.g., K–1, 2–3, 4–5), with help and support for texts at the highest end of the grade range. There also are writing standards for K–5, speaking and listening skills for K–5, and language skills for K–5.

These standards should assist literacy leaders and teachers as they further define and teach the literacy curriculum. All but two states have either been initial members of the Common Core State Standards Initiative or have formally adopted these standards (Common Core State Standards, 2010). This represents a clear movement by states to come to consensus about what elementary-age students should know and be able to do in reading and the other language arts.

Literacy leaders need to provide opportunities for teachers to learn about the Common Core State Standards (2010) as well as any additional standards adopted by the state and assist teachers in periodically reviewing their literacy curriculum. It is important that teachers know the extent to which that curriculum is consistent with the standards in use in a given school or district. Teachers need to know and understand the content of what they teach over the course of the year and know that they can match up that content to what is covered in the standards.

Curriculum Maps

Literacy leaders can provide teachers with assistance in examining their content in light of the standards through the use of "curriculum maps" specifically designed for this purpose. Curriculum maps are most often graphic organizers that identify the critical elements of a curriculum laid out over a period of time in visual form (Jacobs & Johnson, 2009). Curriculum maps allow teachers to see the "big picture" in terms of what they are teaching over the course of 6 months or a year. They provide snapshots of the critical standards that are covered. While there is little literature on curriculum mapping in general and virtually none in reading (but see Remillard, 1999, for math), districts have used curriculum mapping successfully to help teachers understand the overall content of what they teach.

Understanding and reviewing curriculum standards can take place in grade-level meetings, in study groups, or in faculty meetings. Some literacy leaders conduct such meetings before the start of the school year. But these meetings could be ongoing throughout the school year as well. The point is that grade-level teachers work together to ensure consistency in the curriculum being taught and in the extent to which the curriculum matches the standards adopted by the district.

COMPETENCE IN LEADING
LITERACY INSTRUCTION

Most often we refer to instruction as "how to teach." Instructional strategies for literacy include the various ways in which the literacy curriculum is presented to students. In this section, we focus on element 2.2 (Use appropriate and varied instructional approaches, including those that develop word recognition, language comprehension, strategic knowledge, and reading–writing connections; IRA, 2010, p. 20) of IRA's *Standards for Reading Professionals.*

Assisting Teachers in the Use of Appropriate
and Varied Instructional Approaches

Literacy leaders know that the instructional delivery of the curriculum is one of the most critically important elements of teaching. The curriculum, or content, of what is taught is established by clear standards. But *how* that curriculum is taught does not have a set of carefully defined rules and procedures. Do teachers sit on a stool at the front of the room and lecture to students? Do teachers have small, cooperative learning groups where students are provided with specific tasks related to the curriculum? Does the teacher simply assign worksheets for students and give them directions to complete the worksheets? How well things are taught is just as important as what is taught. *The very best curriculum taught poorly is no better than the worst curriculum taught well.*

An important role for literacy leaders is to know what is actually taking place in classrooms. Even though literacy leaders may think they know what is happening in classrooms, classroom instruction largely remains a black box until leaders make frequent, even if brief, visits in classrooms to observe the daily instruction in literacy.

The most effective way to know what is happening in classrooms is through daily observations called "walkthroughs" (Pitler with Goodwin, 2008). In a walkthrough, literacy leaders spend brief amounts of time in each classroom in a school, moving briskly from one classroom to the next. One of the aspects of instruction that leaders need to look for is whether the standards are being met through the instruction. Are teachers teaching what they are supposed to be teaching? Are they spending time wisely? Are objectives and goals for the lesson clearly laid out, and do these match important standards at specific grade levels? The difficulty for some literacy leaders is in knowing how to answer these questions.

One approach to answering these questions is to look broadly at the general instructional approach for a school. For example, throughout the National Reading Panel (NRP), one message is clear: for students to learn to read, they must be explicitly taught the components of reading and given plenty of opportunities to practice these components. So what exactly does that mean? For one, it means that teachers should be comfortable with the gradual release of responsibility model (Pearson and Gallagher, 1983). In this instructional delivery model, instruction moves from teacher modeling to guided and supported reading and writing to the final goal of releasing the students to independent practice. (Sometimes this model is described as "I do, we do, you do.") This model exists in variations, including the Madeleine Hunter approach (Hunter, 2004). In any case, the ultimate goal is that students utilize what they have learned independently in their reading and writing.

So, how might literacy leaders use this information? They would want to look for the gradual release of responsibility as they watch teachers teach. Are teachers modeling how to think about a strategy or skill? Are they guiding students to use a strategy by working with them and providing them with feedback? If students are working on their own, is there credible evidence that students can do it on their own? Leaders can check in on individual students to make sure they can do the exercise or activity independently. If not, then the teacher has not provided the appropriate amount of support and guided practice for the students.

Another approach is to come to the walkthrough with a checklist of expectations for various types of literacy instruction. Someone with a strong understanding of the reading research can develop such a checklist. So that, for the component of reading instruction called phonemic awareness, one would look for students manipulating sounds and words, such as through segmenting and blending. For phonics instruction, one would look for students blending and segmenting but now with letters instead of sounds alone. Phonics instruction would include the studying of words and their spelling patterns. This may mean practice with adding onsets onto rimes such as adding the letter *j* to -*et* to make *jet* and so on. Students also would spend time sorting words according to their common characteristics such as those ending with *ore,* as in *store* and *more.*

For fluency instruction, one would look for students reading text out loud at least twice alone and to partners. One also would want to hear teachers talking about and modeling the qualities of fluent reading, such as a "just right" tempo. For comprehension instruction, one would look for teachers to be teaching students strategies for understanding their reading such as asking and answering questions. For vocabulary instruction, one would look for teachers to be teaching the meanings of specific words through various methods including examples and nonexamples. (See Figure

8.1 for a list of resources that may be useful to those who want to know more about elementary reading curriculum and instruction.)

Literacy leaders also will want to make sure that the instructional strategies teachers are using engage students in learning. Figure 8.2 provides seven examples of research-based strategies that teachers might use. These strategies enable students to work collaboratively and become engaged in the learning process. Leaders want to see students engaged in various activities with their peers rather than sitting passively and independently listening or completing numerous workbook pages. That is not to say teachers should not teach—sometimes students do sit passively and listen, but not for long. That is not to say students should not complete workbook pages

Bean, R. M., Heisey, N., & Roller, C. M. (2010). *Preparing reading professionals* (2nd ed.). Newark, DE: International Reading Association. (Supplement to IRA Standards document.)

Beck, I. L., McKeown, M. G., & Kucan, L. (2002). *Bringing words to life: Robust vocabulary instruction.* New York: Guilford Press.

Beck, I. L., McKeown, M. G., & Kucan, L. (2008). *Creating robust vocabulary: Frequently asked questions and extended examples.* New York: Guilford Press.

Beck, I. S. (2005). *Making sense of phonics: The hows and whys.* New York: Guilford Press.

Buhl, D. (2008). *Classroom strategies for interactive learning* (3rd ed.). Newark, DE: International Reading Association.

Fletcher, R., & Portalupi, J. (2001). *Writing workshop: The essential guide.* Portsmouth, NH: Heinemann.

Gear, A. (2008). *Nonfiction reading power: Teaching students how to think while they read all kinds of information.* Portland, ME: Stenhouse.

Graves, M. F. (2006). *The vocabulary book: Learning and instruction.* New York: Teachers College Press.

Gunning, T. G. (2010). *Creating literacy instruction for all students* (7th ed.). Boston: Allyn & Bacon.

Jacobson, J. (2010). *No more "I'm done": Fostering independent writers in the primary grades.* Portland, ME: Stenhouse.

Kelley, M. J., & Clausen-Grace, N. (2007). *Comprehension shouldn't be silent: From strategy instruction to student independence.* Newark, DE: International Reading Association.

McGill-Franzen, A. (2006). *Kindergarten literacy: Matching assessment and instruction in kindergarten.* New York: Scholastic Press.

Morrow, L. M., & Gambrell, L. (2010). *Best practices in literacy instruction* (4th ed.). New York: Guilford Press.

Razinski, T. (2008). *The fluent reader: Oral reading strategies for building word recognition, fluency and comprehension.* New York: Scholastic.

Tompkins, G. E. (2010). *Literacy for the 21st century: A balanced approach* (4th ed.). Boston: Allyn & Bacon.

FIGURE 8.1. Suggested resources for elementary reading curriculum and instruction.

Instructional Strategy	How Helpful?	Additional Comments
Think–pair–share	Provides an opportunity for all learners to talk, rehearse, and share.	
Teachers' use of gestures, role playing	Provides all learners with an additional kind of support and assistance that aids understanding.	Essential for English language learners. Students can also role-play concepts, vocabulary, readings, etc.
Graphic organizers	Provides another medium for students to learn. Helps students organize information.	There are many different kinds of graphic organizers for all different occasions. Google graphic organizers and see a host of different kinds for all age levels. There are also good resource books (*Classroom Strategies for Interactive Learning,* Buhl, 2008) that have graphic organizer ideas in them.
Cooperative learning groups	Provides additional support and guidance to practice newly acquired skills and strategies.	There is much research evidence that students learn from one another. Students can work in groups of four. Students can work in pairs with a single assignment that they jointly contribute to.
Shared reading/ shared writing	Provides support and assistance as students read and write with the teacher.	This activity provides students with the additional support and assistance they may need in order to read and write well.
Writing to learn	Provides students with time to write about what they want to learn or have learned. This includes short responses and more extended responses to questions, ideas, etc.	There is much research evidence to demonstrate that students learn by writing. This is different from writing simple answers on a workbook page.
Anticipation guides	Provides students with motivation for and engagement in reading an upcoming text.	Anticipation guides must be carefully developed in order to be effective. With careful development, students will engage in a text to find out answers. Also, not all texts are appropriate for using anticipation guides.

FIGURE 8.2. Seven important instructional strategies that literacy leaders should look for.

either. When appropriately given, workbook pages can provide important practice that students need. It is to say that students should spend most of their time engaged in meaningful activities that contribute to their new learning.

COMPETENCE IN LEADING THE SELECTION AND IMPLEMENTATION OF HIGH-QUALITY LITERACY MATERIALS

Finally, to be effective instructional leaders, literacy leaders need to have expertise in assisting teachers in selecting and implementing high-quality literacy materials. This qualification is related to IRA's *Standards for Reading Professionals*, Standard 2: Curriculum and Instruction, 2.3 (Use a wide range of texts [e.g., narrative, expository, and poetry] from traditional print, digital, and online resources; IRA, 2010, p. 20).

Assisting Teachers in Using a Wide Range of Texts

Effective literacy leaders know that as we progress into the second decade of the 21st century, a wide variety of instructional materials need to be used to ensure that students are learning. Gone are the days where primary-grade students read and listen to fairy tales and folktales all day long. Students in the 21st century are going to be exposed to and need to be able to read, comprehend, and learn from many different kinds of texts and materials— informational texts, brochures, bus schedules, trade books, magazines, novels, books on tape, electronic books, multimedia texts, visual organizers, and so forth. These materials must be introduced to children as early as kindergarten and carried throughout the primary and intermediate grades. These varied materials need to be a consistent part of a child's reading. They also must be taught different writing genres, again beginning in kindergarten.

How do literacy leaders work with teachers to support them in the use of a wide range of reading materials? First, evaluations can be made of reading materials to see the extent to which they teach important content found in the standards. For example, literacy leaders can examine carefully the Common Core State Standards (2010) for reading informational text and then see the extent to which various instructional materials assist teachers in teaching those standards. Leaders might examine how much informational text can be found in core reading programs and evaluate whether the instruction is supportive of students learning how to read informational text.

Selecting High-Quality Core Reading Programs

Many districts and schools use a core reading program to assist schools in the vertical and horizontal alignment of curriculum and instruction in literacy. Such programs typically cover reading and the language arts, including writing, spelling, and other conventions. The programs consist of student anthologies along with leveled books at three or four different ability levels and a teacher's edition to go along with the anthologies and leveled books.

Literacy leaders should look for high-quality research-based core reading programs that are integrative and balanced so that the books and materials associated with it work together to provide an instructional program that can serve all readers. The curriculum should align with the district's standards and contain solid core instruction. In addition, it should include instructional materials for students who need additional support and intervention from the teacher as well as those who would benefit from acceleration. Materials should include decodable and high-interest trade books accessible to various readers.

Many core reading programs contain books and instructional materials to meet the needs of various types of students, including those who are English language learners (ELLs). Some intervention programs also contain books and materials that align with the core program for use by special educators. The importance of integration of all these materials cannot be overemphasized. When materials are integrated, it means that all students are receiving the grade-level content they need to master and the materials similar to those on which they will likely be tested. It also means that teachers can better serve the students' individual needs because materials and instructional plans for them are readily available.

Another component of a comprehensive core reading program is that it spirals and builds on itself. A spiraling curriculum is one in which critical content and strategies come around more than once in a school year, as well as in subsequent years. Literacy leaders need to select core reading programs that spiral in logical and progressive ways, from simple to complex, and from concrete to abstract. This is important for two reasons: (1) some students will need additional exposures to skills and strategies before they learn them, and (2) skills and strategies should build in complexity over time.

Over the last decade, as a result of the NRP, several resources and tools have become available for literacy leaders to assist them in their selection of high-quality research-based reading curricula. The U.S. Department of Education has developed a website, the *What Works Clearinghouse* (*www.whatworks.ed.gov/*), and three technical assistance centers with websites in Oregon, Texas, and Florida to help implement best practices in reading instruction. At these sites, consumers can examine the already completed evaluations of some reading programs. In addition, at least two practical tools have been developed at the Oregon (Simmons & Kame'enui, 2002) and Florida (Al Otaiba, Kosanovich-Grek, Torgesen, Hassler, & Wahl, 2005) centers. Other resources are books that include information on this topic (see, e.g., Dewitz, Leahy, Jones, & Sullivan, 2010; Wepner & Strickland, 2008). These tools are accessible to educators and can be used to assist them in knowing what to look for in core reading programs. Literacy leaders may wish to work with teachers to modify one of these available tools so that it is appropriate for a specific school or district.

Implementation of Core Reading Programs

It is the job of the literacy leader to ensure that all those who are using them implement core materials appropriately and effectively. The general educator, specialists, and interventionists should know how different materials fit together to provide more than one access point for students who need additional exposure to core curriculum to master it. It also is important that literacy leaders ensure that teachers are correctly matching materials to the needs of their students. Otherwise, materials appropriate for a specific purpose or population may be inappropriately used for other purposes. For example, suppose a teacher was found to be using a special education phonics program for all his or her regular education and ELL students. That program was designed specifically for a special education population rather than for a general population. Further, it is unclear whether the program would be appropriate for an ELL population. Literacy leaders with a critical stance toward materials know that programs cannot be picked up randomly and used for different populations and for purposes for which they were never intended.

Other Reading Materials

Literacy leaders must understand that core reading programs by themselves are unlikely to provide a complete literacy program for all students. In addition to the core reading program, students need easy access to many, many different kinds of books at their appropriate reading level—both traditional print and electronic/digital materials (see, e.g., *activities.macmillanmh.com/reading/treasures/stories/teachcls.html*; *www-k6.thinkcentral.com/ePC/start.do*). Students must read a lot each day, and read a lot of different kinds of materials, to improve their reading. Easy and frequent use of the library (more than 30 minutes a week) is helpful; a classroom full of trade books is better. Many exemplary teachers provide stacks of books in bins at different reading levels, along with books tagged on different topics, for their students. These additional books are essential materials for a comprehensive reading program.

CONCLUSION

Using IRA's *Standards for Reading Professionals* (2010), we identified the three elements for Standard 2: Curriculum and Instruction, and discussed each one from the standpoint of literacy leadership. For a literacy curriculum, we discussed the responsibilities of literacy leaders as they lead teachers in teaching to standards, particularly the Common Core State Standards (2010) that have been adopted by many states in the nation. For instruction, we highlighted the importance of walkthroughs where literacy leaders visit classrooms to observe the instructional activities going on each day. For materials, we discussed how literacy leaders could help in selecting and implementing high-quality literacy materials. We believe that these three elements used judiciously and wisely will go a long way toward promoting effective instruction in elementary school literacy programs that increases literacy achievement.

ENGAGEMENT ACTIVITIES

1. Consider the case example, and what was discussed in the chapter about effective curriculum and instruction and the appropriate selection and implementation of literacy materials, and make a list of the steps or actions that a literacy leader could take to build a comprehensive, integrated, and balanced school literacy program at that Title I school.

2. What questions should literacy leaders ask teachers to help them think about and reflect on the materials and programs they use?

3. Based on reading this chapter and your own experiences, what are some barriers likely to arise as literacy leaders implement the standards described herein? How can these barriers be overcome?

REFERENCES

Al Otaiba, S., Kosanovich-Grek, M. L., Torgesen, J. K., Hassler, L., & Wahl, M. (2005). Reviewing core kindergarten and first-grade reading programs in light of No Child Left Behind: An exploratory study. *Reading and Writing Quarterly, 21*(4), 377–400.

August, D., & Shanahan, T. (2006). *Developing literacy in second-language learn-*

ers: Report of the National Literacy Panel on language-minority children and youth. Mahwah, NJ: Erlbaum.

Barr, R., Kamil, M. L., Mosenthal, P., & Pearson, P. D. (Eds.). (1991). *Handbook of reading research* (Vol. 2). White Plains, NY: Longman.

Buhl, D. (2008). *Classroom strategies for interactive learning* (3rd ed.). Newark, DE: International Reading Association.

Common Core State Standards for English Language Arts and Literacy in History/ Social Studies, Science and Technical Subjects. (2010). Retrieved April 26, 2011, from *www.corestandards.org/the-standards/english-language-arts-standards.*

Dewitz, P., Leahy, S. B., Jones, J., & Sullivan, P. M. (Eds.). (2010). *The essential guide to selecting and using core reading programs.* Newark, DE: International Reading Association.

Elmore, R. (2002.) *Bridging the gap between standards and achievement: The imperative for professional development in education.* Washington, DC: Albert Shanker Institute.

Hunter, R. (2004). *Madeline Hunter's mastery teaching: Increasing instructional effectiveness in elementary and secondary schools (Updated ed.). Newbury Park, CA: Corwin Press.*

International Reading Association. (2010). *Standards for reading professionals: A reference for the preparation of educators in the United States* (Rev. ed.). Newark, DE: Author.

Jacobs, H. H., & Johnson, A. (2009). *The curriculum mapping planner: Templates, tools, and resources for effective professional development.* Alexandria, VA: ASCD.

Kamil, M. L., Mosenthal, P. B., Pearson, P. D., & Barr, R. (Eds.). (2000). *Handbook of reading research* (Vol. 3). Mahwah, NJ: Erlbaum.

Marks, H. M., & Printy, S. M. (2003). Principal leadership and school performance: An integration of transformational and instructional leadership. *Education Administration Quarterly, 39*(3), 370–397.

National Institute of Child Health and Human Development. (2000). *Report of the National Reading Panel: Teaching children to read: An evidence-based assessment of the scientific research literature on reading and its implications for reading instruction.* (NIH Publication No. 00-4769). Washington, DC: U.S. Government Printing Office.

Pearson, P. D., Barr, R., Kamil, M. L., & Mosenthal, P. (Eds.). (1984). *Handbook of reading research* (Vol. 1). White Plains, NY: Longman.

Pearson, P. D., & Gallagher, M. (1983). The instruction of reading comprehension. *Contemporary Education Psychology, 8,* 317–344.

Pitler, H., with Goodwin, B. (2008). Classroom walkthroughs: Learning to see the trees *and* the forest. *Changing Schools,* Summer, 9–11.

Remillard, J. T. (1999). Curriculum materials in mathematics education reform: A framework for examining teachers' curriculum development. *Curriculum Inquiry, 29*(3), 315–345.

Simmons, D. C., & Kame'enui, K. J. (2003). *A consumer's guide to evaluating a core reading program Grades K–3: A critical elements analysis.* Retrieved April 26, 2011, from *www.nysrti.org/docs/cons_guide_instr_2003.pdf.*

Snow, C. E., Burns, M. S., & Griffin, P. (1998). *Preventing reading difficulties in young children.* Washington, DC: National Academy Press.

Spillane, P., Halverson, R., & Diamond, J. B. (2001). Investigating school leadership practice: A distributed perspective. *Educational Researcher, 30*(3), 23–28.

United States Department of Education, Institute of Education Sciences. *What works Clearinghouse.* Retrieved April 26, 2011, from *www.whatworks.ed.gov.*

Wepner, S. B., & Strickland, D. S. (Eds.). (2008). *The administration and supervision of reading programs* (4th ed.). New York: Teachers College Press.

9

Adolescent Language, Literacy, and Learning

Implications for a Schoolwide Literacy Program

PATRICIA L. ANDERS
RENÉE T. CLIFT

Guiding Questions

- What notable characteristics of adolescent cognitive, social, and linguistic development inform adolescent literacy programs in these new times?

- What educational structures promote literacy development through collaborations among educators and their students?

- What are the recommended practices and policies that enable literacy leaders to develop and implement literacy programs within contemporary secondary schools?

The context for theorizing about literacy and for developing effective literacy practices in today's secondary schools is dramatically different from that of the mid-20th century. As Allen Luke and John Elkins (1998) noted in their editorial for the *Journal of Adolescent and Adult Literacy,* the "historical lesson is that changes in communications technologies set out the conditions for shifts in economic systems, cultural practices, and social institutions" (p. 5). As policy recommendations urge educators to capitalize on these new communication technologies and new literacies to develop a competitive workforce, teachers and administrators in both middle and high schools are grappling with the implications for curriculum, teaching, and school programs and policies.

For example, the U.S. Department of Labor's 1992 report, *What Work Requires of Schools,* which is still referenced on their website as a key document for workforce development, encourages schools to develop students' abilities to work on teams, to teach others, to negotiate, and to work well with people from culturally diverse backgrounds. Additionally, curricula should promote acquiring and evaluating data and using computers to process information while, at the same time, enabling students to understand social, organizational, and technological systems and apply technology to specific tasks, and maintaining and troubleshooting technologies. Surely, this is no small task.

The Partnership for 21st Century Schools, founded in 2002, "to position 21st century readiness at the center of US K–12 education by building collaborative partnerships among education, business, community and government leaders," reinforces the Department of Labor's recommendations. As explained on their website (*www.p21.org/index.php*), the Partnership recommends that student outcomes include learning and innovation skills, which they refer to as the four "C's": creativity, critical thinking, collaboration, and communication. Information literacy, media literacy, and knowledge of information and communication and technologies are major components of the Partnership's vision. Increasingly, secondary educators are challenged to "sift through the maze of ways with words of new technologies and new cultural forms, to decide how to best situate and position our teaching, our curricula, and our learners in relation to these new worlds—these tasks indeed will require new kinds of critical literacy of all of us" (Luke & Elkins, 1998, p. 6).

In this chapter we acknowledge the complexities of both the processes and products of literacy, especially in light of the expectations described above. In so doing, we argue that not only are today's adolescents grappling with new times—forms of communication and the social and cognitive dimensions that arise from new communicative avenues—but they are doing so in an educational milieu in which curriculum, instruction, programs, and policies represent the pretechnology era and teachers are often less experienced or knowledgeable about the opportunities, and the limitations, inherent in the new literacies (Lankshear & Knobel, 2003) and technologies. Given this reality, in the following sections we address issues related to the development of secondary schoolwide literacy programs and make recommendations for instruction, curriculum, and policies. We begin by sharing a brief case example, focusing on the content of an e-mail— highlighting the evolving dilemma school administrators face in addressing technology for adolescents. The example below illustrates the need for policies about technology—one of the most obvious current challenges to those responsible for literacy in secondary schools.

CASE EXAMPLE

In our role in higher education, we are many times asked to observe, comment, develop, and evaluate programs and policies of our local school. Recently, the following e-mail came to our attention.

> *District administrator to an electronic mailing list for collaborating across districts:* We are reviewing our Internet use policy and plan to develop a new social networking policy. I remember that some districts shared their internet usage agreement several months ago ... has anyone else revised their policy and/or agreement? Does anyone have a separate policy for regulations specifically covering social media, texting, sexting, cell phones, Facebook, Twitter, etc? (Administrator A, personal communication, July 17, 2010)

What steps can the literacy leaders in the school take to address the administrator's e-mail request? What elements must be considered so educators at the school fairly address this concern while also respecting the out-of-school literacies of the adolescents? Our e-mail reply to the administrator's e-mail request would be:

> Dear administrator, Your concerns about Internet usage are valid and right on target, because our young people must be very wise about the ways in which individuals or groups can use the anonymity of the virtual world to take advantage of others. School policies that embrace the appropriate use of technology can capitalize on students' knowledge; policies that severely limit or ban Internet-based technology may protect against inappropriate use, but they also deny students the opportunity to become more sophisticated readers, writers, and analysts. School and district literacy leaders, along with teachers and their students, must simultaneously advance and guide learning that acknowledges new literacy tools and new literacy environments. We do believe that reaching out to collaborate across districts is very, very important. However, we would like to talk with you about a question that is related to your question: How can we work with our own students, teachers, and literacy specialists to develop policies that are informed by their experiences and that capitalize on Twitter, Facebook, Skype, etc? How can we transform our curricula to promote 21st century literacy and to assess our students growing and increasingly sophisticated use of these technologies to learn and to create knowledge? How can we use the new media and the literacies regarding use of these new media to promote communication with parents and the community in order to showcase what is right with today's schools and to counteract the detrac-

tors who do not have the confidence in today's students and teachers that you do?

But what if the district administrator were to share our reply with the secondary school principals, department heads, and literacy specialists? How might he or she use our chapter as a springboard for appropriating technology to advance literacy across the schools?

WHAT ADOLESCENT COGNITIVE, SOCIAL, AND LINGUISTIC CHARACTERISTICS GUIDE SECONDARY LITERACY PROGRAM DEVELOPMENT?

In this section, we review recent literature related to the nature of adolescents' thinking (cognition), the influence of social relationships and context, and issues of language—especially in light of new literacy environments. These considerations are powerfully influential on the development of a schoolwide literacy program.

Cognition

We begin with a bit of the old—influential ideas from the 1980s and 1990s that are relevant in the new times. During the 1980s psychologists shifted from describing the reading process as primarily an individual behavior using skills to acquire the author's message to describing reading as an active process in which a reader constructs meaning through the integration of prior and new knowledge and uses strategies to foster, monitor, regulate, and maintain comprehension (Dole, Duffy, Roehler, & Pearson, 1991). Two ideas relevant to new times and secondary literacy programs emerged from this line of research. First, an adolescent reader constructs knowledge by integrating prior knowledge and experiences (schema) with new knowledge.

Second, adolescents in control of their reading and writing are metacognitive. That is, they know about their processes of successful thinking, composing, and comprehending and have the mental tools to make sense of what they are reading and to communicate effectively with others. This requires an ability to evaluate the quality of one's understanding and communicating (Paris, Lipson, & Wixson, 1983) and to access resources to meet the demands of a specific task (Baker & Brown, 1984). As a result of these two theoretical advancements, a line of instructional research was launched to provide teachers with strategy instruction to help students, particularly adolescents in content-area classes, to comprehend (e.g., Buehl, 2009).

Expanding on cognitive perspectives, Alexander (2005), proposed a lifespan developmental perspective with three parts: acclimation, competence, and proficiency/expertise. Acclimation refers to the early beginnings of becoming acquainted with new content knowledge. Adolescents, indeed any learner who is on the verge of learning new content, are faced with the challenge of constructing "a cohesive and well integrated body of knowledge" (p. 11) in each of the content areas studied in school. Individual interest is critical—it sets the stage for meaningful questions and for generating the stamina necessary for "digging in" and becoming competent. Competence is the transformation that takes place as both the quality and quantity of understanding increases. As one's competence develops, personal interest increases and learning is internally driven, with less reliance on external motivation. A learner, who is an expert or proficient in a particular domain, is one who contributes new knowledge to the domain. Secondary schools are charged with the task of acclimating and developing a modicum of competency in the content-area domains.

The implications of cognition-related notions are foundational to the recommendations discussed in the last section of this chapter. Here are the key ideas, based on cognitive research, underlying those recommendations.

- Student learning in the secondary school builds on prior knowledge and experience (schema) that students bring to the content areas they study.
- Student interest reflects the quality of prior knowledge and interacts with the learning opportunities and possibilities offered across the curriculum.
- The secondary school is a place where young people engage in the amazing wonders of the world through their study of the disciplines.

Motivation

Motivation is a multifaceted topic with many years of expansive scholarship (see McCombs, 1996). The National Reading Research Center (NRRC; Alvermann & Guthrie, 1993) conceptualized motivation as "engagement," based on

> the assumption that students acquire the competencies and motivations to read for diverse purposes, such as gaining knowledge, performing a task, interpreting an author's perspective, sharing reactions to stories and informational texts, escaping into the literary world, or taking social and political action in response to what is read. An engagement perspective, recognizes the social nature of cognition. (p. 2)

The NRRC produced studies describing engagement from differing perspectives and in varying contexts. Chief among their findings was that students were motivated when they had choice of reading materials, opportunities to actively collaborate with peers, and challenging meaningful content to investigate (Gambrell & Morrow, 1996).

Reeves (2004) wondered why adolescents resisted reading. To learn more about adolescents' motivation to read, she interviewed 25 students and selected five for extensive interviews and observations. The resulting case studies reveal several interesting findings. For example, many of the students told Reeves that they had enjoyed reading when young, but at about the age of 12 or 13, reading became much less interesting, both because it was hard to find books of interest (this finding is confirmed by Ivey, 1999) and because of the demands of social relationships. Students reported resisting assigned book reports about books they did not choose to read. Another finding was that by high school, their literary interests narrowed: "The omnivorous curiosity of childhood has been distilled into a more mature concentration of attention into fewer areas. These teenagers have begun to specialize, as all people do with age" (Reeves, p. 241). Finally, students reported not needing to read in order to get decent grades. Most of the time, class discussions and teacher's notes provided enough information to "get by" (p. 242).

Lemke (2007) claims that students go outside of school to support their literacy interests; mostly they go to online peer networking communities. He maintains that curriculum, as indicated by the alienated resistant youth described by Reeves (2004), is uninspiring; as a result, youth turn to the new literacies, multimodal and multimedia sources, to find what they need.

What do these findings suggest for schoolwide literacy program development, curriculum, and instruction? The following implications come to mind:

- Youth view reading and its role in their life differently than do elementary-age children. Programs, curriculum, and instruction need to honor and respect the maturing young adult.
- Offering students meaningful choices with authentic reasons for reading go a long way toward motivating students to engage in reading.
- Curriculum writers and teachers should bridge between standards and student interests.

Identity Development

The role that adolescent identity development plays in literacy and learning is related to both cognition and motivation. McCarthey and Moje (2002) suggest "teaching literacy could be considered acts of supporting and challenging learners' identities and providing spaces for learners to explore their identities" (p. 233). Furthermore, Moore (2002) posits that "a productive literate identity means that (adolescents) consider themselves insiders amid a fellowship of readers and writers" (p. 149). Another finding in the Reeves (2004) study was that the students she interviewed talked about their interest in becoming a person who would be happy, successful, loving, and a contributing member of society. That is, each of these youth was conscious of and intentionally developing an identity. They wanted to read about people who would provide them such models.

McCarthey (2002) explored literacy identities of nine upper-elementary students in three different sites. Her conclusions emphasize "the influence of power and authority as communicated through the teacher's role and classroom curriculum, issues of purposes and audiences for writing," and the need for creating spaces for students to invent their identities (p. 107). Literacy identity development happens when youth have the opportunity to participate in a literacy discourse community (Gee, 2008).

Recognizing the importance of youth identity development implies that schoolwide literacy programs:

- Make space and opportunity for students' literacy identity to develop.
- Invite youth to learn the language of different discourse communities.
- Provide models of the power and influence of literacy on the lives of people they admire and respect.

Social Relationships

A powerful influence on identity development, discussed above, is the social experiences and relationships of youth. This has been the case throughout the history of secondary schooling, but the new literacies expansively broaden social opportunities for youth. When we think of social relationships, it is likely that we think of the social life in the secondary school. Eckert (1989), in *Jocks and Burnouts,* dramatically describes the familiar social structure of a high school, but the new literacies are rapidly changing the possibilities and parameters of youth's opportunities to form social relationships.

Youth are members of an evolving society that is global in a way that has never before been seen in history. A Marge Piercy novel, *Sex Wars,* (2005) describes young immigrants from England to the United States in

1868. On the streets of New York, these young immigrants experienced challenges to their identity: their personal beliefs and the norms of their homeland were challenged as they made their way in a society very different from their homeland. Through social relationships, they re-created their lives in ways that were barely recognizable by their relatives and acquaintances who arrived later. In the beginning years of the 21st century, a parallel situation exists, but now global contacts are virtual—interactions occur synchronously and asynchronously through digital media. Young people are increasingly in contact with one another on a global basis, not just on local streets.

The consequences of this global virtual migration are tremendous. George Lipsitz captures the dawning of this age in his inspirational forward to *Youthscapes* (Maira & Soep, 2005), "the category of youth … as a social achievement, [is] not so much a given category based on biological age but a social position structured by the simultaneous powers of consumption, creativity, schooling, citizenship, surveillance, and social membership" (p. xiv). Globalization and the relationships that result from social networks, virtual worlds, and synchronous and asynchronous communications around the world and in the local community are a part of adolescents' reality. Because of the Internet, national borders and different languages are not barriers to a youthful global community. (See Chapter 15 for more information about technology.)

This has implications for the schoolwide literacy program, curriculum, and instruction. Acknowledging that many of today's adolescents can and do experience myriad ways of communicating with others and, at the same time, acknowledging that some do not have the technologies to do so must be factored into curricula, specific assignments, and available access to technologies. Indeed, one of the school districts in the greater Tucson area has abandoned textbooks—using handheld devices or laptop computers instead. Some examples of ways in which educators have taken advantage of global communications include:

- Cross-national projects wherein students from different cultures read and discuss the same books.
- Virtual visits between classrooms where students from one country communicate with students from another country about popular culture, history, literature, etc.
- Projects that identify ways in which new forms of communication engender new forms of miscommunication.
- Collaborative inquiries into environmental issues such as air and water quality.

Language

Consideration of youth language characteristics is also central to planning for the schoolwide literacy program. In this section, language is considered in two ways: (1) the variability of language used by youth in their personal lives; and (2) the language of the secondary school, especially in terms of the goal of acclimating youth to disciplinary knowledge.

Projections in demographics of the United States make it clear that many secondary schools are experiencing a substantial increase in both the numbers of languages being brought to school by students and the number of students speaking languages other than English. Valdés, Bunch, Snow, and Lee (2005) summarize language-related ideas fundamental to understanding what this means for language development:

- Speakers of every language use different dialects depending on regional and class origins … these differences are a natural result of human language development and are not a "problem" to be rectified.
- Speakers of more than one language commonly use "code switching," a linguistic phenomena that "mixes" two languages in syntactically appropriate ways and "code shifting," the "mixing" of appropriate lexicon. Both switching and shifting are normal and acceptable among multilingual speakers.
- Youth come to school as competent speakers, but not necessarily readers and writers, of the varieties of language spoken in their homes and communities.
- All speakers use different registers and styles of language, which vary by context and purpose. The disciplinary classroom, for example, is a context for academic English and students, whatever their home language, need to learn the conventions of school language such as the ways to discuss ideas, to understand and to respond to texts, both critically and creatively.

These principles are relevant to secondary teachers who need to not only navigate the languages students bring to the classroom but are also responsible for helping students to become literate and use academic English, in each of the disciplines. These language principles are also relevant to those responsible for creating the literacy program. School is more than just academic, it is also social and the schoolwide secondary literacy program should be established to recognize, acknowledge, and honor the many kinds of languages in the school—making spaces and places for students to use language.

HOW CAN WE ENCOURAGE COLLABORATIONS AMONG EDUCATORS TO PROMOTE LITERACY DEVELOPMENT AND TEAM BUILDING?

Secondary educators are challenged to provide students language and literacy opportunities to learn disciplinary knowledge across the curriculum in multimodal ways. This is exciting but also daunting. It is exciting because the Internet and media provide resources previously only available to the most elite. For example, students are able to join National Aeronautics and Space Administration scientists as they explore Mars, simply by uploading a website. Virtual interviews are available with authors, and students can interact with other students anywhere in the world. Yet, the limitations of most secondary school contexts are well known. Jay Lemke (2007) elaborates on several of these daunting limitations:

- Curricula exclude domains of interest to students, especially in terms of popular culture and social networking.
- Schooling structures enforce superficiality, with timescales too short for in-depth learning.
- Commercial media are winning the hearts and minds of our students and we do little in curriculum to encourage criticism of the commercial.

Lemke's (2007) arguments are compelling, but even more compelling, and more hopeful, is the case of collaboration to improve literacy among educators, students, and parents in Brockton High School.

> A decade ago, Brockton High School was a case study in failure. Teachers and administrators often voiced the unofficial school motto in hallway chitchat: students have a right to fail if they want. And many of them did—only a quarter of the students passed statewide exams. One in three dropped out. Then Susan Szachowicz and a handful of fellow teachers decided to take action. They persuaded administrators to let them organize a schoolwide campaign that involved reading and writing lessons into every class in all subjects, including gym. Their efforts paid off quickly. In 2001 testing, more students passed the state tests after failing the year before than at any other school in Massachusetts. The gains continued. This year and last, Brockton outperformed 90 percent of Massachusetts high schools. (Dillon, 2010, September 28)

The Brockton example is 1 of 15 high schools highlighted in a recent report by the Achievement Gap Initiative at Harvard University (Ferguson, Hackman, Hanna, & Ballantine, 2010). High schools identified as exemplary, based on value-added achievement gains from eighth to tenth grade and on closing the achievement gaps between racial groups over several years, made presentations in June 2009 at the Initiative's Fifth Annual Research-to-Practice Conference. The authors of the conference report noted that the schools used internal leadership teams to make a plan and take action over several years—sometimes at the school level and sometimes at a department level.

At Brockton, a leadership committee asked for input from students and community members on those skills that each group felt were most important. From there they identified core learning skills in reading, writing, speaking, and reasoning, which are now embedded in the entire curriculum—including art and physical education. They began with a focus on writing related to course content and saw the failure rate on tests drop from 44 to 23%, and the failure rate has since dropped to 5%. Brockton decided to embed literacy instruction as opposed to adding extra, required classes. "The school has found that it needs to keep kids invested in the subjects they really liked: these are the hook. Staff members engage students by enabling them to take the subjects and participate in the activities they like, rather than pushing them toward those they don't like" (Dillon, 2010, p. 64).

Each year the school focuses on one or two elements of a core learning skill and provides ongoing professional development for teachers. The professional development focus is, at once, top-down and bottom-up and involves the entire staff. Data from students' work products, as well as teachers' observations, inform both professional development and curriculum redesign. Less dramatic but equally instructive are the examples of teacher collaboration in DiPardo's (1999) book, *Teaching in Common*. She studied four secondary schools, highlighting four pairs of teachers who worked in widely varying contexts. Her case studies document the ways in which teachers supported one another to find resources, face challenges, and improve learning environments for students. "As they wondered together about classroom events they posed new questions as well as new strategies. ... The effects of these collaborations rippled into the wider contexts as well, stimulating the potential for larger scale change in practice and in values" (pp. 158–159). She argues that schools must provide time and opportunity for teachers to work together and also that teachers must have a voice in the subject and substance of any collaborative activity.

Westheimer's (2008) review of research on teachers' learning within professional communities corroborates much of what DiPardo (1999) concluded. He noted that the continuing norms of teacher isolation in schools cannot be overcome solely because teachers have more decision-making authority and encouragement to work together. The work must be organized around a meaningful professional goal. Furthermore, schools must create shared/communal spaces in which teachers feel welcome to work together and to develop norms for negotiating disagreements and tough discussions about competing practices or ideologies.

Langer's (2001) research on "beating the odds" fits well with the above exemplary school recommendations and also speaks to the professional lives of teachers in schools with successful language and literacy instruction. Each of the schools studied found teachers who coordinated efforts to improve achievement, fostered teacher participation in professional communities, created activities that provided teachers with agency, valued commitment to professionalism, engendered caring attitudes, and fostered respect for learning. (See Chapter 2 for more about teacher leadership.)

At this point, there are many promising studies validating the benefits of teachers working together, but there are formidable historical and structural barriers to this potential benefit. A troubling reality is that some state policies actively discourage schools and teachers from developing locally driven initiatives. Maria and Soep (2005) note that as young people leap nationalistic boundaries by exploring virtual spaces around the globe, those with an investment in the status quo are likely to promote nationalism. This is evident in some states such as Arizona where implementing curricula that teach about students' ethnic and racial heritage may subject a district to heavy fines. This local example of nationalism is in sharp contrast to recommendations for developing global awareness, an appreciation for diversity, or negotiation and collaboration with colleagues. It is also an example of an attempt to curtail schools' freedom to design programs, curricula, and instruction to meet students' interests and needs.

Reform through collaboration suggests the importance of attending to the local conditions for promoting a schoolwide literacy program. Reform is not "cookie-cutter," nor is it a commercial product; rather it is dependent on knowledgeable and committed educators who apply understandings of adolescents, teacher creativity and collaboration, and successful schools to create a sustainable and generative all-school literacy program.

The suggestions below are meant to spark ideas by teachers, literacy specialists, and administrators as they consider the particular situations in which they work. The exemplary schools and beating the odds literature cited above lead us to believe that there is no one perfect plan or program for all schools, but there are tenets that are helpful to those who strive to establish a schoolwide literacy program. These suggestions are generated from both our experience as secondary literacy professionals and from the literature discussed in this chapter.

WHAT ARE RECOMMENDED POLICIES AND PRACTICES FOR CREATING, IMPLEMENTING, AND SUSTAINING A SCHOOLWIDE SECONDARY LITERACY PROGRAM?

We are convinced that student literacy improvement relies on a schoolwide, comprehensive literacy program. We promote this recommendation because of the social constructivist nature of literacy. Literacy is a tool that is used to navigate and negotiate ideas, relationships, and experience. As such, it cannot be diced and narrowed to bits and pieces engaged here and there; rather it must permeate all the nooks and crannies of the school.

The following four goals are central:

1. Create and maintain a *literate environment* in the school.
2. Use the *tools* of reading and writing to engage *meaningful ideas, to develop relationships, and to solve problems.*
3. Energize colleagues and other stakeholders to solve problems through *reflection and inquiry.*
4. Create spaces and opportunities for the development of *literacy for all.*

A Literate Environment

A literate environment means that evidence of literacy activity permeates the school. A casual observer sees evidence of language and literacy from the very moment of approaching and entering the school. The school signs, documents, and mailings are attractive examples of meaningful communication. The hallways and rooms are rich literacy environments with examples of students' and teachers' literate productivity in clear evidence. Public spaces use all forms of literacy in positive and informative ways—for example, message boards, TV monitors, and bulletin boards convey information and entertainment in clear, constructive, and attractive ways. Other examples of activities to establish a literate environment might include having the athletic coaches brainstorm ways they could affect literacy in the school—ideas such as having paperbacks readily available (a cart in the gym or locker room) for youth to borrow, sports magazines available with occasional conversations/lessons about how to read them critically, and book reviews in the school newspaper or on the Web about famous athletes. These examples suggest how even those who are not traditional academics can contribute to a literate environment. Other ideas for a literate environment include inviting local or national authors to the school to speak and interact with students and teachers, establishing a time in the school when everyone reads (sustained silent reading or drop everything and read) and/or when everyone writes (sustained silent writing), making routine the sale of books and magazines to the whole school, keeping the library open before and after school, and many similar ideas. (See Chapter 10 for more information about the literate environment.)

The Tools of Literacy Are Used to Engage Meaningful Ideas

Reading and writing provide humans with opportunities to gain information and construct knowledge, to increase appreciation of aesthetic experiences, and to provide tools for reflection, analysis, and problem solving. Opportunities for using these tools should abound in the secondary school. A good beginning place is the classes students attend. Throughout the 1900s, secondary reading has focused on helping students read in the content areas (see Anders & Guzzetti, 2005, for a history). At the turn of the century, the term *disciplinary literacy* is the term *du jour,* emphasizing that teachers across the curriculum are not responsible for teaching adolescents *how* to read; rather, they are responsible for teaching students the language and ways of reading and writing in each of the particular disciplines. For example, the history teacher understands the particular ways that language and text "works" in the field of history and is able to help students read and write in history (Moje, 2008; Shanahan & Shanahan, 2008). That is, secondary teachers are asked to socialize their students to the language and culture of their particular content area.

Literacy tools should be used to enrich the lives of the adults in the school also. Teachers, as well as students, need opportunities to share their writing orally and on the Internet, to join book clubs in which the books are selected according to the members' interests, to participate in interest groups such as photography clubs, hiking adventures, science clubs, or cooking classes, to download books and audio files, and to develop websites and use social networking to share what they are learning with others around the district, state, nation, or world.

Also, the new literacies provide for expanded uses of the tools of literacy in the classroom. Teachers are experimenting with ways to incorporate multimodal means of exploration and presentation to promote student learning. For example, Wilson, Chavez, and Anders (in press) investigated teaching principles of multimodal design and the reading and writing of memoir and autobiographical literature to language-learning middle school students. The students designed podcasts to represent and present their responses to that literature. Their study concluded that as multilingual, multicultural middle school students create podcasts they experience improvements in both their use of English and sense of literacy identity.

The above is an example of research needed in the use of the new literacies in secondary schools and classrooms. Dressman et al. (2006), when writing about the "potential and practical implications of computer-based technology within the lives and learning of youth" (p. 152), called for

> a great deal more research at the level of case study across a broad and international range of academic, para-academic, and non academic contexts and an equally wide range of individual and grouped participants, from multiple cultures, religions, social classes, genders, and economic backgrounds. In addition, we call for the analysis of findings from these studies through multiple perspectives or frames, including those of traditional academic measures, postmodern social theory, subject-oriented perspectives, cost–benefit analyses, and other approaches. (p. 153)

Colleagues Are Energized to Solve Problems through Reflection and Inquiry

Each school has its own issues and problems to solve. When colleagues gather to discuss these issues, a theme running through the discussion should be the quality of empirical evidence brought to the discussion. Too many times problems are addressed emotionally or on little evidence. Data-driven decision making is a popular topic for professional development right now, and high schools such as Brockton are collecting local data to inform local decisions about their students' progress. Some examples include doing a student survey of reading preferences to help the librarian order new materials, or to select students for interviews or focus groups to learn about the sorts of out-of-school literacies students are engaging, or to learn how much time students are spending on homework and how it fits with their life. Obviously, the actual data collection depends on the questions faculty have, but the point is that externally mandated assessments address some needs for data, but they are not sufficient for answering important local questions.

School Leaders Create an Environment for the Development of Literacy for All

Most schools face issues of student language variation and students who, for whatever reasons, do not read or write well enough to successfully navigate the requirements for high school graduation or their literacy needs. Issues of language must be dealt with from a position of valuing the home language (and culture) of students. The marginalization of these students leads to a socially dysfunctional school and limits learning opportunities for *all* students. Because we know that students are vastly different from each other, we must offer multiple opportunities in a variety of contexts for students to engage in Standard English. Ample opportunities should be provided for community members (e.g., parents, business owners, and political leaders) to help integrate these students into the school. These opportunities should be reciprocal with those from other cultures sharing their life experience with all the students in the school. Counselors and community leaders might serve as liaisons. This approach recognizes diversity and multilingualism as a resource rather than as a deficit (Ruiz, 1997).

Supports for English language learners (ELLs) include small content-area classes with opportunities for ELL students to partner with English speakers to learn disciplinary language. These classes should be characterized by much discussion and collaboration. Teachers might collaboratively plan for the ELL students so that their language development is monitored and they are provided with essential language instruction. Someone—the literacy or language specialist—should collaborate with teachers to help differentiate instruction and to make adaptations for the ELL students. Language clubs might be formed where English-speaking students can coach the ELL students as the ELL students teach the English speakers about their language and culture.

Adolescent "struggling" or "striving" readers are often assumed to need "basic" instruction. Some schools require that students who struggle take a "reading" class, which often uses a commercial product that is taught by a teacher with little or no knowledge of teaching reading or writing. Some commercial programs include teacher professional development, but few are supported by empirical evidence documenting the success of either the professional development or the student instruction. C. Shanahan (2005) reviewed commercial reading intervention programs designed for grades 4–12. She reported that little to no research supports the use of the programs and only a few programs use technology.

It might be that a particular commercial program is more successful than providing little to nothing for students. A qualified reading specialist should make this instructional decision, however. A reading specialist conducts an individualized assessment and selects a commercial program that meets students' needs.

An exciting noncommercial innovation is collaborative retrospective miscue analysis (CRMA; Goodman & Marek, 1996), which teaches students about the reading process and helps them to understand what they do and why. Students often claim not to be readers because they do not know words, cannot pronounce them, or are bad spellers. They use these perceived lack of skills to convince themselves that they "can't read." CRMA, an adaptation of retrospective miscue analysis, has been used with middle school students (Costello, 1996) and high school students (Anders, 2010). In this adaptation, students collaborate with one another to discuss and reflect upon the quality of miscues made during a previously taped oral reading, using knowledge about language and the reading process.

As students participate in CRMA, their beliefs about reading and language are challenged and they become more confident readers, which results in more reading for meaning. They attribute CRMA to helping them read in their classes and to passing the high-stakes graduation test. In a recent pilot study, 16 of 16 students who had previously failed the test needed for graduation were successful. Students reported: "This class has helped me understand my reading. I think I passed my AIMS test. I passed my driver's permit test. I never felt that I actually passed something [before]" (Student A, personal communication, April 21, 2010). A second said, "I seriously see a big difference in my reading. I can see great improvement; I just wish that someone would have taught me sooner. I feel good to be able to find miscues … it helped me make sense of the reading" (Student B, personal communication, April 21, 2010). And a third, "It's like experiencing freedom" (Student C, personal communication, April 21, 2010). These preliminary investigations are encouraging; other larger-scale studies are on the drawing board (Anders, 2010).

The above CRMA work corresponds well with Dennis's (2009) critique of interventions typically designed for adolescent struggling readers. She argues that "struggling young adolescents demonstrate complex, heterogeneous reading abilities requiring significantly different instructional interventions" (p. 290). Successful interventions are widely described for elementary students, but little attention has been paid to appropriate interventions for secondary students. This is another need for research, and thoughtful, reflective, inquiry-oriented instruction in the secondary school.

In addition to appropriate interventions, students who struggle to meet the reading and writing demands of the secondary school should be supported across the curriculum by teachers who incorporate content-based language and literacy instruction into their curriculum and teaching practices. Literacy across the curriculum means that *all* students are socialized to the culture and language of each discipline. Academic teachers need to be supported by a reading specialist or literacy coach with the resources and practices needed to differentiate instruction for students whose native language is not English and for those students who need support to read, write, discuss, and present academic ideas.

NEXT STEPS FOR LITERACY LEADERS: FORMS OF LEADERSHIP

The recent literature on secondary school reform suggests that leadership is not top-down; nor is it externally driven. Rather, a schoolwide literacy program should be created and guided by a team of teachers, including the librarian or media specialist, and led by a reading specialist or literacy coach (see Chapter 4 on literacy coaches in secondary schools). This team collaborates and has ongoing dialogue toward the goal of creating a literacy program tailored to the needs of the students and the schoolwide community. The goals discussed above provide a framework; a collaborative knowledgeable leader provides the resources and professional development.

A Literacy Council

Such a team might establish a literacy council. Irwin, Meltzer, Mickler, Phillips, and Dean (2009) describe literacy councils and provide multiple suggestions for establishing a council. Anders and Guzzetti (2005) list the advantages of a literacy council: it distributes responsibility across various members and programs in the school community; it increases the faculty and staff buy-in to the literacy program; and the program is adapted according to input and suggestions made by the council members. Members of the council are extensions of the literacy leader's influence and serve as the literacy leader's ears, eyes, and helpful hands. A literacy council ensures that the schoolwide program is "bottom-up" and suited to their particular school.

The literacy council is established in different ways, depending on the school culture. In one school, volunteers from the professional staff were asked for and the principal wrote a letter of invitation to one teacher who volunteered from each department. In another school, each department decided who would be best to serve. The member needs to be well respected by his or her peers, be interested in contributing to the schoolwide literacy program, and be willing to learn and pass that learning on to others. Some schools also involve student representatives from each class, counselors and other nonteaching staff, and members of the community, such as business leaders.

The literacy council members receive intensive professional development from the literacy leader. The inservice program consists of information in response to the most pressing questions of the faculty. The council members are expected to take this information back to their departments to help "spread the word." Once the members of the literacy council have some common experiences and knowledge, the literacy leader and council members can develop specific objectives to be achieved in the short term (1-year objectives) and in the long term (a strategic plan with goals and objectives for the next 5 years). These plans are vetted with the faculty, administration, and other constituents in the community. The objective is to get as many members of the community as possible to buy into the evolving program. Their personal investment pays off as the program gets under way. The literacy council also initiates and leads the needed professional development. This is similar to how Brockton High School achieved their remarkable change.

Another responsibility of the literacy council is to help develop an evaluation plan for the literacy program. Using the four goals described above, the council members might do an asset inventory of the strengths, possibilities, and concerns about the current status of literacy in the school. Possible categories include data on student interests and attitudes toward literacy, interviews with teachers to ascertain their perceptions, attitudes and beliefs about literacy, the quantity and quality of books checked out of the library, the availability of computers, especially for those students who are likely to have difficulty accessing technology, and the quality of opportunities for students who need literacy instruction. Then, through discussion and consultation with department members and other stakeholders, council members arrive at a plan for building on current successes, taking advantage of possibilities and addressing concerns.

CONCLUSION

As we were writing this chapter, we read the following quote, which encapsulates much of what we have been discussing: "today's kids are way smarter than we give them credit for: They know how to change a photo caption on a digital photo and send it to a friend. They can add the smiley face without the colon and parentheses! They never took typing but they can type faster than I can!" (Harpaz, 2010). Secondary school curricula in general and literacy development in particular are effective when students' interests, talents, and knowledge offer reciprocal opportunities for teachers' and administrators' continued learning. We advocate for a secondary school plan that brings students into the professional learning community as partners, for a leadership structure that is responsive to both *how* students and teachers learn and *why* they find learning meaningful and engaging.

We have an opportunity to shape the ways in which students' progress can be assessed in relation to the literacy curriculum and to reshape the curriculum as we learn from the assessments. We also have the opportunity to work with the people who are directly affected by the curriculum. Today's adolescents are smart and they are curious. They are the 21st century and they can help us enable them to be successful.

ENGAGEMENT ACTIVITIES

1.   The administrator in the opening case example chose to appeal to other district administrators to address the problem. What examples from this chapter might he or she use with school literacy specialists to turn what is perceived to be a problem into an opportunity?

2.   Invite a content-area teacher who has not had any preparation about

literacy development and instruction to read and respond to this chapter. You might also want to use this chapter with a study group of content-area teachers. What points are sensible and which are contentious? Share responses to formulate explanations for both positive responses and negative responses to the chapter.

3. Discuss why students are often described as not being able or interested in reading by the time they reach high school. Include curricular, linguistic, and psychological reasons in your discussion. Make a linkage between these reasons and the way literacy is treated in school structures with which you are familiar. If possible, discuss the empirical support for the positive and negative responses.

4. Discuss the ways in which students' voices are and are not present in discussions of literacy curriculum development. Draft a plan for using student input productively.

5. Use this chapter in conjunction with others in this book. Next, compare the content of Chapter 4 on literacy coaching with the content of this chapter. What commonalities are there? Any differences in how the authors view the role of literacy leaders? What are the key implications about how literacy leaders might work in middle or secondary schools? What do you think are the important qualifications for literacy leaders in these schools?

REFERENCES

Alexander, P. A. (2005). *The path to competence: A life-span developmental perspective on reading.* Retrieved September 15, 2010, from *www.nrconline.org.*

Alvermann, D. E., & Guthrie, J. T., (1993). Themes and directions of the National Reading Research Center. *Perspectives in reading research, no. 1,* Washington DC: Office of Research, United States Department of Education.

Anders, P. L. (2010). Adolescent literacy: Secondary students' language, literacy and learning. *Imagine Research* (pp. 7–10). Tucson, AZ: College of Education.

Anders, P. L., & Guzzetti, B. (2005). *Literacy instruction in the content areas.* Hillsdale, NJ: Erlbaum.

Baker, L., & Brown, A. L. (1984). Metacognitive skills and reading. In P. D. Pearson, R. Barr, M. Kamil, & P. Mosenthal (Eds.), *Handbook of reading research* (pp. 353–394). New York: Longman.

Buehl, D. (2009). *Classroom strategies for interactive learning.* Newark, DE: International Reading Association.

Costello, S. (1996). A teacher/researcher uses RMA. In Y. M. Goodman & A. M. Marek (Eds.), *Retrospective miscue analysis: Revaluing readers and reading* (pp. 165–175). Katonah, NY: Owen.

Dennis, D. V. (2009). "I'm not stupid": How assessment drives (in) appropriate reading instruction. *Journal of Adolescent and Adult Literacy, 53*(4), 283–290.

Dillon, S. (2010, September 28). 4,100 students prove "small is better" rule wrong. *New York Times.* Retrieved [DATE] from *www.nytimes.com.*

DiPardo, A. (1999). *Teaching in common: Challenges to joint work in classrooms and schools.* New York: Teachers College Press.

Dole, J. A., Duffy, G. G., Roehler, L. R., & Pearson, P. D. (1991). Moving from the old to new: Research on reading comprehension instruction. *Review of Educational Research, 61,* 239–264.

Dressman, M., O'Brien, D., Rogers, T., Ivey, G., Wilder, P., Alvermann, D., et al. (2006). Problematizing adolescent literacies: Four instances, multiple perspectives. In J. V. Hoffman, D. L. Schallert, C. M. Fairbanks, J. Worthy, & B. Maloch (Eds.), *55th yearbook of the National Reading Conference* (pp. 141–154). Oak Creek, WI: National Reading Conference.

Eckert, P. (1989). *Jocks and burnouts: Social categories and identity in the high school.* New York: Teachers College Press.

Ferguson, R. F., Hackman, S., Hanna, R., & Ballantine, A. (2010). How high schools become exemplary: Ways that leadership raises achievement and narrows gaps by improving instruction in 15 public high schools. *Report on the 2009 Annual Conference of the Achievement Gap Initiative at Harvard University.* Retrieved [DATE] from *www.agi.harvard.edu.*

Gambrell, L., & Morrow, L. (1996). Creating motivating contexts for literacy learning. In L. Baker, P. Afflerbach, & D. Reinking (Eds.), *Developing engaged readers in school and home communities* (pp. 115–136). Mahwah, NJ: Erlbaum.

Gee, J. (2008). *Social linguistics and literacies: Ideology in discourses* (3rd ed.). New York: Routledge Taylor & Francis.

Goodman, Y. M., & Marek, A. M. (1996). *Retrospective miscue analysis: Revaluing readers and reading.* Katonah, NY: Owen.

Harpaz, B. J. (2010, September 28). Can we blame tech for turning kids into dolts? *Arizona Daily Star.* Retrieved [DATE] from *azstarnet.com.*

Irvin, J., Meltzer, J., Dean, N., & Mickler, M. J. (2010). *Taking the lead on adolescent literacy: Action steps for schoolwide success.* Thousand Oaks, CA: Corwin Press.

Ivey, G. (1999). A multicase study in the middle school: Complexities among young adolescent readers. *Reading Research Quarterly, 34*(2), 172–192.

Langer, J. A. (2001). Beating the odds: Teaching middle and high school students to read and write well. *American Education Research Journal, 38*(4), 837–880.

Lankshear, C., & Knobel, M. (2003). *New literacies: Changing knowledge and classroom learning.* Philadelphia: Open University Press.

Lemke, J. (2007, February). *New media and new learning communities.* Paper presented at the annual meeting of the National Council of Teachers of English Assembly for Research, Nashville, TN.

Luke, A., & Elkins, J. (1998). Reinventing literacy in "new times." *Journal of Adolescent and Adult Literacy, 42*(1), 4–7.

Maira, S., & Soep, E. (2005). *Youthscapes: The popular, the national, the global.* Philadelphia: University of Pennsylvania Press.

McCarthey, S. (2002). *Students' identities and literacy learning.* Newark, DE: International Reading Association.

McCarthey, S., & Moje, E. (2002). Identity matters. *Reading Research Quarterly, 37*(2), 228–238.

McCombs, B. L. (1996). Alternative perspectives for motivation. In L. Baker, P. Afflerbach, & D. Reinking (Eds.), *Developing engaged readers in school and home communities* (pp. 67–89). Mahwah, NJ: Erlbaum.

Moje, E. B. (2008). Foregrounding the disciplines in secondary literacy teaching and learning: A call for change. *Journal of Adolescent and Adult Literacy, 52*(2), 96–107.

Moore, D. (2002). Adolescent literacy for all means forming literate identities. In C. M. Roller (Ed.), *Comprehensive reading instruction across grade levels: A collection of papers from the Reading Research 2001 Conference* (pp. 148–157). Newark, DE: International Reading Association.

Paris, S. G., Lipson, M. Y., & Wixson, K. K. (1983). Becoming a strategic reader. *Contemporary Educational Psychology, 8,* 293–316.

Piercy, M. (2005). *Sex Wars.* New York: HarperCollins.

Reeves, A. R. (2004). *Adolescents talk about reading: Exploring resistance to and engagement with text.* Newark, DE: International Reading Association.

Ruiz, R. (1997). The empowerment of language-minority students. In A. Darder, R. Torres, & H. Gutierrez (Eds.), *Latinos and education: A critical reader* (pp. 319–328), New York: Routledge.

Shanahan, C. (2005). *Adolescent literacy intervention programs: Chart and program review guide.* Naperville, IL: Learning Point Associates.

Shanahan, T., & Shanahan, C. (2008). Teaching disciplinary literacy to adolescents: Rethinking content area literacy. *Harvard Educational Review, 78*(1), 40–59.

United States Department of Labor. (1992). *What work requires of schools. A SCANS report for America 2000.* Retrieved September 20, 2010, from *wdr.doleta.gov/SCANS/whatwork/.*

Valdéz, G., Bunch, G. C., Snow, C. E., & Lee, C. (2005). Enhancing the development of students' language(s). In L. Darling-Hammond, J. Bransford, P. LePage, K. Hammerness, & H. Duffy (Eds.), *Preparing teachers for a changing world? What teachers should learn and be able to do* (pp. 126–168). San Francisco: Jossey-Bass.

Westheimer, J. (2008). Learning among colleagues: Teacher community and the shared enterprise of education. In M. Cochran-Smith, S. Feiman-Nemser, D. J. McIntyre, & K. E. Demers (Eds.), *Handbook of research on teacher education: Enduring questions in changing contexts* (3rd ed., pp. 756–783). New York: Routledge.

Wilson, A. A., Chavez, K., & Anders, P. (in press). *"From the Koran and Family Guy": The expression of identity in English language learners' digital podcasts. Journal of Adolescent and Adult Literacy.*

10

Establishing a Print-Rich Classroom and School Environment

MISTY SAILORS
JAMES V. HOFFMAN

Guiding Questions

- What is the role of a print-rich environment in student achievement?
- What types of texts inform achievement?
- What is the role of literacy leaders in the creation of print-rich schools and classrooms?

Signs surround us. Some of these signs are placed in our environment by others to constrain (like that speed limit sign we ignored once too often), to motivate (like that billboard telling us that to look young forever, you just have to rub on the right kind of cream), to inspire (like that quote on the volleyball team's practice shirt that reminds us there is no *I* in *team*), to inform (like that terrifying list of "potential side effects" on medicine prescriptions), or to humor (like that bumper sticker on the car in front that says "Thank heaven for spell chack."). Some of the signs in our environment help us focus (like the "to-do list" that never seems to get done), to remind us (like the appointment calendar on one of those electronic pocket organizers), to capture ideas and thoughts (like the journal kept on a special trip overseas), or to celebrate (like the favorite poem of a young first-grade child that gets posted on the refrigerator door).

As literate members of a literate culture, we almost never focus on the symbols but on the messages these signs carry. Not so for the very young who must work to gain access to the meanings hidden beneath the physical appearances. As parents, we surround our children with signs and messages that are jointly interpreted and valued. We fill our homes with these texts and we revisit them again and again. As teachers, we fill our classrooms with signs and messages that can be used to guide young minds toward the skills and strategies they need to access meaning. We create a world of texts for and with our students that can become the basis for conversation, instruction, inspiration, and ultimately independence as learners. The texts we make available in our classrooms form a bridge to the literacies that are useful in the world outside. The literate environment of the classroom is (or should be) developed out of a conscious effort on the part of the teacher. In developing this supportive literate environment the teacher draws on his or her knowledge of the students, of development, and of literacy.

Our purpose in writing this chapter is to share what we have discovered through several studies into the qualities and characteristics of effective elementary classroom text environments. We begin with a brief review of research into effective classroom literacy environments with a specific focus on the research that provides the basis for our chapter. We follow with a description of the assessment instrument and procedures that we have used in our research since this provides the basic framework for our recommendations. We then describe the characteristics and qualities of the text environment that are linked to student growth in literacy. Finally, we offer thoughts on the ways literacy leaders can support the growth of print-rich schools and classrooms. Below are the thoughts of Ms. Anguiano, a literacy coach at Strong Elementary School, about what she sees during her visit to a second-grade classroom.

CASE EXAMPLE

"Stepping into Mr. Lopez's classroom was like stepping into an almost-ideal classroom. His children loved him and so did their families. He is a well-respected teacher by the administration and me. His second-grade children were always on task; everywhere you looked, you saw children engaged in acts of literacy. As I observed this morning, I noticed children at the guided reading table with Mr. Lopez, eagerly beginning another book with him. He was well prepared for the lesson—as he passed out the books, he showed the children a poster he had created titled, 'Strategies We Use When We Come to Words We Don't Know. ... ' He began the lesson by telling the students that they were going to practice the strategies that he had identified for them; he then proceeded to read the poster to the children, reminding them to look at the poster if they encountered an unknown word in their new book. 'Hmm,' I wondered to myself. I wonder why he didn't generate that list of strategies *with* the children?

"Looking around the room, I began to notice other texts in his classroom in which his children were engaged. Above the writing center was a commercially produced poster that listed the steps in the writing process. Next to the pencil sharpener was a poster that explained how to sharpen pencils. A bulletin board was located near the door that announced, 'Look who made a 100'; that bulletin board contained six spelling tests from the previous week. Last, but not least, every single one of the many instructional posters that I noticed was either commercially produced (such as colors and color words; names of shapes; organizational classifications of animals; and different types of houses around the world, to name a few) or made by Mr. Lopez (such as the weather report; the birthday chart; and the daily schedule, to name a few).

"As I examined the room, I was struck by the lack of input *of the children* into the print environment. I was surprised at my discovery as Mr. Lopez's practices are so in tune with the instructional needs of his students and he is always so supportive of them during his reading instruction. Perhaps Mr. Lopez would be willing to discuss his print environment with me. How would his practices improve even more if we critically examined his print environment, looking specifically at the role of the many different types of text he could offer his students (there are no journals in this classroom!) and the role of the children in *creating* those texts! It's worth a try. ...."

STUDENT ACHIEVEMENT
AND PRINT-RICH ENVIRONMENTS

Converging evidence from multiple research sources (Metsala et al., 1997; Morrow, Tracey, Woo, & Pressley, 1999; Pressley, Rankin, & Yokoi, 1996; Snow, Barnes, Chandler, Goodman, & Hemphill, 1991; Taylor, Pearson, Clark, & Walpole, 2000; Wharton-McDonald, Pressley, & Hampston, 1998) provides evidence that learning to read occurs best in classrooms where children are provided multiple opportunities to read, write, and talk about text within print-rich environments. However, research studies (Duke, 2000; Fractor, Woodruff, Martinez, & Teale, 1993; Morrow, 1991) and our own experiences in classrooms across the country leads us to believe that much needed "print laboratories" (Searfoss & Readence, 1983) that are "filled" (Pressley et al., 1996) or "flooded" (Cambourne, 2000) with print are simply not a ubiquitous part of classroom literacy practice, even though the literature has demonstrated for years the importance of a print-rich environment for literacy development.

The earliest studies of this body of literature were descriptions of literacy environments (or the lack of; Duke, 2000; Fractor et al., 1993; Morrow & Weinstein, 1982), the use of those environments by children and teachers (Morrow, 1991, 1992), the role of teacher philosophies and beliefs on print environments (Dowhower & Beagle, 1998), and the ways in which text environments represent a particular ideology of literacy instruction (Taylor, Blum, & Logsdon, 1986). Further, this body of literature evolved as the tools used to document print environments evolved (Hoffman, Maloch, & Sailors, 2010). There is now a growing set of instruments developed specifically to capture, describe, and/or measure the literacy environment (e.g., see Baker, Gersten, Haager, & Dingle, 2006; Hoffman, Sailors, Duffy, & Beretvas, 2004; Loughlin & Martin, 1987; Ross, Smith, Lohr, & McNelis, 1994; Wolfersberger, Reutzel, Sudweeks, & Fawson, 2004) and as a way to self-examine literacy practices for classroom teachers (Hoffman & Sailors, 2004). It comes as no surprise within such a growing body of literature that print-rich environments are associated with student achievement.

For example, Taylor et al. (1986) conducted a study in which prekindergarten and kindergarten teachers implemented a classroom environment where children's initial literacy concepts were developed easily and naturally. The researchers examined the implementation of the staff development as it manifested itself in the print environment of these classrooms. The texts in the high-implementing classrooms were student generated, reflected ongoing activity, and were displayed prominently. Observations across the classrooms revealed that print in the high-implementing classrooms was centered on children's interests, language and purposes; the creation of print was an integral part of the classroom routine and integrated across classroom activities; and the print represented multiple and varied stimuli for reading and writing. Children in the high-implementing classrooms outperformed children in the nonimplementing classrooms on two of the subtests (visual, which measures letter recognition, and visual matching and language, which measures school language and listening) on the Metropolitan Readiness Test.

A few years later, Ray Reutzel and his colleagues (Reutzel, Oda, & Moore, 1989) capitalized on these findings and studied the effects of three instructional approaches for developing kindergarteners' print awareness and concepts. Groups in the study were assigned to one of three approaches: (1) traditional readiness approach, (2) print immersion, and (3) print immersion plus teacher-led instruction. Findings from this study indicated that children in the treatment groups (print immersion and print immersion plus teacher-led instruction) outperformed children in the traditional group on measures of readiness and word reading abilities. Children in the print immersion plus teacher-led instruction group demonstrated significantly greater print concept development than the other two groups.

In her seminal study of "book floods" in impoverished classrooms in day care centers in 10 regions of the United States, Neuman (1999) studied the effects of almost 18,000 books with accompanying instruction for teachers on how to use the books. According to Neuman, the book floods set off a series of events that led to physical changes in the classrooms, further enhancing the children's access to and engagement with print in these classrooms. Children in the intervention group scored statistically significantly higher than the control group on four of six assessment measures (concepts of print, letter name knowledge, concepts of narrative, and concepts of writing) with gains still evident 6 months later in kindergarten.

McGill-Franzen and her colleagues (McGill-Franzen, Allington, Yokoi, & Brooks, 1999) conducted a similar experimental study. This team examined the effects of providing books to kindergarteners while enhancing their teachers' instructional routines involving books. Three groups of classrooms participated: the first group received books and instruction on how to use the books, the second group received books only (no instruction), and the third group received neither books nor instruction (control group). The research team found that the first group of teachers read significantly more to their students than did teachers in the second or third group and displayed the books more attractively than did the second group of teachers. In addition, the teachers in the training group (first group) provided more extensive and planned displays of a variety of print materials, including examples of student-written work when compared with teachers in the second and third groups. More important, the children in the first group achieved significantly higher scores on every measure of literacy development when compared to children in the other groups. The authors concluded that although it is important to provide classrooms with books, it is critical that teachers know what to do with the books.

In summary, studies have demonstrated the importance of a print-rich environment for literacy development. Children who are engaged in a print-rich environment simply achieve better than those children who are not. And, the evidence also points to the need for teachers to not only create a print-rich environment with their children; those same teachers must know how to use the environment in strategic ways. In the next section, we continue to explore the role of a print-rich environment for literacy teaching and learning, while advocating for a more through definition of what "counts" in a print-rich environment.

REPRESENTATION OF LITERACY
AS A SOCIAL PRACTICE:
RETHINKING PRINT ENVIRONMENTS

Our work has also followed the line of research around the importance of a print-rich environment and literacy instruction and development. That line of research is evident in recent educational standards, such as the Standards 2010, written by the International Reading Association (IRA). Standard 5 focuses explicitly on the creation of a "literate environment that fosters reading and writing by integrating foundational knowledge, instructional practices, approaches and methods, curriculum materials, and the appropriate use of assessments" (p. 13). IRA's stance is holistic; our stance in this chapter focuses primarily on the print environment of classrooms and is driven by the social practice of literacy. In this section, we define our stance around the social nature of literacy and explain the importance of this stance through several studies we have conducted.

Literacy as a Social Practice

Literacy is not a natural state but is a social construct (Cole & Scribner, 1974). As a social construct, all literacy acts (reading and writing), are inherently historical, social, cultural, situated, and contextual. Literacy acts arise out of the ways in which people in a particular society think about, use, understand, and value literacy (Barton, 1994). The definition of literacy as set forth by Barton and Hamilton (2000) guides our work:

> Literacy is a social practice. Literacy practices are the general cultural ways of utilizing written language, which people draw upon in their lives. In the simplest sense literacy practices are what people do with literacy. (p. 7)

Literacy practices are inclusive of values, attitudes, feelings, and social relationships and include people's awareness of literacy, how they talk about literacy, and how they make sense of literacy. Although these processes are internal to the individual they are, at the same time, social practices connect people to each other (Barton & Hamilton, 2000).

The texts located within a community and the ways in which people in that community use those texts are the simplest and most obvious places to begin a description of the literacy practices of a community. However, the texts in the community are not a static set of physical objects but part of a dynamic social context that impacts as well as is impacted by those around it (Brandt & Clinton, 2002). When combined, the observable and "interpretivistic aspects" (how the members of the community use, think about, are aware of, construct, talk about, and how those members make sense of the texts; Barton & Hamilton, 2000) become an inference to the larger global patterns of literacy practices within a particular community. These inferences then become indicative of the role literacy plays in the lives of the members of the society (Barton & Hamilton, 1998; Barton, Hamilton, & Ivanic, 2000; Langer, 1987).

Ormerod and Ivanic (2000) maintain that literacy practices can be inferred from the characteristics of the "texts" located in the environment. Texts are not just a form of verbal and visual representation, but also "permanent and material evidence" (Tusting, 2000, p. 43) consisting of distinct physical features. Borrowing from anthropological studies, Hamilton refers to those materials, tools, and accessories as "artefacts" [sic] (Hamilton, 2000, p. 17). From her research, Hamilton demonstrated that artifacts are constituents of literacy practices inside the observed interactions between people and written texts. Hamilton, as well as others within the New Literacy Studies, keeps practices central to her work, examining how texts fit into the practices of people's lives, rather than the other way around (Barton & Hamilton, 2000).

Documenting and Describing the Social Literacy Practices of Classrooms

How does one capture and describe the literacy practices of a community? We have relied heavily on the works of the New Literacy Studies group (Barton & Hamilton, 2000; Barton, 1994; Barton et al., 2000; Brandt & Clinton, 2002) as we constructed an instrument, the TEX-IN3 (Hoffman & Sailors, 2002). The TEX-IN3 is an acronym for the three principal components of the instrument, the text inventory, the text in-use observation, and the text interview. The TEX-IN3 is designed to (1) capture and represent the range and qualities of texts in classrooms; (2) observe teachers and students as they engage with these texts during instruction; and (3) record the understandings of the forms, functions, and uses of these texts by teachers and students. Although we have written extensively about the instrument elsewhere (see Hoffman & Sailors, 2002b; Hoffman et al., 2004, 2005; Sailors & Hoffman, 2010), here we offer a brief explanation of each of its three components.

Text Inventory

The text inventory is a description and a valuing of the physical text environment in the classroom. We have identified a set of 17 broad text types that help us organize the inventory of the texts in the classroom. Within these categories of texts there are several broad dimensions of texts we examine: public, personal; extended and limited; local and commercial; process, product; and extended and limited. We thoroughly document all of the text types in a classroom and then we apply 5-point rubrics to rate the quality of the texts in each category for a classroom. There are two additional rubric ratings we apply during the inventory. The first applies to the overall effectiveness of the text environment. The second holistic rating scale applies to the quality of the "local text" environment. "Local texts" are those texts within a classroom that are created by the teacher and or the student as part of the literacy environment (Maloch, Hoffman, & Patterson, 2002).

Our inventory of the texts in a classroom is a starting point for us in peeling back the layers of the classroom literacy environment. However, on the basis of Barton (1994), we must at some point move to the next step of examining the practices of use of these texts in the classroom environment. How, when, and by whom are these texts used? This brings us to the second component of the TEX-IN3: texts in-use.

Texts In-Use

The texts in-use part of the process allows us to step out of the inferring mold of the anthropologist and actually watch the students and the teachers as they engage with the texts in the classroom. Within the TEX-IN3 we have opted for a relatively low-inference observation scheme in which engagements with texts in specific time bands are counted and sorted based on the types of texts engaged with and the context in which they are used. We typically focus our observations on the teacher and three students in the class: a highly skilled reader, an on-grade-level reader, and a below-grade-level reader. We are interested in understanding the range of use of the variety of texts by different skill levels within the class. The low-inference coding scheme is modeled after the work of Jane Stallings (e.g., Stallings, Amy, Resnick, & Leinhardt, 1975) and is used to allow us to make a direct connection to the effective teaching literature, where levels of sustained engagement are seen as closely tied to achievement growth. The narrative notes that describe the overall activity structure in the classroom complement the low-inference observation using sweeps and snapshots. We actually calculate an "in-use" score from our observations that is considerate of the amount of engaged time weighted by the quality rating for the texts the student is using.

Through the observations we come closer to understanding the literacy environment but there are still aspects of it that we cannot access through direct observation; this is what Barton referred to as the inner processes. We simply cannot observe what is inside the student's head. We have to talk to the student to reveal these understandings. The third and final component of the TEX-IN3 refers to the text interviews.

Text Interviews

Because students are the prime users of text in classrooms, we begin our interview with students, and finish the interview process with the teacher. The interview structure for the students is akin to a reading the room exercise. The student is asked to lead the observer on a tour of the print in the room. Interviews with students might begin with a focus on the texts observed during the lesson, but this is just the starting point. From there the conversation is focused on all print in the room. What is this? What is it for? Who uses it? How is it used? Based on these interviews the researcher assigns a rating to the students' understanding and valuing of each of the text types in the classroom.

Last, but not least, the teacher interview is conducted in a manner of a sorting strategy. We present the teacher with 17 cards each with the name of a text category (trade book, textbook, assessment, journal, etc). We talk about these briefly in terms of the terminology we are using, pointing out whenever we can how these texts appear in his or her classroom. We asked him or her to rank them from most to least important and we ask the teacher to then rate each of them individually in terms of their importance. As they are ranking and rating, we ask him or her to talk aloud, in much the same way as we ask the students to read the room. What's this? Why is it important? Who uses it? How is it used? Based on the interviews, the researcher assigns a rating for the teacher's understanding and valuing of each of the text types in the classroom.

Literacy as a Social Practice Perspective and Student Achievement

Based on findings from our previous work, reported elsewhere (Hoffman et al., 2004) and summarized here, each of the three components of the TEX-IN3 instrument correlate to literacy achievement. For example, statistical analyses revealed that the holistic inventory and the local text inventory were individually significant predictors of the comprehension posttest scores of children in the study. Likewise, the average measures (across data collection time periods) describing the teacher's engagement and the measure averaged across three representative students were significantly related to the adjusted posttest comprehension score. Finally, both the average students' text understanding and that of the teacher, as measured with the TEX-IN3, were significant predictors when entered individually into the equation.

For the purposes of this chapter, we have conducted follow-up analysis of data gathered in the Hoffman et al. (2004) study. This analysis focus explored the types of text found in the highest-performing classrooms in our data pool across first through sixth grades. For the identification of

the qualities of characteristics of effective literacy environments, the teachers were rank ordered based on the residualized gain scores (pre/post)
of their students on the reading comprehension measure of the GRADE
(Group Reading Assessment and Diagnostic Evaluation) (American Guidance Services, 2001). Next we compared the scores on the TEX-IN3 for the
high-comprehension-gain classrooms (the top-ranked 15 teachers) with the
low-comprehension-gain classrooms (the lowest-ranked 15 teachers). The
results of this analysis are summarized in Table 10.1. The average scores
on all but two of the subtests favored the high-gain classrooms in ways predicted by the TEX-IN3, although not all of these differences reached a level
of statistical significance.

Our next step in the analysis was to examine the specific observation
protocols to identify the specific features within the categories that might
explain (in qualitative terms) the quantitative differences in scores. We organize our reporting of the findings around the "big idea" constructs represented within the TEX-IN3.

TABLE 10.1. Text Inventory: High- versus Low-Gain Classrooms

TEX-IN3 category	Low ($N = 15$)	High ($N = 15$)	p values (Low vs. high)
Holistic Rating for the Physical Texts Environment	2.9	3.6	Yes ($p = .01$)
Computers/Electronics	2.5	3.1	No ($p = .12$)
Extended Text Process Charts	2.5	3.0	No ($p = .17$)
Games/Puzzles/Manipulatives	2.4	3.4	Yes ($p = .01$)
Instructional Aids	3.0	4.1	Yes ($p < .01$)
Journals	2.7	3.2	No ($p = .14$)
Leveled Books	3.0	3.7	Yes ($p < .01$)
Limited Text Process Charts	2.3	3.6	Yes ($p < .01$)
Organizational/Management Charts	3.7	4.1	No ($p = .13$)
Portfolios	2.2	2.3	No ($p = .75$)
Reference Materials	3.4	3.1	No ($p = .30$)
Serials	2.2	2.4	No ($p = .62$)
Social/Personal/Inspirational Text Displays	2.8	2.9	No ($p = .72$)
Student–Teacher Published Works	1.4	2.7	Yes ($p < .01$)
Textbooks	3.9	3.3	No ($p = .14$)
Trade Books	3.0	4.2	Yes ($p < .01$)
Work Product Displays	2.3	2.8	No ($p = .11$)
Writing on Paper	3.1	3.5	No ($p = .09$)
Holistic Rating for the Local Texts	2.9	3.6	Yes ($p < .01$)

The Text Environment

All of the text environment scores presented in Table 10.1 represent the averages of the three scores (from the fall, winter, and spring data collection periods) for each of the categories. In some instances, it was revealing to compare the differences during the fall (the start of the year) with the winter (school in full swing) and the spring (approaching the end of the academic year). These differences are noted as they appear.

The holistic score for the physical text environment favors the high-gain classrooms. There were six specific text categories where the differences were statistically significant: games/puzzles, instructional aids, leveled books, limited text process charts, student–teacher published works, and trade books. We were surprised that more types of text did not show up as significant; however, upon further investigation, we believe that these other types were either common across classrooms (e.g., textbooks are supplied to schools for all students) or were nonexistent across classrooms (e.g., portfolios). In short, the next section of this paper is in no way intended to suggest that the 11 text types that did not show up as significantly different are not important—they are. We report, however, only on the text types that were statistically significantly different across high- and low-gain classrooms and discuss qualitatively what we found in high-gain classrooms.

GAMES/PUZZLES/MANIPULATIVES

These are instructional materials designed for student use (often as independent or small-group work). To be considered in this category they must feature text prominently. This category includes both limited and extended uses of text (e.g., Scrabble, as limited text; Monopoly, as extended text) and may be constructed either locally or commercially. Upon our qualitative examination of these texts in high-gain classrooms, we found that almost all classrooms had them (94%). Of the classrooms that had them, all of the games that were reading and language arts related with other subject areas were also represented (science, math, and social studies). The vast majority of the classrooms (71%) contained games that were locally constructed, such as word sorts that engaged children in making word activities and/or sorting for rhyming patterns. These word-sort games contained limited texts (texts that are at the letter or word level) in the vast majority of the classrooms (94%) and included such games as BINGO, and magnetic poetry, to name a few. All high-gain classrooms that had texts of this category were neatly stored and organized in bags, bowls, boxes, folders, bins, and shelves.

INSTRUCTIONAL AIDS

These enlarged/public texts are used to support instruction in classrooms, both subject area and literacy learning. They may be commercial charts (e.g., story charts provided by basal publishers), created by the teacher for the students, or co-constructed by the teacher and student. Often these texts are referred to as posters and are an artifact of past instruction. These texts may remain displayed in the classroom after a lesson or a unit as a reference point for students (e.g., a color chart in kindergarten). Our qualitative analysis of this text type in high-gain classrooms revealed that there were an average of 18 posters in each of the classrooms (range of 8 to 34); two-thirds were locally created. The vast majority of the classrooms contained instructional aids focused toward math (82%), science (82%), and social studies (82%), whereas 60% of the instructional aids we documented and examined were focused on reading and/or language arts. Of these instructional aids, a large majority of them supported comprehension (88%), writing instruction (82%), and word identification (59%). Some texts that we documented appeared to be for immediate or current use, such as a document on an overhead projector or written on the chalkboard, while other texts were more permanent in nature such as poems that hung in the poetry center, labels throughout the classrooms, and vocabulary lists. However, this is not to say that these instructional aids never changed. On the contrary, we noticed a marked difference in the instructional aids offered to children across our three visits; that is to say, the instructional aids in these classrooms were dynamic and changed with the instruction in the classroom.

LIMITED TEXT PROCESS CHARTS

This category includes letter/word-level texts that are procedural and guide the students in the use of a particular strategy or set of strategies. They tend to focus at the letter or word level. They are typically locally created and are added to as part of instructional processes. They may be enlarged, public texts, as in word walls, or they may be personal (word walls found inside folders at students' desks). They may be local or commercial in design. Our analysis of the limited texts found in high-gain classrooms indicated that the vast majority of them were word walls (88%) that included student names (in the kindergarten classes) and sight words. More than two-thirds of the classrooms had alphabet charts, and 59% of the classrooms had lists of phonogram families. Many of the words on these word walls were locally created by the teacher to map onto words in readers or on spelling lists. Over and over in our data, the word walls were described as filled and clearly organized. Across our site visits, these limited text charts changed as the instruction changed—there were no word walls in the high-gain classrooms that were static (i.e., same at end of year as they were at the beginning).

STUDENT–TEACHER PUBLISHED WORKS

This category consists of locally authored (by a student, a teacher, or a combination of the two) books or publications and is, consequently always a local text. When we examined the nature of the student–teacher published works in the high-gain classrooms, we found that 88% of our classrooms contained them. Individual children were the authors of the vast majority of the books (80%), but many of the classrooms (60%) contained class-authored works. The majority of these books were written with traditional tools (pencils and pens) and illustrated with colors or markers; only a few classrooms used technology to publish these materials (Kid Pix or Word). All classrooms that contained this type of text displayed them prominently—in centers, on display shelves, and/or in the classroom library.

TRADE BOOKS

We defined trade books as those texts that are typically found in "book format" and do not have any obvious instructional design features. They are commonly referred to as "library books" although this is somewhat misleading as a reference point. The trade book collections in the high-gain classrooms were a pervasive part of the text environment. There was an average of 667 books per classroom (ranging from 106 to 2,503 in a kindergarten and first-grade classroom, respectively) and there were on average 36 books per child across the high-performing classrooms. Our analysis showed that more than half of the classrooms (53%) contained multicultural books and 69% offered informational books to children. There were a variety of formats located across these classrooms—all of the classrooms offered picture books to children; more than half (56%) offered chapter books (including the classrooms in the primary grades). Additionally, there were an average of 18 Big Books in these classrooms, more than two-thirds of the classrooms. Our analysis also revealed differences in the ways in which these trade books were organized (e.g., by themes, authors) and the ways in which they were linked to content-area studies. The trade books in the high-gain classrooms were everywhere—in the library corner, on bookshelves, in learning centers, and in freestanding displays. Teachers in these classrooms displayed the books in thoughtful ways that put them in the foreground throughout the classroom, not simply stacked on shelves in a library corner. For example, across the classrooms books were organized by the developmental level of the books ("easy" chapter books), the content or subject ("volcano" books), genre ("biographies"), author ("Eric Carle"), theme ("friendship"), and/or format ("Big Books").

LEVELED TEXTS

The statistically significant ways in which the teachers in the high-gain classrooms attended to the needs of developing readers are revealed in the differences in the categories of leveled texts for the students and limited text process charts. The leveled text collections in the high-gain classrooms were larger in number and quality, and better organized than in the low-gain classrooms providing students with texts that were readily accessible to their reading abilities. These leveled texts were organized in ways that teachers could access them easily and were located in places where students could access them, should they choose to.

Local Texts

Perhaps the most revealing finding related to the texts in the environment came with our examination of "local texts" in the classroom. Local texts are those created by the teachers/and or the students in the classroom. The average holistic rating for local texts favored the high-gain classrooms. There are some texts categories that are exclusively local in nature (e.g., journals, student–teacher published works, and work product displays). With local texts in particular, it was revealing to look at the patterns from the start of the year to midyear. Journals were not statistically different between the two groups when looking at the average score across the three observations. However, the differences were statistically significant at the midpoint of the year suggesting that there was an increasing use of local texts as the year progressed. The same pattern of no difference at the start of the year but statistically significant differences at midyear was true for the category of work product displays (displays of children's written work). The differences in student–teacher published work were statistically significant at every data collection period. The average score of 1.7 for this category in the low-gain classrooms suggests that there was almost no attention to publishing work within the classroom. There was no student–teacher published work present in over half of the low-gain classrooms.

Based on our examination of the protocols we drew three dominant impressions with respect to the contrasting physical text environment between the high- and low-gain classrooms. First, in the high-gain classrooms there was far greater representation of texts created within the classroom than in the low-gain classrooms. Second, the number, variety, and quality of print materials was much greater in the high-gain classrooms. And third, there appeared to be more texts in the classroom to meet students where they were academically, and to support them to success with text. Simply stated, teachers in these classrooms appeared to know the instructional level of their students and provided texts that met their needs.

Text In-Use

The data related to the text in-use observations presented in Table 10.2 reflect the combined data from the observation focused on reading and the observation focused on language arts with the exception of the last category.

All numbers in each of the cells reflect a weighting of the proportion of students or the proportion of time students are observed interacting with text. These proportions are weighted by the ratings of the quality of the texts the students are engaged with in that classroom. The maximum score possible is 100.

The average snapshot score of 61.7 in the high-gain classrooms contrasts with the average score of 35.1 in the low-gain classrooms. The snapshot score reflects the proportion of all students in the classroom interacting with text at the time the snapshot is taken. There are three separate snapshot observations reflected in this score (two from the reading observation period and one from the language arts observation period). The "sweep" scores reflect a close observation of three students and the teacher over two 20-minute observations (one in reading and one in language arts). Each student and the teachers are observed for interaction with text every 20 seconds. The overall engagement scores for the students in the high-gain classrooms during both the snapshot and sweep observations are approaching double the level of engagement for the low-gain classrooms. The data on the teacher suggest that it is not just the engagement of the students but the engagement of the teacher as well with text that marks the differences between these classrooms.

The findings related to engagement are not surprising in light of all the classroom research that has revealed close connections between student "time on task" and student achievement growth (see Brophy & Good, 1986). However, these data go further in suggesting that it is engagement

TABLE 10.2. Texts In Use: High- versus Low-Gain Classrooms

Texts In-Use	Low (N = 15)	High (N = 15)	p values (low vs. high)
Average Snapshot Score (reading and language arts)	35.1	61.7	Yes (p = .05)
Average rating discussion (quantity)	2.8	3.1	No (p = .89)
Average rating discussion (quality)	2.6	3.1	No (p = .53
Average Sweep Score for above-grade-level standard	33.7	59.5	Yes (p = .05)
Average Sweep Score for on-grade-level standard	29.0	56.2	Yes (p = .05)
Average Sweep Score for below-grade-level standard	32.4	55.8	Yes (p < .05)
Average Sweep Score for all students	31.6	56.7	Yes (p < .05)
Average Sweep Score for teacher	36.1	56.2	No (p = .09)
Average Sweep Score for teacher (reading obs.)	46.7	68.8	Yes (p = .05)

with text that is of high quality that accounts for the differences. Further, the findings add the teacher into the equation of engagement as critical.

Text Interviews

As part of the TEX-IN3 interview process the teachers were asked to rank the various text types in terms of their importance to the classroom instructional plan. The lists of the teachers are more alike than they are different in the rankings with two noticeable contrasts. First, and perhaps the most glaring contrast, came with respect to journals, ranked third highest in importance by the teachers in the high-gain classrooms and ranked tenth by the teachers in the low-gain classrooms. A second contrast we would point out is the relatively high ranking (second) for instructional aids in the high-gain classrooms as contrasted with the ranking of seventh for instructional aids in the low-gain classrooms.

The similarity in talk about the valuing of texts within classrooms is not always consistent with the other evidence gathered. For example, the three highest-rated text categories in the inventory for the low-gain classrooms were reference material, management charts, and textbooks. Reference materials and textbooks did not rank in the top eight on the teachers' valuing scale. In contrast, the rankings made by the teachers in the high-gain classrooms closely matches the ratings of quality from the inventory. Three of the top four ranked categories by the teachers in the high-gain classrooms were those ranked highest on the actual inventory (trade books, leveled books, and instructional aids).

The data from the student interviews regarding the text environment were among the most revealing sources we tapped. The mean differences consistently favored the students from the high-gain classrooms over the low-gain classrooms although there were no significant differences between the two groups. Students in the high-gain classrooms were passionate and knowledgeable about the print in their environments. They could verbalize who created the texts, why they were created, who used them, and how. We have come to believe that one of the best insights into the use of the print environment is through discussions with students about that environment.

IMPLICATIONS FOR TEACHING
AND THE ROLE OF THE LITERACY LEADER
IN THE SCHOOL'S PRINT ENVIRONMENT

Because classrooms are unique to their context, there are no templates for a print-rich environment that we can offer. The effective classroom literacy environments we explored in this analysis have certain similarities but they are also as different as the teachers and the students who learn in them. The important similarities are to be found in a set of principled understandings that guide teacher decision making:

- Local texts must be valued and in the foreground of the classroom literacy environment.
- The texts in the classroom must be functionally linked to "inquiry" that is ongoing in the curriculum.
- The texts must be accessible to and supportive of a variety of reading skill levels; children must have access to and be able to locate texts that they can and want to read.
- The teacher is the primary mediator of "how texts work" for the learners; teachers in effective classrooms model and explain to students the ways in which we use texts and the role of texts in our lives.

Rather than a template for the perfect classroom, we need a process to support teachers as they enrich their classroom literacy environment. This process begins with an examination of what is in classrooms. And, it might be the literacy leader who guides that process, concerned not only with the print environments of classrooms, but also that of the school environment, too. We once worked with a new literacy leader who, upon arrival at the school, noticed that there was a scarcity of texts in the school and classroom environments. Together through a partnership (Miller, 2011), we supported teachers in creating the kind of environment that supports literacy development.

First, we invited the teachers to take panoramic pictures of their classrooms, print those images, and bring them to a workshop. At the workshop, we labeled all the text types in their classrooms and talked about the importance of texts in those classrooms. We challenged these teachers to go back into their classrooms and observe the uses of those texts and to talk to their children about the ways in which the texts are valued and used. Each of the participating teachers reported back at faculty meetings about their growing print environment, including their successes and challenges. Additionally, each selected three text types that they would implement in their classrooms across the school year. Many teachers invited their literacy leader into their classrooms to model the creation of locally constructed texts with their students.

Over the course of the school year, we saw not only improvements in the classroom environments, we also saw attitudes of teachers shift from "I can't do that. The fire marshal will yell at me," to "Well, I've learned to be very careful with the selection of what texts I put on my walls and when I put them there. The kids really help me choose." Over the course of that same year, we saw the emergence of public texts in and around the school that marked it as a place where reading and writing was taking place. In essence, the school had become a literate, social environment.

Following our recommendations (for additional guidance see Hoffman & Sailors, 2004, 2008), a literacy leader might decide to use our instrument (or any other available instrument) as a tool to help teachers evaluate their own literacy practices. Teachers can use the instrument by themselves or can employ the assistance of their literacy leader. Taking a systematic and critical approach to one's own practice can be quite revealing. There are many times we wonder ourselves about the rating and quality of our practices had we applied these instruments to our own print environment (of days gone by). For us as teacher educators, our heightened awareness of the importance of print has led to print-rich classrooms when we conduct professional development workshops for teachers, whether or not those workshops center around print environments. This heightened awareness had led us to "see" classrooms through print-rich lenses; teachers and literacy leaders with whom we have worked say the same thing—once you "see" a print-rich classroom, the print becomes the focus in all classrooms.

The school and Ms. Anguiano, the literacy leader described earlier, are not unique. Through a process of self-study, schools and teachers can adopt a social practice perspective that looks deeper than the physical text environment to include an exploration of the uses and understandings (valuing) of texts in the environment. First steps, small stages of change, and the study of these changes will follow. In this way, information (as presented in this chapter) might be transformed into knowledge that enables effective teaching and literacy development through the support of print-rich environments.

ENGAGEMENT ACTIVITIES

1. Reread the case example. How would you respond to Mr. Lopez's classroom if you were the literacy leader? Where would you begin your work with him to improve this aspect of his practices?

2. Select a classroom in a school in which you work. What are the strengths in terms of the print-rich environment in this classroom? What texts are there? Who has created them? What do the children say about the texts? What texts are missing? What suggestions do you have for the teacher as a way of making the classroom more print rich? What is the role of the children in a co-constructed environment?

3. Visit and read the IRA's Standards (2010) for Reading Professionals (*www.reading.org/General/CurrentResearch/Standards.aspx*). These standards clearly spell out what beginning teachers should know and be

able to do. Look at the standards that address the literate environment of the classroom (Standard 5). What other elements are critical to the development of a literate classroom in addition to the print elements? As a literacy leader, how would you assist a beginning teacher in ensuring that his or her classroom meets these standards?

REFERENCES

American Guidance Services (AGS). (2001). *Group reading assessment and diagnostic evaluation (GRADE)*. Circle Pines, MN: Author.

Baker, S. K., Gersten, R., Haager, D., & Dingle, M. (2006). Teaching practice and the reading growth of first-grade English learners: Validation of an observation instrument. *Elementary School Journal, 107,* 199–221.

Barton, D. (1994). *Literacy: An introduction to the ecology of written language.* Oxford, UK: Blackwell.

Barton, D., & Hamilton, M. (1998). *Local literacies: Reading and writing in one community.* New York: Routledge.

Barton, D., & Hamilton, M. (2000). Literacy practices. In D. Barton, M. Hamilton, & R. Ivanic (Eds.), *Situated literacies: Reading and writing in context.* London: Routledge.

Barton, D., Hamilton, M., & Ivanic, R. (Eds.). (2000). *Situated literacies: Reading and writing in context.* London: Routledge.

Brandt, D., & Clinton, K. (2002). Limits of the local: Expanding perspectives on literacy as a social practice. *Journal of Literacy Research, 34,* 337–356.

Brophy, J., & Good, T. (1986). Teacher behavior and student achievement. In M. C. Wittrock (Ed.), *Handbook of research on teaching* (3rd ed.). New York: McMillan.

Cambourne, B. (2000). Observing literacy learning in elementary classrooms: Twenty-nine years of classroom anthropology. *Reading Teacher, 53,* 512–515.

Cole, M., & Scribner, S. (Eds.). (1974). *Culture and thought: A psychological introduction.* New York: Wiley.

Dowhower, S. I., & Beagle, K. G. (1998). The print environment in kindergartens: A study of conventional and holistic teachers and their classrooms in three settings. *Reading Research and Instruction, 37,* 163–190.

Duke, N. K. (2000). 3.6 minutes per day: The scarcity of informational texts in first grade. *Reading Research Quarterly, 35,* 202–224.

Fractor, J. S., Woodruff, M., Martinez, M., & Teale, W. H. (1993). Let's not miss opportunities to promote voluntary reading: Classroom libraries in the elementary school. *Reading Teacher, 46,* 476–484.

Hamilton, M. (2000). Expanding the New Literacy Studies: Using photographs to explore literacy as a social practice. In D. Barton, M. Hamilton, & R. Ivanic (Eds.), *Situating literacy: Reading and writing in context* (pp. 16–34). New York: Routledge.

Hoffman, J. V., Maloch, B., & Sailors, M. (2010). Observations of literacy instruction. In P. D. Pearson, E. Moje, & M. Kamil (Eds.), *Handbook of Reading Research* (4th Edition).

Hoffman, J. V., Roller, C. M., Maloch, B., Sailors, M., Duffy, G. G., Beretvas, S. N., et al. (2005). Teachers' preparation to teach reading and their experiences and practices in the first three years of teaching. *Elementary School Journal, 105*(3), 267–289.

Hoffman, J. V., & Sailors, M. (2002). *Texts Inventory, Texts In-Use and Text Interviews Observation System.* Unpublished manuscript, University of Texas at Austin.

Hoffman, J. V., & Sailors, M. (2004).Studying the literacy environment and literacy practices as the basis for critical reflection and change. In J. V. Hoffman & D. L. Schallert (Eds.). *The role of texts in elementary classrooms* (pp. 191–216). Ann Arbor, MI: Center for the Improvement of Early Reading Achievement.

Hoffman, J. V., & Sailors, M. (2008). Evaluation and change: The role of the literacy specialist in guiding program improvement. In D. Strickland & S. Wepner (Eds.), *The administration and supervision of reading programs* (4th ed., pp. 231–254). New York: Teachers College Press.

Hoffman, J. V., Sailors, M., Duffy, G. G., & Beretvas, S. N. (2004). The effective elementary classroom literacy environment: Examining the validity of the TEX-IN3 Observation System. *Journal of Literacy Research, 36,* 303–334.

International Reading Association. (2010). *Standards for Reading Professionals— Revised 2010.* Newark, DE: Author.

Langer, J. A. (1987). *Language, literacy, and culture: Issues in society and school.* Norwood, NJ: Ablex.

Loughlin, C. E., & Martin, M. D. (1987). *Supporting literacy: Developing effective learning environments.* New York: Teachers College Press.

Maloch, B., Hoffman, J. V., & Patterson, B. (2002). Local texts: Reading and writing "of the classroom." In J. V. Hoffman & D. Schallert (Eds.), *Texts in elementary classrooms.* MI: Center for the Improvement of Early Reading Achievement.

McGill-Franzen, A., Allington, R. L., Yokoi, L., & Brooks, G. (1999). Putting books in the classroom seems necessary but not sufficient. *Journal of Educational Research 93,* 67–74.

Metsala, J. L., Wharton-McDonald, R., Pressley, M. J., Rankin, J., Mistretta, J., & Ettenberger, S. (1997). Effective primary-grades literacy instruction = Balanced literacy instruction. *Reading Teacher, 50,* 518–521.

Miller, C. (2011). Capitalizing on a relationship with a university faculty member to form a successful partnership. In S. B. Wepner & D. Hopkins (Eds.), *Collaborative leadership in action: Partnering for success in schools* (pp. 44–45). New York: Teachers College Press.

Morrow, L. M. (1991). Relationships among physical design of play centers, teachers' emphasis on literacy in play, and children's literacy behaviors during play. In J. Zutell & S. McCormick (Eds.), *Fortieth yearbook of the National Reading Conference: Learner factors/teacher factors: Issues in lit-*

eracy research and instruction (pp. 127–140). Chicago: National Reading Conference.

Morrow, L. M. (1992). The impact of a literature-based program on literacy achievement, use of literature, and attitudes of children from minority backgrounds. *Reading Research Quarterly, 27, 250–275.*

Morrow, L. M., Tracey, D. H., Woo, D. G., & Pressley, M. (1999). Characteristics of exemplary first-grade literacy instruction. *Reading Teacher, 52,* 462–476.

Morrow, L. M., & Weinstein, C. S. (1982). Increasing children's use of literature through program and physical design changes. *Elementary School Journal, 85*(2), 133–137.

Neuman, S. B. (1999). Books make a difference: A study of access to literacy. *Reading Research Quarterly, 34,* 286–311.

Ormerod, F., & Ivanic, R. (2000). Texts in practices: Interpreting the physical characteristics of children's project work. In D. Barton, M. Hamilton, & R. Ivanic. (Eds.), *Situated literacies: Reading and writing in context* (pp. 87–104). London: Routledge.

Pressley, M. J., Rankin, T. & Yokoi, L. (1996). A survey of instructional practices of primary teachers nominated as effective in promoting literacy. *Elementary School Journal, 96,* 363–384.

Reutzel, D. R., Oda, L. K., & Moore, B. H. (1989). Developing print awareness: The effect of three instructional approaches on kindergarteners' print awareness, reading readiness, and word reading. *Journal of Reading Behavior, 21*(3), 197–217.

Ross, S. M., Smith, L. J., Lohr, L., & McNelis, M. (1994). Math and reading instruction in tracked first-grade classes. *Elementary School Journal, 95,* 105–119.

Sailors, M., & Hoffman, J. V. (2010). The text environment and learning to read: Windows and mirrors shaping literate lives. In D. Wyse, R. Andrews, & J. Hoffman (Eds), *The international handbook of English, language and literacy teaching* (pp. 294–304). New York: Taylor Francis.

Searfoss, L. W., & Readence, J. E. (1983). Guiding readers to meaning. *Reading Psychology, 4,* 29–36.

Snow, C. E., Barnes, W. S., Chandler, J., Goodman, I. F., & Hemphill, L. (1991). *Unfulfilled expectations: Home and school influences on literacy.* Cambridge, MA: Harvard University Press.

Stallings, J., Amy, M., Resnick, L. B., & Leinhardt, G. (1975). Implementation and child effects of teaching practices in follow through classrooms. *Monographs of the Society for Research in Child Development, 40,* 1–133.

Taylor, B. M., Pearson, P. D., Clark, K., & Walpole, S. (2000). Effective schools and accomplished teachers. *Elementary School Journal, 101,* 121–165.

Taylor, N. E., Blum, I. H., & Logsdon, D. M. (1986). The development of written language awareness: Environmental aspects and program characteristics. *Reading Research Quarterly, 21,* 132–149.

Tusting, K. (2000). The new literacy studies and time. In D. Barton, M. Hamilton, & R. Ivanic (Eds.), *Situated literacies: Reading and writing in context.* London: Routledge.

Wharton-McDonald, R., Pressley, M., & Hampston, J. M. (1998). Literacy instruction in nine first-grade classrooms: Teacher characteristics and student achievement. *Elementary School Journal, 99,* 101–128.

Wolfersberger, M. E., Reutzel, D. R., Sudweeks, R., & Fawson, P. C. (2004). Developing and validating the classroom literacy environmental profile (CLEP): A tool for examining the "print richness" of early childhood and elementary classrooms. *Journal of Literacy Research, 36,* 211–272.

11

—

Differentiating
Literacy Instruction

HEIDI ANNE E. MESMER
JENNIFER JONES
LAUREN CATHERWOOD
LAURA M. LESTER

Guiding Questions

- Why is differentiated instruction important in K–5 literacy instruction?
- When and how is whole-class and small-group instruction beneficial?
- What are the four guiding principles needed to understand differentiation?

Imagine that you have decided that you would like to learn to play tennis. You buy a racket, go to the local community center, and show up for the first evening of class. You are a beginner but as you walk onto the courts, you get the sneaking suspicion that not everyone is. The class begins with the tennis instructor asking everyone to form one line at the baseline of the tennis court. Taking turns, each person is to return the balls that the tennis instructor hits to him or her. You look around, feeling a little confused. You are a beginner. You don't know how to hold a racket. You are not exactly sure how to swing. Somehow there is a mistake; this is not the right class. The instructor is assuming that you know things, when you do not. But when it is your turn, you walk up to the baseline and swing the best you can. You keep waiting for something to change, but tennis balls just whiz by you as the instructor moves to the next drill. The class content has been determined and you just have to fit it. So you go on attending this class and then trying to muddle through some games. At the end of the session the instructor has a little awards ceremony and presents each of the players with a certificate indicating that they can move up to the next level. When it is your turn to get a certificate, the instructor quietly pulls you aside and says, "I would really like to move you up but there are some things that you just have not gotten right. You are not holding your racket properly and you are not following through in your swing." You are shocked. No one taught you how to hold your racket or swing. How could you learn those things? Deep inside, you feel like a failure. You never want to play tennis again.

This is the case for many students in our schools. They come to school and the curriculum just whizzes by them. They come to school with books and materials in hand, but they aren't told how to use them. They are not exactly sure what is going on. For some students the opposite occurs. They go to the tennis class expecting intermediate instruction that will improve their game and the instructor is telling them how to hold the racket, so to speak. They are simply endlessly rehearsing something that they can already do. For both the student who has mastered the standard curriculum and the student who is not ready for the standard curriculum, the situation is the same—the center of the educational endeavor is the standard curriculum and not the students.

Best educational practices in literacy place the students, not the curriculum, at the center of teaching and learning process (Allan & Tomlinson, 2000). Differentiated instruction is instruction that responds to what students need to know and then connects instruction with students' knowledge. The overarching goal of this chapter is to provide literacy leaders with both the research supporting differentiation as well as pragmatic solutions about how to differentiate. The chapter is divided into two major sections with the first section providing the research support for differentiation and the second section illustrating how this research can be put in place.

LITERATURE SUPPORTING DIFFERENTIATION

There is a rich and diverse research literature that supports differentiated literacy instruction that focuses on the characteristics of effective schools and exemplary teachers (Adler & Fisher, 2001; Hoffman, 1991; Taylor, Pearson, Clark, & Walpole, 1999). From the effective schools literature we have identified four pillars or principles of differentiated instruction: (1) knowledge of literacy development, (2) use of literacy assessments, (3) creation of small groups, and (4) use of classroom models.

Differentiation Is Supported by a Knowledge of Literacy Development

Given the range of abilities in any one classroom and the nature of development, it is simply not reasonable to expect that all elements of the curriculum will apply to everyone, all of the time. Teachers must understand the continuum of literacy development because it helps them understand what their students need and where their students are going. There is a robust line of research that converges upon at least four stages of literacy development—emergent, beginning, transitional, and reading to learn. The emergent stage begins at birth and runs through ages 5 or 6 and is marked by a child's development of oral language, vocabulary, phonological awareness, and print concepts (Chall, 1983; Brown, 2003). Until about age 3 children in the emergent stage are mostly developing their oral language skills. From ages 3 to 6, children are continuously building their oral language and vocabulary, which supports their listening comprehension and their later reading comprehension. Listening comprehension skills also build through exposure to both narrative and expository texts, book discussions, and development of conceptual knowledge. In addition, children are also beginning to recognize print conventions, develop phonological awareness, and may learn some letters, especially those in their name. If children in this stage attempt to recognize words, their strategies are often idiosyncratic and they rely on visual cues such as pictures, word length, or memory (Brown, 2003; Gaskins & Ehri, 1996/1997). By the end of the emergent stage in late kindergarten children have acquired the concepts of print, letter, and phonological awareness knowledge that will support their initial attempts at reading. (See Chapter 7 for more information on emergent literacy.)

In the beginning stage, around age 6, children show an essential understanding of the alphabetic principle—visual symbols represent phonemes that map onto printed words (Chall, 1983). Chall called this stage "glued to the print" because so much effort is devoted to *applying* foundational letter–sound and phonological knowledge to decode words. Using the acquired skills, children access simple spelling patterns such as short vowels, consonant blends, consonant digraphs, and silent *e*. They also learn some of the most frequently occurring words (e.g., *the, at, is, was*; Brown, 2003). After learning how to decode, children move into a transitional stage of reading, around ages 7 to 8 and in this stage "unglue from the print," as the focus on decoding decreases and children begin to build their fluency. Having acquired a more advanced level of decoding, children are able to handle multisyllabic words and consolidate letter units to read words more quickly (e.g., *-ed, -ment, -ly, pre-*). At this stage word recognition becomes more automatic, which allows more attention to be placed on the improvement of comprehension and fluency—accuracy, rate, and expression.

Children from approximately ages 8 and up move into a fourth stage, often called "reading to learn" (Chall, 1983). In this stage children are using reading as a tool to gain new information and lots of it. Up to this point, the focus has been learning to read, and the content has included mostly information and words that children already know but are learning to decode. However, in this stage, word reading becomes fully automatic and children must learn how to extract information from text (Chall, 1983). The main accomplishment during this stage for proficient readers is comprehension development with exposure and engagement with new and known vocabulary and therefore, prior knowledge plays a critical role. It is important to keep in mind that the age ranges associated with stages are general and do not apply to all students; therefore, examining assessment data will help pinpoint the stages of development of students and help predict where they will go next (Brown, 2003). Because students of similar ages move through the reading stages at different times and may perform differently even within the stages, there is a need to differentiate reading instruction.

Differentiation Is Supported by Teachers Who *Use* Assessment Data to Inform Instruction

Effective schools begin differentiation by assessing students' literacy development, and what distinguishes them from ineffective schools is that they *use* the collected data to guide their teaching. In 1971, Weber named *continuous evaluation of pupil progress* as a key factor among successful schools, with Edmonds (1979) gleaning similar findings. Hoffman (1991) highlighted eight attributes of effective schools from the late 1970s and 1980s, with one being *frequent monitoring of student progress.* In their comprehensive study of beating-the-odds schools and classrooms, Taylor and colleagues pinpointed that classroom-based assessments and curriculum-based assessment were systematically utilized three to five times a year in effective schools (Taylor et al., 1999). Cunningham (2006) examined six beating-the-odds schools using the Flour Blocks framework and found the intentional use of data in a systematic way to inform instructional choices. Data were used to establish instructional goals designed to meet students' needs in both reading and writing. Booker, Invernizzi, and McCormick (2007) likewise found that four beating-the-odds schools exhibited greater gains than other schools using the same assessments.

Specifically, schools collect data that provide them with students' reading levels, phonological awareness, fluency, spelling, letter knowledge, or comprehension. Data in these excelling schools determine instructional reading levels, drive small-group instruction, and differentiate whole-class instruction. In one school, various data sources were triangulated to make instructional adjustments throughout the school year as well (Booker et al.,

2007). Results of the assessments were shared to monitor students' progress and to regroup: "These data provided teachers with regular, recurring opportunities to reflect on the validity of their instructional groupings and modify the membership accordingly" (Taylor et al., 1999, p. 33). Teachers and school leaders had "learned to make performance data a useful ally, rather than a cause of constant alarm or frustration" (p. 26).

Differentiation Requires Small, Flexible Instructional Groups

The natural result of assessing students, and discovering that they have different needs, is teaching them in small groups. Although legitimate cautions about tracking and self-esteem have been raised related to ability grouping, the best thing that can be done for children's self-esteem is to teach them to read. The effective school's literature supports data-based, flexible grouping (Booker et al., 2007; Elbaum, Vaughn, Hughes, Moody, & Schumm, 2000; Langler, 2001: Papanastasiou, 2008; Taylor et al., 1999; Taylor, Pressley, & Pearson, 2000). As early as the 1970s, Anderson noted that schools with higher achievement provided students with more reading group time and lower socioeconomic groups benefited the most from small groups (Anderson, 1979). A recent meta-analysis showed that students taught in small groups learned significantly more than students who received whole-class instruction (Elbaum et al., 2000). Cunningham's study (2006) of six beating-the-odds schools noted that struggling readers received some extra small-group instruction, geared toward their specific reading needs. Likewise, in the case studies of high-performing schools, Booker and colleagues gleaned that one school in the study used small-group rotations to meet students' needs, differentiating instruction according to data (Booker et al., 2007).

Effective schools continually reassess their students' needs so that groups are flexible and change based on needs. Taylor et al. (1999) highlighted the importance of flexible grouping and the importance of data guiding decision making along the way. In the Taylor et al. (1999) classrooms, students changed groups on the basis of performance because students learn at different rates. Effective schools and teachers also collaborate to ensure that logistical issues (i.e., scheduling) do not erode flexible grouping because often it is lack of coordination and planning that leads to fragmented instruction and/or ineffective grouping. In their report to the National Education Association, Taylor and colleagues noted that in the majority of schools, tailored, small-group instruction was facilitated by collaboration among teachers (Taylor et al., 2000). In Cunningham's study (2006), collaboration among classroom teachers and resource teachers in the school allowed *extra* small-group instruction to take place. Such collaboration efforts can prove challenging, as professionals must find time to plan together and make collaborative decisions regarding students' progress. Reading teachers, literacy coaches, and reading specialists must compromise and respect the individual expertise of other professionals, interacting with humility and understanding their own expertise and limitations. Challenging as it may be, such collaboration efforts among specialized professionals, such as special education teachers, reading specialists, speech/language pathologists, and/or school psychologists serve as an important part of the solution to the differentiated classroom. Bringing all professionals to the table provides a wealth of expertise and works toward the achievement of all students (Mesmer & Mesmer, 2008). Effective schools thoughtfully use data to efficiently teach small groups of students with similar instructional needs. These schools have procedures to reanalyze data and carefully coordinate small-group content.

Differentiation Requires a Model for Classroom Organization

Teachers most often voice concerns about logistically handling multiple instructional groups asking us, "What do the other children do while I am working with a small group? How can I keep them focused on meaningful, engaging work, while I focus on the needs of one group?" In this section we provide an overview of four different models as a way to illustrate important considerations for organizing the differentiated classroom with meaningful small-group and independent activities (i.e., guided reading, the Daily Five, Four Blocks, word study). These are illustrative only because we cannot begin to enumerate the many different models for literacy instruction and organization. What is important is identifying a model that allows teachers to create flexible groups and students to engage in meaningful work.

Guided reading is small-group instruction organized around students' instructional reading levels (Guastello & Lenz, 2005; Iaquinta, 2006; Schirmer & Schaffer, 2010; Tobin & McInnes, 2008). Prior to guided reading instruction, teachers obtain students' reading levels by taking running records using a set of leveled benchmark passages. Students are then placed in small groups based on their reading levels and teachers choose texts that match the reading levels of small groups. The foundation of guided reading is a collection of leveled books that correspond to the reading assessment system used, such as the Fountas and Pinnell (2006) A–Z Leveling System. In this system, Bill Martin's classic book, *Brown Bear, Brown Bear, What Do You See?* (1983) is considered a level C text, whereas at the other end of the spectrum, Judy Blume's *Superfudge* (1980) is a Q. During small-group guided reading, teachers focus on developing specific reading strategies based on the assigned text level of the group (Fountas & Pinnell, 2006). Unlike traditional reading groups, guided reading groups do not involve round-robin reading. Instead, children receive explicit instruction in word recognition, text structure, fluency, or comprehension and then apply the reading strategies independently (Fisher, 2008). During the majority of the lesson students are reading while the teacher conferences with individuals. The last 5 minutes usually includes group discussion, pointed comprehension questions, and review. Guided reading provides clear information about exactly how to form and run groups.

The Daily Five (Boushey & Moser, 2006) is an increasingly popular organizational scheme for various elements of literacy instruction. The classroom organizational scheme includes five student activities, read to self, read to someone, listen to reading, work on writing, and word work. It is strikingly similar to the Four Blocks plan (self-selected reading, guided reading, writing, and word work; Cunningham, Hall, & Sigmon, 2008). In both of these approaches, students are engaged in four to five activities based on their instructional needs. Self-selected reading or read to self is individualized, independent-level reading. Writing typically follows a writer's workshop model, with teachers presenting minilessons and students writing and conferencing. Guided reading or read to someone are both differentiated instructional times in which teachers are selecting instructional-level materials for small groups and supporting students as they comprehend these materials. Word work in these two models differs somewhat with Four Blocks tending to emphasize whole-class phonics and morphology activities and the Daily Five suggesting small-group phonics and morphology work. Both the Daily Five and Four Blocks divide the literacy block into 30-minute increments and students rotate through activities, with focused whole-class activities offered for specific work. Both models set up clear routines for students and predictable activities in the classroom. Both focus on engaging students in authentic reading and writing. Although these models focus more on organizing the language arts block than differentiation, they provide powerful structures for supporting differentiated small groups with meaningful independent activities for students not working with teachers.

Word study is an approach to teaching phonics, spelling, and vocabulary that organizes students into small groups based on the orthographic features that they need to learn (Bear, Invernizzi, Templeton, & Johnston, 2008; Ganske, 2000; Williams, Phillips-Birdsong, Hufnagel, Hungler, & Lundstrom, 2009). Spelling assessments help teachers identify the stages in which students are functioning beginning at an emergent stage, continuing through letter-name stage, within word pattern, syllables and affixes, and eventually landing in the derivational relations stage. Small-group instruction is then planned around students' needs. The *Words Their Way* curriculum is designed to engage students in word-sorting activities where they can manipulate and examine word patterns as well as read and spell them (Bear et al., 2008). There are many different types of sorts that differentiate word learning for students. Picture sorts may include pictures targeting specific sounds, which force students to focus on the sounds in words. Word sorts include words, which allow students to focus on visually classifying spelling/pattern features used to represent specific sounds. Picture or words may be sorted blindly (the student must determine the category after only *hearing* the words read aloud and therefore must practice remembering the letter–sounds).

Open sorts allows the student to determine his or her own categories after reading all of the provided words. Students may also engage in word hunts, searching in meaningful texts for specified word features, such as long vowel patterns. Advanced sorters even race for speed and accuracy against a teacher or a friend (Ganske, 2000). In *Words Their Way*, Bear et al. (2008) describe a simply organizational scheme for delivering differentiated word study called Seat–Circle–Center. Using this scheme, students rotate through three stations: seat (independent work), circle (work with the teacher), and center (pointed activities with peers). The teacher designs circle and seat work to align with weekly literacy objectives. While some students are engaged in independent work during seat time, other students might work with the teacher on word study and/or small-group reading. Thus, not all stations pertain to word study, but word study might be a central component several times per week in rotation with other literacy activities.

Individually, each of these models offers specific advantages but collectively they highlight important considerations in organizing classrooms for differentiation. Assessments are closely matched to the creation of groups and are the key to creating groups. Clear routines, procedures, and activities are in place to guide both teachers and students as they work in small groups or independently. Independent activities are meaningful, appropriate, and require minimal teacher intervention. It has been our experience that most schools start with a model for instruction and then gradually shape the model to make it their own. Whatever the approach, organizational models are essential for supporting differentiated instruction.

STEPS FOR DIFFERENTIATING INSTRUCTION

We have worked with a number of schools and we found that leaders who provide teachers and staff with specific steps for differentiating instruction are most successful. Figure 11.1 illustrates the four steps in our differentiation cycle. The first step is assessment. Just as a good tennis instructor carefully observes the mechanics of his or her students' forehand, backhand, and serve, the classroom teacher must carefully assess and evaluate his or

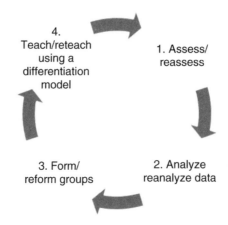

FIGURE 11.1. Four steps of the differentiation cycle.

her students' reading abilities. In our opinion there needs to be at least three points of in-depth diagnostic assessment: (1) beginning of the year, (2) midyear, and (3) end of the year. After the administration of assessments, analysis of the data is required to determine areas in which differentiation should occur and developmentally what the students require. In a tennis class, the instructor carefully analyzes the entire class's skills to determine what skills and strategies may be addressed in a whole-class format, and what skills need more attention in a small-group or individual setting. In the classroom, the teacher uses this step to analyze areas that may be addressed to the whole class and strategies that need more attention, perhaps in small-group settings. The teacher prepares these data to share with additional professionals in the school building for further discussion. During the third step, reading specialists, teachers, literacy coaches, and administrators come together to think about how students should be grouped. These first three steps should be completed as quickly as possible, preferably within the first 3 weeks of school, so that instructional time is not wasted and the bulk of teachers' time is focused on the fourth step, teaching. Although the graphic shows each of these parts of the cycle as equivalent, in fact the first three steps should subsume 5–10% of the school year and instruction should subsume 90% of the cycle. We have very purposefully expressed differentiation as a cycle because schools must have an approach to continually reassess students, reanalyze data, and reorganize groups at *regular intervals* because these activities prevent tracking. As we describe this process we will illustrate its practical application by discussing Linda, a third-grade teacher.

Linda is in her eighth year of teaching and like many teachers, she has become overwhelmed by the many assessment demands placed on her:

> "It's crazy. The first month of school all I do is assess. I give an individually administered state reading screening test to all of my students, a spelling assessment, the Developmental Reading Assessment (DRA), the STAR test, the Otis–Lennon test, and I turn it all in to my principal or the reading supervisor and then, in October, I start teaching. It's just too much."

Linda did not see the assessments that she was giving as being useful, she wasn't sure how to organize and analyze the data, and like many teachers was fed up with crushing assessment mandates. When we observed her third-grade literacy block, we found some instructional activities that were not coordinated with the assessments being given. Student were reading basal selections or novels as a class, completing activities for a spelling program, doing projects, learning comprehension strategies, reading Accelerated Readers books, and participating in writer's workshop. Essentially, most of the instruction was whole class, many of the assessments were redundant, and few informed instruction. What are some of the challenges that Linda faces? How are they similar to challenges that you face? How can she use the data more effectively? Where should Linda begin?

Step 1: Assessment

There are many different types of assessments and all have important but different purposes. All states in the United States have state literacy outcome measures, which are used for accreditation and accountability. Generally, most districts have a literacy screening measure that helps in identifying children who might need interventions. Schools also use assessments for special education and gifted program referrals. The type of assessment that is most critical to differentiation is diagnostic assessment. The purpose of diagnostic assessment is to ascertain what prior knowledge and skills a student possesses so that instructional modifications can be made to meet needs. These formative, diagnostic assessments directly inform what teachers teach.

In Table 11.1 we provide a minimal list of diagnostic information that we believe should be collected at the beginning of each school year in various grade levels. In kindergarten and first grade, the beginning reading years, teachers need to know about children's letter knowledge, phonemic awareness, and concepts of print. In the latter part of each grade, first through

TABLE 11.1. List of Essential Diagnostic Assessments

Grade level	Letters	Phonemic awareness	Concepts of print	Spelling	Reading level	Fluency
Kindergarten	• Names • Sounds	• Initial sounds • Blending sounds	• Finger pointing • Identifying a word	• Sampling a range of orthographic patterns (e.g., beginning consonants, short vowels, consonant clusters)		
First grade	• Names • Sounds	• Initial sounds • Blending sounds • Segmenting sounds	• Finger pointing • Identifying a word	• Sampling a range of orthographic patterns (e.g., beginning consonants, short vowels, consonant clusters)	• (Midyear) Students' instructional reading level	• (midyear) Words correct per minute
Second–Fifth Grades				• Sampling a range of orthographic patterns (e.g., beginning consonants, short vowels, consonant clusters)	• Students' instructional and independent reading levels	• Words correct per minute

fifth, we suggest obtaining a reading level with comprehension questions on every student, both at the independent level (books read without assistance) and at the instructional level (books read with assistance). It is also important to know the level at which each child becomes frustrated (books too difficult to read, even with assistance). Texts at a frustration level should be avoided, as reading growth is not likely to occur at these levels. It defies imagination that anyone could properly teach reading without knowing the reading levels of their students. Lastly, we suggest obtaining an estimate of a student's fluency in words correct per minute. Such a fluency measure can be easily compared to national norms to inform teachers about the need for fluency instruction. We recommend that all students K–5 be given a spelling inventory because they provide a wealth of information about which orthographic patterns students know (e.g., short vowels, digraphs, inflected endings). Given the vast differences in vocabulary knowledge that children enter school with, we are strong proponents of strong vocabulary instruction and assessment. However, because childrens' vocabulary can number in the thousands and because there are no diagnostic vocabulary instruments of which we know, we are unable to recommend a vocabulary assessment (Pearson, Hiebert, & Kamil, 2007). We suggest that prior to large units of reading, science, or social science instruction, teachers pretest vocabulary to ascertain words from the unit that their students already know. In our opinion each of these assessments should be administered at the beginning of the year within the first 3 weeks of school. Figure 11.2 provides a tool to examine assessments being used in your school and at each grade level. Building leaders may choose to use Figure 11.2 to gain an overall view of the assessments being used and the component of literacy each assessment addresses, as well as the frequency of use for each assessment. Having all of this information visible in one place may bring to light issues surrounding assessments being used in a single school. For example, it may become evident that some components of reading are not being measured at all, whereas others are being assessed in a redundant way. In such cases, adjustments should be made.

As we applied this part of the process to Linda and her school, it became clear that there were both missing assessments and redundant assessments. Teachers were being asked to assess students' reading levels using three different measures. The statewide literacy screening in third grade actually took the form of an informal reading inventory and provided teachers with whole-grade estimates of students' reading levels. In addition to this reading-level measure, teachers were also using the DRA, which provided estimated reading levels in an alphabetical system (e.g., A, B, C) , and the STAR test, which provided a reading level in grades and months (e.g., 3.4, 3.6). No fluency measures were being administered. Linda's school decided to include a simple fluency measure with words correct per minute and a

FIGURE 11.2. Building level assessment summary.

Assessments at a Glance

Grade Level	Assessment Name	Frequency of Use	Component of Literacy/Instructional Connection						
			Spelling	Phonemic Awareness	Alphabet Knowledge	Decoding	Fluency	Comprehension	Other

prosody rating. They also decided to drop the DRA because they did not use that leveling system to select books for students and it was duplicating the required state assessment.

In surveying the assessments used by grade levels within your school, consider:

- Are the assessments being used at specific grade levels consistent with the components of literacy that are most critical at this stage of reading development?
- Is there evidence of redundancy across assessments used at each grade level for any of the components of literacy?
- How often are assessments administered? What does this frequency indicate about how the assessment is used to inform instruction?
- Are assessments in place, in appropriate grade levels, to determine students' functional reading levels?

Step 2: Analyzing Data

In our experience, we find that much data is being collected and much data is being entered into databases or recorded on sheets *but then never accessed again*. One of the most difficult parts of analyzing assessment data is that teachers have so many different pieces of data and no approach for handling all the pieces. In a series of professional development grants we have worked closely with teachers to help them *use* data and present a three-part procedure based on that work. We call the process SDB for *same, different, bring it together*.

Before beginning the SDB process, teachers must have organized summaries of their students' assessment data in each separate area that they assessed. For each of the areas listed in Table 11.1 (e.g., fluency, phonemic awareness, reading level) teachers should have a summary sheet of the data. A summary sheet is simply a printout, table, graph, or worksheet that shows all student scores on a given measure. In our experience most diagnostic literacy tests provide a form for teachers to organize their entire classes' scores. For instance, the elementary spelling inventory provides a summary that rank orders students' scores and charts the orthographic patterns that students have mastered. As an example, a second-grade teacher should have a summary for student reading levels, spelling development, and fluency scores.

In the first part of the procedure teachers analyze data to find the areas in which their students are the *same* and in the second part they look for the areas in which their students are *different*. At the same step of SDB, teachers review each of the summary tables to identify content that just about all of their students know or just about all of their students do not know.

Interestingly this first step is really directed at identifying areas in which differentiation is *not* needed. In other words, to suggest that a teacher must be delivering fully differentiated instruction all day long to 20 or more students in a class, as implied in some articles and book chapters, is not realistic. This is both unnecessary and logistically impossible and any pragmatic discussion about how to differentiate instruction must clarify when whole-class literacy instruction *is* appropriate. So, we ask teachers to list areas in which all children might need help. A third-grade teacher might notice that none of her students are reading at a sixth-grade level, but that their vocabulary and listening comprehension would benefit from listening to read-alouds of books at the fifth-grade level.

At the different step of SDB, teachers are looking at each of their assessment summaries with a focus on how the students differ in a particular area. Although the explicit purpose of this step is not forming groups, teachers are analyzing with an eye toward the areas in which students would require differentiated instruction in small groups. The key at this step is to look at the content areas where students differ and the magnitude of the differences. For example, a third-grade teacher inspecting a Qualitative Spelling Inventory might find that most of his or her students are in the within-word pattern stage but differ in the orthographic patterns with which they need instruction. Some students might need help with long vowel patterns (e.g. *ai/ay/eigh*), whereas others might need help with *r*-controlled patterns (e.g., *or, ar, ur/ir/er*), and others with diphthongs (e.g., *oi, ow*). In other situations a teacher may find that students differ a great deal. For instance, a third-grade teacher might have students who are reading at a first-grade level and students reading at a fifth-grade level. It is helpful for teachers to make a list of the areas that fall into the same and different steps of the SDB process before moving on to the last step, bring it together.

The last step of SDB is for teachers to bring it together, and this is the most difficult step because it requires integration of data and synthesis. However, if teachers invest the time to organize all their data and think about what their students need, they simply fly through the process of creating groups. To bring the data together, teachers must prioritize one assessment or piece of data that will be the basis for creating groups. This prioritized measure will be listed first on a summary sheet and the students' names listed in order from lowest scores to highest based on this prioritized score. In the case of our example, students' names are listed according to their instructional reading levels, starting with the lowest instructional level, preprimer, and ending at the highest level, fifth grade. In second through fifth grades we recommend that either a spelling assessment or reading-level measure be used and in kindergarten and first grade (beginning of year) letter knowledge or spelling be used. We recommend prioritizing spelling or reading-level assessments because students who read at a similar level will be doing word study at a similar level and vice versa. We believe that the best use of fluency data is to support reading level and spelling data. For instance, a student who is not showing the ability to accurately represent patterns in multisyllabic words might show a lack of fluency relative to his or her peers. We also suggest some kind of color coding to allow for a quick visual "picture" of the data.

As you walk through the SDB process consider the following guiding questions:

- Have I color coded student data to help provide a quick visual of the students' performance?
- In what components of literacy, such as alphabet knowledge, phonemic awareness, fluency, word knowledge/decoding, fluency, or comprehension are my students the same?
  - Plan to implement whole-class instruction in these areas.
- In what components of literacy do students' scores differ most?
- Within the differing components are there specific needs?
  - Plan to deliver small-group instruction in these areas.

Step 3: Grouping

After assessment data have been collected, organized, and analyzed some of the most difficult work has been done, but we always caution people not to rush through forming their instructional groups. In an ideal world, teachers would look at their data, identify the groups of students who need similar instruction, and form groups based upon that solely. However, the number of groups that a teacher creates will be influenced by other factors such as the time available for group work, the organizational model being used (e.g., guided reading, word study), the classroom environment, and the independence of the students. There is always some tension among the number of groups that the data suggest and the number of groups a teacher can handle and the time available. For example, the data might show that students seem to cluster into five different instructional groups, but the teacher does not have the requisite time to meet with five groups or does not feel comfortable meeting with five groups. We recommend that first-year teachers or those not experienced with grouping start with three groups until they feel comfortable with management. If classroom management is lost, then no instruction will take place for students. We also recommend that the highest-need students be placed in smaller groups. An additional consideration in identifying the number of groups to create is the independence of students. If, for instance, a teacher must stop in between meeting with small groups to refocus the class, answer questions, or provide directions, then not as many groups can be created. Similarly, if a teacher has a 1½-hour language arts block, as opposed to a 2-hour language arts block, then he or she cannot meet with as many small groups.

Table 11.2 provides an example of Linda's third-grade data organized by instructional reading level (far left column). In addition, the students' fluency (words correct per minute), STAR reading level, and DSA score (Developmental Spelling Assessment) are included. After doing the SDB process, Linda and her teammates were relieved to have their data organized and useful. They decided to organize their groups by reading level based on the state assessment because this assessment is also used for literacy screening, but they liked having a closer estimate of reading level provided by the STAR test. The color coding represents the guided reading groups that were formed with comments indicating students who receive additional support or enrichment. The students coded with the darker gray shading are students who are in most need of support and who receive additional one-on-one tutoring. The students with the lighter gray shading receive additional classroom support and those without any shading are meeting grade-level expectations. Linda appreciated having all the data on one sheet and felt like it was being put to use: "Before, I felt like I had been working like a dog to get all these assessments, but after using this process, I felt like *the data were working for me.*"

When forming small groups for targeted instruction, we suggest teachers consider the following questions:

- Are there specific needs in regard to the components of literacy among specific students? For example, is it feasible to form small groups to specifically work on fluency skills? Decoding? Comprehension?
- Also consider, is it feasible to form small groups according to students' functional reading levels?
  - Further, what levels of texts will I need for reading instruction? Social studies? Science? For example, will I need to have materials on two to three different grade levels available for students?

Step 4: Teaching

After small groups have been formed, planning for instruction for each small group takes precedence. In planning the instruction for small groups, it is important to set goals and determine learning objectives focusing on the types of instruction most suited to helping students achieve the learning objectives. Before setting objectives for small-group instruction, we recommend taking a step back to examine the students in each group. Collectively, determine the strengths of the group in the areas you will be addressing. Then, determine what aspect of this component needs targeted attention. List these in the first two columns of Figure 11.3, which has been adapted

TABLE 11.2. Sample Assessment Summary for Third Grade.

Instructional reading level	First name	Fluency	DSA spelling	STAR reading level
PP	Tendra	15	1.05	0.50
1	Anita	24	2.05	1.00
1	Rachel	30	2.70	1.20
1	Kwuan	22	3.11	1.20
1	Jarrett	32	2.15	1.30
1	Josiah	25	2.15	1.50
1	Dale	27	2.15	1.50
1	Tiffany	27	3.06	1.70
2	Emilia	64	3.07	2.00
2	Taylor	64	3.12	2.10
2	Jon	68	3.12	2.10
2	Heather	59	3.09	2.20
2	Kaitlyn	63	3.11	2.00
2	Darrel	75	3.13	2.40
2	Letisha	76	3.14	2.40
2	Michael	80	3.10	2.60
2	Jesus	79	3.09	2.60
3	Maria	79	3.09	3.10
3	Cal	83	4.02	3.10
3	Emily	84	3.17	3.20
3	Jacobe	87	3.16	3.20
3	Britany	79	3.16	3.30
3	Leandra	101	3.15	3.40
4	Tom	112	4.11	4.50
4	Divonta	120	4.08	4.50
4	Hunter	128	4.05	4.80
5	Stephanie	152	4.16	5.70

from the one used at the McGuffey Reading Center at University of Virginia. In completing this first step, teachers will enhance instruction by building upon students' strengths and targeting areas in their zone of proximal development. For example, a group needing fluency instruction may be strong in their sight-word knowledge and automaticity; however, they may need to

Grading Period: _____	Group: _____
Strengths	**Targeted Instruction**

Objectives for the Grading Period	Instructional Strategies	Evaluation
		Weekly: • Measure to be used: _____ • Performance: _____ Grading Period: • Measure to be used: _____ • Performance: _____

FIGURE 11.3. Planning for instruction.

improve reading rates and/or reading prosody. At this point in the planning process, the following questions serve as helpful guides:

- What aspects of this reading component (e.g., fluency, word study, comprehension) seem to be strongest for this group of students? Be specific.
- What aspects of this reading component need instruction? Be specific.

Using the strengths and targets for instruction for the group, determine objectives for each group. We recommend writing objectives that can be achieved within the framework of a grading period, which is usually 6 to 9 weeks. One to two objectives are suitable for targeted instruction within a grading period. For example, the group needing targeted instruction for reading rate might have an instructional objective stating, "The students will read with increased speed and accuracy in third-grade-level texts, both fiction and expository." Not only is it important to include the learning objective, but also the level and types of texts. Of course, daily instructional objectives should also be used, but for these purposes, we address grading period objectives as a mode of goal setting and planning overall group instruction. After completing the instructional objectives, reflect and consider:

- Do the objectives for this grading period tie directly to the targeted area of instruction?
- Is it reasonable to expect that the stated objective(s) can be achieved in one grading period?
- Do the stated objectives include the text levels and genres?

Next, list four to five instructional strategies that the teacher will employ to help students achieve the stated objective(s). The teacher must take care that the instructional techniques included in this column match directly with the stated objective. For example, including sight-word games on the list of instructional strategies for improving reading rates would not be appropriate. Instead, instructional techniques such as timed repeated readings would be more suitable for an objective focused on reading rate. After completing the objectives and instructional strategies portion of the planning guide, it is important to consider:

- Do the instructional techniques and strategies directly relate to the instructional objective? *If there is any mismatch, work to revise and connect the objectives and instructional strategies.*
- Reflecting upon the objectives and the instructional techniques chosen, what materials will be needed for the grading period?

Finally, in order to differentiate effectively, ongoing assessment must take place and we suggest that teachers identify a short, quick measure that they will use on a weekly basis to evaluate progress. This (re)assessment begins our four-page cycle again as teachers reassess, reanalyze, and reteach or move on to new teaching. The reassessment is what prevents small groups from becoming entrenched in tracks. To identify the appropriate assessments for the group reflect upon the objectives and revisit the assessment summary (see Table 11.1). Use available assessments or create simple assessments that match the instruction in the group. For example, to measure an objective focusing on increasing reading rate, an assessment that involves calculation of reading rate will be needed. To address an objective focused on long vowel consonant–vowel–consonant+e (CVCe) patterns, a measure that requires students to spell and/or read CVCe patterns is called for. After an assessment has been selected, determine the level of performance at which the stated objective would be met. How well will the students need to perform in order to have successfully achieved the stated objective? At this phase in the planning for instruction process, ask:

- What assessment tools are available for this component of literacy?
  - Does the assessment reflect the specific areas for targeted instruction focused upon during the grading period?
- What assessment will I use to measure the specific stated objective?
- Can the measure be administered on a weekly basis and in a timely manner?
- Do I have a system in place to record students' progress over the 6- to 9-week grading period?
- What level of performance on this assessment is expected for students to successfully meet the objective?
- Is the system considerate of teacher time and easily accessible?

As teachers are working with small groups and collecting weekly assessments we also suggest that they meet with other teachers, reading specialists, or special educators on their team for a weekly grade-level team assessment meeting. We cannot state too emphatically the importance of this weekly meeting because it is this meeting that structures the continual review of data and the recycling of the differentiation cycle. During this meeting teachers share the results of their small-group assessments with their colleagues and discuss how students in small groups are meeting the objectives of the group. If most students begin to exhibit progress during the small-group instruction, then it is having desired effects. Sometimes adjustments are needed to make sure that everyone is moving forward. If most students respond to the adjusted instruction, but one student does not, then it might be that a student actually needs a different group to better meet his or her needs. Obviously, there are various degrees of action, and data and instruction need to be taken into careful consideration when making such decisions. The result of this process is that at the end of a 9-week period, 6–9 data points are available for decision making about whether or not to move a child to a different group, intensify instruction, or request additional individual formal testing, perhaps by the school's reading specialist. The key is that data are being used to guide instruction in a systematic way, which saves time as well as frustration on the part of the teacher and the students.

Linda, our third-grade teacher, explained:

> "When we first started doing the weekly grade-level team meeting, I rolled my eyes. Here we go again, I thought, another hoop to jump through and another piece of paper. But I have to say that those conversations were really helpful. I had to make sure that I had my assessments done and I sometimes had to look a little more carefully at students in groups. I remember with one student I had drawn the conclusion, based

on what I thought was off-task behavior, that the student wasn't learning, but my assessment showed him to be acing the instruction. I think that I moved him to another group after about 4 weeks."

Linda also explained that she felt that the process really helped the newer teachers on the team, who benefited from hearing the analyses that the more experienced teachers offered.

In sum, as planning for instruction takes place, teachers along with other key personnel (e.g., reading specialist/literacy coach, special educators) should visualize a threaded process in place. The process begins with noting strengths within a group and then moves into areas in which targeted instruction is needed. As instructional goals and objectives are created, strengths should be built upon and areas for targeted instruction focused upon. Objectives are written for the grading period and should ideally include text levels and/or genres. Instructional strategies should mirror the stated objectives. Listing instructional strategies helps with planning, ultimately saving time. Finally, evaluation of the objective(s) must take place. Measures for weekly progress monitoring, as well as for the grading period, should be in place to determine whether students have met the stated objectives. Weekly progress monitoring allows for instructional adjustment, as well as a way to collect data points for each child, one a week. If students do not respond to adjusted instruction, evidence is present to consider alternatives to better meet the needs of the child. Each step in the planning process threads into the next, ultimately providing a clear plan that is data driven, founded in best practice, and evaluated through assessment.

ENGAGEMENT ACTIVITIES

1. Examine the sample assessment summary (see Table 11.2) for Linda's third-grade class. Construct instructional plans for each group in her classroom. Use the questions within this chapter to guide yourself through the process. For example, what strengths and areas of targeted instruction are evident among the data? For one grading period, name your objectives for each group and instructional strategies you would use to achieve these goals. Discuss how you will measure your objectives with assessments already found in your building.

2. Considering the instructional needs and your instructional plans for each group of students, how would you manage instruction in Linda's classroom? Discuss when and how you would conduct whole-class instruction, as well as small-group instruction.

3. Engage in a Diagnostic Assessment Audit at your school, grade level, or classroom. Use Figure 11.2 to evaluate the assessments being used and ask yourself:

   a. Is there evidence of redundancy across assessments used at each grade level for any of the components of literacy?

   b. How often are assessments administered? What does this indicate about how the assessment is used to inform instruction?

   c. Are assessments in place, in appropriate grade levels, to determine students' functional reading levels?

4. By engaging in data-driven instruction, Linda's students will progress at different times and at different rates. What system or methods would you use to alter your reading groups based on weekly assessments to ensure flexible grouping?

REFERENCES

Adler, M. A., & Fisher, C. W. (2001). Early reading programs in high-poverty schools: A case study of beating the odds. *Reading Teacher, 54*(6), 616–619.

Allan, S. D., & Tomlinson, C. A. (2000). *Leadership for differentiating schools and classrooms.* Alexandria, VA: Association for Supervision and Curriculum Development.

Bear, D., Invernizzi, M., Templeton, S., & Johnston, F. (2008). *Words their way: Word study for phonics, vocabulary, and spelling instruction* (4th ed.). Upper Saddle River, NJ: Pearson.

Blume, J. (1980). *Superfudge.* New York: Dutton.

Booker, K. C., Invernizzi, M. A., & McCormick, M. (2007). "Kiss your brain": A closer look at flourishing literacy gains in impoverished elementary schools. *Reading Research and Instruction, 46*(4), 315–339.

Boushey, G., & Moser, J. (2006). *The daily five: Fostering independence in the elementary grades.* Portland, ME: Stenhouse.

Brown, K. J. (2003). What do I say when they get stuck on a word? Aligning teachers' prompts with students' development. *Reading Teacher, 56*(8), 222–243.

Chall, J. S. (1983). *Stages of reading development.* New York: McGraw-Hill.

Cunningham, J. S., Hall, D. P., & Sigmon, C. M. (2008). *Teachers guide to the Four Blocks Literacy Model.* Greensboro, NC: Carson-Dellosa.

Cunningham, P. M. (2006). High-poverty schools that beat the odds. *Reading Teacher, 60*(4), 382–385.

Edmonds, R. (1979). Effective schools for the urban poor. *Educational Leadership, 37*(1), 15. Retrieved [DATE] from EBSCO*host*.

Elbaum, B., Vaughn, S., Hughes, M., Moody, S. W., & Schumm, J. S. (2000). How reading outcomes of students with disabilities are related to instructional grouping formats: A meta-analytic review. In R. Gersten, E. Schiller, & S. Vaughn (Eds.), *Contemporary special education research* (pp. 105–135). Mahwah, NJ: Erlbaum.

Fisher, A. (2008). Teaching comprehension and critical literacy: Investigating guided reading in three primary classrooms. *Literacy, 42*(1), 19–28.

Fountas, I., & Pinnell, G. S. (2006). *The Fountas and Pinnell leveled book list, K–8 2006–2008 Edition.* Portsmouth, NH: Heinemann.

Ganske, K. (2000). *Word journeys: Assessment-guided phonics, spelling, and vocabulary instruction.* New York: Guilford Press.

Gaskins, I. W., & Ehri, L. C. (1996/1997). Procedures for word learning: Making discoveries about words. *Reading Teacher, 50*(4), 312–328.

Guastello, F. E., & Lenz, C. (2005). Student accountability: Guided reading kidstations. *Reading Teacher, 59*(2), 144–156.

Hoffman, J. V. (1991). Teacher and school effects in learning to read. In R. Barr, M. L. Kamil, P. B. Mosenthal, & P. D. Pearson (Eds). *Handbook of reading research, vol. 2* (pp. 911–950). New York: Longman.

Iaquinta, A. (2006). Guiding reading: A research-based response to the challenges of early reading instruction. *Early Childhood Education, 33*(6), 413–418.

Langler, J. A. (2001). Beating the odds: Teaching middle and high school students to read and write well. *American Educational Research Journal, 38*(4), 837–880.

Martin, B. (1983). *Brown bear, brown bear, what do you see?* New York: Holt, Rinehart, and Winston.

Mesmer, E. M., & Mesmer, H. E. (2008). Response to intervention (RTI): What teachers of reading need to know. *Reading Teacher, 62*(4), 280–289, Retrieved [DATE] from EBSCO*host*.

Papanastasiou, C. (2008). Factors distinguishing most and least effective schools in terms of reading achievement: A residual approach. *Educational Research and Evaluation, 14*(6), 539–549.

Pearson, P. D., Hiebert, E. H., & Kamil, M. L. (2007). Vocabulary assessment: What we know and what we need to know. *Reading Research Quarterly, 42,* 282–296.

Schirmer, B., & Schaffer, L. (2010). Guiding reading approach. *Teach Exceptional Children, 42*(5), 52–58.

Taylor, B. M., Pearson, P. D., Clark, K. F., & Walpole, S. (1999). *Beating the odds in teaching all children to read.* Ann Arbor, MI: Center for the Improvement of Early Reading Achievement.

Taylor, B. M., Pressley, M., & Pearson, D. (2000). *Effective teachers and schools: Trends across recent studies.* Ann Arbor, MI: Center for the Improvement of Early Reading Achievement.

Tobin, R., & McInnes, A. (2008). Accommodating differences: Variations in differentiated literacy instruction in grade 2/3 classrooms. *Literacy, 42*(1), 3–9.

Williams, C., Phillips-Birdsong, C., Hufnagel, K., Hungler, D., & Lundstrom, R. (2009). Word study instruction in the K–2 classroom. *Reading Teacher, 62*(7), 570–578.

12

Culturally Responsive Literacy Instruction

ALLISON SKERRETT
AFRA AHMED HERSI

Guiding Questions

- What are the cultural and linguistic resources and literacy practices that students bring to the classroom?
- What are the curricula, instructional, and assessment practices that link these resources to literacy learning in school?
- What are the implications of this research for literacy educators who work with culturally and linguistically diverse students?

Our goals in this chapter are to present current research on how the cultural and linguistic resources that diverse students bring to school can be used for literacy teaching and learning, and for developing and implementing the curriculum, instructional approaches, and assessment practices that facilitate culturally responsive literacy instruction. All literacy leaders, including classroom teachers, principals, reading specialists, and special educators can add this knowledge to what they are continuously learning with and from their students.

Many of today's classrooms can be described as culturally and linguistically complex classrooms (CLCCs; Ball, 2009) in which students from two or more cultural or linguistic groups receive literacy instruction in English. The students in these classrooms, and their learning needs, certainly represent great complexity. There are students who are second-language learners, students who speak several varieties of one or more languages, and learners

230

who represent an array of cultural backgrounds (Ball, Skerrett, & Martínez, 2010). The pervasiveness of CLCCs has created an unprecedented urgency to respond to the literacy learning needs of students in these classrooms. One indicator of this strong emphasis on culturally responsive literacy instruction is the International Reading Association's (IRA) revised *Standards for Reading Professionals* (International Reading Association, 2010) to which a new and distinct Diversity Standard has been added. This standard calls for teachers to draw out and capitalize on the productive relationships between diversity and literacy teaching and learning.

In constantly evolving CLCCs, where the particularities of student demographics and attendant learning needs are always in flux, we question what "best practices" of culturally responsive literacy instruction might mean. Rather than a static set of strategies or approaches, teachers today need to draw on key research, theory, and practice-based principles to provide a dynamic form of culturally responsive literacy instruction. Ball (2009) wrote of teachers' generativity in CLCCs. By this she meant that teachers combine their knowledge of theory, best practices, and their daily work with their diverse populations to facilitate their own theorizing and generative thinking about how to approach teaching in CLCCs. We present the case example of Susan, a reading specialist in a culturally and linguistically diverse school, who struggles with her school's approach to addressing the needs of culturally and linguistically diverse students.

Case Example

Susan, a second-grade teacher with 4 years of experience, finished her course work for her reading specialist certification and applied for a reading specialist position in her district. After a 3-week-long summer training hosted by her large suburban school district, Susan was assigned back to her (K–8) school—one of the district's most culturally and linguistically diverse and lowest-performing schools. As Susan was well aware, this school and its surrounding community had experienced significant demographic changes as more middle class African American and recent immigrant families from East Asia, East and West Africa, and Latin America settled into the community. While the school had a cadre of experienced teachers who had worked at the school for more than 5 years, most of them were white and middle class and did not have prior experience teaching diverse populations. In a series of meetings before the school year began, the administration and literacy team pledged to implement culturally responsive literacy practices within the school. While completely supportive of the initiative, Susan was concerned about implementation and whether or not the literacy leadership team was prepared. What should they, as a team, know about culturally responsive curricula, pedagogy, and assessment practices? How can they help their largely white, middle-class teachers gain the knowledge and skills necessary to successfully implement these practices? How can she support teachers and students to teach and learn effectively in a diverse learning environment?

In the remainder of the chapter, we present research addressing the following major topics related to literacy instruction in CLCCs: culturally responsive curriculum materials; instructional practices related to language use; learning activities that involve social justice inquiry; instructional practices related to technology and multimodality; and, assessment practices that attend to cultural and linguistic diversity, including professional development support for teachers. We highlight practical implications, links to the case study, and suggestions for further reading. In so doing, we seek to support literacy leaders' efforts to implement successful strategies for meeting the literacy needs of culturally and linguistically diverse learners.

WHAT WE KNOW ABOUT CLCCs

Students in CLCCs bring rich resources and repertoires of practice to their classrooms that can facilitate literacy teaching and learning. Their linguistic repertoires include bilingualism and multilingualism that allow them to serve as translators and language brokers for family and community members. They possess knowledge of, and abilities to use, language varieties such as African American Vernacular English (AAVE) and Spanish–English mixing (Spanglish) and they code switch among formal and informal language registers (Cooks & Ball, 2008; Lee, 2006; Martínez, 2010). These students' cultural heritages, membership in transnational communities, and the local communities in which they live afford complex understandings of, and experiences with, diversity and its attendant benefits and challenges (Martínez-Roldán & Fránquiz, 2008; Hersi, 2005, in press). Students acquire in-depth knowledge of, and facility with, an array of social practices for navigating the social, economic, and geographic landscapes of their communities (Martínez-Roldán & Fránquiz; Hersi, in press). Research has shown how these linguistic and cultural resources and repertoires of practice can be drawn upon for literacy teaching and learning, thereby providing a culturally responsive literacy instruction.

Culturally Responsive Curriculum Materials

Research findings encourage teachers to use literature and popular culture materials that represent the cultural and linguistic experiences of their diverse students (Becker, 2001; Lee, 2006, 2007). In a longitudinal curriculum project, Lee studied how students' local cultural knowledge and cultural artifacts such as rap lyrics could be used to facilitate teaching and learning the English language arts. She called this approach *cultural modeling*, which she defined as "a framework for the design of curriculum and learning environments that links everyday knowledge with learning academic subject matter, with a particular focus on racial/ethnic minority groups, especially youth of African descent" (2006, p. 308). Other research supports the use of popular culture materials such as trade books, magazines, movies, TV shows, music, tagging and graffiti art, and other materials from students' community and cultural backgrounds as curriculum materials (Becker, 2001; Duncan-Andrade & Morrell, 2005; Fisher, 2005; Weinstein, 2007). For example, Duncan-Andrade and Morrell showed how hip-hop music and popular films can be used to teach critical analysis skills as well as to teach other academic knowledge and skills called for in state and national standards. Fisher examined how using spoken-word poetry, a literacy practice in African American students' communities, in two language arts classrooms expanded the writing practices of teachers and students beyond writing and into speaking and performing. Weinstein organized her teaching of poetry around her students' extensive writing and performance of rap. She identified important links between students' cultural knowledge and practices in this area and aspects of poetry that she needed to teach. For instance, she noted the uses of allusion and intertextuality in students' rap compositions and the poetry used in the formal curriculum. The research is clear that using culturally responsive curriculum materials signals appreciation of students' home dialects and cultural resources and facilitates links between school literacy tasks and students' everyday literacy knowledge and practice.

Implications

• Provide students with multiple opportunities to see materials and activities that represent their experiences in the literacy curriculum. Literacy leaders like Susan, the reading specialist in our case study, can begin by working with teachers to examine their existing official curriculum to identify what materials and learning activities already accurately reflect the cultural and linguistic experiences of their students and what other kinds of materials might be needed.

• Teachers and other literacy leaders can learn about the home and community language and literacy resources that students bring to school. For instance, at the beginning of the school year, students can conduct ethnographic inquiries of the language and literacy practices in their homes and their communities. The knowledge generated by such learning activities could be used to develop curriculum units that reflect students' cultural and linguistic knowledge and practices.

• Teachers can also identify the knowledge and skills within the official curriculum that students need to acquire and think together about how the resources for learning that their students already possess can be used to scaffold their acquisition of these knowledge and skills. For example, teachers could begin teaching literary analysis skills by using students' interpretations of rap lyrics or popular TV shows that require similar analysis processes and then move students into studying official curriculum texts.

• Literacy leaders like Susan should provide teachers with support, guidance, and models of curriculum and instructional practices that respond to students' language and culture in a variety of ways. Susan may not have the specific knowledge to work with English language learners, but she can seek outside support from her district's bilingual coordinator as a start. If she is to serve as a resource for teachers, she should do some reading about current research on culturally and linguistically responsive teaching. Working with her administrator, Susan can form a study group with other teachers in order to learn more about how to plan and implement a culturally and linguistically responsive curriculum. In Figure 12.1, we provide a list of resources that provide additional information about culturally responsive curriculum.

Instructional Practices Related to Language Use

Using Language Dialects and Code Switching in Speaking, Reading, and Writing

Using language dialects and code switching in speaking, reading, and writing promotes students' acquisition of Standard English (SE) and academic literacy while maintaining and enhancing their linguistic and cultural identities (Cooks & Ball, 2008; Godley & Minnici, 2008; Greene & Walker, 2004; Herrero, 2006; Hill, 2009; Lee, 2006; Martínez, Orellana, Pacheco, & Carbone, 2008; Martínez-Roldán & Sayer, 2006; Sealey-Ruiz, 2007; Wheeler & Swords, 2010). In their review of the literature on AAVE and adolescents' literacy learning, Cooks and Ball reported that teachers' positive attitudes toward students' use of AAVE in the classroom encouraged students' positive identities and self-concepts related to AAVE use and supported their school achievement. Lee (2006) also found that sanctioning students' use of AAVE in classroom talk encouraged high levels of engagement and participation that supported their learning. She found that students' reasoning was highest when they dominated classroom talk. Lee showed that as teachers and students used AAVE in instructional talk about curriculum texts that

Further Readings on Culturally Responsive Curriculum

Lee, C. D. (2007). *Culture, literacy, and learning: Blooming in the midst of the whirlwind.* New York: Teachers College Press.

Marshall, E., Staples, J., & Gibson, S. (2009). Ghetto fabulous: Reading black adolescent femininity in contemporary urban street fiction. *Journal of Adolescent and Adult Literacy, 53*(1), 28–36.

Stevens, L. P. (2001). South Park and society: Instructional and curricular implications of popular culture in the classroom. *Journal of Adolescent and Adult Literacy, 44*(6), 548–555.

Further Readings on Instructional Practices Related to Language Use

Martínez, R. A. (2010). Spanglish as literacy tool: Toward an understanding of the potential role of Spanish–English code-switching in the development of academic literacy. *Research in the Teaching of English, 45*(2), 124–149.

Rickford, J. R. (1999). *African American vernacular English: Features and use, evolution, and educational implications.* Oxford, UK: Blackwell.

Further Readings on Conducting Social Justice Inquiry

Bomer, R., & Bomer, K. (2001). *For a better world: Reading and writing for social action.* Portsmouth, NH: Heinemann.

Pescatore, C. (2008). Current events as empowering literacy: For English and social studies teachers. *Journal of Adolescent and Adult Literacy, 51*(4), 336–339.

Rogers, R., & Mosley, M. (2006). Racial literacy in a second grade classroom: Critical race theory, whiteness studies, and literacy research. *Reading Research Quarterly 41,* 462–495.

Further Readings on Integrating Technology and Multimodality

Black, R. W. (2009). English-language learners, fan communities, and 21st century skills. *Journal of Adolescent and Adult Literacy, 52*(8), 688–697.

Long, T. W. (2008). The full circling process: Leaping into the ethics of history using critical visual literacy and arts-based activism. *Journal of Adolescent and Adult Literacy, 51*(6), 498–508.

Richardson, W. (2010). *Blogs, wikis, podcasts, and other powerful web tools for the classroom.* Thousand Oaks, CA: Corwin Press.

Further Readings on Assessment and Professional Development

Ball, A. F., & Lardner, T. (2005). *African American literacies unleashed: Vernacular English and the composition classroom.* Carbondale: Southern Illinois University Press.

Horan, D., & Hersi, A. A. (2010). Knowledge of language and the teaching of reading: What should preservice teachers know and be able to do? In S. Elis, J. Bourne, & E. McCartnery (Eds.), *Insight and impact: Applied linguistics and the primary school* (pp. 44–52). Cambridge, UK: Cambridge University Press.

Skerrett, A. (2009). Biographical orientations to secondary English teaching within a mosaic context of diversity. *English Education, 41*(3), 281–303.

FIGURE 12.1. Suggestions for further reading.

contained AAVE, teachers were able to assist students in transferring their AAVE discourse about their cultural resources and practices into the discourse of academic language.

Greene and Walker (2004) recommended that teachers themselves code switch to promote students' engagement in effective code switching and that they model for students how meaning can be affected by language choice. Wheeler and Swords (2010) adopted contrastive analysis theory from second-language acquisition as a way for teachers to build on students' existing linguistic knowledge (the pattern of community English or the second language of students) to add new knowledge of academic English. Through analysis of linguistic patterns, students develop explicit conscious understanding of the difference between their home language and the formal language of school, with the goal of empowering students to become code switchers—able to make conscious, effective choices—to choose their language and writing to fit the time, audience, and purpose. Godley and Minnici (2008) provided an example of code-switching instruction in their design of instructional activities. Within one instructional unit, students practiced code switching in writing and other linguistic tasks. They found that such exercises improved students' understandings about the grammatical patterns of privileged and stigmatized dialects while helping them identify and critique underlying issues of power that privileged SE.

Moreover, bilingual struggling students benefit from instruction that draws on the oral literature and language patterns of their native language (Gort, 2006; Herrero, 2006). Dominican students were able to produce more elaborate texts in English as well as Spanish when they were invited to draw on the patterns of language and discourse that they used in their language practices outside school. In a study of Spanish–English code switching of bilingual elementary school students, Becker (2001) found that students who engaged in code-switching during a story retelling activity demonstrated stronger narrative skills. Likewise, Martínez-Roldán and Sayer (2006) found that bilingual third-grade students displayed greater comprehension of stories when they used Spanglish to mediate their retellings rather than relying on English only.

Teaching about Language Ideologies and Linguistics

One recommendation for teachers in CLCCs is to implement critical language pedagogy, which means instruction that guides students to critically examine language ideologies that stigmatize their home languages (Cooks & Ball, 2008; Godley & Minnici, 2008; Greene & Walker, 2004; Sealey-Ruiz, 2007). Drawing from their synthesis of research on Black English and dialect shift, Greene and Walker laid out several strategies through which teachers can support AAVE-speaking students' acquisition and use of SE while recognizing and embracing the value of AAVE. They called for teachers to demonstrate an understanding and respect of Black English and to learn about and teach students the history of AAVE and its development in relation to SE. Implementing these principles, Sealey-Ruiz experienced how validating the language backgrounds of her African American students served as a catalyst for the students' writing. Sealey-Ruiz engaged students, all of whom spoke AAVE, in conversations about their language varieties and ideologies. They also read scholarship about AAVE as a rule-governed language. The intent was to have students recognize that their goal of becoming better writers could only be achieved if they used their entire set of language resources. One strategy was to encourage students to use AAVE to sound out and write words for which they were unsure of the SE pronunciation or spelling (Sealey-Ruiz, 2005). Another was the use of a range of curriculum materials that represented students' languages and sociocultural experiences.

Godley and Minnici's (2008) work also demonstrated how teaching about language ideologies can help African American students use AAVE as a resource for learning. Godley and Minnici taught a week-long unit on language varieties to African American students. Their goals for the unit were to encourage students to develop critical perspectives on language by (1) critiquing dominant language ideologies, (2) emphasizing the diversity of dialects spoken in the United States and in the students' communities, and (3) raising students' awareness of the ways that they used language for different purposes and audiences. Godley and Minnici introduced students to the notion of language ideologies through viewing a film *American Tongues*. They then facilitated discussions where students were guided in critiquing dominant language ideologies. They also held conversations with students about their beliefs and practices in relation to the varieties of language that they used both in and out of school.

Implications

• As a first step, teachers and other literacy leaders can create environments that value the language and cultures students bring to school. For example, sanctioning, and indeed, encouraging students' use of AAVE in classroom discussions can foster student learning, engagement, and participation.

• Literacy leaders and classroom teachers need to develop knowledge of language in order to enhance the code-switching strategies of linguistically diverse students and accelerate their literacy development. Susan, the reading specialist in our case example, may not have the specific knowledge about language variation or code-switching instructional strategies. However, as a literacy leader, she can facilitate a teacher book group to broaden her and her colleagues' knowledge of the rule-based structures of different language varieties as well as their rich metaphorical, poetic, and often lyrical language and styles.

• By examining linguistic patterns, grammatical structure of students' home language and the language of school, teachers can help students to make conscious, effective choices—to choose their language and writing to fit the time, audience, and purpose.

• Teachers can develop language activities where students practice writing in and switching among SE and other language varieties in their writing activities. They can examine samples of student writing, discuss the examples of code switching in them, and ask students to talk about their purposes for using different language varieties and the possible effects of their language choices on their texts and their readers. See Figure 12.1 for suggestions for additional reading about instructional practices related to language use.

Learning Activities Involving Social Justice Inquiry, Technology, and Multimodality

Social Justice Inquiry

Instructional strategies that support social justice help students to recognize oppressive and unjust circumstances, structures, or systems of inequalities; learn about their origins and effects; take steps to confront and dismantle them; and work toward implementing more just conditions or systems. Teachers are encouraged to design inquiry projects where students conduct research into the historical and contemporary social, political, or economic conditions or challenges that their families and communities face (Cooks & Ball, 2008; Martínez-Roldán & Fránquiz, 2008; Morrell & Rogers, 2006). Morrell and Rogers described a project in which urban youth conducted original historical research on the 1954 *Brown v. Board of Education Supreme Court* decision and thereby entered a significant conversation about the historical and contemporary issues surrounding this landmark event. They further documented how the youth developed their reading and writing skills by participating in this project. In their review of effective literacy instruction for Latina/Latino youth, Martínez-Roldán and Fránquiz noted the success of inquiry projects where teachers help youth identify, investigate, and report on social issues that concern them and their communities.

In the social justice inquiry projects discussed above, teachers guided students to reflect on their family and community experiences, identify a particular concern or problem they are facing, systematically learn about the origins of these problems and avenues for redressing them, and take decisive steps toward ameliorating or solving the problems. The projects foster school–home–community partnerships about authentic concerns and issues. These projects involve substantial reading, writing, speaking, and research skills and thus develop a range of important literacy skills in students. By implementing inquiry projects with an orientation toward social activism and social justice, teachers address not only the benefits of living in a diverse society but the entrenched inequities. Teachers prepare students to be active citizens who work toward securing greater equity for all members of a diverse society (Cooks & Ball, 2008; Martínez-Roldán & Fránquiz, 2008; Morrell & Rogers, 2006). Indeed, this element of literacy instruction, in which teachers and students address the social justice dimension of literacy learning, is a prominent feature of the IRA's newly added Diversity Standard (International Reading Association, 2010).

IMPLICATIONS

• Teachers can design inquiry projects where students use journal writing and discussion to reflect on conditions in their communities, schools, city, or other contexts that they believe are unfair or unjust. Teachers would guide students in conducting research to learn more about the conditions of inequity that concern them, why they exist, what is being done about them, and what might be done. From there, teachers and students can plan to take some focused action toward addressing these circumstances. For example, they can raise awareness about particular injustices by writing letters to a local newspaper or elected official or speaking with community members and leaders, or students, teachers, and administrators at their school. A class can plan for specific activities to confront, eradicate, or ameliorate the unjust condition that they have been studying. For instance, if they are studying homelessness or hunger in their city, they might conduct food drives or other regular activities of providing supplies to the homeless and hungry. They could plan a series of rallies or meetings with local elected officials to advocate for increased funding for community organizations that provide job training and other support for homeless members of society.

• Teachers and students could also examine the inequities that exist within organizational or structural features of the school itself and take steps to redress them. For example, they can look into disciplinary procedures, academic tracking, or the quality and amount of educational resources at their school to identify whether inequities exist and develop plans for addressing these problems.

• Literacy leaders can work with school administrators to help them understand the importance of social justice inquiry projects in literacy teaching and learning. Literacy leaders, like Susan, the reading specialist in our case example, can work to provide supportive conditions for teachers who desire to do this work with their students. They can also help teachers locate materials, resources, and knowledgeable others in the community who can support students' research and social organizing activities. See Figure 12.1 for suggestions for further reading about social justice.

Technology and Multimodality

Technology, which facilitates the use and composition of multimodal texts, is an underutilized instructional tool in CLCCs (Ball et al., 2010). Integrating technology into literacy instruction can help linguistically diverse students draw on their language resources to acquire digital literacy and other language skills (Brass, 2008; Hall & Damico, 2007; Kirkland, 2009; Redd, 2003). Hall and Damico examined how using culturally relevant pedagogy with African American youth in teaching them how to construct digital media texts allowed students to employ various features of AAVE: tonal semantics, sermonic tone, call and response, and signifying in producing digital texts that contained complex meanings. Brass showed how a group of culturally and linguistically diverse students were able to create a sophisticated video where they critiqued the popular culture materials and attitudes they consumed or subscribed to. Within this production process, she documented how the students used their home languages and dialects to develop ideas for their digital composition.

Kirkland (2009) concluded from his study of African American young men's participation in online social communities that the youth expanded their uses of language to include social, cultural, and political purposes. Students engaged in online discussions with their peers to form and deepen friendships while also discussing political and social issues that were important to them. Redd (2003) encouraged her students to use AAVE in online discussions to help them expand their literacy communities. She initiated relationships with South African students in a composition course to enable her students to discuss South African literature with these cultural insiders. Her students also engaged in culturally relevant multimodal literacy activities, for example, collaboratively building an African American literature website with students from another university. Redd's students also used various informational websites to foster their understanding of literature throughout the course.

Researchers have shown particular benefits for second-language learners from writing in online communities such as fan-fiction sites—websites containing the writings of fans (Black, 2005; Yi, 2008). Membership in these communities allow students to develop their writing skills in a second language within a safe and supportive community and to request and receive feedback on a variety of aspects of their writing—content, grammar, and mechanics, to name a few. These online spaces afford second-language learners important tools for composing rich texts, for instance, the ability to link their texts across various websites and to use image, sound, and other multimodal communication devices. Moreover, students can develop strong literate identities in these communities as their offerings of content expertise (e.g., in story-line development) and sharing of feedback based on their knowledge of the story contribute to the overall improvement of their peers' texts.

Students' engagement with technology and multimodality in outside-school contexts has important implications for literacy learning in school. Multimodal texts are a powerful resource for enhancing the literacy engagement and comprehension of linguistically diverse students (Ajayi, 2009; Chun, 2009). Graphic novels that express meaning in writing as well as image are effective instructional tools (Ajayi; Chun). Additionally, teachers can capitalize on students' visual literacies, particularly through using multimodal texts that relate to cultural and linguistic diversity and its attendant benefits and challenges (Chun). Likewise, multigenre writing is a powerful approach for making available to students multiple modalities for expressing meaning (Gillespie, 2005). Students may bring together expository writings, interviews, music lyrics, poetry, advertisements, drawings, photographs, and a host of other compositional forms to deliver complex understandings of literature they have read or history- or science-based research they have conducted. Offering students multiple modes and genres for learning and demonstrating their learning is essential in CLCCs (Skerrett, 2011).

IMPLICATIONS

- Use all modalities to increase student learning. Students should have opportunities to read, write, listen to, and view the curriculum. Teachers could examine their existing instructional and assessment materials to identify areas where they could include a wider range of modalities to help students learn and demonstrate their learning of particular knowledge and skills.

- Multigenre projects, webquests, digital stories, blogs, wikis, and podcasts are just some examples of products that students could create as part of their work in literacy classrooms. In designing these multimodal and technology-rich projects, teachers need to take on roles as co-learners with their students. These projects tend to work well when undertaken in small groups so that students can share their knowledge and skills with each other while they learn about and produce multimodal texts together.

• Given the untapped potential of technology in diverse schools, literacy leaders have much to do in learning about and supporting teachers in integrating available sources of technology into their curriculum—both school-based and outside-school (e.g., fan fiction) contexts. They should keep teachers apprised of professional development opportunities related to specific digital literacies or technology tools within their school district or community. See Figure 12.1 for suggestions for further readings on integrating technology into instructional practices.

Assessment

There are limitations to using standardized assessments with culturally and linguistically diverse students; alternative and more multifaceted assessments should accompany standardized measures (Cooks & Ball, 2008; Greene & Walker, 2004). Opportunities for students to use technology and multimodality (including digital and oral communication tools) should also be integrated into assessments (Hall & Damico, 2007; Fisher, 2005). In relation to writing, Greene and Walker encouraged teachers to use criteria addressing appropriate language use, organization of thoughts and ideas, delivery, and other communications competencies when developing assessments. Assessments, they proposed, should be structured and incorporated over the scope of a course. These researchers further suggested creating culturally reflective assignments such as tribute speeches that allow students opportunities to further develop proficiency in code switching while affirming their cultural identities.

Furthermore, the voices of teachers from diverse cultural backgrounds should be included in assessing the work of linguistically diverse students (Cooks & Ball, 2008). For example, Ball found that African American teachers, more so than European American teachers, emphasized the content and quality of students' ideas and balanced these with writing conventions and forms (Ball, 1997, in Cooks & Ball). Hence, teachers' wider cultural and sociolinguistic knowledge and beliefs have a significant influence on what students learn and how teachers assess student learning. Fogel and Ehri (2006) demonstrated how teaching teachers the language patterns of AAVE fostered positive dispositions, knowledge, and skills in the teachers in relation to drawing on students' linguistic resources in teaching them. Ball also identified the importance of teachers gaining an understanding of the language patterns of their students and working intensively with them to communicate about and assist them with meeting each other's writing expectations (Ball, 1997, in Cooks & Ball). Greene and Walker (2004) also recommended communicating expectations for language use in the classroom to students including explaining which varieties of English are appropriate for different classroom occasions or activities.

Implications

• Encourage formative assessments that are sensitive to cultural differences. Written and oral tribute speeches, spoken-word poetry, drama, music, and other performing arts that allow students to draw on their cultural and linguistic backgrounds should be encouraged in the classroom. Teachers can provide opportunities for students to use their language dialects and code switch not only during instructional talk and learning activities but also in assessments.

• Working collaboratively with students, teachers should develop clear expectations and criteria about the format, structure, language varieties, and other conventions to be used for particular assessments.

• Students should be offered multiple opportunities across the course of instruction to demonstrate their learning in a range of modalities, for example, oral and written language, drawing, and digital literacies. These could be designed as long-term projects that span a number of weeks and teachers can confer with and give students feedback on their developing work.

• Literacy leaders can facilitate teachers' analysis of student work as they learn about the language varieties of their students to help them effectively assess their students' work. Literacy leaders can work with teachers to develop a range of criteria and competencies for assessing student work in order to recognize and affirm all of students' strengths while attending to their ongoing academic development.

• In relation to professional development about teachers' beliefs about language diversity, literacy leaders like Susan, the reading specialist in our case example, can facilitate teacher study groups where teachers write about, and discuss with their colleagues, their own language and cultural backgrounds; their experiences with and beliefs about how language diversity should be addressed in society and in the classroom; and how they see these beliefs influencing their teaching. They can read research about language ideologies and language use such as presented in this chapter and consider their beliefs and practices in light of what the research identifies as productive or problematic beliefs and practices.

• Literacy leaders can locate additional research for teachers to read and discuss about how teachers' beliefs about language and cultural diversity affect teaching and learning in CLCCs. These professional development opportunities provide space for individual reflection and change while fostering a community of teachers that understand and continuously consider how beliefs about language diversity affect teaching and learning. See Figure 12.1 for suggestions for further reading about assessment.

CONCLUSION

At the beginning of the chapter, we summarized Ball's (2009) discussion of teachers' generativity in which teachers combine what they learn in the community with their colleagues, their students and their families, and from educational research and best practice to devise a dynamic form of instruction in their CLCCs. Through a focus on deep understanding of teaching and learning as a contextualized practice and influenced by culture and language, literacy leaders can help classroom teachers to draw on the language and literacy traditions that their students bring into the classroom to provide a culturally responsive literacy education. This chapter has provided insight into some ways in which these learning environments might be attained.

ENGAGEMENT ACTIVITIES

1. Reread the case example of Susan, the experienced teacher/new reading specialist in a CLCC school. How can she serve as a resource to teachers in her current position? How might she plan and design a long-term professional development effort at the school?

2. Brainstorm with a colleague or two about the cultural and linguistic resources your students are bringing to school. How might you go about learning even more about your students' cultural and language practices?

3. How might you incorporate a code-switching activity into your instructional planning?

4. What are the technology resources available at your school? How might a literacy leader like Susan support teachers' use of available technologies to increase multimodal learning opportunities for culturally and linguistically diverse students?

5. Locate some readings on culturally and linguistically diverse literacy practices (see Figure 12.1) in which your students engage, discuss with a peer, and consider the implications for teaching practices. What kind of support can a literacy leader provide?

REFERENCES

Ajayi, L. (2009). English as a second language learners' exploration of multimodal texts in a junior high school. *Journal of Adolescent and Adult Literacy, 52*(7), 585–595.

Ball, A. F. (1997). Expanding the dialogue on culture as a critical component when assessing writing. *Assessing Writing, 4*, 169–202.

Ball, A. F. (2009). Toward a theory of generative change in culturally and linguistically complex classrooms. *American Educational Research Journal, 46*(1), 45–72.

Ball, A. F., & Lardner, T. (2005). *African American literacies unleashed: Vernacular English and the composition classroom.* Carbondale: Southern Illinois University Press.

Ball, A. F., Skerrett, A., & Martínez, R. (2010). Research on diverse students in culturally and linguistically complex language arts classrooms. In D. Lapp & D. Fisher (Eds.), *Handbook of research on teaching the English language arts* (3rd ed., pp. 22–28). Erlbaum-Taylor Francis.

Becker, R. R. (2001). Spanish–English code switching in a bilingual academic context. *Reading Horizons, 42*(2), 99–115.

Black, R. W. (2005). Access and affiliation: The literacy and composition practices of English-language learners in an online fanfiction community. *Journal of Adolescent and Adult Literacy, 49*(2), 118–128.

Black, R. W. (2009). English-language learners, fan communities, and 21st century skills. *Journal of Adolescent and Adult Literacy, 52*(8), 688–697.

Bomer, R., & Bomer, K. (2001). *For a better world: Reading and writing for social action.* Portsmouth, NH: Heinemann.

Brass, J. J. (2008). Local knowledge and digital movie composing in an after-school literacy program. *Journal of Adolescent and Adult Literacy, 51*(6), 464–473.

Chun, C. W. (2009). Critical literacies and graphic novels for English-language learners: Teaching Maus. *Journal of Adolescent and Adult Literacy, 53*(2), 144–153.

Cooks, J., & Ball, A. F. (2008). Research on the literacies of AAVE-speaking adolescents. In L. Christenbury, R. Bomer, & P. Smagorinksy (Eds.), *Handbook of adolescent literacy research* (pp. 140–152). New York: Guilford Press.

Duncan-Andrade, J. M. R., & Morrell, E. (2005). Turn up that radio, teacher: Popular cultural pedagogy in new century urban schools. *Journal of School Leadership, 15*(3), 284–304.

Fisher, M. T. (2005). From the coffeehouse to the schoolhouse: The promise and potential of spoken word poetry in schools. *English Education, 37*(2), 115–131.

Fogel, H., & Ehri, L. C. (2006). Teaching African American English forms to standard American English-speaking teachers: Effects on acquisition, attitudes, and responses to student use. *Journal of Teacher Education, 57*(5), 464–480.

Gillespie, J. (2005). "It would be fun to do again": Multigenre responses to literature. *Journal of Adolescent and Adult Literacy, 48*(8), 678–684.

Godley, A. J., & Minnici, A. (2008). Critical language pedagogy in an urban high school English class. *Urban Education, 43*(3), 319–346.

Gort, M. (2006). Strategic code-switching, interliteracy, and other phenomena of emergent bilingual writing: Lessons from first grade bilingual classrooms. *Journal of Early Childhood Literacy, 6*(3), 323–354.

Greene, D. M., & Walker, F. R. (2004). Recommendations to public speaking instructors for the negotiation of code-switching practices among black English-speaking African American students. *Journal of Negro Education, 73*, 435–442.

Hall, D. T., & Damico, J. (2007). Black youth employ African American vernacular English in creating digital texts. *Journal of Negro Education, 76*(1), 80–88.

Herrero, E. A. (2006). Using Dominican oral literature and discourse to support literacy learning among low-achieving students from the Dominican Republic. *International Journal of Bilingual Education and Bilingualism, 9*(2), 219–238.

Hersi, A. A. (2005). Educational challenges and sociocultural experiences of Somali students in an urban high school. *NABE: Journal of Review of Research and Practice, 3,* 125–143.

Hersi, A. A. (in press). Immigration and resiliency: Unpacking the experiences of high school students from Cape Verde and Ethiopia. *Journal of Intercultural Education.*

Hill, K. D. (2009). Code-switching pedagogies and African American student voices: Acceptance and resistance. *Journal of Adolescent and Adult Literacy, 53*(2), 120–131.

Horan, D., & Hersi, A. A. (2010). Knowledge of language and the teaching of reading: What should preservice teachers know and be able to do? In S. Elis, J. Bourne, & E. McCartney (Eds.), *Insight and impact: Applied linguistics and the primary school.* Cambridge, UK: Cambridge University Press.

International Reading Association (2010). *Standards for reading professionals—Revised 2010.* (pp. 44–52). Newark, DE: Author.

Kirkland, D. E. (2009). Standpoints: Researching and teaching English in the digital dimension. *Research in the Teaching of English, 44*(1), 8–22.

Lee, C. D. (2006). "Every good-bye ain't gone": Analyzing the cultural underpinnings of classroom talk. *International Journal of Qualitative Studies in Education, 19*(3), 305–327.

Lee, C. D. (2007). *Culture, literacy, and learning: Blooming in the midst of the whirlwind.* New York: Teachers College Press.

Long, T. W. (2008). The full circling process: Leaping into the ethics of history using critical visual literacy and arts-based activism. *Journal of Adolescent and Adult Literacy, 51*(6), 498–508.

Marshall, E., Staples, J., & Gibson, S. (2009). Ghetto fabulous: Reading black adolescent femininity in contemporary urban street fiction. *Journal of Adolescent and Adult Literacy, 53*(1), 28–36.

Martínez, R. A. (2010). Spanglish as literacy tool: Toward an understanding of the potential role of Spanish-English code-switching in the development of academic literacy. *Research in the Teaching of English, 45*(2), 124–149.

Martínez, R. A., Orellana, M. F., Pacheco, M., & Carbone, P. (2008.) Found in translation: Connecting translating experiences to academic writing. *Language Arts, 85*(6), 421–431.

Martínez-Roldán, C. M., & Fránquiz, M. E. (2008). Latina/o youth literacies: Hidden funds of knowledge. In L. Christenbury, R. Bomer, & P. Smagorinksy (Eds.), *Handbook of adolescent literacy research* (pp. 323–342). New York: Guilford Press.

Martínez-Roldán, C. M., & Sayer, P. (2006). Reading through linguistic borderlands: Latino students' transactions with narrative texts. *Journal of Early Childhood Literacy, 6*(3), 294–322.

Morrell, E., & Rogers, J. (2006). Becoming critical public historians: Students study diversity and access in post "Brown v. Board" Los Angeles. *Social Education, 70*(6), 366–369.

Pescatore, C. (2008). Current events as empowering literacy: For English and social studies teachers. *Journal of Adolescent and Adult Literacy, 51*(4), 336–339.

Redd, T. M. (2003). "Tryin to make a dolla outa fifteen cent": Teaching Composition with the Internet at an HBCU. *Computers and Composition, 20*(4), 359–373.

Richardson, W. (2010). *Blogs, wikis, podcasts, and other powerful webtools for the classroom.* Thousand Oaks, CA: Corwin Press.

Rickford, J. R. (1999). *African American vernacular English: Features and use, evolution, and educational implications.* Oxford, UK: Blackwell.

Rogers, R., & Mosley, M. (2006). Racial literacy in a second grade classroom: Critical race theory, whiteness studies, and literacy research. *Reading Research Quarterly 41,* 462–495.

Sealey-Ruiz, Y. (2005). Spoken soul: The language of black imagination and reality. *Educational Forum, 70*(1), 37–46.

Sealey-Ruiz, Y. (2007). Wrapping the curriculum around their lives: Using a culturally relevant curriculum with African American adult women. *Adult Education Quarterly: A Journal of Research and Theory, 58*(1), 44–60.

Skerrett, A. (2009). Biographical orientations to secondary English teaching within a mosaic context of diversity. *English Education, 41*(3), 281–303.

Skerrett, A. (2011). A case of generativity in a culturally and linguistically complex classroom. *Changing English: Studies in Culture and Education, 18*(1), 85–97.

Stevens, L. P. (2001). South Park and society: Instructional and curricular implications of popular culture in the classroom. *Journal of Adolescent and Adult Literacy, 44*(6), 548–555.

Weinstein, S. (2007). A love for the thing: The pleasures of rap as a literate practice. *Journal of Adolescent and Adult Literacy, 50*(4), 270–281.

Wheeler, R., & Swords, R. (2010). *Code-switching lessons: Grammar strategies for linguistically diverse writers.* Portsmouth, NH: Heinemann.

Yi, Y. (2008). Relay writing in an adolescent online community. *Journal of Adolescent and Adult Literacy, 51*(8), 670–680.

13

—

English Learners
Developing Their Literate Lives

MaryEllen Vogt

Guiding Questions

- What do we know about effective literacy instruction for English learners?
- What are some instructional considerations for the literacy development of adolescent English learners?
- What should a literacy leader see in a classroom where effective instruction for English learners occurs?
- How can literacy leaders support teachers in implementing the recommendations in this chapter?

Throughout the United States, as well as in other countries, increasing numbers of students are entering schools where the language of instruction (L2) differs from the students' home languages (L1). In our increasingly global village, it is estimated that by 2025 approximately one of four students in the United States will be English learners (National Clearinghouse for English Language Acquisition, 2010). At present, in several regions of the country, this percentage has already been exceeded. Who are these students?

Some English learners arrive in school with very little language and literacy development in their L1, and they may have little or interrupted formal education. Frequently, these students have difficulty learning to read in English because they have few literacy skills to transfer to their new language. Other English learners are native-born U.S. citizens who have been to school but have not developed sufficient academic English to be successful. Still other English learners arrive as immigrants, and they are fully literate in their L1 with a history of successful, comprehensive formal education. These students are able to apply what they know about academic language and literacy to reading, writing, and speaking in English. Because of these vastly differing educational backgrounds, personal and experiential factors, and current educational contexts available for these students, an academic gap persists between non- or limited-English-speaking students and their more proficient English-speaking peers.

It is not enough for these students to just learn "English words." Rather, there are specific content vocabulary, procedural steps for classroom tasks and activities, language functions (such as requesting information or summarizing), English grammar and structure, and content concepts that must be taught to English learners (Cummins, 2003; Echevarria, Vogt, & Short, 2010a, 2010b; Vogt & Shearer, 2011). Despite the challenges, there are schools and districts in the United States where English learners are performing satisfactorily. What characterizes these successful learning environments is that the English learners are active participants in learning and they are set up for success with scaffolds that enable them to learn English while they comprehend and complete academic tasks (Echevarria & Vogt, 2010). What also describes these schools is that their teachers have received targeted and ongoing preparation and professional development in how to meet the language, literacy, and academic needs of their students (Snow, Griffin, & Burns, 2005; Vogt, 2009). In the case below, I provide an example of the issues faced by personnel in a school with a large number of English learners.

CASE EXAMPLE

Henry Tyler has been teaching for 23 years, primarily in the upper elementary grades. Currently, he's teaching grade five and has 31 students in his class, 9 of whom are English learners, students whose L1 differs from the L2. During the past few years, the number of English learners in Henry's school has increased substantially, from just a few to nearly 20% of the student population. Professional development opportunities highlighting factors that affect second-language acquisition or effective teaching approaches for teaching English learners have not been made available to the teachers.

Henry and the other teachers realize they're floundering, and their English learners are not making satisfactory progress in language arts or the other content areas. They decide they cannot wait until the district's newly established ESL department can give them a hand. So, during a staff meeting, the teachers and administrators commit to learning how they can better meet the language, literacy, and learning needs of the English learners in their school.

Several teachers are taking graduate classes and they pledge to seek some advice and resources from their professors. Others volunteer to do Internet searches, while some commit to checking with neighboring districts to see what they've been doing to accommodate the needs of English learners. Henry's school administrators and support staff, including two reading specialists and three special educators, are delighted with the teachers' decision to tackle this topic, but they're also concerned about what their own roles in the process will be. After all, as with the teachers, they have little background in teaching students whose L1 is not English. They fear that the enthusiasm engendered by the discussion during the staff meeting will wane as everyone realizes the challenges awaiting them all. What are the issues that Henry and his colleagues are facing? What will happen when the ESL department does get involved? What if their ideas are different from plans designed by the teachers? What are some alternative actions that they might consider at this point, and the pros and cons of each?

WHAT DO WE KNOW ABOUT EFFECTIVE LITERACY INSTRUCTION FOR ENGLISH LEARNERS?

Although there is still a need for high-quality research studies on assessing and teaching English learners, several recent research syntheses have focused on what we do know about the language, literacy, and academic development of English learners (August & Shanahan, 2008; Genesee, Lindholm-Leary, Saunders, & Christian, 2006; Gersten et al., 2007). The recommendations that follow are from these syntheses and are adapted from Goldenberg (2008), and Vogt and Shearer (2011, pp. 142–143).

Many experts believe that teaching students to read in their first language promotes higher levels of reading achievement in English because skills and other knowledge about literacy transfer across languages (Bauer, 2009; Cummins, 1981). "That is, if you learn something in one language you either already know it in (i.e., transfer it to) another language or can more easily learn it in another language" (Goldenberg, 2008, p. 15). Other experts suggest that studies advocating for either L1 reading instruction prior to L2 reading instruction, or English-only reading instruction for second-language learners, have methodological flaws. Therefore, the relationship between L1 and L2 literacy development is not entirely clear (Gersten et al., 2007). (For a theoretical overview and discussion of specific research studies, see Genesee, Geva, Dressler, & Kamil, 2008). The good news is that there is evidence that English learners can develop adequate literacy skills and strategies in

English-only classrooms given appropriate, modified instruction (August & Shanahan, 2008; Echevarria, Short, & Powers, 2006).

While the five core reading elements (phonological awareness, phonics, reading fluency, vocabulary, comprehension), as identified by the National Reading Panel (2000), are the same elements that English learners must master, the development of and practice with oral language is also of critical importance. Therefore, core reading instruction and intensive, small-group intervention based on assessment data should focus on the five core elements plus oral language development.

High-quality vocabulary instruction should be provided throughout the school day, with an in-depth focus on essential content words, language processes, and language functions. Additionally, instructional time should be allotted for teaching common words, phrases, and expressions in English.

English learners should also have extra practice in silently and orally reading words, sentences, paragraphs, and stories to develop fluency and automaticity. To facilitate comprehension, challenging words and passages within texts should be identified, highlighted, defined, paraphrased, and clarified as needed. Beginning in the primary grades, the development of academic English should be a targeted instructional goal for English learners.

Predictable classroom routines should be maintained so that English learners can depend on a degree of consistency throughout their day, including easy-to-read daily agendas, posted and reviewed content and language objectives for each lesson, procedures for transitioning between subjects or periods, and so forth. Redundancy of key information can be provided with visual cues, pictures and diagrams, modeling, physical gestures, and graphic organizers, for example.

WHAT ARE SOME INSTRUCTIONAL CONSIDERATIONS FOR THE LITERACY DEVELOPMENT OF ADOLESCENT ENGLISH LEARNERS?

Whereas the instructional recommendations made in the previous section are applicable for both elementary and secondary English learners, there are additional challenges for students and teachers alike at the secondary level. Nearly 56% of adolescent English learners are native born (Capps et al., 2005). These are students who have been educated exclusively in the United States, but they have not developed adequate English proficiency for success in school.

Many immigrant students at varied levels of English proficiency and educational backgrounds also have a very difficult time reaching academic standards. Because language and literacy are critical to academic success, English learners with poor reading and writing skills have little chance of performing satisfactorily in secondary school subjects (Ehren, n.d.). Reading demands at the secondary level include the complex prose found in content-area texts and reference books, the need to write persuasively, support a point of view, hypothesize, predict, analyze, and so forth, all of which is required in other than the student's L1. Proficiency in academic language requires three sophisticated knowledge bases: knowledge of content vocabulary, knowledge of English-language processes and functions, and knowledge of English morphology and syntax. For many students who are "stuck" at the intermediate level of English proficiency, the academic language of multiple content areas presents incredible challenges (see Vogt, Echevarria, & Short, 2010; and Zwiers, 2008, for practical ideas for teaching academic language).

Further, some current instructional practices impinge on English learners' chances for academic success in the secondary schools, and they include the following (Echevarria & Vogt, 2011):

• Literacy development is particularly challenging for adolescent English learners who enter U.S. schools in the secondary grades because of the complex course content and the fact that they have less time to learn English (Short & Fitzsimmons, 2006).

• When literacy practices are embedded into subject-area teaching, lessons are sometimes mediated by students' expectations and responses to them (Vogt & Shearer, 2011). For example, consider a teacher's efforts to involve adolescents in a generative, creative writing activity. Capable readers and writers most likely will engage themselves, whereas students with weak literacy skills might balk or refuse to do the activity. The teacher is then influenced by the students' responses and acts accordingly—the most proficient readers and writers tackle the assignment and become better readers and writers. The least proficient students may not be expected to complete generative writing assignments and they receive little scaffolding to be successful; therefore, they do not improve their writing skills.

• Many adolescent classrooms are not aligned with students' interests and out-of-school literacies. Students who are highly engaged in searching on the Internet, participating regularly on Facebook, Twitter, and blogs, may be the same students who are disengaged with school literacy practices. With native-speaking adolescents, disengagement may be perceived as apathy and frustration. With adolescent English learners, it may be thought of as a lack of ability.

• Adolescents needing intensive reading intervention outnumber the support personnel, such as reading specialists, who are available to provide it.

• Most adolescent English learners who have reached an intermediate level of English proficiency receive little or no ESL or language development instruction in secondary schools (Gedney, 2007).

• The configuration of most secondary schools results in no one teacher "owning" students, as contrasted to the elementary grades with one teacher per classroom. Many English learners with poor literacy skills can easily slip through the cracks until they come to the attention of a counselor when they are already experiencing academic failure.

• Many secondary classrooms provide little to no differentiated instruction for English learners and other students who need accommodations and modifications. One-size-fits-all instruction for English learners who have diverse backgrounds, needs, and levels of English proficiency is frequently inappropriate and ineffective.

• At the time of this writing, only five states require preservice teachers to take coursework in effective instruction for English learners. Many secondary teachers report they are unprepared to meet the language, literacy, and content needs of their English learners (Short & Fitzsimmons, 2006).

• The assessment of English learners' language and literacy skills continues to be a challenge, especially for non-Spanish-speaking students. There is also a lack of common criteria for identifying English learners and for tracking their academic progress.

It is incumbent on secondary literacy leaders to develop appropriate and flexible program options for adolescent English learners. In addition, modifying instructional practices to accommodate students' language, literacy, learning, and experiential backgrounds is of utmost importance. (See Chapter 9 for more information about secondary reading programs.)

WHAT SHOULD A LITERACY LEADER SEE IN A CLASSROOM WHERE EFFECTIVE INSTRUCTION FOR ENGLISH LEARNERS OCCURS?

Since 1995, we have been conducting research to develop and refine the SIOP Model based on the Sheltered Instruction Observation Protocol (Echevarria, Vogt, & Short, 2008, 2010a, 2010b). Sheltered instruction is a means for making content comprehensible for English learners while they are developing English proficiency, and SIOP is an empirically validated model of sheltered instruction. Sheltered classrooms may include a mix of native English speakers and English learners, or only English learners.

From our research, we have learned that consistent, systematic implementation of effective sheltered techniques in all lessons for English learners results in academic and language gains (Echevarria et al., 2006; Short, Echevarria, & Richards-Tutor, 2011). Elementary and secondary teachers who implement the SIOP Model to a high degree plan their lessons based on 30 instructional features that are grouped within eight components. These features include accommodations and modifications that have been found to increase language development and content knowledge for English learners. When observing a classroom with English learners, mentors, coaches, and administrators who are well versed in the SIOP Model can use questions, organized by the SIOP components, to determine the degree to which effective sheltered instructional practices are being implemented for English learners in the classroom (see Figure 13.1).

The features of the SIOP Model are not all new educational ideas. Rather, they are best educational practices that when implemented in lessons to a high degree, consistently and systematically result in language and academic growth for English learners. (See Chapter 12 for more information about working with culturally diverse students.)

HOW CAN LITERACY LEADERS SUPPORT TEACHERS IN IMPLEMENTING THE RECOMMENDATIONS IN THIS CHAPTER?

One of the first steps leaders can take in implementing effective literacy instruction for English learners is to consider the following when examining student performance data (Short, Echevarria, & Vogt, 2008, p. 48):

- How well are the English learners in your school or district performing?
- Is there a particular subject area or grade level where they are doing well or very poorly?
- What has been the trend over the past few years?
- On average, are the English learners making expected progress? Or have their scores stagnated from year to year?

An additional measure of a school's success with English learners is to examine the data on students who have exited the language development program by passing the state test, but have not been redesignated as language proficient because they cannot meet reading (and/or math) standards. Another aspect to consider is whether the students who have been redesignated falter academically once they are placed in mainstream classes.

These scenarios may point to inappropriate language-development classes, ineffective language and academic assessments, a lack of a comprehensive plan for teaching English learners, and/or teachers who have not

Lesson Preparation

- Does the lesson have separate content and language objectives that are posted and discussed with students at the beginning and ending of the lesson?
- Are the content and language objectives linked to the curricula and/or standards?
- Are the content concepts suited to the grade and developmental level of the students?
- Does the lesson include meaningful activities that integrate content concepts with language practice?
- Are supplementary materials used to support the academic text?

Building Background

- Does the teacher make explicit connections between new concepts and students' personal or cultural experiences?
- Does the teacher explicitly discuss prior lessons and link them to the new concepts?
- Is the teacher explicitly teaching key academic vocabulary and providing multiple opportunities for English learners to use this vocabulary in meaningful ways?

Comprehensible Input

- Does the teacher modulate his or her rate of speech, choice of words, use of idioms, and complexity of sentence structure according to the proficiency level of the English learners?
- Does the teacher explain academic tasks clearly, both orally and in writing, providing models and examples?
- Does the lesson make content accessible to students through multiple ways, such as the use of visual aids, demonstrations, graphic organizers, vocabulary previews, predictions, cooperative learning, peer tutoring, and native language support?

Strategies

- Does the teacher explicitly teach and model learning strategies for students?
- Does the teacher scaffold instruction with verbal prompting (such as asking students to elaborate a response) and instructional tools (such as an outline of major topics in a chapter)?
- Does the lesson incorporate higher-order thinking questions and tasks that challenge students?

Interaction

- Does the lesson provide frequent opportunities for interaction and discussion between teacher and students, and among students?
- Are the grouping configurations appropriate to the lesson's content and language goals?
- Does the teacher provide sufficient wait time after questioning so that students can process the information and respond accordingly?
- Does the teacher allow and facilitate clarification (through the teacher, an aide, or peer) in the native language when needed?

Practice and Application

- Does the lesson have hands-on practice opportunities with newly learned material?
- Are students asked to practice and apply both the content and language skills they are learning?
- Do the activities integrate all language skills (reading, writing, listening, and speaking)?

FIGURE 13.1. (continued on next page)

Lesson Delivery
- Does the lesson as implemented clearly support the content and language objectives?
- Is the pacing appropriate for English learners? How can you tell?
- Are students actively engaged throughout the class period?

Review and Assessment
- Does the teacher review key vocabulary and concepts during and at the end of the lesson?
- Does the teacher provide ongoing feedback to students on their work that is specific and academically relevant (not just praise)?
- How does the lesson assess student learning? Are multiple options to demonstrate learning included?

FIGURE 13.1. Guiding questions when observing classroom instruction for English learners. (Adapted from Short, Vogt, and Echevarria (2008, pp. 43–44). Copyright 2008 by Allyn & Bacon. Adapted by permission.

been adequately prepared to teach this population of students. So, what can literacy leaders do to create effective literacy programs for English learners?

1. Leadership is about learning and is a shared endeavor (Lambert, 1998). If you or the other literacy leaders in your school have not received adequate preparation in working with language minority students, it is imperative that you either receive preparation or you and your colleagues engage in book study and the review of research studies on effective practices for English learners. Areas to study should include second language acquisition, the stages (or phases) of second language development, what constitutes effective sheltered instruction, and how to assess and monitor the academic progress of English learners.

2. Work together with other literacy leaders (e.g., teachers, reading specialists, literacy coaches, support staff, and administrators) to develop a professional development plan for everyone who will be working with English learners. Our work with the SIOP Model has taught us that becoming a knowledgeable and highly effective teacher for English learners is a process that may take up to 3 years, and it involves, in combination, workshops, book study, and coaching. Leaders should join professional development sessions, not as observers, but as active participants.

3. Avoid competing initiatives when embarking on a professional development plan. Too often, schools endeavor to implement several major initiatives at one time. In our SIOP work, we have learned that teachers are more likely to become high implementers of the SIOP Model when they are focusing only on incorporating the SIOP components and features into their teaching, not on several other professional development initiatives at the

same time. Of course, teachers usually don't have much say in which initiatives a district undertakes, but if you are leading professional development efforts for teaching English learners, then convey to the powers that be that competing initiatives can doom the implementation of any one (or more) of them.

4. Assist teachers, reading specialists, literacy coaches, and special educators in making effective use of adopted reading programs. Most states require that the programs include provisions for working with English learners. However, the suggestions in the teacher's edition may be superficial, focusing more on how the teacher should explain something, rather than involving students in generating, practicing, and applying what they are learning about English. Therefore, when you review instructional materials that will be used with English learners, make sure anything that is selected is congruent with the research-based best instructional practices as described in this chapter.

5. Become an advocate for English learners, both those who are native born and those who are immigrants. These students deserve effective instruction that is appropriate for their language, literacy, and other academic strengths and needs. English learners, increasing in numbers throughout the country, represent the U.S. citizens and leaders of the future, and it behooves all of us to provide them with the best education possible.

FINAL THOUGHTS

Not long ago, I had the opportunity to interview some adolescent English learners about what makes learning in English either easy or difficult in their various classes. These astute teens didn't hesitate to tell me their thoughts. "One teacher does everything she can to make us understand. She'll explain something and then will give examples, draw pictures, even slide across the floor to show us what 'slippery' means. She doesn't give up until we get it. Other teachers just tell us to do stuff and we're supposed to do it. It doesn't seem like they really expect us to understand it ... just get it done."

My final question for these students was "If you could tell teachers one thing that they could do to make it easier for you as an English learner, what would it be?" A young woman from India said, "Don't just talk to the kids who speak English. Talk to us, too." A boy from Ukraine said, "Tell us what to do in the order we have to do it." Finally, a girl from Guatemala paused and then quietly added, "I would tell them to not forget we're here."

Henry Tyler and his colleagues might begin their exploration of how to effectively teach their English learners by talking to their students about how they wish to develop their literate lives. By assessing and understanding their students' language needs, the teachers can build on their interests, talents, abilities, and English proficiency. In addition, the teachers also need to prepare themselves to provide instruction that has been found to be effective with English learners. Their students, like their native-English-speaking peers, will thus have a better chance of becoming literate, capable, contributing adults.

ENGAGEMENT ACTIVITIES

1.   In the case example, Henry Tyler and his colleagues took the first step in providing an appropriate and equitable education for their students who were English learners: They acknowledged that what they had been doing instructionally for these students was not working. They then began to plan how they could become better informed and more effective in providing language, literacy, and content instruction for English learners. What is your response to their plans? Are there other options that they might consider?

2.   Reflect on your present educational context, whether it is a school, district office, county office, university, or other workplace. What do you see as obstacles or challenges to providing effective language, literacy, and content instruction for English learners?

3.   What are the possibilities and chances for success in your district (or other workplace) for implementing an initiative focusing on language, literacy, and content teaching for English learners?

4.   Who are the people with whom you work who need to take a leadership stance in bringing about effective instructional programs for English learners? What role do you see yourself taking? What will your first step be to prepare yourself to take on a leadership role in such an initiative?

5.   What similarities are there in the implications suggested in Chapter 12 on culturally relevant instruction and this chapter? Any differences?

REFERENCES

August, D., & Shanahan, T. (Eds.). (2008). *Developing reading and writing in second-language learners: Lessons from the Report of the National Literacy Panel on Language-Minority Children and Youth*. New York: Routledge; Newark, DE: International Reading Association; Washington, DC: Center for Applied Linguistics.

Bauer, E. B. (2009). Informed additive literacy instruction for ELLs. *Reading Teacher*, 62(5), 446–448.

Capps, R., Fix, M., Murray, J., Ost, J., Passel, J., & Herwantoro, S. (2005). *The new demography of America's schools: Immigration and the No Child Left Behind Act.* Washington, DC: Urban Institute.

Cummins, J. (1981). The role of primary language development in promoting educational success for language minority students. In C. F. Leyba (Ed.), *Schooling and language minority students: A theoretical framework* (pp. 3–49). Los Angeles: Evaluation, Dissemination, and Assessment Center, California State University.

Cummins, J. (2003). Reading and the bilingual student: Fact and fiction. In G. G. Garcia (Ed.), *English learners: Reading the highest level of English literacy.* Newark, DE: International Reading Association.

Echevarria, J., Short, D., & Powers, K. (2006). School reform and standards-based education: An instructional model for English language learners. *Journal of Educational Research, 99*(4), 195–210.

Echevarria, J., & Vogt, M. E. (2010). Using the SIOP Model to improve literacy for English learners. *New England Reading Association Journal, 46*(1), 8–15.

Echevarria, J., & Vogt, M. E. (2011). *RTI for English learners: Making it happen.* Boston: Pearson.

Echevarria, J., Vogt, M. E., & Short, D. (2008). *Making content comprehensible for elementary English learners: The SIOP Model* (2nd ed.). Boston: Allyn & Bacon.

Echevarria, J., Vogt, M. E., & Short, D. (2010a). *Making content comprehensible for elementary English learners: The SIOP Model.* Boston: Pearson.

Echevarria, J., Vogt, M. E., & Short, D. (2010b). *Making content comprehensible for secondary English learners: The SIOP Model.* Boston: Pearson.

Ehren, B. J. (n.d.). *Response to Intervention in secondary schools: Is it on your radar screen?* Retrieved February 5, 2010, from *www.rtinetwork.org.*

Gedney, S. (2007). *Structuring language instruction to advance stalled English learners. Aiming high.* Santa Rosa, CA: Sonoma County Office of Education. Retrieved June 20, 2010, from *www.scoe.org.*

Genesee, F., Geva, E., Dressler, C., & Kamil, M. L. (2008). Cross-linguistic relationships in second-language learners. In D. August & T. Shanahan (Eds.), *Developing reading and writing in second-language learners: Lessons from the Report of the National Literacy Panel on Language-Minority Children and Youth.* New York: Routledge; Newark, DE: International Reading Association; Washington, DC: Center for Applied Linguistics.

Genesee, F., Lindholm-Leary, K., Saunders, W., & Christian, D. (2006). *Educating English language learners: A synthesis of research evidence.* New York: Cambridge University Press.

Gersten, R., Baker, S. K., Shanahan, T., Linan-Thompson, S., Collins, P., & Scarcella, R. (2007). *Effective literacy and English language instruction for English learners in the elementary grades: A practice guide* (NCEE 2007-4011). Washington, DC: National Center for Education Evaluation and Regional Assistance, Institute of Education Sciences, U.S. Department of Education. Retrieved July 15, 2010, from *ies.ed.gov/ncee.*

Goldenberg, C. (2008). Teaching English language learners: What the research does and does not say. *American Educator, 32*(2), 8–23, 42–44. Retrieved July 20, 2010, from *www.aft.org/pubs-reports/american-educator/index.htm.*

Lambert, L. (1998). *Building leadership capacity in schools.* Alexandria, VA: Association for Supervision and Curriculum Development.

National Clearinghouse for English Language Acquisition. (2010). Frequently asked questions. Retrieved July 10, 2010, from *www.ncela.gwu.edu/faqs.*

National Reading Panel. (2000). *Teaching children to read: An evidence-based assessment of the scientific research literature on reading and its implications for reading instruction.* Washington, DC: National Institute of Child Health and Human Development, National Institutes of Health.

Short, D., Echevarria, J., & Richards-Tutor, C. (2011). Research on academic literacy development in sheltered content classrooms. *Language Teaching Research, 15*(3), 363–380.

Short, D., Echevarria, J., & Vogt, M. E. (2008). *The SIOP Model for administrators.* Boston: Allyn & Bacon.

Short, D., & Fitzsimmons, S. (2006). *Double the work: Challenges and solutions to acquiring language and academic literacy for adolescent English language learners.* A Report to the Carnegie Corporation. New York: Alliance for Education.

Snow, C., Griffin, P., & Burns, S. (Eds.). (2005). *Knowledge to support the teaching of reading: Preparing teachers for a changing world.* Washington, DC: National Academic of Education, Reading Sub-Committee.

Vogt, M. E. (2009). Teachers of English learners: Issues of preparation and professional development. In F. Falk-Ross, S. Szabo, M. B. Sampson, & M. M. Foote (Eds.), *Literacy issues during changing times: A call to action* (pp. 23–36). Commerce, TX: Texas A&M University. The Thirtieth Yearbook of the Association of Literacy Educators & Researchers.

Vogt, M. E., Echevarria, J., & Short, D. (2010). *The SIOP Model for teaching English-language arts to English learners.* Boston: Pearson.

Vogt, M. E., & Shearer, B. (2011). *Reading specialists and literacy coaches in the real world* (3rd ed.). Boston: Pearson.

Zwiers, J. (2008). *Building academic language: Essential practices for content classrooms.* San Francisco: Jossey-Bass.

14

Literacy Assessment in Schools

SUZANNE LANE
DEBRA MOORE

Guiding Questions

- In what ways have changes in educational legislation influenced comprehensive assessment systems in schools?
- What sources of validity evidence can be used to develop a comprehensive and coherent literacy assessment system?
- What are some recent advances in assessment design that have the potential to positively affect literacy assessment?
- What are some advantages and limitations of widely used assessments of beginning literacy skills?

Assessments are considered to be valuable tools for educational reform. Both policy makers and educators have argued that the use of assessments that measure students' thinking and reasoning skills and their ability to apply knowledge to solve realistic, meaningful problems will help shape sound instructional practices by modeling to teachers what is important to teach and to students what is important to learn (Lane & Stone, 2006). The use of assessments, including performance assessments that capture complex thinking skills in large-scale assessment and accountability systems, declined with the requirements of the No Child Left Behind Act of 2001 (U.S. Department of Education, 2005). With the advent of the Common Core Standards initiative (Council of Chief State School Officers [CCSSO] and National Governors Association Center for Best Practices [NGACBP],

2010) and the Race to the Top initiative (U.S. Department of Education, 2009) there is a renewed interest in using large-scale state assessments that capture complex thinking skills that are grounded in academic standards.

The goal of this chapter is to provide literacy leaders with information that will help them use assessments and interpret assessment results in a manner that that will promote sound instructional practice and student learning. Current assessment practices in schools are impacted by federal and state legislation; therefore a school's assessment system reflects decisions regarding assessment practices not only made at the school and district level but also at the state and federal level. Extra effort is needed by all involved in using assessments that provide accurate and meaningful information for improving student achievement and learning.

The chapter begins with a short case example of a teacher's concern about assessment, followed by a discussion of national efforts that have affected assessment systems such as the Common Core Standards (CCSSO & NGACBP, 2010), Race to the Top funding (U.S. Department of Education, 2009), the No Child Left Behind Act (U.S. Department of Education, 2005), and the Reading First legislation (U.S. Department of Education, 2008). It also addresses the different types of assessments that are used in schools for various purposes. The second section addresses the need to construct a validity argument for a school's comprehensive assessment system. The third section discusses some recent advances in the design of assessments that are particularly relevant for literacy assessment, including the use of learning progressions in assessment design, and computer-based tasks and scoring. The fourth section discusses assessments that are used to evaluate the beginning reading skills of students, some of which have been used as part of the Reading First programs. These assessments can have a significant impact on the nature of literacy instruction students receive and therefore are pivotal in shaping their literacy opportunities in school. Below is a case example of a teacher concerned about the emphasis on a single assessment tool used to plan instructional programs in his school.

CASE EXAMPLE

Jamal, a first-grade teacher with 2 years of experience had just completed a graduate course on educational measurement and became concerned with his school's practice of using an assessment of developing reading skills as the sole source for planning the literacy programs for low-achieving students. From his graduate course he learned that no one educational assessment should be the sole source for making important decisions about individual students. He recognized that his school needed to adopt a more comprehensive assessment system and to be more diligent about using tests for their intended purposes. Jamal was also troubled by the fact that the school was administering to low-achieving students this one assessment of developing reading skills to predict their reading comprehension skills in the later elementary grades. He wasn't sure whether this assessment could accurately make such predictions. Many of the first-grade students who performed poorly on this assessment were being grouped for remedial instruction on foundational skills, and in his opinion they were missing valuable classroom instruction on vocabulary and reading comprehension. He questioned the soundness of taking these students out of the classroom for intensive instruction on foundational skills. From his preparation and limited experience, he believed that the foundational skills could be taught in conjunction with vocabulary and reading comprehension. Jamal decided to do some research on best assessment practices in literacy and then have a discussion with the literacy coach in his school. What are Jamal's major assessment and instruction concerns? What should he focus on in examining best assessment practices in literacy? What other sources are needed to help plan a student's educational program in literacy?

ASSESSMENT SYSTEMS IN SCHOOLS

The Common Core Standards in English language arts for K–12 (CCSSO & NGACBP, 2010) will provide the foundation for the next generation of state assessment systems in literacy and therefore will affect the nature of the classroom assessments used by teachers and schools. The Common Core Standards in English language arts (ELA) represent a set of expectations for the literacy knowledge and skills students need so that when they graduate from high school they are prepared for success in college and careers. These Standards emphasize students' ability to reason, synthesize information from various sources, and think critically. The K–12 ELA Common Core Standards are in reading, writing, speaking and listening, and language. In addition, there are grades 6–12 Common Core Standards for literacy in history/social studies, science, and technical subjects, stressing the importance of literacy in other subject domains. Most states have agreed to adopt the Common Core Standards and have competed for federal funding from the U.S. Department of Education's (2009) Race to the Top initiative.

The U.S. Department of Education has provided funding for a consortia of states to develop new assessments that measure the Common Core Standards (CCSSO & NGACBP, 2010). The reauthorization of the Elementary and Secondary Education Act (U.S. Department of Education,

1965) will set guidelines for assessments and their use in the future. For a state to have been eligible for Race to the Top funding, a state needed to show a commitment to improving the quality of its state assessment system, measure student achievement and student growth, and ensure cohesiveness among formative, interim, and summative assessments (U.S. Department of Education, 2009). Moreover, states needed to show how the assessment system will measure "standards against which student achievement has traditionally been difficult to measure" and include "items that will be varied and elicit complex student demonstrations or applications of knowledge and skills" (p. 8).

Two consortiums have been funded to support this new generation of content standards and state assessment systems, the Partnership for Assessment of Readiness for College and Career and the Smarter Balanced Assessment System. As an example, the Smarter Balanced Assessment System calls for formative assessments, periodic through-course performance tasks (i.e., interim assessments) and an end-of-year reference exam that are used together for both summative and accountability purposes (Darling-Hammond & Pecheone, 2010). The through-course performance tasks are to be curriculum embedded (e.g., exhibitions, product developments), standardized, and administered and scored by teachers, with moderation. The end-of-year reference exams are intended to include various item formats (e.g., selected response, short and extended answer, complex electronic items), be computer adaptive, scaled vertically across a range of learning progressions, and use both computer-automated scoring and moderated human scoring. Although there are challenging assessment design and psychometric issues that need to be addressed for this new generation of assessment systems, this opportunity needs to be embraced so as to ensure that assessments not only reflect meaningful tasks, but are positioned to inform and enhance both teaching and student learning (Lane, 2010).

The Reading First legislation, a part of the No Child Left Behind Act, 2001), has had a large impact on instruction and assessment of students' developing reading skills (U.S. Department of Education, 2005). As indicated by Paris (2005), a direct result of this legislation was an increased use of alphabet knowledge, phonemic awareness, and oral reading fluency as predictors of later reading achievement, with little attention given to vocabulary and reading comprehension in the early elementary grades. Paris argued that these former reading skills are constrained skills, in that these skills develop from "nonexistent to high or ceiling levels in childhood" (p. 187), and as a consequence the developmental trajectories of mastery for these constrained skills are based on highly variable and unstable data over time. Thus, the validity of the interpretations of scores from assessments that assess constrained skills needs further evaluation.

Literacy leaders in schools, including principals, literacy coaches, teachers, and other literacy educators, are pivotal in shaping literacy instruction and assessment and promoting student learning under these new initiatives. Literacy leaders need to have a vital role in designing a comprehensive assessment system that includes formative, interim, and summative assessments.

Framework for Assessments

Formative, interim, and summative assessments all play a vital role in a school's assessment system. Formative assessments are embedded within curriculum and instruction to promote student learning and they are used by teachers to diagnose where students are in their learning, identify gaps in student understanding, and promote student learning. Black and William (1998) argue that formative assessments are part of the whole educational system that uses the information from the assessments to adapt teaching to meet students' needs. An important outcome of the use of formative assessments in classrooms is their positive effect on student achievement and learning (William, 2010). Literacy leaders should become familiar with Stiggins's (2010) delineation of the competencies teachers and school leaders need to adopt, develop, and implement formative assessments that support learning. Interim or periodic assessments are administered by the school or district several times a year; the results can be meaningfully aggregated to the school or district level and they can inform decisions not only at the student level but at the class, school, and district level (Perie, Marion, & Gong, 2009). Their purposes include predicting student scores on large-scale assessments, evaluating an educational program, identifying gaps in student learning, or providing information for an accountability program. Summative assessments are used at the end of the school year or term to assess student performance against content standards. States have developed and implemented summative assessments as part of their accountability program to inform policy. Summative assessments also include teacher-administered end-of-semester tests that are for grading purposes only. Regardless of the nature of the assessment, evidence is needed to ensure that they promote valid score interpretations. Both large-scale assessments and teacher made or used assessments require evidence to support the accuracy of score interpretations.

Another way to conceptualize the many purposes of assessments is by the types of educational decisions for which they are used. Educational assessments may be used for informing decisions about policy at the district, state, and national levels; decisions about curricula, educational programs, and schools including formative interim and summative evaluations; and decisions about students including managing instruction and placement of students into programs (Nitko & Brookhart, 2007).

Nitko and Brookhart (2007) expand on the decisions about students that involve managing instruction. Under managing instruction they include (1) formative evaluations for the purposes of planning instruction activities, placing students into learning sequences, monitoring students' progress, diagnosing learning difficulties, and feedback to students on how to improve; and (2) summative evaluations for the purposes of reporting to students about achievement and to teachers about effectiveness, and of assigning grades to students. As discussed above interim assessments can inform various decisions at the student, school, and district level.

DEVELOPING A VALIDITY ARGUMENT

Literacy leaders need to recognize that the most fundamental technical consideration in the evaluation of educational assessment systems is validity. Validity pertains to the meaningfulness, appropriateness, and usefulness of test score interpretations (Messick, 1989). As stated in the Standards for Educational and Psychological Testing (American Educational Research Association [AERA], American Psychological Association [APA], & National Council on Measurement in Education [NCME], 1999), validity is the "degree to which evidence and theory support the interpretations of test scores entailed by proposed uses of tests" (p. 9). Test score interpretations therefore need to be verified by both empirical evidence and a logical argument. This requires the design of systematic validity plans for evaluating the efficacy of comprehensive validity arguments (Kane, 2006), and entails the synthesis of empirical results against a theory of action and validity argument.

Kane's (2006) argument-based validation framework assumes that the "proposed interpretations and uses will be explicitly stated as an argument, or network of inferences and supporting assumptions, leading from observations to conclusions and decisions" (p. 17). Validation involves an "appraisal of the coherence of this argument and of the plausibility of its inferences and assumptions" (p. 17). Kane's framework involves both an interpretative argument and a validity argument. An interpretative argument "specifies the proposed interpretations and uses of test results by laying out the network of inferences and assumptions leading from the observed performances to the conclusions and decisions based on the performances" (p. 23), whereas the validity argument allows for an evaluation of the interpretative argument. As an example, in the interpretative argument for a reading test in the early elementary grades, one of a number of inferences may take the form: If a first-grade student scores relatively low on this reading skills test, then the student will have problems in reading comprehension in later grades. As Kane points out, the validity argument provides an evaluation of the interpretative argument and begins with an evaluation of the argument as a whole to make sure it is reasonable, and if it is reasonable, then its inferences and assumptions would be evaluated using appropriate evidence. In this example of the reading skills test inference, evidence would be needed to support or possibly refute the inference. In summary, a validity argument requires specifying the proposed interpretations and uses of the assessment system, using measurement procedures consistent with these proposed uses, and then critically evaluating and providing evidence for the merits and worth of the initial assumptions and resulting inferences. Further, the consequences of the decisions made based on the test scores must also be evaluated. As stated by Cronbach (1988), "validation speaks to a diverse and potentially critical audience, therefore the argument must link concepts, evidence, social and personal consequences, and values" (p. 4).

Literacy leaders in schools need to be involved in delineating the proposed purposes and uses for their comprehensive assessment system, including formative, interim, and summative assessments. It might be helpful for literacy leaders to consider a "theory of action" in developing interpretative arguments for their assessment systems. A theory of action will help guide the development of a more complete interpretative argument. In the Race to the Top Assessment Program Application for New Grants (U.S. Department of Education, 2009) a theory of action was required and evaluated based on whether it was "logical, coherent, and credible and will result in improved student academic outcomes" (p. 31). Proposals for Race to the Top funding needed to propose a theory of action that included a description of and rationale for

> (a) each component of the proposed assessment system and the relationship of the component to other components in the system; (b) how the assessment results produced by each component will be used; (c) how the assessments and assessment results will be incorporated into a coherent educational system (i.e., a system that includes standards, assessments, curriculum, instruction, and professional development); and (d) how the educational system as a whole will improve student achievement and college- and career-readiness. (U.S. Department of Education, 2009, p. 31)

Within this theory of action for an assessment system, the goals of the assessment system, the purposes and uses of the assessment system, the outcomes of the system (e.g., increase the rates of college and career readiness for all students), and the mediating outcomes necessary to achieve the ultimate outcomes (e.g., students will score higher on the assessments, instruction and curriculum will improve) need to be articulated (Marion, 2010). The final step is to prioritize the key components of the theory of action and to further delineate them to support assessment design and the validity argument.

Sources of Validity Evidence

A meaningful way to organize the collection and examination of evidence for a validity evaluation has been proposed by the *Standards for Educational and Psychological Testing* (AERA, APA, & NCME, 1999). They include evidence based on test content, evidence based on response processes, evidence based on internal structure, evidence based on relations to other variables, and evidence based on consequences of testing. Although the *Standards* were developed for more formal measures, such as standardized summative and interim achievement tests, many aspects of it are relevant to tests constructed and administered by teachers for their own use in the classroom and tests that accompany curriculum and instructional materials. Thus, it is important for literacy leaders to be familiar with the fundamental aspects of validity when considering the adoption, development, and implementation of student assessments.

It is common for a test to have more than one purpose such as monitoring individual student progress and evaluating the quality of the educational program at the school, district, or state level. The type of evidence that is needed is dependent on a particular purpose so the validity evidence needed for one purpose will differ for another purpose. Tests that provide information about individual student performance can be used to evaluate a student's achievement and progress, diagnose student strengths and needs, plan interventions and instructional efforts, identify appropriate education programs, and certify individual achievement. Tests that provide information at the aggregate level, such as the state, school district, or school level, are used to evaluate and monitor educational programs and to make decisions about the success of policies and programs that are being evaluated. Tests can provide information at both student level as well as at the state, district, or school level. It is important, however, to ensure that there is validity evidence to support each use. In evaluating the quality of a test for its intended purpose, the stakes associated with a given test's use needs to be considered. If the stakes are particularly high, such as making a decision about whether a student is promoted or placed into a particular program, the more important it is that the test score inferences are supported by strong technical and validity evidence. It is also essential that the users of tests interpret test results in light of other relevant information about the student or group of students. Using tests to make important decisions about an individual student or a group of students entails "collecting sound collateral information both to assist in understanding the factors that contributed to test results and to provide corroborating evidence that supports inferences based on test results" (AERA, APA, & NCME, 1999, p. 140). Further, it is important to recognize that it is not enough to consider individual pieces of validity evidence; instead an evaluative judgment based on the synthesis of the validity evidence is needed to evaluate the worth of the interpretative argument (Haertel, 1999; Kane, 2006).

The evaluation of the fairness of an assessment is inherently related to all sources of validity evidence. Bias can be conceptualized "as differential validity of a given interpretation of a test score for any definable, relevant subgroup of test takers" (Cole & Moss, 1989, p. 205). This conception of bias as differential validity suggests that ensuring a fair assessment requires evidence to support the meaningfulness, appropriateness, and usefulness of the inferences made from test scores for all groups of students. The intended population and subpopulations of examinees should be considered in the design of assessments. For example, the validity of score inferences from an assessment is dependent on its capability of evoking the same intended level of cognitive activity for all groups of students regardless of their gender, cultural, or linguistic backgrounds. Therefore, task context should not interfere differentially with student performance. As another example, if an assessment requires students to compose an essay on the computer, equitable opportunity for practice in using the computer for writing is an important consideration. The amount of writing required on reading assessments can be examined to help ensure that writing ability will not unduly influence the ability of the students to demonstrate what they know and can do on these assessments. Scoring rubrics can be designed to ensure that the relevant reading skills are the focus, and not students' writing ability. The use of other response formats, such as graphic organizers, on reading assessments may alleviate the concerns of writing ability confounding student performance on reading assessments (O'Reilly & Sheehan, 2009).

Evidence Based on Test Content

Evidence based on test content includes "logical or empirical analyses of the adequacy with which the test content represents the content domain and of the relevance of the content domain to the proposed interpretations" (AERA, APA, & NCME, 1999, p. 11). It is important that the test samples the range of knowledge and elicits the thinking skills reflected in the target domain. Evidence based on test content can also be obtained by experts examining the relationship between the content of the test and the target domain as well as its intended use and score interpretations. As an example, prior to selecting a literacy assessment for identifying young students with reading difficulties, literacy experts should evaluate whether data have been obtained to support the relationship between the test content and the domain it is intended to measure as well as its intended use. If a test is to be used for a purpose other than that for which it was initially developed, it is essential to examine the appropriateness of the content domain and the proposed new use (AERA, APA, & NCME). As an example, if an added purpose of a test is to help monitor student progress in reading, it would be essential to obtain data that the test content can support that purpose and provides meaningful and accurate information about a student's progress. If an added purpose of a literacy test is to measure growth in identifying multisyllabic words, evidence is needed to support this added use of the test. This would most likely include evidence that the content of the test allows for the measurement of growth. Evidence would be needed to indicate that there are adequate samples of multisyllabic words to support this added test use.

Evidence Based on Response Processes

Evidence based on response processes requires the theoretical and empirical analyses of the processes students are engaged in when taking the test and extent to which the test elicits the intended processes (AERA, APA, & NCME, 1999). Several methods have been used to examine whether tasks are assessing the intended cognitive skills and processes (Messick, 1989), including protocol analysis, analysis of reasons, and analysis of errors. Students are asked to think aloud as they solve a task or describe retrospectively how they solve the task in *protocol analysis*. In the method of *analysis of reasons*, students are asked to provide rationales to their responses to the tasks. The method of *analysis of errors* requires an analysis of the procedures, concepts, or representations of the problems so as to make inferences about students' misconceptions in their thinking. This latter approach, analysis of errors, is a fundamental aspect of measures such as running records and oral readings.

As an example, if the intention of a reading comprehension test is for students to make inferences based on one or more reading passage, it is important to determine the extent to which students are engaged in inferential reasoning and not merely identifying material directly from text. For classroom assessment purposes, teachers can ask students to describe what information they used to respond to the reading comprehension question for verification that the assessment elicited inferential skills. For a writing task, monitoring and examining students' written drafts provides evidence regarding students' writing processes.

As indicated in the *Standards* (AERA, APA, & NCME, 1999), it is important to examine the response processes of those who evaluate student performances or products. It is also important to ensure that raters are applying the scoring criteria appropriately and consistently, and are not being influenced by irrelevant factors when evaluating students' responses on writing assessments and reading assessments that require students to produce a verbal or written response.

Evidence Based on Internal Structure

Evidence based on internal structure requires analyses of the extent to which relationships among test items and test parts are consistent with the targeted domain (AERA, APA, & NCME, 1999). As an example, if a reading assessment has multiple reading passages that are intended to be comparable in complexity and are used on different occasions to monitor student progress, evidence is needed to demonstrate the comparability of the reading passages. If they are not comparable, the student may be showing progress or lack of progress due to differences in difficulty of the passages being used on different occasions. Also, if a literacy assessment provides multiple scores that are used for instructional decision making, evidence is needed to ensure that the scores are not highly related, instead each is assessing some unique aspect of the domain. As an example, if a writing assessment provides scores for voice, organization, structure, and mechanics, evidence is needed that each of the scores reflects some unique aspect of the writing construct.

Evidence Based on the Relationship of Test Scores to Variables External to the Test

The relationship of test scores to variables external to the test can also serve as important validity evidence (AERA, APA, & NCME, 1999). External variables that may be of interest include measures of some criteria that the test is intended to predict as well as measures that assess similar and different domains. For example, if a reading fluency test that is administered in the early elementary school years claims to predict reading comprehension in the latter elementary years, evidence supporting this claim is needed. As another example, if the goal of a reading comprehension test that consists of constructed-response items is to measure students' reading achievement only, then scores on the test should be related to scores on other similar reading comprehension tests and to a lesser degree scores on writing assessments. Otherwise, the reading comprehension scores may unduly reflect a student's writing ability.

Literacy experts need to consider the extent to which the validity evidence for a test's predictive capability can be generalized to a new situation. Predictive validity may vary due to the way the criterion performance (e.g., reading comprehension) is defined, the type of curriculum involved, the measure used to assess the criterion performance, and the time period that the evidence was collected. The extent to which these factors vary in a particular testing situation will impact on predictive validity evidence.

Evidence Based on Consequences of Testing

Evidence based on consequences of testing requires the examination of both the intended positive consequences and the potentially negative consequences that occur when using a test and making decisions about individual students or groups of students based on test results (AERA, APA, & NCME). The values inherent in a testing program should be delineated and the consequences, both positive and negative, of the decisions made based on the test scores should be examined. This is essential for users of assessments to consider. For example, if a score from a reading fluency test is being used to develop an individual student's educational plan, it is important to consider the outcomes for the student, both negative and positive. The student's performance on a reading fluency test might suggest that the student be placed in a small reading intervention group that would provide assistance in developing fluency, but at the same time, the student may miss essential class instruction that addresses the student's vocabulary and comprehension needs. Moreover, in using the test results in instructional planning, collateral information must be considered along with the test results.

Studies have documented the relationship between changes in instructional practice and improved performance on assessments that measure complex thinking skills. A study by Stecher and his colleagues compared teachers' reported instructional practices in schools with low- and high-gain scores on Kentucky's state assessment (Kentucky Instructional Results Information Systems; KIRIS; Stecher, Barron, Kaganoff, & Goodwin, 1998). Although their study revealed few consistent findings across subject areas and grades, there was a positive relationship between standards-based practices in writing and the KIRIS direct writing assessment at the middle school level. As an example, more seventh-grade writing teachers in high- versus low-gain score schools reported integrating writing with other subjects and increasing their emphasis on various aspects of the writing process. Other studies that have examined the relationship between changes in instructional practice and improved performance have been conducted using Maryland's state performance-based assessment (MSPAP) that tapped high-level thinking skills (Lane, Parke, & Stone, 2002; Stone & Lane, 2003). The relationship between changes in MSPAP scores for schools and classroom instruction and assessment practices, student motivation, and students' and teachers' beliefs about and attitude toward MSPAP and school characteristics was examined. Results indicated that teacher-reported instruction-related variables explained differences in performance on MSPAP in writing and reading. Schools in which teachers reported that their instruction over the years reflected more reform-oriented problem types and learning outcomes similar to those assessed on MSPAP had higher levels of school performance on MSPAP than schools in which teachers reported that their instruction reflected less reform-oriented problem types and learning outcomes. More importantly, for the writing and reading domains, teacher-reported reform-oriented instruction-related variables also explained differences in rates of change in MSPAP school performance on writing and reading over time. That is, an increase in reported use of reform-oriented tasks in writing and reading and focus on the performance-based reading and writing learning outcomes in instruction were associated with greater rates of change in MSPAP school performance over a 5-year period. These results indicate that performance-based instruction has a positive impact on student learning and attainment of high-level thinking skills.

Threats to Validity

Two sources of potential threats to the validity of test use and score interpretations are construct underrepresentation and construct irrelevant variance (Messick, 1989). Construct underrepresentation occurs when an assessment does not fully capture the targeted construct, resulting in score interpretations that may not be generalizable to the larger domain of interest. Examples include a reading skills test with a limited number of items and a reading comprehension test with too few reading passages or perhaps reading passages that only reflect one genre. It is important for users of tests to ensure that the test itself is measuring the content and the cognitive skills that it claims to assess. If the test is not representing the domain of interest, the interpretations based on the test scores are jeopardized.

Construct-irrelevant variance occurs when one or more irrelevant constructs is being assessed along with the intended construct. Sources of construct-irrelevant variance for assessments may include task wording, task context, response mode, and raters' attention to irrelevant features of responses. As an example, if performance on a writing assessment is unduly influenced by the students' familiarity of the context of the writing prompt, students who have similar writing proficiency will perform differently due to their familiarity with the context. In this case, the assessment is measuring in part a construct that is not the assessment target—context familiarity. Construct-irrelevant variance may also occur when raters score student responses to tasks according to features that do not reflect the scoring criteria and are irrelevant to the construct being assessed (Messick, 1994). This can be addressed by clearly articulated scoring rubrics and qualified scorers. For classroom purposes, teachers who apply scoring rubrics to student work appropriately and consistently help ensure that the targeted domain is being evaluated and not some irrelevant feature.

Studies have examined the extent to which raters accurately apply the criteria in scoring rubrics. One study examined relevant and irrelevant scoring rubric features that may affect holistic scores on the 7th- and 10th-grade reading state assessment for Kansas (Pomplun, Capps, & Sundbye, 1998). Based on a regression analysis, the researchers found that the correctness of the answer was the primary feature reflected in holistic scores. The correct answer across grade levels and subject areas accounted for over 50% of the holistic score variance. With regard to irrelevant rubric features, the length of response (i.e., number of words) was most influential. Number of words was a significant predictor of holistic score variance when the other rubric features were held constant in reading at both 7th- and 10th-grade. Further research needs to determine the construct relevancy of the length of the response.

Other studies that have examined the extent to which construct-irrelevant features affect student performance have studied the comparability of scores assigned to handwritten essays and versions of the same essays typed on a word processor. One study found that typed versions of essays obtained lower scores than handwritten essays using the Massachusetts Comprehensive Assessment Systems Language Arts Tests for grades 4, 8, and 12 (Russell & Tao, 2004). In this study, the raters indicated that they detected more mechanical errors in the computer-printed responses and some raters suggested that for the handwritten essays, they identified more with the students and could see the effort students put into their writing. However, a study conducted by Wolfe, Bolton, Feltovich, and Welch (1993) contradicted the findings of this study. They found that transcribed computer versions received higher scores than the handwritten original essays. The results of these studies suggest that if assessment programs allow students to either handwrite essays or use a word processor, an irrelevant source of variance may be introduced into the rating of student responses if expert raters are used. Moreover, if programs have raters change from scoring handwritten versions to scoring word-processed versions, the comparability of scores over time may be jeopardized.

Construct-irrelevant variance may also occur when examinees are given a choice of prompt or task. Proponents who support student choice of tasks advocate that choice allows examinees to select a task that has context they are more familiar with, which may lead to better performance than if they are assigned a task (Powers, Fowles, Farnum, & Gerritz, 1992). Some have argued, therefore, that allowing for choice may minimize any potential negative impact of irrelevant contextual variables. If the purpose of an essay is to assess students' ability to organize evidence and craft a coherent argument or position on a familiar topic, and not to assess specific content, then choice may be preferable (Bridgeman, Morgan, & Wang, 1997). Wainer, Wang, and Thissen (1994) argued, however, that choice not only measures the student's proficiency in a given subject area but also measures the student's conception of his or her ability to pick the easiest problem to answer. In this manner, choice introduces a source of construct-irrelevant variance and potentially diminishes the validity of the score interpretations. Nevertheless, not providing choice may disadvantage some students who are unfamiliar with the topic and if the topic is not relevant to the construct being assessed, it will be a source of irrelevant score variance.

ADVANCES IN ASSESSMENT DESIGN AND SCORING

A number of advances in assessment design and scoring are particularly relevant for literacy assessments, including the use of learning progressions in assessment design, computer-based tasks, and automated scoring systems.

Use of Learning Progressions in Assessment Design

The deeper the understanding of how students acquire and structure knowledge and cognitive skills, and how they perform cognitive tasks, the better we are at assessing students' cognitive thinking and reasoning skills and to obtain information that will lead to improved learning. The extent to which theories and models of cognition and learning are used in the design of assessments will therefore have an impact on how well they can monitor student progress and provide meaningful information to guide instruction. Literacy assessments that are designed to reflect learning progressions that describe successively more sophisticated ways of understanding and reasoning in a domain will improve the meaningfulness and usefulness of assessment results for monitoring student learning and informing instruction (National Research Council, 2006). The Australians have been effective in using learning progressions as a basis for student assessment and instruction. An example of a reading comprehension learning progression developed by the Australian Council for Educational Research (Forster, 2009) is provided in Figure 14.1.

It is important to note that for many subject domains cognitive models of how competency develops have not been fully developed (National Research Council, 2006), including models in the reading and writing domains. As a consequence, the specification of learning progressions needs to be supplemented by what expert literacy educators know about student learning.

Computer-Based Task Design

Computer-based simulation tasks allow for the assessment of complex reasoning and inferential skills that cannot be measured by more traditional assessment formats. Students' strategies, as well as their products, can be captured, which can be valuable in monitoring the progress of student learning and guiding instruction (Bennett, Persky, Weiss, & Jenkins, 2007).

Several issues arise in the design of computer-based tasks, including the extent to which the assessment is measuring factors that are irrelevant to the construct that is intended to be assessed. For example, the computer interface should be familiar to examinees and they should have had the opportunity to practice with it. It is also important to ensure that the range of cognitive skills and knowledge assessed not be narrowed to those that are more easily assessed using computer technology.

Computer-based simulation tasks in reading and writing domains are being designed and evaluated for their potential inclusion in an integrated accountability and formative assessment system (Bennett & Gitomer, 2009; O'Reilly & Sheehan, 2009). As an example, in the reading domain, a cognitive model of reading competency has been proposed to serve as the basis for both assessing learning and advancing learning (O'Reilly & Sheehan, 2009). As part of this cognitive model, three design features that are aimed at assessing deeper processing by requiring students to actively construct meaning from text have been delineated. First, in the assessment a scenario is provided that describes the purpose of reading. The purpose of reading is clearly articulated because students engage in the reading process in mean-

Level	Description of Reading Comprehension
5	Students can tackle difficult texts and complete sophisticated reading tasks; deal with information that is difficult to find in unfamiliar texts, demonstrate detailed understanding of these texts, and determine which information is relevant to the task; and evaluate texts critically, draw on specialized knowledge to formulate hypotheses, and deal with concepts that are contrary to expectations
4	Students can tackle difficult tasks, such as identifying embedded information, constructing meaning of part of a text by considering the text as a whole, and handling ambiguities; and demonstrate accurate understanding of complex texts and evaluate texts critically.
3	Students can handle moderately complex reading tasks, such as identifying several pieces of information and sorting out detailed competing information requiring consideration of many criteria to compare, contrast, or categorize; draw links between different parts of a text; and understand text in a detailed way in relation to knowledge acquired in daily life.
2	Students can handle basic reading tasks, such as locating straightforward information, making low-level inferences, using some outside knowledge to understand a well-defined part of a text, and using their own experiences to help explain aspects of text.
1	Students can deal with only the least complex reading tasks, such as finding explicitly stated pieces of information and recognizing the main theme or author's purpose in a text on a familiar topic when the information is readily accessible in the text; and make a connection between common, everyday information in the text.

FIGURE 14.1. Example of a reading comprehension learning progression. Based on Forster (2009).

ingfully different ways dependent on the purpose of reading. Second, students are required to read multiple texts so as to encourage the integration and synthesis of information across texts. Last, to assess students' evaluation skills texts of varying quality are provided. One of the four important components assessed in this reading competency model is the student's ability to extract discourse structure (the other three are understanding vocabulary, drawing necessary inferences, and identifying important details). The assessment provided graphical representations to students so they can map out the structure of the text, including graphic hierarchical organizers and construct maps. As O'Reilly and Sheehan point out, requiring students to construct a lengthy written summary may be more appropriate in the assessment of writing as the quality of students' response to a reading task can be affected by their writing ability. The use of graphical representations instead of written summaries helps ensure that a student's writing ability does not affect his or her performance on the reading tasks. Further, the use of graphical representations will more easily allow for computer-automated scoring procedures to be used in the scoring of students' competency in organizing and summarizing information that they have read from one or more texts. This research program draws on models of cognition and learning and advances in technology and measurement to design assessments that capture students' complex thinking skills and thus will provide meaningful information to guide instruction. As the researchers have indicated there are numerous issues that need to be addressed in the design of these computer-based simulation tasks, such as issues related to the format of response, content and cognitive skill representativeness, and scoring of student performances.

Automated Scoring Systems

Automated scoring systems for evaluating student performance to computer-based tasks, including computer-delivered writing assessments, allow for timely feedback and address the cost and demands of human scoring. Further, automated scoring procedures are consistent in their application of the scoring rubric, explicitly allow for the test designer to control what features are attended to in scoring student responses, and allow for the collection and recording of multiple features of student performance (Williamson, Behar, & Mislevy, 2006). However, the scores generated from computer-automated scoring systems may be somewhat inaccurate if the scoring procedures do not reflect important features of proficiency (Bennett & Gitomer, 2009). Validation studies for automated scoring systems can provide evidence for appropriate score interpretations and uses. There are three categories of validation approaches for automated scoring systems: approaches focusing on the consistency among scores given by different scorers (human and computer), approaches focusing on the relationship between test scores and external measures of the construct being assessed, and approaches focusing on the scoring process (Yang, Buchendahl, Juszkiewicz, & Bhola, 2002). Studies have focused on the first category, on the relationship between human and computer-generated scores, typically indicating that the relationship between human scores and those generated by the computer is very similar to the relationship between the scores produced by two humans. Validation studies that focus on the latter two categories are scarce. Further, both construct-irrelevant variance and construct underrepresentation may affect the validity of scores generated by automated scoring systems in that the systems may be influenced by irrelevant features of students' responses and assign a higher or lower score than deserved or the systems may not fully represent the construct being assessed that can affect score interpretations (Powers et al., 1992).

STRENGTHS AND LIMITATIONS
OF ASSESSMENT MEASURES
OF EARLY READING SKILLS

The use of assessments for evaluating students' beginning reading skills is prolific. This section briefly discusses some literacy assessments of early reading skills that are being used for multiple purposes such as determining functional reading levels, designing interventions, and monitoring student progress. As previously indicated, it is imperative for users of assessments to ensure that there is sufficient validity evidence when using a test for a given purpose. Paris (2005) has raised concern regarding the capability of some assessments of beginning reading skills to monitor student progress because of the underlying differences in developmental trajectories of reading skills. Reading skills such as alphabetic knowledge, phonemic awareness, and oral reading fluency are constrained in that they develop from "nonexistent to high or ceiling levels" (p. 187) in young children. In contrast, vocabulary and reading comprehension are considered unconstrained in that they have no ceiling effect. Thus, developmental trajectories differ across these skill types. Some of the validity evidence that has been obtained for constrained skills needs to be interpreted cautiously because the statistical methods used assume distributions that are not obtainable for constrained skills (Paris).

The difference between predictive ability and causation also needs to be considered when interpreting test scores. As Paris (2005) states, "knowing letter names in kindergarten is probably not the mediator of reading comprehension at grades 3 and 4. Instead, home environment and many variables associated with parent–child interactions probably account for better reading comprehension in later grades, especially if those same family and home factors continue to be influential several years later" (p. 197). When using test scores to make inferences about students, contextual information is needed to inform the score inferences and actions (Haertel, 1999). Although scores on phonemic awareness, alphabet knowledge, oral reading rate and fluency assessments in grades K–1 are related to current and future reading comprehension scores, they are all related to one another and many environmental and social variables. The inclusion of these three enabling skills on early reading assessments instead of vocabulary and reading comprehension is based on correlation coefficients that do not account for contextual variables. Further, inappropriately attributing the causation to a correlation and ignoring contextual variables that contribute to the correlation has led to potentially negative consequences of using these tests in the early years. As Paris has indicated, some have inappropriately argued that "children should be taught constrained skills first and often, rather than other reading skills, because measures of alphabet knowledge, print concepts, and phonemic awareness identify children who later read well or poorly" (p. 197). Paris also pointed out that "interventions on these skills are important, but, ironically, the instruction may also provide ancillary benefits for practice on related skills, motivation, and guided reading. In other words, the assessment and instruction of constrained skills may be confounded with multiple variables, and they may be effective for reasons other than a causal relation" (p. 198).

Given these concerns raised by Paris (2005) and others, a few of the reading assessments for beginning readers are be reviewed. The brief review illustrates the importance of evaluating the validity evidence obtained to support the use of a test for a particular purpose.

Running Records

While originally used to identify the functional reading level of students, running records are now being used to monitor student progress, to diagnose reading needs, and even to serve as a benchmark or an interim measure (Fawson, Reutzel, Smith, Ludlow, & Sudweeks. 2006). There is little validity evidence, however, that demonstrates the utility of running records for these other purposes. Fawson and colleagues found that the most reliable way to determine a student's functional reading level is to have the student read three passages and average the error score. These authors noted that the observed variability in texts that were identical in reading level suggests that identifying the level of texts can be inaccurate, especially when using leveled texts from different sources (Fawson et al.). Consequently, more than one text of the same level is needed when determining the functional reading level of a student so as to ensure accurate instructional decisions that result from the use of the assessment.

Ardoin and Christ (2009) suggest that readability indexes are not the best measures for identifying passages of equal difficulty because of the variability in difficulty of any one passage that results, yet this procedure is consistently relied upon as the sole means to determine passage equivalency for many reading programs. These authors further suggest that, in addition to a readability index, other methodologies, including empirical evidence from actual students, be used to verify the readability of a passage. Examining the results from programs that have verified equivalent difficulty levels through additional processes may afford some confidence in using these assessments. The variability in difficulty of passages is of particular concern when using running records to monitor student growth over time (Ardoin & Christ). If an easier passage is used initially, followed by the use of a more difficult passage, and a student's resulting scores are similar, erroneously it may be concluded that a student is not progressing over time when in fact the student has progressed but the scores are impacted by the differential easiness of the passages.

Informal Reading Inventories

Informal reading inventories (IRIs) were designed to evaluate specific aspects of a reading performance (Nilsson, 2008). In recent years, reading inventories have expanded in purpose and are now being used to match students with appropriate reading materials, place students in reading groups, design interventions, and monitor student progress over time (Nilsson). As with running records, limited validity evidence is available for any of the purported uses, particularly the monitoring of student progress over time. Similar to running records, the administration of these inventories is predicated on frequent administrations of identically leveled reading passages; therefore, passage equivalency is important and using more than one passage to determine functional reading level is recommended. In addition, because the passage a student reads is determined by the graded word lists included in the inventory, the source of the lists and the appropriateness to the intended grade level is also important and is not always included in the technical report (Nilsson). A lexical analysis of the word lists for six currently published IRIs found considerable overlap in words for the preprimer to grade 2 levels, but virtually no overlap in words between inventories for grades 3 through 6 (French, 2005). This indicates that there is no expectation of comparability in functional reading levels between inventories at the upper grade levels, but some comparability might be expected at the lower grades where more overlap in words occurs. The samples used to establish the norms for IRIs tend to be very small, and neither representative of grade levels for which the inventory is intended nor the variety of demographics (e.g., ethnicity, racial) one would expect from a nationally representative sample, therefore, careful examination of the sample would need to be used to determine whether the suggested interpretations of these scores is applicable to a given situation.

Paris and Hoffman (2004) note that IRIs, as well as running records, are legitimate formative tools for assessing student growth and program evaluation due to their authenticity and alignment with classroom practices. However, in their experience, extensive training and professional development are needed to ensure teachers are using them consistently and accurately (Paris & Carpenter, 2003). Also, they indicated that analyzing student growth across leveled texts required scaling with item response theory, a psychometric procedure unlikely to be accessible to a wide variety of schools (Paris & Hoffman).

Developmental Reading Assessment (2nd Edition)

The Developmental Reading Assessment (2nd Edition; DRA2) was designed to help teachers determine a student's functional reading level and identify his or her strengths and weaknesses in relation to reading engagement, oral fluency, and comprehension skills so teachers can design instructional interventions (Pearson Education, 2009). The technical manual indicates that the DRA2 also can be used to "understand a student's strengths and weaknesses, monitor student growth and development, prepare students for standardized accountability assessments, and help teachers communicate with stakeholders" (p. 4). The manual provides moderately high predictive validity evidence with selected standardized reading tests in support of the claim that the assessment prepares students for standardized tests. Although the predictive validity evidence suggests that the DRA2 has some predictive power, one cannot conclude that this evidence indicates that the test "prepares" students for a standardized test. As Paris (2005) has pointed out, it is important to differentiate between prediction and causation, and recognize evidence that supports one over the other. The misinterpretation of validity evidence can have unintended consequences for instruction and student learning.

Again, if being used in a situation with repeated administrations, the equivalency of passages deemed to be identical in reading level is important. For this version, there is some evidence, although not explained in specific detail, that the difficulty level of the passages was empirically verified. Some evidence in support of this claim is that the variability within passages is greater than the variability between passages and that mean scores decrease as a student reads passages beyond his or her functional reading level (Pearson Education, 2009).

Maze Technique

For second grade and higher, the Maze technique (MZ), a modified Cloze technique, is used to assess reading comprehension (Rathvon, 2004). The MZ has strong criterion validity and is considered to be adequate in monitoring student progress over time (Fuchs & Fuchs, 1999). The MZ has also been found to have moderately high to high correlations with several popular standardized reading tests (Marcotte & Hintze, 2009; Shinn, Deno, & Epsin, 2000; Jenkins & Jewel, 1993). In addition, the strength of relationship between MZ and achievement test performance, in one study, did not show a decline as the grade level increased; a phenomenon seen with oral reading fluency measures (Jenkins & Jewel). Even though correlations on MZ assessments showed no clear trend, the standard deviations increased across grades, which may suggest that the assessment is measuring different constructs at higher grade levels rather than a single global construct (Jenkins & Jewel).

Marcotte and Hintze (2009) found the MZ assessment when combined with a simple "words read correctly per minute" oral reading fluency count predicted 61% of the observed variability in scores on a standardized reading assessment. They also suggest that the MZ may be a good measure to identify students who have mastered decoding, but are still struggling readers. They caution, however, that the validity of individual decisions made based on growth measured across short periods of time (as little as 4 weeks) needs to be examined.

Dynamic Indicators of Basic Early Literacy Skills

The Dynamic Indicators of Basic Early Literacy Skills (DIBELS) is a series of tests designed to identify students at risk to score below proficient on state accountability measures, monitor their progress toward proficiency, and evaluate the effectiveness of reading instruction (Brunsman, 2005; Shanahan, 2005; Rathvon, 2004). The test, however, is not meant to be used as the only assessment for students with reading disabilities (Brunsman). No technical manual exists for the assessments, but there are many studies cited on the website that can be accessed by the public (*dibels.uoregon. edu/*).

Readability levels of the passages were determined by the Spache index, which was chosen based on a pilot study with second-grade students (Rathvon, 2004). Passages at other levels were not verified empirically. The authors of the DIBELS noted that any one passage differed widely in readability level depending on the index used (Rathvon), which again highlights the concerns with comparability of readability levels among different programs and tests, and the need to use more than one passage when determining a student's functional reading level and the instructional decisions that will be made based on it. In addition, Rathvon noted that the difference in readability level between second and third grade is minimal. Since the DIBELS is used as a benchmark assessment or as a monitoring tool (Brunsman, 2005; Shanahan, 2005), enough passages of equivalent difficulty to support the desired assessment frequency needs to be available.

The Oral Reading Fluency (D-ORF) measure has the strongest empirical support because of decades of research into fluency measures associated with curriculum-based measurement (Riedel). The criticism leveled at the words read correctly per minute measure is that it measures speed rather than comprehension (Riedel, 2007). The DIBELS offers the Retell Fluency (RTF) measure to guard against this phenomenon and suggests an RTF to D-ORF ratio be computed to validate the D-ORF scores; however, it is considered optional (Shelton, Altwerger, & Jordan, 2009). It is unclear how many teachers are basing instructional decisions solely on the D-ORF score or how many of those students do not have ratios that would validate their D-ORF scores (in Shelton et al. this was 57% of one small sample). However, even if the protocol was consistently administered, suggestions on how best to serve students with an RTF to D-ORF ratio between 25 and 50% are not offered (Shelton et al.).

Evidence concerning the reliability and discriminate validity of using the D-ORF cut scores to determine instructional categories is absent (Brunsman, 2005; Shanahan, 2005). This can lead to misclassification of students, resulting in some students getting remediation who do not need it and others who need remediation not getting it. Riedel (2007) noted that 15% of his sample that was classified as low risk by their D-ORF cut scores, in fact, had poor comprehension. This was later linked to poor vocabulary and the recommendation to assess vocabulary so as to make better informed decisions. In this instance, if students were determined not to need intervention based only on one D-ORF score, they would not get the intervention they needed to be successful in reading. The authors of the DIBELS in a position paper specifically refer to this practice as a misuse of the purposes of the measures (Dynamic Measurement Group, 2008). The authors state that "because DIBELS are only one piece of information that teachers have access to when making educational decisions, it is recommended that teachers use additional assessment information and knowledge about a student to validate a score and the decision to provide additional support" (Dynamic Measurement Group, 2007, p. 2).

The RTF is the only measure of comprehension in the DIBELS (Shelton et al., 2009). In the few studies examining the RTF, the D-ORF has been more highly correlated with other comprehension measures than the RTF (Riedel, 2007). Also, Marcotte and Hintze (2009) found that the RTF did not compare favorably with the D-ORF, three other measures of comprehension (Maze, sentence verification technique, and written retell technique), or the Group Reading Assessment and Diagnostic Evaluation for measuring comprehension. These authors attribute less than optimal correlations (.49 and lower) to the poor interrater reliability they observed using the measure. In fact, there have been concerns raised about the lack of interrater reliability data reported for any DIBELS measure given the complex administration and scoring rules (Rathvon, 2004; Brunsman, 2005). If the reliability of the scores is a concern, it raises a question about the validity of the score interpretations and resulting decisions based on the scores. Rathvon strongly recommends several practice sessions with a trained colleague before administering the RTF.

Letter Naming Fluency appears to be moderately or strongly correlated with other measures of reading proficiency for kindergartners, including teacher ratings, and is comparatively the most reliable of the measures, besides the ORF (Rathvon, 2004). There is evidence (Hintze, Ryan, & Stoner, 2003) that the benchmark goals for this test may be too high and falsely identify too many students as having issues with phonological awareness. Riedel (2007) observed that cut scores used to identify low-risk students may need to be raised for urban populations. This again highlights the need to examine the sample used for determining the cut scores to determine whether it is applicable to a specific population.

Attempts to provide predictive and concurrent validity evidence for the Phonemic Segmentation Fluency (PSF) and the Nonsense Word Fluency (NWF) measures have met with mixed results and make it difficult to generalize results, especially given the homogeneity of the samples used for these studies (Riedel, 2007). Additionally, Riedel noted that administering the PSF and NWF in addition to the D-ORF from the end of first grade forward provides no additional predictive power. There is also evidence (Good, Simmons, & Kame'enui, 2001) that the benchmark goals for the PSF are not useful due to low predictive validity. There is a lack of reliability and validity evidence for the Initial Sound Fluency (ISF) and Word Use Fluency (WUF) measures. It is recommended, however, that one has several practice sessions with a trained colleague before trying to administer both the ISF and WUF (Rathvon, 2004).

It is important to stress that while these assessments, as do all assessments, have limitations, they can be used with confidence for their intended purposes given validity evidence to support those purposes. As the Standards for Educational and Psychological Tests (AERA, APA, & NCME, 1999) indicate, if an assessment is to be used for a different purpose than originally intended, it is necessary to ensure that there is evidence to support the appropriateness for using the assessment for that purpose. It is also important to stress that the sole use of one test score to make important educational decisions for a student is not recommended.

CONCLUSION

Assessment is a process of reasoning from evidence that should be driven by theories and data on student cognition and learning (National Research Council, 2001). Cognitive theories of student proficiency and learning in the literacy domain provide a foundation for the design of literacy assessments and the interpretation of the results. Technological developments such as computer-based tasks and automated scoring procedures have emerged and hold promise for improvements in the design and use of assessments. In the evaluation of an assessment system, evidence to support the validity of the score inferences is at the forefront. Assessment validation requires the specification of the purposes and uses of an assessment, the use of an assessment that has been designed to fit the intended purposes, and the collection of evidence to support the proposed uses of the assessment and the intended score inferences. The Common Core Standards (CCSSO & NGACBP, 2010) and the Race to the Top initiative (U.S. Department of Education, 2009) provide an opportunity for literacy leaders to have a substantial voice in decisions regarding the next generation of assessment systems so as to ensure that they provide valid information regarding student achievement and learning, and support the instructional process.

Literacy leaders need to be competent in assessment practices, that is, they must have assessment literacy. Prior to selecting an assessment, it is important to articulate the types of decisions that will be made based on the assessment results. Thus, it is necessary to become familiar with the purpose, content, and accompanying validity evidence for an assessment that may be used. Technical manuals and guidelines that accompany assessments can provide literacy leaders with this information. School psychologists are trained in administering, selecting, and evaluating tests so they can also be an invaluable source for assessment information. Many schools of education at universities have measurement programs that offer introductory courses on educational assessments and have measurement faculty who may be consulted. There are also valuable books on assessment written especially for school leaders, including *Educational Assessment of Students* (Nitko & Brookhart, 2007). Further, the *Mental Measurement Yearbook* (Baros Institute, n.d.), which has an online version, contains content and technical reviews of numerous educational tests that can be an invaluable source for literacy leaders. Regardless of the source, literacy leaders who become literate in assessments can have a profound impact on student learning.

ENGAGEMENT ACTIVITIES

1. For the case presented earlier in this chapter, explain the types of evidence that are needed to support or refute the use of the assessment as the sole source for planning a students' literacy educational program in the early grades.

2. For the different types of decisions that assessments can inform, think about your schools' assessment system and whether it is comprehensive and provides information that informs these decisions. If not, identify how your school's assessment system could be more comprehensive.

3. How could your school's assessment system provide a better balance between assessing foundational skills and more complex reasoning and

thinking skills? What additional types of assessments could be used to ensure a good balance?

4. Consider the types of measures used at the middle and high school levels for assessing literacy skills: In what ways do they meet the validity criteria discussed in this chapter? What decisions do they help inform?

5. Compare the information on assessment in this chapter with that provided in Chapter 11. How can literacy leaders use the findings from each to inform practices?

REFERENCES

American Educational Research Association, American Psychological Association, & National Council on Measurement in Education. (1999). *Standards for educational and psychological testing.* Washington, DC: American Educational Research Association.

Ardoin, S. P., & Christ, T. J. (2009). Curriculum-based measurement of oral reading: Standard errors associated with progress monitoring outcomes from DIBELS, AIMSweb, and an experimental passage set. *School Psychology Review, 38*(2), 266–283.

Bennett, R. E., & Gitomer, D. H. (2009). Transforming K–12 assessment: Integrating accountability testing, formative assessment and professional support. In C. Wyatt-Smith & J. Cumming (Eds.), *Educational assessment in the 21st century* (pp. 44–61). New York: Springer.

Bennett, R. E., Persky, H., Weiss, A. R., & Jenkins, F. (2007). *Problem solving in technology-rich environments: A report from the NAEP Technology-Based Assessment Project* (NCES 2007-466). Washington, DC: National Center for Education Statistics, U.S. Department of Education. Retrieved May 2, 2009, from *nces.ed.gov/pubsearch/pubsinfo.asp?pubid=2007466*.

Black, P., & William, D. (1998). Assessment and classroom learning. Educational Assessment: *Principles Policy and Practice, 5*(1), 7–74.

Bridgeman, B., Morgan, R., & Wang, M. (1997). Choice among essay topics: Impact on performance and validity. *Journal of Educational Measurement, 34*(3), 273–286.

Brunsman, B. A. (2005). Test review of the DIBELS: Dynamic Indicators of Early Literacy Skills. In R. A. Spies & B. S. Plake (Eds.), *The sixteenth mental measurements yearbook.* Retrieved July 31, 2010, from *www.unl.edu/buros*.

BUROS Institute. (no date). *Tests reviewed in Mental Measurements Yearbook series.* Retrieved May 3, 2011, from *www.unl.edu/buros/bimm/html/00testscomplete.html*.

Cole, N. S., & Moss, P. A. (1989). Bias in test use. In R. L. Linn (Ed.), *Educational Measurement* (3rd ed., pp. 201–220). New York: American Council on Education and Macmillan.

Council of Chief State School Officers and National Governors Association Center for Best Practices. (2010). *Common Core Standards for English Language Arts.* Retrieved June 25, 2010, from *www.corestandards.org*.

Cronbach, L. J. (1988). Five perspectives on validity argument. In H. Wainer & H. Braun (Eds.), *Test validity* (pp. 3–37). Hillsdale, NJ: Erlbaum.

Darling-Hammond, L., & Pecheone, R. (2010). *Developing an internationally comparable balanced assessment system that supports high-quality learning.* Retrieved April, 2010, from *www.k12center.org/rsc/pdf/Darling-Hammond-PechoneSystemModel.pdf.*

Dynamic Measurement Group. (2007). *DIBELS myths and facts.* Retrieved August 8, 2010, from *www.dibels.org/papers/Myths_0208.pdf.*

Dynamic Measurement Group. (2008). *Using DIBELS for student accountability decisions.* Retrieved August 7, 2010, from *www.dibels.org/papers/staccount_0908.pdf.*

Fawson, P. C., Reutzel, D. R., Smith, J. A., Ludlow, B. C., & Sudweeks, R. (2006). Examining the reliability of running records: Attaining generalizable results. *Journal of Educational Research, 100*(2), 113–126.

Forster, M. (2009). *Informative assessment: Understanding and guiding learning.* Australian Council for Educational Research. Retrieved August 4, 2010, from *www.acer.edu.au.*

French, M. P. (2005). *A lexical analysis of informal reading inventory graded word lists.* Retrieved July 29, 2010, from *www.americanreadingforum.org/Yearbooks/05_yearbook/pdf/arf_05_french.pdf.*

Fuchs, L. S., & Fuchs, D. (1999). Monitoring student progress toward the development of reading competence: A review of three forms of classroom-based assessment. *School Psychology Review, 28*(4), 659–671.

Good, R. H., Simmons, D. C., & Kame'enui, E. J. (2001). The importance and decision-making utility of a continuum of fluency-based indicators of foundational reading skills for third-grade high-stakes outcomes. *Scientific Studies of Reading, 5*(3), 257–288.

Haertel, E. H. (1999). Performance assessment and education reform. *Phi Delta Kappan, 80*(9), 662–667.

Hintze, J. M., Ryan, A. L., & Stoner, G. (2003). Concurrent validity and diagnostic accuracy of the Dynamic Indicator of Basic Early Literacy Skills and the Comprehension Test of Phonological Processing. *School Psychology Review, 32,* 541–566.

Jenkins, J. R., & Jewell, M. (2004). Examining the validity of two measures for formative teaching: Reading aloud and Maze. *Exceptional Children, 59*(5), 421–435.

Kane, M. T. (2006). Validation. In R. L. Brennan (Ed.), *Educational measurement* (4th ed., pp. 17–64). New York: American Council on Education/Macmillan.

Lane, S. (2010). *Performance assessment: The state of the art.* Stanford, CA: Stanford University, Stanford Center for Opportunity Policy in Education.

Lane, S., Parke, C. S., & Stone, C. A. (2002). The impact of a state performance-based assessment and accountability program on mathematics instruction and student learning. *Educational Assessment, 8*(4), 279–315.

Lane, S., & Stone, C. A. (2006). Performance assessments. In B. Brennan (Ed.), *Educational measurement* (pp. 387–432). Westport, CT: American Council on Education and Praeger.

Marcotte, A. M., & Hintze, J. M. (2009). Incremental and predictive utility of formative assessment methods of reading comprehension. *Journal of School Psychology, 47*, 325–335.

Marion, S. (2010, April 16). *Developing a theory of action: A foundation of the NIA response.* Retrieved August 2, 2010, from *www.nciea.org/papers-Theory ofAction_041610.pdf.*

Messick, S. (1989). Validity. In R. L. Linn (Ed.), *Educational Measurement* (3rd ed., pp. 13–104). New York: American Council on Education and Macmillan.

Messick, S. (1994). The interplay of evidence and consequences in the validation of performance assessments. *Educational Researcher, 23*(2), 13–23.

National Research Council. (2001). *Knowing what students know: The science and design of educational assessment.* Pellegrino, J., Chudowsky, N., & Glaser, R. (Eds.), Board on Testing and Assessment, Center for Education. Division of Behavioral and Social Sciences and Education. Washington, DC: National Academy Press.

National Research Council. (2006). *System for state science assessment.* M. R. Wilson & M. W. Bertenthal (Eds.), Board on Testing and Assessment, Center for Education, Division of Behavioral and Social Sciences and Education. Washington, DC: National Academy Press.

Nilsson, N. L. (2008). A critical analysis of eight informal reading inventories. *Reading Teacher, 61*(7), 526–536.

Nitko, A. J., & Brookhart, S. M. (2007). *Educational assessment of students.* Upper Saddle River, NJ: Pearson.

O'Reilly, T., & Sheehan, K. M. (2009). Cognitively based assessment of, for and as learning: A framework for assessing reading competency (RR-09-26). Princeton, NJ: Educational Testing Service.

Paris, S. G. (2005). Reinterpreting the development of reading skills. *Reading Research Quarterly, 40*(2), 184–202.

Paris, S. G., & Carpenter, R. D. (2003). FAQs about IRIs. *Reading Teacher, 56*(6), 578–580.

Paris, S. G., & Hoffman, J. V. (2004). Reading assessments in kindergarten through third grade: Findings from the Center for Improvement of Early Reading Achievement. *Elementary School Journal, 105*(2), 199–217.

Pearson Education. (2009). *Technical manual for the Developmental Reading Assessment* (2nd ed.). Upper Saddle River, NJ: Pearson.

Perie, M., Marion, S., & Gong, B. (2009). Moving toward a comprehensive assessment system: A framework for considering interim assessments. *Educational Measurement: Issues and Practice, 28*(3), 5–13.

Pomplun, M., Capps, L., & Sundbye, N. (1998). Criteria teachers use to score performance items. *Educational Assessment, 5*(2), 95–110.

Powers, D. E., Fowles, M. E., Farnum, M., & Gerritz, K. (1992). *Giving a choice of topics on a test of basic writing skills: Does it make any difference?* (ETS Research Report No. 92–19). Princeton, NJ: Educational Testing Service.

Rathvon, N. (2004). *Early reading assessment.* New York: Guilford Press.

Riedel, B. W. (2007). The relation between DIBELS reading comprehension, and vocabulary in urban first-grade students. *Reading Research Quarterly, 42*(4), 546–567.

Russell, M., & Tao, W. (2004). Effects of handwriting and computer-print on composition scores: A follow-up to Powers, Folwes, Farnum, and Ramsey. *Practical Assessment, Research and Evaluation, 9*(1). Retrieved May 2, 2010, from *PAREonline.net/getvn.asp.*

Shanahan, T. (2005). Test review of the DIBELS: Dynamic Indicators of Early Literacy Skills. In R. A. Spies & B. S. Plake (Eds.), *The sixteenth mental measurements yearbook.* Retrieved August 5, 2010, from *www.unl.edu/buros.*

Shelton, N. R., Altwerger, B., & Jordan, N. (2009). Does DIBELS put reading first? *Literacy Research and Instruction, 48,* 137–148.

Shinn, J., Deno, S. L., & Epsin, C. (2000). Technical adequacy of the Maze task for curriculum-based measurement of reading growth. *Journal of Special Education, 34*(3), 164–172.

Stecher, B., Barron, S., Kaganoff, T., & Goodwin, J. (1998, June). *The effects of standards-based assessment on classroom practices: Results of the 1996–97 RAND survey of Kentucky teachers of mathematics and writing* (CSE Tech. Rep. No. 482). Los Angeles: University of California, National Center for Research on Evaluation, Standards, and Student Testing.

Stiggins, R. (2010). Essential formative assessment competencies for teachers and school leaders. In H. L. Andrade & G. J. Cizek (Eds.), *Handbook of formative assessment* (pp. 233–250). New York: Taylor & Francis.

Stone, C. A., & Lane, S. (2003). Consequences of a state accountability program: Examining relationships between school performance gains and teacher, student, and school variables. *Applied Measurement in Education, 16*(1), 1–26.

U.S. Department of Education. (April 11, 1965). Elementary and Secondary Education. Retrieved April 27, 2001, *www2.ed.gov/policy/elsec/leg/esea02/beginning.html.*

U.S. Department of Education. (2005). *The nation's report card.* Washington, DC: Retrieved December, 2009, from *nationsreportcard.gov/science_2005/s0116.asp.*

U.S. Department of Education. (July 12, 2008). *Reading First.* Retrieved April 27, 2011, from *www2.ed.gov/programs/redingfirst/lestlation.html.*

U.S. Department of Education. (2009). Race to the top program executive summary. Retrieved on April 15, 2010, from *www.ed.gov/programs/racetothetop/resources.html.*

Wainer, H., Wang, H., & Thissen, D. (1994). On examinee choice in educational testing. *Review of Educational Research, 64,* 159–195.

William, D. (2010). An integrative summary of the research literature and implications for a new theory of formative assessment. In H. L. Andrade & G. J. Cizek (Eds.), *Handbook of formative assessment* (pp. 18–90). New York: Routledge Taylor & Francis Group.

Williamson, D. M., Behar, I. I., & Mislevy, R. J. (2006). Automated scoring of complex tasks in computer-based testing: An introduction. In D. M. Williamson, I. I. Bejar, & R. J. Mislevy (Eds.), *Automated scoring of complex tasks in computer-based testing* (pp. 1–14). Mahwah, NJ: Erlbaum.

Wolfe, E., Bolton, S., Feltovich, B., & Welch, C. (1993). *A comparison of word-processed and handwritten essays from a standardized writing assessment.* RR. 93-8. Iowa City, IA: American College Testing.

Yang, Y., Buchendahl, C. W., Juszkiewicz, P. J., & Bhola, D. S. (2002). A review of strategies for validating computer-automated scoring. *Applied Measurement in Education, 15*(4), 391–412.

PART III

PERSPECTIVES ON SPECIAL ISSUES

15

Technology in the Literacy Program

JILL CASTEK
CAROLYN B. GWINN

Guiding Questions

- In what ways are new technologies transforming how we teach reading, writing, and communication in K–12 classrooms? How are these changes affecting what it means to be literate in the digital age and, as a result, how must our instruction be reconceptualized to address a broader notion of literacy?

- In what ways do the Common Core State Standards for English Language Arts and Literacy in History/Social Studies, Science and Technical Subjects (2010) and the International Reading Association Standards for Reading Professionals (2010) create new opportunities for teaching literacy using the Internet and new technologies?

- How can professional development efforts that address online reading comprehension help cultivate literacy leaders who are skilled in teaching literacy with technology?

The Internet has become increasingly central to our daily lives (Johnson, Levine, Smith, & Smythe, 2009) and is changing the way we read, interact, teach, and learn (Malloy, Castek, & Leu, 2010). The emergence of the Internet as today's defining technology for literacy and learning (Castek, Zawilinski, McVerry, O'Byrne, & Leu, 2011), and the rapid shift in literacy practices from page to screen (Lankshear & Knobel, 2006), require literacy leaders to think differently about the ways in which literacy is taught and practiced in school classrooms.

Today's students have spent their lives surrounded by technology—using computers, playing online games, listening to digital music, sharing YouTube videos, social networking on sites like Facebook, and texting on smartphones. They have grown up in a networked world in which texts are multimodal, interactive, and socially distributed (Coiro, Knobel, Lankshear, & Leu, 2008; Kress, 2003; New London Group, 2000). As a result of ubiquitous interactions with new technologies, Prensky (2001) suggests that young people's online immersion has made this generation of "digital natives" think and process information differently.

Although students are skilled with social networking, texting, video, and music downloads, most are less skilled with online information use, including locating and critically evaluating information (Bennett, Maton, & Kervin, 2008; Leu, O'Byrne, Zawilinski, McVerry, & Everett-Cocapardo, 2009). Internet reading and learning requires skills and strategies that are complex, and in some cases unique, to online reading and writing contexts (Afflerbach & Cho, 2008; Coiro & Dobler, 2007).

While some might conceptualize the use of new technologies in school classrooms as a natural outgrowth of the use of technology in our daily lives, few teachers are knowledgeable about how to guide students in developing online reading skills and strategies in today's networked world. We need to cultivate leaders who understand the profound changes taking place in literacy and its ripple effect on educational settings spanning preschool to grades K–12 and beyond (American Association of Colleges for Teacher Education, 2010).

This chapter is designed to nurture literacy leaders to become more knowledgeable and prepared to expand literacy teaching and learning and make the most of the Internet in their literacy and content-area instruction. We begin by introducing a case example that illustrates the dynamic, creative, and innovative ways teachers are using the Internet to support new forms of reading comprehension in today's networked world. Next we address the overall aim of the chapter by offering a short discussion of computer and Internet access in today's schools. Then we discuss how new technologies are redefining literacy, ways technology use creates motivation for literacy learning, and essential strategies involved in online reading comprehension. Finally, we describe the characteristics of professional development that support online reading comprehension and offer suggestions for implementation.

CASE EXAMPLE

Mrs. Jamison's 5th grade class consists of a wide range of academically diverse learners. She begins a weather and water unit by administering two short formative assessments—one informs her about her students' experience using the Internet and the other addresses students' background knowledge about the content they are preparing to learn. At the end of the first week of instruction, she shows a 20-minute water cycle video from United Streaming, an extensive online video library to which her school district subscribes. After debriefing the content, students are given time to engage in small-group discussions about the importance of water in sustaining life on Earth. Marcelina, a Spanish-speaking English language learner, and three other students discuss what they have learned about precipitation, evaporation, and condensation, while other groups explain to one another the various ways that water is recycled. Students are organized into small groups to promote proficiency with the tasks that follow. Each group takes a turn on the classroom's Internet-connected computer replaying sections of the video and searching for interactive online resources to extend their understanding.

Marcelina and her group locate an animated water cycle diagram created by Earth Guide (*earthguide.ucsd.edu/earthguide/diagrams/watercycle*), Discovery Education's water cycle simulation (*player.discoveryeducation.com/views/hhView.cfm?guidAssetId=087777c8-4ff0-45d2-878f-e7cd90f7ee19*), and the Environmental Protection Agency's interactive water cycle model (*www.epa.gov/safewater/kids/flash/flash_watercycle.html*). After evaluating the resources for quality and veracity, a process modeled by Mrs. Jamison, the group saves them on Gaggle (*www.gaggle.net*), a suite of collaboration tools for use in schools, so they can be shared with others. Then, Marcelina's group presents their ideas to the class. Next, students log on to TeXT (*text. teachingmatters.org*), their classroom blog, and the dialogue continues.

As is typical in classrooms nationwide, Mrs. Jamison integrates literacy and content area learning. What is less typical is her strategic use of the Internet to address this goal. As a result of Mrs. Jamison's efforts, her students have learned how to search for Web resources that match their learning needs, navigate within websites to locate the information they need, critically evaluate the reliability of these websites, and synthesize key ideas from the many resources they have read. In addition to the traditional literacy skills commonly taught in schools, these skills are essential for full participation in higher education and the workplace.

Mrs. Jamison was not always this skilled in using the Internet to support teaching and learning. In fact, she considered herself a casual technology user until her school took part in a professional development effort that introduced ways to incorporate online reading comprehension into classroom instruction. To date, Mrs. Jamison has spent 2 years refining her implementation of instructional approaches with the aid of her professional learning community (four grade-level teachers, a literacy specialist, a library media teacher, and her principal). This group meets face-to-face monthly and regularly dialogues in their shared virtual discussion space—a teaching literacy with technology blog they created as a means to pose questions and share ideas. This digital community offers expanded contact hours, sustained opportunities to problem solve implementation issues, and promotes engagement in active learning with peers.

Mrs. Jamison's confidence in teaching online reading comprehension has grown exponentially, not only because of sustained interactions with her professional learning community, but also due to her willingness to learn from the interactions among students that regularly take place within her own classroom. She provides time and opportunity for students to share and exchange online reading comprehension strategies.

As Mrs. Jamison demonstrates, integrating the Internet into literacy and content learning opens doors that make it possible for her students to realize their learning potential. Recognizing the changing literacy landscape emerging with the advent of new technologies requires teachers to teach in new ways and fully incorporate online reading comprehension into the curriculum.

Within this chapter, we provide several ways teachers like Mrs. Jamison can expand students' literacy experiences and make use of new technologies for reading, writing, and communication in K–12 classrooms. We contend that implementing a lasting approach to professional development will aid teachers in transforming their teaching, which will go a long way toward preparing students to effectively engage in literacy and content learning in the 21st century. As a means to consider next steps, how might Mrs. Jamison and her colleagues continue to explore the use of technology in their literacy classrooms, in honor of student needs and in response to standards? What might Mrs. Jamison and her school leadership team consider as they expand professional development opportunites for both technology bold and reluctant teachers?

HOW WIRED ARE TODAY'S SCHOOLS?

Access to the Internet is nearly universal among public elementary and secondary schools in the United States. In 2005, 100% of public schools had Internet access, and 97% of these schools used broadband connections to access the Internet (Wells & Lewis, 2006). Approximately 94% of classrooms in public schools had computers with Internet access, and the ratio of students to instructional computers was one computer to 3.81 students (National Center for Education Statisitics, 2005; Wells & Lewis, 2006). In 2010 and beyond, we can assume that access to information and communications technologies (ICTs) will continue to improve with the increased availability of inexpensive mobile devices and the Department of Education's support of technology as an important component of education reform (International Reading Association [IRA], 2009; National Education Technology Panel, 2010). Though many teachers may lack experience in using digital technologies in literacy instruction, it is nonetheless our responsibility to provide an educational context in which all students gain experience with the Internet, since this opportunity is central to them becoming participatory citizens who are well versed in academic language and who seek to achieve success in elementary and secondary school, higher education, and the workplace (National Center on Education and the Economy, 2007).

In 2008, at least half of all school districts in the United States had a one-to-one laptop program in at least one grade level, in at least one school (Greaves & Hayes, 2008). Yet, these initiatives lack a research-based model of professional development to draw on (Lawless & Pellegrino, 2007). They are often short in duration and focus on simple tool use (Warschauer, 2006), despite the fact that studies of technology integration universally conclude that extensive professional development on higher-level learning is required before academic gains can be realized (Silvernail & Buffington, 2009; Silvernail & Gritter, 2005; Penuel, 2006; Warschauer, 2006). The need to develop a systematic model of professional development designed to address ways teachers can infuse digitial literacy in their literacy program is becoming increasingly essential (Leu et al., 2009; Penuel, 2006).

HOW IS TECHNOLOGY REDEFINING TEACHING AND LEARNING?

The Internet has become the defining technology for literacy and learning in the 21st century (Coiro et al., 2008), transforming the ways we access, use, and exchange information. To maximize the Internet's potential as an educational context, we need to ensure that all students have opportunities to develop the literacy skills required in today's networked world (Watts-Taffe & Gwinn, 2007). We also need to support teachers in designing and delivering instruction that makes the most of what the Internet has to offer (Smolin & Lawless, 2003; Wallace, 2004). Implementation requires the development of a new generation of literacy leaders who are able to support their students in learning and their colleagues in teaching new forms of literacy essential on the Internet.

Reading on the Internet requires additional skills beyond those needed for traditional print reading (Leu, Kinzer, Coiro, & Cammack, 2004; Coiro & Dobler, 2007). Many of these higher-order, online reading comprehension skills now appear in the Common Core State Standards for English Language Arts and Literacy in History/Social Studies, Science and Technical Subjects (2010) and will be essential for success in both literacy and content-area classrooms (IRA, 2009). Making online reading an integral part of classroom instruction motivates students to access information quickly, explore a range of multimedia resources, and share ideas as part of a socially networked classroom community.

The Common Core State Standards provide an overview of the capacities of 21st-century-literate individuals. These new standards assert that students are expected to use technology and digital media strategically and capably and employ technology thoughtfully to enhance their reading, writing, speaking, listening, and language use. For example, students are expected to (1) conduct online searches to acquire useful information; (2) draw information from multiple print or digital sources to locate an answer or solve a problem; (3) gather relevant information from multiple print and digital sources and assess the credibility and accuracy of each source; (4) use technology, including the Internet, to produce, publish, and interact with others, while also recognizing the strengths and limitations of various technological tools; and (5) select digital tools that are suited to meeting specific communication goals. Research-based models of professional development are needed to support teachers' important work in developing student's skills in these areas (Desimone, 2009), especially as classrooms address the new reading, writing, and communication demands required by the Internet.

HOW DOES TEACHING WITH THE INTERNET AND NEW TECHNOLOGIES CREATE MOTIVATION FOR LEARNING?

Although the research regarding the relationship between technology use and academic achievement is limited, working with a range of digital technologies appears to increase motivation (IRA, 2009; National Council of Teachers of English [NCTE], 2007). Most teachers who have used the Internet to extend literacy learning can attest to the positive relationship between technology use and student engagement. Projects and group work that include strategic use of technology seem to increase engagement in schoolwork (Castek, 2008; Dwyer, 2010) and provide a context in which students produce work they care about and take pride in (Malloy et al., 2010). Digital technologies also offer expanded access to content through video, multimedia, visual aids, and text-to-speech options.

Technology use for literacy and content learning extends new social contexts for developing knowledge (Dalton & Proctor, 2008). These social contexts influence how learners make sense of, interpret, and share understandings. Participation in these social contexts motivates students to read for a range of purposes, use knowledge gained from previous experiences to generate new understandings, and actively engage in meaningful literacy interactions. Incorporating collaborative learning experiences that make use of digital technologies in classrooms fulfills an important need as many students, especially adolescents, are driven by social interaction. For more information about technology in secondary classrooms, see Chapter 9.

Henry, Castek, O'Byrne, and Zawilinski (in press) found that using the Internet and creating digital projects such as podcasts, videos, and inquiry projects appeared to engage students who were less skilled with traditional literacy in new ways. Given their technology expertise, these often marginalized students became valued collaborators and contributors in digital activities. Working in groups appeared to encourage active participation and created community among learners who worked toward a common purpose. High levels of engagement, if sustained over time, may lead to improved literacy and content learning (Castek, 2008).

Not only is using technology motivational, it also forges a tangible connection to students' out-of-school lives. By drawing in and making use of the technology experiences students bring to the classroom from outside of school, we acknowledge students as valuable contributors to learning. This recognition has the potential to transform the classroom learning environment by encouraging students to collaborate, guide one another, and engage fully in literacy activities. As teachers, we need to tap into this powerful potential and provide students with the means for such strategic engagement.

WHAT STRATEGIES ARE ESSENTIAL FOR ONLINE READING COMPREHENSION?

To fully participate in a globally networked society, every student needs to develop strategies for locating, comprehending, and responding to text in ways that take advantage of ICTs (Educational Testing Service [ETS], 2003; IRA, 2009; NCTE, 2007). Most of these literacy strategies cluster in four areas: (1) reading to locate online information; (2) reading to critically evaluate online information; (3) reading to synthesize online information, often from multiple media sources; and (4) reading to communicate information, often in social networks (Leu et al., 2009). The sections that follow briefly outline these areas.

Reading to Locate Online Information

A critical component of successful Internet reading is the ability to read and locate information that meets one's needs (ETS, 2003). New online reading skills and strategies are required to generate effective keyword search strategies (Kuiper, 2007), to infer which link may be most useful within a set of search engine results (Henry, 2006), and to efficiently locate relevant information within websites (Rouet, 2006). To accomplish these goals students need to learn strategies that will help them become flexible and adaptable searchers. These strategies include selecting appropriate key words, determining whether searches are yielding pertinent results, and knowing when to revise search terms to arrive at a more targeted set of results. In classrooms, effective searching allows students to navigate to useful websites efficiently so that time can be spent reading, discussing, and learning from the information found on the sites located (Dwyer & Harrison, 2008).

Reading to Evaluate Online Information

A second component of successful Internet use is the ability to critically evaluate information encountered on the Internet. Such evaluation presents challenges greater than traditional print and media sources (Burbules & Callister, 2000). The content of online information is even more diverse, often driven by commercial purposes. Source information about authorship and expertise is frequently difficult to determine. Reading online materials requires skillful recognition and interpretation of potential bias. Political campaigns, different newspapers reporting on the same event, or seemingly neutral advertisements introduce understated commercial motives and stances that students must navigate, negotiate, and sort. Reading to critically evaluate information is an important area in which to target instruction because students are typically unskilled (Bilal, 2001; Henry, 2006).

Reading to Synthesize Online Information

Successful Internet use also requires the ability to read and synthesize information from different online sources, often with multiple media (Goldman, Wiley, & Graesser, 2005; Jenkins, 2008). Innovative teachers are tackling synthesis by expecting that students will draw information from more than one online source. Providing several articles on the same subject, some expository and others narrative, and asking students to read across them to inform their own perspective is one way to promote this important skill. The ability to manage, process, and filter multiple electronic documents is a key component of online literacy (Bulger, 2006) and is another challenging aspect of online reading comprehension (Goldman et al., 2005; Lawless & Schrader, 2008).

Reading to Communicate Online Information

A fourth component of successful Internet use is the ability to read and respond via the Internet while seeking information or sharing what has been learned (Britt & Gabrys, 2001). The interactive processes of reading and communicating have become so intertwined on the Internet that they often happen simultaneously (Leu et al., 2009). Thus, the communication processes involved in using online tools to ask and answer questions on the Internet appear to be inextricably linked to aspects of online reading comprehension. Moreover, each communication tool on the Internet has different affordances and presents a range of necessary new skills, strategies, and social practices to use them effectively (Greenhow, Robelia, & Hughes, 2009).

WHAT CHARACTERIZES CLASSROOMS THAT INCORPORATE INSTRUCTION IN ONLINE READING COMPREHENSION?

Castek's (2008) mixed-method study examined the contexts and conditions through which fourth- and fifth-grade students acquired online reading comprehension strategies. Themes that describe instructional scaffolding within a technology-rich classroom are summarized in Figure 15.1.

This study illustrates the very new and different roles teachers and students assume when the Internet is a regular part of classroom instruction. For example, instruction transitioned from largely teacher-directed to student-directed with peers providing just-in-time support to assist classmates in completing a wide range of online reading tasks. In addition to students scaffolding each other, they discovered new strategies independently and shared them with one another. There were also instances when students showed the teacher strategies they independently discovered.

The role students played in scaffolding each other was particularly important for developing online reading comprehension. Because the teacher could not anticipate every context that would arise, students looked to each other for additional support at all junctures. This ongoing student-to-student collaboration enhanced understanding of the context in which the strategy was being implemented, the intent behind the use of the strategy, and the purpose for its use. This knowledge helped students implement scaffolds that were supportive. They reported relying on each other to help make decisions about the usefulness of any particular

	The Teacher's Role Appeared to Change When Scaffolding Online Reading Comprehension

Restructured the classroom	• The teacher restructured the classroom environment:
	  ° To maximize student-to-student interactions
	  ° To provide ample time for students to apply new learning

Designed instructional activities	• The teacher carefully designed instructional activities:
	  ° To expose students to new online applications
	  ° To create opportunities for students to immediately put to use strategies demonstrated

Facilitated demonstration	• The teacher facilitated discussion, demonstration, and sharing:
	  ° To distribute a range of approaches throughout the class
	  ° To empower students as experts

	Students Scaffolded Each Other's Application of Online Reading Comprehension Strategies
Pooled strategies	• Students pooled information and ideas informally: ° They followed the processes other students used to accomplish similar tasks
Worked collaboratively toward goals	• Students supported each other in meeting goals: ° They located other students who could help them meet their needs
	The Transition from Teacher Scaffolding to Students Scaffolding Each Other Was Swift

Teacher modeling was brief	• Teacher modeling was kept brief:
	  ° Too lengthy or detailed explanations appeared to lose impact
	• Just-in-time support was guided by students' needs:
	  ° Support by teacher promoted task completion
	  ° Support by knowledgeable peer promoted student independence

FIGURE 15.1. Themes that characterized scaffolding in a technology-rich literacy classroom.

strategy and alternate ways to reach their goals if a given strategy was not useful in the context they were navigating.

Explicit instruction that supports offline reading comprehension is not typically organized in the way just described; rather it emphasizes extensive teacher modeling and a gradual release of responsibility (Pearson & Gallagher, 1983). Therefore, teaching online reading introduces a new way of delivering comprehension instruction for nearly every teacher. This discontinuity in offline and online reading approaches further illustrates the need for high-quality professional development experiences designed to support teachers in making these leaps.

WHAT SPENDING PRIORITIES
WILL HAVE A LASTING IMPACT?

Despite the fact that schools have made great strides in student-to-computer ratios (Wells & Lewis, 2006), the digital divide, a situation in which different groups do not have the same degree of access to digital information and communication technologies, is still prevalent and, for this reason, some groups do not have the same opportunities for social and economic development. However, digital divide discussions among educators are moving beyond physical access to computers and are paying closer attention to differentiated uses of the Web (Hargittai, 2002). The emergence of this second wave of attention to issues of digital inequality has been called the second-level digital divide. We interpret this emerging research to suggest that simply providing schools with funds to purchase updated equipment, software, and reliable access to Internet in schools does not go far enough because extending access does not mean that students will become skilled at online reading comprehension. We believe that investing in sustained professional development for teachers is an essential and integral part of providing high-quality and relevant instructional experiences for students. In a 2008 survey of 111 middle school teachers, 66% indicated a need for professional development in "integrating technology within the existing curriculum"—the highest self-identified need (Silvernail & Buffington, 2009). These results suggest that when funds are available, professional development and coaches may in fact be more of a priority than additional hardware and software.

WHY THE SENSE OF URGENCY WITH
PROFESSIONAL DEVELOPMENT IN GENERAL
AND MORE SPECIFICALLY FOR TEACHING
ONLINE READING COMPREHENSION?

Professional development is a gatekeeper to meaningful educational implementations designed to impact student learning; this aspect becomes increasingly complex with the infusion of technology into learning opportunities. Thus, what characterized more traditional professional development must now be reexamined in light of the changing landscape of learning. The impact of technology on learning is noted in the IRA Position Statement addressing New Literacies and 21st Century Technologies (IRA, 2009). This document calls for professional development that provides opportunities for teachers to explore online tools and resources expected for use with students, suggesting it isn't enough to just make new technologies available. The IRA

Standards for Reading Professionals (2010) encourages teachers to integrate technology into student learning experiences across planning, implementing, assessing, and reflecting, which Watts-Taffe and Gwinn (2007) refer to as the instructional cycle. More specifically, learners are expected to engage in learning with traditional print, digital, and online resources from various genres and perspectives, as well as media and communication technologies. As previously mentioned, the integration of technology into literacy learning is called for in the Common Core State Standards (2010). Students who meet the standards are able to, among other aspects, use technology and digital media strategically and capably.

With the call for students to develop a full range of digitial literacies, including online reading skills and strategies, we are challenged to consider the impact of these new forms of literacy on reading professionals, as they must be competent in this area (IRA Standards for Reading Professionals, 2010). In response to this charge, we address the following questions: (1) What characterizes effective professional development in general? and (2) How are these characteristics infused into effective professional development when preparing teachers to engage students in digital literacy and online reading comprehension?

WHAT CHARACTERIZES EFFECTIVE PROFESSIONAL DEVELOPMENT?

High-quality professional development increases teacher knowledge and skills, changes teacher practice, and improves student achievement (Borko, 2004; Desimone, Smith, & Ueno, 2006; Richardson & Placier, 2001). The design of such professional development is characterized by (1) expanded contact hours; (2) sustained opportunities across time; (3) shared engagement by teachers from the same grade, school, or subject; (4) active learning experiences; (5) connections to various reform efforts; and (6) a focus on subject-matter content (Desimone, Porter, Garet, Yoon, & Birman, 2002; Desimone et al., 2006; Garet, Porter, Desimone, Birman, & Yoon, 2001).

WHAT CHARACTERIZES EFFECTIVE PROFESSIONAL DEVELOPMENT FOR ONLINE READING COMPREHENSION?

With the integration of technology into literacy, it is essential that we remain true to the aforementioned characteristics as well as consider those more tailored to 21st-century learning; thus, we examine three guiding principles, as outlined by Coiro (2005). One of the most commonly used continuums was proposed by the Apple Classrooms of Tomorrow (Cennamo, Ross, & Ertmer, 2009).

First, teachers move across a developmental continuum as they progress in their thoughts and actions regarding literacy technology integration. More specifically, continuum stages include (1) adoption, with technology used to support traditional instruction; (2) adaptation, with technology embedded within current classroom practices; (3) appropriation, with strengths of technology capitalized on as new instructional approaches are used; and (4) innovation, with technology used in new ways. It is critically important to recognize that teachers begin their journeys at various points on the continuum and travel across it at varying paces. Research suggests that it may take 3 to 5 years for teachers to move from novice to expert technology integrators, capable of supporting student learning (Wasser & McNamara, 1998).

Second, it is essential to understand the impact of teacher perception regarding technology integration on how recommendations for its use are interpreted. As suggested by Labbo and Reinking (1999), there are five lenses from which teachers view the potential value and worth of the use of technology, moving from that which is traditional in nature to that which is designed to transform. These varying perspectives influence how online reading comprehension may or may not be embedded within learning experiences and point to the need for tailored professional development, rather than one size fits all, which can lead to little or no change in instruction (Gora & Hinson, 2003).

Third, job-embedded professional learning, described by DuFour, DuFour, Eaker, and Many (2010) as essential for improved student learning, is a meaningful alternative to training presentations delivered to large groups. More specifically, a professional learning community is an "ongoing process in which educators work collaboratively in recurring cycles of collective inquiry and action research to achieve better results for the students they serve" (p. 11); such a community is characterized by members who commit to a focus on learning, collaborative teams, collective inquiry, action orientation, and continuous improvement, all of which are assessed based on results, not objectives (DuFour et al.). An integral way to embed new literacies within a professional learning community is to test the potential of Web 2.0 tools (e.g., Moodle, wikis, social networking forums, blogs, and Nings) to expand collective inquiry. These tools provide opportunities for teachers to collaborate, share, and develop content (Huber, 2010). Communities such as the Technology in Literacy Education Special Interest Group (*tilesig.wikispaces.com*), affiliated with the IRA; the 21st Century Literacies Group (*ncte2008.ning.com/group/21stcenturyliteracies*), affiliated with the NCTE; and the New Literacies Collaborative, affliated with North Carolina State University (*newlitcollaborative.ning.com*) help teachers be in touch with an extended network of colleagues with whom to discuss instructional approaches, share resources, and collaborate.

Professional development efforts, such as the New Literacies Teacher Leader Institute (*newlitinstitute2010.wikispaces.com*), offer transformative models that expand beyond the school level and help build extended learning communities that promote lasting change. This week-long institute addresses ways that new digital tools can create challenging and engaging learning opportunities for students and teachers in K–12 and higher education. Participants come together to network, share ideas, boost their leadership skills, and create technology-infused curriculum units they can implement in their own classrooms. For teachers who are unable to attend such an institute in person, online resources can be explored and discussed with colleagues to support implementation. Available resources include videos, instructional suggestions, readings that link theory to practice, and online networking tools that allow teachers to connect with others who have similar goals and interests. School leaders who tap into the social networking tools in particular can participate in virtual learning experiences that can be customized based on the needs in their own setting.

Despite growing interest and participation in these online professional learning networks, many educators lack familiarity with or preparation in teaching the skills and strategies required for online reading, writing, and collaboration (Wallace, 2004). Even those who consider themselves experienced in this arena recognize that the online literacy landscape is complex and constantly changing. Barone and Wright (2008) suggest that teachers face many challenges, including a lack of resources (e.g., technology, time, or technical support), a lack of knowledge and skills (insufficient technological and pedagogical knowledge), and a lack of school leadership (e.g., inadequate planning or scheduling). In addition, teachers' attitudes and beliefs are often limiting. Some educators are fearful of the use of new technologies. A lack of valid and reliable assessments that match the skills and strategies for online reading comprehension also present limitations (Malloy et al., 2010). To offer support to educators at primary, intermediate, and secondary levels, we turn our attention to discussing job-embedded professional development for teachers who seek to engage students in digital literacy and online reading comprehension.

Primary Level

Given primary students' needs, early grade teachers in particular may identify strongly with traditional notions of literacy. However, incorporating new technologies and digital resources in literacy and content instruction involves adopting expanded views of reading, writing, and communicating. Professional development efforts that emphasize how teachers can model the skills and strategies involved in using the Internet and demonstrate ways to locate information online, evaluate Internet sources, synthesize information found across sites, and communicate with digital tools such as e-mail, blogs, and wikis are critically important (see Moss & Lapp, 2009). Not only does this exposure support teachers' pedagogical knowledge, it expands their vision of literacy. Teachers can provide targeted instruction in the early grades to help students learn to read critically online (Assaf & Adonyi, 2009; Share, 2009; Zhang & Duke, in press). Specific focus areas might include strategies for (1) identifying the author or sponsor of a website, (2) determining how current the information is, (3) integrating website content together with background knowledge to judge the usefulness and veracity of the information, and (4) examining the URL to determine whether a site serves commercial or educational interests.

Providing opportunities for students to create digital stories with sound and images, record podcasts, and use the Internet to locate information enriches students' literacy experiences while fostering both traditional and digital literacies. In addition, a variety of digital tools can be widely used in primary classrooms—digital cameras, handheld video cameras, and audio recording devices (iPods), as well as the Internet. Based on this information, we recommend that teacher professional development includes special attention to instructional strategies that promote active participation, inclusion, and diverse roles for working collaboratively in groups.

The relationship between digital literacy and offline literacy is complex; we suggest that a useful approach for teaching young learners is to consider how digital literacies and offline reading and writing skills are connected in everyday use. Offering primary grade students access to online resources to develop their literacy skills is a tangible way for teachers to aid them in learning about the Internet and will promote their independent use of it in the upper grades. Incorporating online reading within learning experiences fosters both traditional and new literacy skills. Starfall (*www.starfall.com*) offers students short fiction and nonfiction books, early scaffolded literacy experiences, and multimodal interactives that support reading and writing. Guiding students' use of this site by exploring resources as a class, before offering access to them individually, will make the most of these highly scaffolded digital literacy experiences. These teacher-directed activities will set the stage for future online reading comprehension activities in which teachers model effective search strategies, Web evaluation techniques, and synthesis across sites.

Intermediate and Secondary Levels

In light of the increased expections of technology-infused literacy teaching and learning at the intermediate and secondary levels, teachers may find it useful to participate in a regular, ongoing learning experience supported by the building-level instructional coach, instructional technology teacher, and/or principal. The focus of the learning experience is to increase teacher understanding of the ways in which to expand students' familiarity with online reading comprehension and to support the teacher as technology is infused in increasing amounts. At the onset of the experience, teachers are reminded of the connections between online reading comprehension and district literacy efforts related in part to the standards. Teachers assume the role of learner as they collaboratively engage in online comprehension; they read to locate information, evaluate information, synthesize information, and read to communicate information. Then, in a scaffolded manner, building on instruction that occurred at the primary level, they teach students the same process gradually, moving from modeled to guided to independent practice. Across this process, teachers participate in meaningful conversations, some online and others offline, to carefully ponder critical questions key to learning in professional communities including the following: (1) What do we want all students to know and be able to do? (2) How will we know if they have learned it? (3) How will we respond when students have not learned it? and (4) What will we do if they already know it? (DuFour et al., 2010).

FUTURE DIRECTIONS

The emergence of the Internet as today's defining technology for literacy and learning (Leu, 2007) and the rapid shift in literacy practices from page to screen (Lankshear & Knobel, 2006) requires that literacy leaders think differently about the ways in which literacy learning is taught and practiced in school classrooms. We introduced ways the Internet can be used skillfully with students to support digital literacy and online reading comprehension and offered suggestions for designing professional development experiences that support teaching and learning in this important area.

We suggest that the Internet provides many opportunities to engage students with content and develop reading and writing, while communicating and learning. However, as important as these literacy skills and strategies are in a digital age, there are few professional development models that support teachers in teaching online reading comprehension. As school communities work toward designing meaningful teacher learning experiences, capitalizing in part on the aforementioned characteristics of high-quality professional development, we encourage teachers to embrace students and colleagues as collaborative learning partners. Together with their students, and in collaboration with their colleagues, teachers will make strides in generating new and innovative ways to teach online reading comprehension and make use of a full range of digital resources that extend literacy and learning.

ENGAGEMENT ACTIVITIES

Literacy educators like Mrs. Jamison play a vitally important role in paving the way for Internet integration in a manner that supports literacy learning. Reflect on Mrs. Jamison's journey toward becoming a teacher who is skilled in making the most of the Internet and new technologies for literacy and content learning.

1. What role does Mrs. Jamison assume as the case study activies unfold? What role do the students assume? How might Mrs. Jamison respond to her students' needs as they work collaboratively to share knowledge and scaffold one another's learning?

2. How might Mrs. Jamison continue to extend students' literacy and content learning with technology? Consider DuFour et al.'s (2010) critical questions that are key to learning in professional communities:
    a. What do we want all students to know and be able to do?
    b. How will we know if they have learned it?
    c. What will we do if they haven't learned it?
    d. What will we do if they already know it?

3. What have you learned from Mrs. Jamison and her students? How might you begin to apply this learning to your own work with students, colleagues, and parents?

4. As a means to extending your learning, visit a classroom during the implementation of a literacy- and technology-based lesson. Engage in a postvisit conversation with the teacher to reflect on what was observed. Make connections that support implementation in your setting and apply new learning to your work with students. Invite the teacher you observed to visit the classroom during your implementation of a literacy- and technology-based lesson. Engage in a postvisit conversation to reflect and apply new learning to your work with students. Discuss insights gained with your professional learning community. A similar process can include an instructional coach.

REFERENCES

Afflerbach, P., & Cho, B. Y. (2008). Identifying and describing constructively responsive comprehension strategies in new and traditional forms of reading. In S. Israel & G. Duffy (Eds.), *Handbook of reading comprehension research* (pp. 6–90). Mahwah, NJ: Erlbaum.

American Association of Colleges for Teacher Education (2010). *21st century knowledge and skills in educator preparation.* White paper produced as part of a collaborative project by the American Association of Colleges of Teacher Education and the Partnership for 21st Century Skills (P21). Retrieved May 4, 2011, from *aacte.org/index.php?/Accreditation-Issues/Accreditation-Update/ aacte-brings-task-force-to-final-report-for-a-unified-accrediting-body.html.*

Assaf, C. L., & Adonyi, A. (2009). Critically reading advertisements: Examining visual images and persuasive language. In B. Moss & D. Lapp (Eds.), *Teaching new literacies in grades K–3* (pp. 209–220). New York: Guilford Press.

Barone, D., & Wright, T. E. (2008). Literacy instruction with digital and media technologies. *Reading Teacher, 62*(4), 292–302.

Bennett, S., Maton, K., & Kervin, L. (2008). The digital natives debate: A critical review of the evidence. *British Journal of Educational Technology, 19*(5), 775–786.

Bilal, D. (2001). Children's use of the Yahooligans! web search engine: II. Cognitive and physical behaviors on research tasks. *Journal of the American Society for Information Science, 52,* 118–136.

Borko, H. (2004). Professional development and teacher learning: Mapping the terrain. *Educational Researcher, 33*(8), 3–15.

Britt, M. A., & Gabrys, G. L. (2001). Teaching advanced literacy skills for the World Wide Web. In C. R. Wolfe (Ed.), *Learning and teaching on the World Wide Web.* Millbrae, CA: Academic Press.

Bulger, M. (2006). *Beyond search: A preliminary skill set for online literacy.* Retrieved May 4, 2011, from *transliteracies.english.ucsb.edu/post/research-project/research-clearinghouse-individual/research-papers/beyond-search-a-preliminary-skill-set-for-online-literacy.*

Burbules, N. C., & Callister, T. A. (2000). *Watch IT: The risks and promises of information technologies for education.* Boulder, CO: Westview Press.

Castek, J. (2008). *How do 4th and 5th grade students acquire the new literacies of online reading comprehension? Exploring the contexts that facilitate learning.* Unpublished doctoral dissertation: University of Connecticut.

Castek, J., Zawilinski, L., McVerry, G., O'Byrne, I., & Leu, D. J. (2011). The new literacies of online reading comprehension: New opportunities and challenges for students with learning difficulties. In C. Wyatt-Smith, J. Elkins, & S. Gunn (Eds.), *Multiple perspectives on difficulties in learning literacy and numeracy* (pp. 91–110). New York: Springer.

Cennamo, K., Ross, J., & Ertmer, P. (2009). *Technology integration for meaningful classroom use: A standards-based approach.* Belmont, CA: Wadsworth, Cengage Learning.

Coiro, J. (2005). Every teacher a Miss Rumphius: Empowering teachers with effective professional development. In R. Karchmer, M. Mallette, J. Kara-Soteriou, & D. J. Leu, Jr. (Eds.), *New literacies for new times: Innovative models of literacy education using the Internet.* Newark, DE: International Reading Association.

Coiro, J., & Dobler, E. (2007). Exploring the online comprehension strategies used by sixth-grade skilled readers to search for and locate information on the Internet. *Reading Research Quarterly, 42,* 214–257.

Coiro, J., Knobel, M., Lankshear, M., & Leu, D. J. (2008). Central issues in new literacies and new literacies research. In J. Coiro, M. Knobel, C. Lankshear, & D. J. Leu (Eds.), *Handbook of research on new literacies* (pp. 17–49). Hillsdale, NJ: Erlbaum.

Common Core State Standards for English Language Arts and Literacy in History/ Social Studies, Science and Technical Subjects. (2010). Retrieved May 4, 2011, from *www.corestandards.org/the-standards/english-language-arts-standards.*

Dalton, B., & Proctor, C. P. (2008). The changing landscape of text and comprehension in the age of new literacies. In J. Coiro, M. Knobel, C. Lankshear, & D. J. Leu (Eds.), *Handbook of research on new literacies.* Mahwah, NJ: Erlbaum.

Desimone, L., Porter, A. C., Garet, M., Yoon, K. S., & Birman, B. (2002). Effects of professional development on teachers' instruction: Results from a three-year study. *Educational Evaluation and Policy Analysis, 24*(2), 81–112.

Desimone, L. M. (2009). Improving impact studies of teachers' professional development: Toward better conceptualizations and measures. *Educational Researcher, 38,* 181–199.

Desimone, L. M., Smith, T. M., & Ueno, K. (2006). Are teachers' who need sustained, content-focused professional development getting it? An administrator's dilemma. *Education Administration Quarterly, 42*(2), 179–215.

DuFour, R., DuFour, R., Eaker, R., & Many, T. (2010). *Learning by doing: A handbook for professional learning communities at work* (2nd ed.). Bloomington, IN: Solution Tree.

Dwyer, B. (2010). *Scaffolding Internet reading: A study of a disadvantaged school community in Ireland.* Unpublished doctoral dissertation: University of Nottingham, UK.

Dwyer, B., & Harrison, C. (2008). There's no rabbits on the Internet: Scaffolding the development of effective search strategies for struggling readers during Internet inquiry. In Y. Kim & V. J. Risko (Eds.), *57th yearbook of the National Reading Conference* (pp. 187–202). Oak Creek, WI: National Reading Conference.

Educational Testing Service. (2003). *Digital transformation: A framework for ICT literacy.* Princeton, NJ: Author. Retrieved May 4, 2011, from *www.ets.org/ Media/Research/pdf/ICTREPORT.pdf.*

Garet, M. S., Porter, A. C., Desimone, L. S., Birman, B., & Yoon, K. S. (2001). What makes professional development effective? Results from a national sample of teachers. *American Education Research Journal, 38,* 915–945.

Goldman, S. R., Wiley, J., & Graesser, A. C. (2005, April). *Learning in a knowledge society: Constructing meaning from multiple information sources.* Paper presented at the annual meeting of the American Educational Research Association, Montreal, Canada.

Gora, K., & Hinson, J. (2003). Teacher-to-teacher mentoring. *Learning and Leading with Technology, 31*(4), 36–40.

Greaves, T., & Hayes, J. (2008). *America's digital schools 2008 report.* Retrieved May 4, 2011, from *ads2008.org/ads/index.php.*

Greenhow, C., Robelia, E., & Hughes, J. (2009). Web 2.0 and classroom research: What path should we take now? *Educational Researcher, 38*(4), 246–259.

Hargittai, E. (2002). Second-level digital divide: Differences in people's online skills. *First Monday, 7*(4). Retrieved May 4, 2011, from *firstmonday.org/htbin/cgi-wrap/bin/ojs/index.php/fm/article/view/942/864.*

Henry, L. A. (2006). SEARCHing for an answer: The critical role of new literacies while reading on the Internet. *Reading Teacher, 59*(7), 614–627.

Henry, L. A., Castek, J., O'Byrne, I., & Zawilinski, L. (in press). Using new literacies to empower struggling readers. *Reading and Writing Quarterly.*

Huber, C. (2010). Professional learning 2.0. *Educational Leadership, 67*(8), 41–46.

International Reading Association. (2009). *New literacies and 21st century technologies: A position statement.* Newark, DE: Author. Retrieved May 4, 2011, from *www.reading.org/General/AboutIRA/PositionStatements/21stCenturyLiteracies.aspx.*

International Reading Association. (2010). *Standards for reading professionals—Revised 2010.* Newark, DE: Author.

Jenkins, H. (2008). *Convergence culture: Where old and new media collide.* New York: New York University Press.

Johnson, L., Levine, A., Smith, R., & Smythe, T. (2009). *The 2009 Horizon Report: K–12 edition.* Austin, TX: New Media Consortium.

Kress, G. (2003). *Literacy in the new media age.* London: Routledge.

Kuiper, E. (2007). The Web as an information resource in K–12 education: Strategies for supporting students in searching and processing information. *Review of Educational Research, 75*(3), 285–328.

Labbo, L. D., & Reinking, D. (1999). Negotiating the multiple realities of technology in literacy research and instruction. *Reading Research Quarterly, 34,* 478–492.

Lankshear, C., & Knobel, M. (2006). *New literacies: Everyday practices and classroom learning* (2nd ed.). Buckingham, UK: Open University Press.

Lawless, K. A., & Pellegrino, J. W. (2007). Professional development in integrating technology into teaching and learning: Knowns, unknowns, and ways to pursue better questions and answers. *Review of Educational Research, 77*(4), 575–614.

Lawless, K. A., & Schrader, P. G. (2008). Where do we go now? Understanding research on navigation in complex digital environments. In D. J. Leu & J. Coiro (Eds.), *Handbook of new literacies* (pp. 267–296). Hillsdale, NJ: Erlbaum.

Leu, D. J. (2007, May). *What happened when we weren't looking? How reading comprehension has changed and what we need to do about it.* Invited keynote address to the Research Conference of the International Reading Association, Toronto, Canada.

Leu, D. J., O'Byrne, W. I., Zawilinski, L., McVerry, J. G., & Everett-Cocapardo, H. (2009). Expanding the new literacies conversation. *Educational Researcher, 38,* 264–269.

Leu, D. J., Jr., Kinzer, C. K., Coiro, J., & Cammack, D. (2004). Toward a theory of new literacies emerging from the Internet and other information and communication technologies. In R. B. Ruddell & N. Unrau (Eds.), *Theoretical models and processes of reading* (5th ed., pp. 1568–1611). Newark, DE: International Reading Association.

Malloy, J., Castek, J., & Leu, D. J. (2010). Silent reading and online reading comprehension. In E. Hiebert & R. Reutzel (Eds.), *Revisiting silent reading* (pp. 221–240). Newark, DE: International Reading Association.

Moss, B., & Lapp, D. (Eds.). (2009). *Teaching new literacies in grades K–3*. New York: Guilford Press.

National Center for Education Statistics (2005). *The condition of education in brief*. Retrieved May 4, 2011, from *nces.ed.gov/pubsearch/pubsinfo. asp?pubid=2005095*.

National Center on Education and the Economy. (2007). *Tough choices or tough times: The report of the new Commission on the Skills of the American Workforce*. Washington, DC: Author. Retrieved May 4, 2011, from *www.skillscommission.org/executive.htm*.

National Council of Teachers of English. (2007). *21st-century literacies: A policy research brief*. Retrieved May 4, 2011, from *www.ncte.org/library/files/Publications/Newspaper/Chron1107ResearchBrief.pdf*.

National Education Technology Panel. (2010). *Transforming American education: Learning powered by technology*. National Educational Technology Plan. U.S. Department of Education. Retrieved May 4, 2011, from *www.ed.gov/technology/netp-2010*.

New London Group. (2000). A pedagogy of multiliteracies: Designing social futures. In B. Cope & M. Kalantzis (Eds.), *Multiliteracies: Literacy learning and the design of social futures*. London, UK: Routledge.

Pearson, P. D., & Gallagher, M. (1983). The instruction of reading comprehension. *Contemporary Educational Psychology, 8*, 317–344.

Penuel, W. R. (2006). Implementation and effects of one-to-one computing initiatives: A research synthesis. *Journal of Research on Technology in Education, 38*(3), 329–348.

Prensky, M. (2001). Digital natives, digital immigrants. *On the Horizon, 9*(5), 1–2. Retrieved May 4, 2011, from *www.marcprensky.com/writing/*.

Richardson, V., & Placier, P. (2001). Teacher change, In V. Richardson (Ed.), *Handbook of research on teaching* (4th ed., pp. 905–947). American Educational Research Association. Washington, DC: AERA,

Rouet, J. F. (2006). *The skills of document use*. Mahwah, NJ: Erlbaum.

Share, J. (2009). Young children and critical media literacy. In D. Kellner & R. Hammer (Eds.), *Media/cultural studies: Critical Approaches* (pp. 126–151). New York: Lang.

Silvernail, D., & Buffington, P. (2009). *Improving mathematics performance using laptop technology: The importance of professional development for success*. Gorham, ME: Maine Education Policy Research Institute.

Silvernail, D., & Gritter, A. (2005). *Maine's middle school laptop program: Creating better writers*. Gorham, ME: Maine Education Policy Research Institute.

Smolin, L. I., & Lawless, K. A. (2003). Becoming literate in the technological age: New responsibilities and tools for teachers. *Reading Teacher, 56*, 570–577.

Wallace, R. (2004). A framework for understanding teaching with the Internet. *American Education Research Journal, 41*(2), 447–488.

Warschauer, M. (2006). *Laptops and literacy.* New York: Teachers College Press.

Wasser, J., & McNamara, E. (1998). *Professional development and full-school technology integration: A description of the professional development model for the Hanau Model Schools Partnership* (Hanau Model Schools Report #5). Cambridge, MA: TERC.

Watts-Taffe, S., & Gwinn, C. B. (2007). *Integrating literacy and technology: Effective practice for grades K–6.* New York: Guilford Press.

Wells, J., & Lewis, L. (2006). *Internet access in U.S. public schools and classrooms: 1994–2005* (NCES 2007-020). Washington, DC: U.S. Department of Education, National Center for Education Statistics.

Zhang, S., & Duke, N. K. (in press). The impact of instruction in the WWWDOT framework on students' disposition and ability to evaluate websites as sources of information. *The Elementary School Journal.*

16

Developing Effective Home–School Literacy Partnerships

Jeanne R. Paratore
Lilly M. Steiner
Susan Dougherty

Guiding Questions

- What is the importance of parental involvement in children's literacy achievement?
- What are the challenges to productive parental involvement?
- What role should literacy leaders play in establishing effective home–school partnerships?
- What are ways that literacy leaders can support teachers and parents in their work together to increase children's opportunities to learn?

THE IMPORTANCE OF EFFECTIVE HOME–SCHOOL LITERACY PARTNERSHIPS

There is robust evidence of a strong, positive relationship between parent involvement and children's school success. Studies indicate that higher levels of parental involvement correlate with higher achievement test scores

(Dearing, McCartney, Weiss, Krieder, & Simpkins, 2004; Dearing, Kreider, Simpkins, & Weiss, 2006; Jeynes, 2003), higher motivation and engagement (Dickinson & Tabors, 1991; Epstein, 1995; Gonzalez-DeHass, Willems, & Holbein, 2005), higher rates of graduation (Rumberger, Ghatak, Poulos, Ritter, & Dornbusch, 1990), and higher secondary school grade-point averages (Fan & Chen, 2001). Moreover, studies indicate that parent involvement has especially strong effects for children of low-income families (Dearing et al., 2004), for children of low-education mothers (Dearing et al., 2006), and for children of minority languages and cultures (Jeynes, 2003). Researchers have also found that sustained and increasing involvement over the years of children's elementary schooling correlated with higher levels of reading achievement (e.g., Dearing et al., 2006).

Literacy leaders (e.g., teachers, reading specialists, principals, special educators) who are knowledgeable about factors that influence productive home–school partnerships and skillful at helping peers to acquire and use a repertoire of strategies for establishing effective relationships with parents are in a position to provide valuable support as they work to optimize students' learning opportunities. In this chapter, our purpose is to help literacy leaders effectively assume this role by describing ways they can act on evidence of effective home–school partnerships as they work to create a school culture of parent–teacher collaboration. The following case provides an example of one parent's experience with the school and a teacher's response to that parent.

Case Example: A Parent

Luis is the father of Jasmine, a first grader attending a public school in a large urban city in the northeast. Luis was born in the Dominican Republic and has lived in the United States for 11 years. His knowledge of English enables him to carry on conversations, but he believes that he lacks a strong overall understanding of the language. Jasmine, who was born in the United States, is bilingual, and speaks Spanish at home with her father. She is a pleasant, happy child who is eager to go to school each day and reports that she likes her teacher and has many friends. Luis is the custodial parent for his daughter and he works long hours. Although he is often tired in the evenings, he does his best to check that his daughter has completed her homework. He also usually reads the books his daughter brings home from her class's once-a-month trip to a public library near the school.

Luis is becoming increasingly discouraged by his interactions with his daughter's teacher. When he attended a fall parent–teacher conference, he was told that his daughter was not meeting the school's expectations for reading. Luis finds this hard to understand, because his daughter entered kindergarten already knowing most of the letters of the alphabet and seemed to be making fine progress throughout kindergarten. Although he was perplexed by the teacher's assessment of his daughter's reading progress, Luis did not question her further. In the days following the conversation he found himself wondering what had gone wrong. He tried to question his daughter directly about her reading, but she reported that she "knew all the sight words and could read the little books in group."

CASE EXAMPLE: A TEACHER

MaryBeth, Jasmine's first-grade teacher, has been teaching in the district for 8 years. She is quite knowledgeable about literacy development, having earned a master's degree in reading from a local university. She describes her approach to teaching reading as "balanced reading instruction." MaryBeth has noticed that although Jasmine has learned to use phonics elements to decode words in leveled texts and has a solid sight vocabulary, she rarely has much to say about the books she reads or those that are read to her. When she does contribute to the discussion, Jasmine either repeats something said by another child or makes a comment that focuses on a small detail in the story.

MaryBeth was pleased that Jasmine's father attended the fall parent–teacher conference, as attendance is often poor and seems particularly low among Latino parents and single parents. However, MaryBeth was disappointed by Luis's apparent lack of interest in his daughter's reading progress. Although she had sent home monthly newsletters describing elements of her classroom activities, Luis appeared to be unfamiliar with many of the activities she described and the terms she used to describe Jasmine's reading performance. She wondered if he read them. When she explained that Jasmine was not meeting expectations, Luis was silent. When she suggested that he read to Jasmine at home, Luis simply nodded. MaryBeth was not certain he had completely understood her, but she concluded that he probably was doing little to support Jasmine through home reading activities.

As we reflected on the information and events Luis and Marybeth shared with us, we noticed the strong commitment each has to Jasmine's school success; and, of course, we noticed the shared misunderstandings and, as a consequence, the likely lost opportunities for improving Jasmine's literacy achievement. Luis understands his responsibility to be involved in his daughter's schooling, and he attends to many of the tasks teachers typically ask of parents: He monitors Jasmine's homework completion, he reads the books that are sent home, he asks her about her school experiences, and he attends parent conferences. In turn, MaryBeth takes actions that typically characterize effective teaching: through additional coursework and professional development, she deepened her expertise in the teaching of reading and she carefully observes and monitors her students' learning and adjusts her instruction accordingly. She also understands the importance of parent involvement and she invites parents to participate through school meetings and by sending home an informational newsletter. Even so, Luis and Mary-Beth work separately, and in so doing, they fail to understand the efforts the other is making to help Jasmine learn. Their relationship with one another is characterized by frustration.

Although this type of misunderstanding between parents and teachers is common (Greene & Compton-Lilly, 2011; Lawrence-Lightfoot, 2004; Tutwiler, 1998), it need not be. There is convincing evidence that, when teachers ground actions and interactions with parents in evidence-based practice, parents and teachers develop strong, collaborative relationships (e.g., Allen, 2007; Chrispeels & Rivero, 2001; González, Moll, & Amanti, 2005; Sheldon, 2003). Unfortunately, few teachers enter the profession armed with requisite knowledge about ways to develop learning partnerships with parents. Preservice education programs dedicate little attention to parent–teacher partnership building (Broussard, 2000; Epstein & Sanders, 2006; Garcia, 2004; Rochkind, Ott, Immerwahr, Doble, & Johnson, 2007), leaving most teachers to draw upon their own previous experiences (e.g., back-to-school nights, conferences, classroom volunteer opportunities) in how to work with families. However, these forms of parental involvement are often a poor fit for many contemporary parents (Lawrence-Lightfoot, 2004; Nieto, 1992).

As evidence supporting the important contributions parents make to children's school success continues to build (e.g., Henderson & Mapp, 2002; Houtenville & Conway, 2008; Jeynes, 2003), and as evidence of the complexity of developing effective home–school partnerships also deepens (e.g., Graue, 2005; Hoover-Dempsey & Sandler, 1995; Hoover-Dempsey et al., 2005; Hoover-Dempsey & Whitaker, 2010) relegating this work primarily to teachers' mostly optional self-study risks squandering an important learning resource. As such, helping teachers to acquire and use effective strategies for working with parents seems a logical priority for literacy leaders. Yet, doing so is often fraught with an array of challenges. In the next section, we turn to evidence that helps us understand (and mediate) some common obstacles.

CHALLENGES TO EFFECTIVE HOME–SCHOOL PARTNERSHIPS

As we move in and out of schools working with teachers around home–school partnerships, teachers often tell us something like this: "Well, we know parent involvement is important. But in our school, we just cannot get parents involved. No matter how hard we try, we can't get cooperation." The difficulty teachers experience as they try to engage parents is widely acknowledged (Allen, 2007; Compton-Lilly, 2003; Lareau, 1989) but unevenly understood. Some teachers interpret parents' absence at school events and meetings as lack of concern or interest in their children's schooling; others assume parents' interest, but simply don't know how to effectively involve them. As a first step, it is important to understand that parents' seeming disregard for school invitations and events may not be a measure of their interest or concern in their children's schooling but, instead, a product of their discomfort and unfamiliarity with the school personnel and culture. As Valdés (1996) explained:

> Even when asked to come, however, it was often the case that parents did not respond. . . . In many families neither of the two parents felt competent enough to deal with school personnel. They were embarrassed, and found almost any excuse not to go to the school and "ponerse en evidencia" (show how ignorant or incapable they were). (p. 162)

Reactions such as these are especially prominent among parents whose own school experiences differed from their children's, which is often the case among immigrant families (Delgado-Gaitan & Trueba, 1991; Compton-Lilly, 2003) and among parents who themselves experienced failure in American schools (Edwards, 2009). This disposition clearly presents a challenge to establishing productive parent–teacher partnerships.

Yet another challenge emerges from a mismatch between parents' and teachers' understandings of roles and responsibilities. In many instances, parents perceive their responsibilities as centering on making certain their children are well fed, well rested, well behaved, and respectful of teachers, administrators, and other children, whereas teachers' responsibilities are instructionally focused: teaching reading, writing, and mathematics (Delgado-Gaitan, 1994; Lapp, Fisher, Flood, & Moore, 2002; Paratore et al., 1995; Rodriguez-Brown, 2010). Even when asked, such parents may not comply with requests to implement particular tasks or activities because they believe that they do not have the knowledge or skills to teach their children properly and they do not want to risk teaching their child incorrectly (Lapp et al., 2002; Rodriguez-Brown, 2010). In these cases, parents view themselves (appropriately) as being involved in their children's schooling because they are following through with their perceived tasks and responsibilities; however, their involvement may not be evident to the teacher.

Parents' reticence to participate in their children's school-based learning that emerges either from unfamiliarity or discomfort with the school setting, from a belief that doing so would be an intrusion on teachers' responsibilities or from a belief that they lack the knowledge or skills necessary to "teach it right" represents one type of challenge to effective home–school partnerships. Such reticence may be compounded by teachers' uncertainty about how to interact with families of students whose backgrounds differ from their own. McCarthey (1997), for example, studied five fourth- and fifth-grade teachers in a high-poverty, urban school with a linguistically and culturally diverse population. McCarthey found that although these teachers effectively connected with the families of students from mainstream backgrounds, they failed to connect as closely with students who were poor or from culturally diverse backgrounds. Teachers knew less about these students and initiated fewer interactions to gain information about their backgrounds. Because teachers lacked knowledge about such students' home literacy experiences or knowledge of the culture, they often were unable to help their students form connections between home and school.

Such challenges notwithstanding, there are teachers and schools serving high-poverty and culturally and linguistically diverse populations that have managed to establish effective parent–teacher partnerships (e.g., Chrispeels & Rivero, 2001; Delgado-Gaitan 2004; Sheldon, 2003). In fact, there is compelling evidence that teacher practices are more crucial than other factors such as race, parent education, family size, and marital status in determining a child's academic success and parents' involvement in a child's education (Delgado-Gaitan & Allexsaht-Snider, 1992; Epstein, 1986, 1995). In the next section, we turn to research that helps us to understand the processes and practices that guide teachers who successfully collaborate with parents to support high levels of student achievement.

THE ROLE OF TEACHERS IN ESTABLISHING EFFECTIVE HOME–SCHOOL PARTNERSHIPS

Successful parent involvement is grounded in deep understanding of three fundamental factors: (1) a match between parental role construction and the tasks teachers ask or expect parents to perform (Delgado-Gaitan, 2004; Hoover-Dempsey et al., 2005; Rodriguez-Brown, 2010); (2) parents' beliefs (i.e., self-efficacy) in their ability to effectively support their children (e.g., Hoover-Dempsey et al., 2005; Lapp et al., 2002; Edwards, 1994); and (3) the match between the forms of involvement expected of parents (e.g., to support high expectations, help with homework, teach skills at home, attend school meetings, volunteer in classroom or school activities) and parents' available or accessible resources (e.g., time, transportation, child care, knowledge and skills; Lareau, 1989; Nieto, 1992; Hoover-Dempsey & Whitaker, 2010). In the next sections, each of these conditions is discussed in turn.

Parental Role Construction

Parental role construction refers to parents' beliefs about the appropriateness of or need for their involvement in their children's education. Evidence that socioeconomic and cultural background and experience influence parents' construction and understanding of their roles and responsibilities relative to their children's schooling is widespread. Studies indicate that parents of Latino and Hispanic background often perceive their roles as primarily related to children's health, hygiene, and social behavior (Chrispeels & Rivero, 2001; Parra & Henderson, 1982; Smrekar & Cohen-Vogel, 2001); that parents with lower levels of education and lower socioeconomic status often emphasize educational aspirations and expectations, but are reluctant to teach their children or help with homework because they doubt their ability to do so correctly (e.g., Lapp et al., 2002; Lareau, 1989; Lawrence-Lightfoot, 1978); that highly educated Chinese American parents are more likely than their European American peers to emphasize explicit teaching at home, but less likely to attend or participate in school meetings (Huntsinger & Jose, 2009); that middle- and high-income parents are more likely to approach teachers as "social equals" (Lareau, 1989, p. 171), asserting themselves at school, requesting information about their children's academic performance or about the teachers' instructional practices and approaches, and questioning instructional practices.

The differences in the ways parents construct their roles related to their children's learning take on even more weight in light of the evidence that most schools leave it up to parents to figure out how to be involved in their children's education (Sheldon & Van Voorhis, 2004). In the particular area of literacy learning, Sheldon and Epstein (2005) cautioned that "leaving parents on their own to create a supportive home environment for reading and literacy" (p. 18) has the potential to lead to inequities between the children of parents who are more familiar with school-based literacy practices and those who require explicit support in learning how to support their children's schooling.

As we considered the evidence, we wondered if specific teaching actions or practices effectively mediate parents' understanding, such that they take on new roles or responsibilities related to their children's learning. We found clear evidence that this, indeed, is the case. For example, Chrispeels and Rivero (2001) studied the effects of the Parent Institute for Quality Education (PIQE), a program intended to increase parent involvement in and understanding of their children's education. Chrispeels and Rivero described PIQE as a forum in which instructors provided parents with the opportunity to "consider current beliefs, role construct [sic], and practices and to explore alternative ideas" (p. 124). They studied program effects within a community characterized by high poverty, high percentages of new immigrants, mostly of Latino heritage, and high rates of school failure (evident in a high dropout rate). Parents were asked to participate in eight 90-minute sessions, each addressing information about the educational system, ways to interact with the school and teachers, and ways to help their children at home. Classes were offered both in the morning and the evening to accommodate parents' differing schedules, instructors were fluent in the parents' first language, and all curricular materials were prepared in the first languages of the parents. The study included 100 parent participants (all but two, Spanish speakers), all low income but with a range of education from grade 3 to a few with some college education in their own countries or in the United States. The parents' pre- and postparticipation survey responses indicated a shift in their role construction and behaviors, including (1) increased parent-initiated communication, (2) more positive support and interaction with their children, (3) greater involvement in homework and literacy activities, and (4) greater levels of advocacy for their children in the school setting.

In another example (Nistler & Maiers, 1999), Maiers, a first-grade teacher, invited the parents of students in her classroom to join their children in her classroom 15 times over the course of the school year. She had a very high level of participation with 95% of all parents visiting at least once. During their visits, parents observed their children in the regular classroom literacy activities, including whole-class, teacher-led activities, such as reading the morning message, and small-group, cooperative activities, as children rotated among literacy stations. They also met with Maiers individually to share information or concerns about each child's literacy development. Data collected during the 2 years of program implementation included a personal journal kept by Maiers, observers' field notes, and audiotaped interviews conducted with each family three times during the school year. During interviews, parents reported that, following participation, they were more aware of the classroom literacy program and they better understood how they could provide similar support at home.

Parental Self-Efficacy

When parents have a high level of self-efficacy, that is, when they believe that by getting involved in a particular way they are likely to provide a positive outcome for their child, they are more likely to engage in the focal activity. Likewise, parents who believe that their efforts will have no effect or a negative effect are far less likely to engage in the activity (Hoover-Dempsey & Sandler, 1995; Hoover-Dempsey et al., 2005). Given these findings, we wondered to what extent teachers and other literacy leaders could influence parents' sense of self-efficacy. We found several convincing examples of instances in which children whose parents were provided with explicit instruction in ways to support their children's literacy and language learning at home experienced significant achievement gains.

In one example, Jordan, Snow, and Porche (2000) studied the impact of Project EASE. This project took place over a 5-month period during which parents of kindergarteners were invited to monthly training sessions and provided with children's books and scripted activities to use at home. During the parent training meetings, information about the importance of various types of language interactions (e.g., building and extending vocabulary knowledge) was presented. Next, the month's activities were modeled by the presenters followed by an opportunity for parents to engage in the activities with their children. Parents took home 3 weeks' worth of materials after each training session and returned 1 month later for another session. The five training sessions addressed vocabulary learning, telling personal narratives, discussing storybook narratives, discussing informational texts, and learning about letters and sounds. In addition to a parent survey, which was used to gather information about home literacy behaviors and the home literacy environment, pre- and postintervention testing examined child outcomes. The gains made by children whose parents participated were statistically greater than those made by children in the control group, with particularly strong effects on measures of language learning.

In another example, Reutzel, Fawson, and Smith (2006) designed a parent involvement program that focused on developing the word-reading and word-writing abilities of first graders. Words to Go! was implemented with first-grade parents from two high-poverty schools (one a treatment school and the other a control group). Both schools offered the same school-based comprehensive family literacy program and both used the same instructional phonics program (Cunningham, 2000) as part of classroom reading instruction. Parents with children attending the four first-grade classrooms in the treatment school were invited to attend a workshop to teach them how to implement at home "making and breaking" word lessons. Sixty-five percent of the parents of first graders attended one of the three training sessions; detailed instructions for implementing the program were sent home to the remaining parents. Once per week, a new program lesson, which included the necessary materials and a script, was sent home. Parents were asked to work with the words daily, and to fill out a report recording what had been completed over the course of a week. The researchers found that parents were highly engaged in this program. Students who participated in the Words to Go! program scored significantly higher on posttests measuring word-reading and word-writing abilities than did their control group peers. Words to Go! children also outperformed control group children on a state-administered "end-of-level" test, suggesting that they were able to apply the word-level skills learned through the program to the reading of connected texts.

In a third example, Rasinski and Stevenson (2005) studied the effects of a fluency-based family literacy program called Fast Start, an approach that combined reading to children and listening to children read. Parents of first graders were invited to attend a 60-minute training program on engaging children in supported and repeated readings of simple texts. Parents practiced a lesson with their children after it had been modeled and explained in the session. Over the course of the next 11 weeks, parents worked with their children daily for approximately 10 to 15 minutes using the same text for a week. Each week, a packet containing a short reading passage and a skill activity based on the words in the passage was sent home. Parents were asked to read the passage aloud to the child a number of times until the child was comfortable with it. Then the child was to read the passage, with parent support as needed. Finally, the parent and child completed the skill activity together. The parents were also called weekly and asked to report the amount of time they spent on the program and given the opportunity to ask questions about the program. Although as a whole the performance of children participating in Fast Start did not differ significantly from that of children in the control group, the initially lower-achieving children in the experimental group had greater gains than those of the lower-achieving children in the control group, suggesting that the intervention was of greatest benefit to the children who entered first grade with lower than expected literacy skills.

In yet another example, in a series of studies, Whitehurst and colleagues (Arnold, Lonigan, & Whitehurst, 1994; Whitehurst et al., 1994; Valdez-Menchaca & Whitehurst, 1992; Whitehurst et al., 1988; Zevenbergen & Whitehurst, 2006) studied the effects of a dialogic reading technique, an approach "based on the theory that practice in using language, feedback regarding language, and appropriately scaffolded adult–child interactions in the context of picture book reading all facilitate young children's language development" (Zevenbergen & Whitehurst, p. 178). Studies conducted with both high- and low-income children and parents, with parents of varied ethnic and racial groups (African American, Latino, European American) and different first-language groups (English and Spanish) found consistent, substantial positive effects on the language skills of children whose parents were trained in the dialogic reading technique. Moreover, when children experienced the book-reading technique both in the classroom and at home, their rates of achievement were even higher (Whitehurst et al., 1994).

The parent involvement initiatives described above, while by no means exhaustive of the types of programs that have been created and studied, demonstrate a range of possibilities for the types of coaching programs that might be implemented with parents. Yet, even well-specified programs that develop parents' self-efficacy related to a particular skill or strategy may not be sustained if insufficient attention is paid to the match between what we are asking parents to do and parents' access to resources (e.g., time, materials, equipment) necessary to maintain the practice over the long term. This is the focus of the next section.

The Match between Forms of Involvement and Parent Resources

Parent involvement has many definitions, including parents' involvement in school activities (e.g., back-to-school night, parent–teacher conferences, classroom volunteering, chaperoning field trips), parent involvement in home–based school activities (e.g., homework completion, reading to the child), and parents' aspirations for their children's academic success and encouragement of the child's academic growth (Epstein, 2001; Fan & Chen, 2001; Hoover-Dempsey et al., 2005). Studies indicate that the category of parents' aspirations and expectations for their children's educational achievement has the strongest relations with academic achievement (Fan & Chen), an especially interesting finding because this particular behavior is largely out of the teacher's view and often undetected. Conversely, involvement with children's schoolwork at home (e.g., monitoring of homework, setting rules for TV watching) had the weakest relationship with academic outcomes, a finding that is counterintuitive. One explanation is that parents may tend to emphasize homework completion and limit TV viewing in response to children's poor grades (Fan & Chen) thereby providing a poor indication of the benefit of parent involvement with schoolwork. There is also evidence that the forms of involvement parents choose relate to parents' education and parents' income levels, with those with higher levels of education and higher income levels more likely to become involved in forms of school-based involvement, such as parent–teacher conferences (e.g., attending formal school conferences, speaking with teachers about academic progress, talking with teachers about schoolwork to practice at home), volunteering in the classroom, and attending field trips (Fantuzzo, Tighe, & Childs, 2000; Ingram, Wolfe, & Lieberman, 2007). Parental involvement choices are at least partially related to time (e.g., lower-income families often work more than one job and are in hourly positions that permit little flexibility) and the availability of resources (e.g., lower-income families may have less access to child care and transportation).

Schools that achieve high levels of parent involvement are characterized by effective outreach to families, and in turn, effective outreach is a function of careful attention to forms of involvement that are consistent with parental needs and resources (Chrispeels & Rivero, 2001; Sheldon, 2003). Sheldon defined effective outreach as eight actions that collectively address ways to communicate with parents, engage parents in their children's schoolwork, and involve parents in school and community leadership activities (see Figure 16.1). Although these actions may be time consuming or challenging, the importance of thoughtful attention to these aspects of parent involvement program planning is underscored by evidence of a significant relationship between parent involvement and student achievement on a state assessment: "The results of the multiple regression analyses indicate that, in any given year, the degree to which schools are working to overcome several challenges to equitable parent involvement is associated with students' performance on state tests after accounting for poverty, mobility, and size of the school population." (p. 161)

ACTING ON THE EVIDENCE: DEVELOPING EFFECTIVE HOME–SCHOOL LITERACY PARTNERSHIPS

Recall the individuals we introduced as we opened this chapter: Luis, a parent with a strong commitment to his daughter Jasmine's education and school success, and MaryBeth, a teacher with an equally strong commitment to ensuring Jasmine's success. Despite their efforts, Jasmine is falling

- Identifying ways for schools, families, and students to contribute to communities
- Getting information to parents/families unable to attend meetings
- Communicating clearly with families, including attention to reading levels and first languages
- Establishing ways for parents to request and provide information
- Providing volunteer opportunities at school or at home
- Assigning interactive homework that prompts children to share what they are learning with family members
- Involving families from all ethnic, income, and racial groups in school leadership councils and committees
- Using community resources to enhance student learning

FIGURE 16.1. Eight actions that define effective outreach to parents (based on Sheldon, 2003).

behind in reading, and Luis and MaryBeth seem to be at an impasse—each believes he or she is doing what is necessary. To move forward, they will likely need some sort of mediation—someone who can help them understand that although they are both working hard to support Jasmine, there are ways they might work together that would increase Jasmine's opportunities to learn and result in higher literacy achievement. In Jasmine's school, Brenda, the literacy specialist, is aware of Jasmine's increasing reading difficulty; she also knows that many of her colleagues are concerned about the level of parent involvement in her school.

CASE EXAMPLE: A LITERACY LEADER

Brenda was formerly a first- and second-grade teacher in the district. She has been a literacy coach in the school for 4 years, and throughout this time she has frequently heard teachers complain that parents aren't doing enough at home to support their children's literacy development. These conversations and comments prompted Brenda to investigate effective home–school partnerships to deepen her understanding and help her support her colleagues' efforts. Now, as she considers the research evidence and reflects on what her colleagues are doing, she suspects that the teachers may be overlooking some ways that might increase parent involvement. Brenda would like to design a project that will bring parents and teachers together in a more productive partnership.

Brenda began by considering the three factors previously described as essential to productive home–school partnerships. First, parents and teachers must have a shared understanding of parents' roles and responsibilities related to children's school learning. Second, parents must have the knowledge and skills necessary to effectively implement the activities or tasks teachers expect them to do. Third, the forms of involvement offered to parents must be congruent with parents' available resources. Then, she planned an 8-week intervention (based on the work of Steiner, 2008) that she hoped would help her address each of these basic elements.

For her work with parents, Brenda designed an intervention that would help them learn about and support school-based literacy practices, particularly storybook reading strategies and talking about books. She scheduled eight 1-hour meetings at two different times of day (morning and evening) so that parents who worked outside the home could participate. She used funding from a grant to provide child care during both sessions and she also used funding from the grant to purchase books for a lending library.

During each session parents were provided training in effective read-aloud strategies and ways to engage their children in response to books, and a book to read with their children at home. Brenda selected books that connected to the classroom curriculum and units of study. Instruction during the sessions included (1) defining focal storybook reading strategies, (2) modeling strategies through a read-aloud, (3) providing guided practice in using strategies, (4) reading books chorally or individually, and (5) discussing the books and strategy use with a partner.

Brenda also worked with teachers to improve their understanding of the factors that relate to parental involvement and their awareness of actions they could take to collaborate more effectively with parents. She hoped that this work would have far-reaching results, as teachers learned to partner more effectively with parents of all their children year in and year out.

During the 8 weeks, Brenda and the teachers met weekly to discuss issues central to productive home–school partnerships. In preparation for each meeting, the teachers and the literacy coach read an article related to understanding and supporting home–school literacy partnerships; during their meeting, they shared their understandings, clarified or elaborated on ideas, and discussed implications for the ways teachers might develop partnerships with parents. They co-planned activities that the teachers would implement to involve parents in children's school-based literacy learning. These activities included parent read-aloud training sessions, a parent workshop to demonstrate how reading is taught in the classroom, and two writing celebrations.

Brenda reported that 20 parents attended the parent workshops, and Luis, in particular, attended several of the evening workshops. After just a few sessions, he said that he recognized how he could help Jasmine with her reading. He explained that he began to talk more with Jasmine about the stories, and he also asked her the types of questions that had been modeled in the coaching sessions. Because Brenda also had invited the teachers to attend these sessions, Luis and MaryBeth had an opportunity to talk one week after a session. MaryBeth later told Brenda that she was surprised to see Luis there, and she now realized that her impression of him as uninterested in supporting his daughter's literacy learning was incorrect. Following their conversation, MaryBeth decided to send home storybooks weekly with all her students, providing Luis and other parents with more materials to use in supporting their children's comprehension.

Following the professional development meetings, teachers reported that as they interacted with parents in the various activities, they increased their knowledge of parents' understanding of their roles and responsibilities related to their children's literacy learning, and they also increased their awareness of parents' knowledge and skills related to the specific tasks and activities teachers expected children to do at home. They also reported that as they interacted with parents more frequently in less formal contexts, they learned more about family backgrounds and experiences and they were able to integrate this information into classroom literacy instruction, in particular by helping parents to make connections to texts read in class.

CONCLUSION

Brenda's approach to coaching teachers and parents represents only one model, and although it met with some success, it cannot, of course, respond to the range of needs that literacy leaders will find as they meet and talk with parents and teachers. Our hope is that in studies cited within the chapter, readers will find many other examples of events, activities, and projects that, when selected and modified with thoughtful attention to focal teachers and families, will have desired outcomes. In closing, as we think and work with teachers to identify pathways to productive partnerships, we find that the stance taken by Shockley, Michalove, and Allen (1995) serves as an important reminder of the fundamental premise that *partnerships* emerge when teaching and learning are viewed as reciprocal processes aimed at "fostering each other's expertise" (p. 95):

> We were not trying to impose our vision of literacy but to develop relationships with families where we could learn about what already existed in the families and connect that with the literacy classroom community. We were trying to learn from parents what literacy events were important in their lives and share with them the important literacy events in their children's school. We recognized that families as well as teachers have busy lives. We needed channels for developing meaningful partnerships that were open, dependable, nonintrusive and nonevaluative. (p. 94)

ENGAGEMENT ACTIVITIES

1. Consider the steps Brenda took as a literacy leader and think about the parents of the children in your school. What types of interventions will help parents develop an understanding of the roles and responsibilities you wish them to assume? What types of interventions will help parents acquire the knowledge and skills necessary to effectively engage in the tasks you ask of them? What are some ideas for helping parents understand how they can be helpful (parental role construction) and for building their sense of self-efficacy?

2. What are the obstacles to family involvement in your school/district? Work with your colleagues to develop a list of actions you might take to overcome the obstacles.

3. Imagine that you are about to meet with teachers who have had largely

negative parental involvement experiences. What information from this chapter might you use to build an argument that, if you work together to design a research-based program, they are likely to meet with better success? Develop two to three PowerPoint slides that frame your argument.

4. In schools with high levels of parental involvement, teachers and literacy leaders are especially active in working with parents. What types of professional development opportunities might help teachers with whom you work develop a deeper understanding of "best practices" in parent involvement?

REFERENCES

Allen, J. (2007). *Creating welcoming schools: A practical guide to home–school partnerships with diverse families.* New York: Teachers College Press.

Arnold, D. H., Lonigan, C. J., & Whitehurst, G. J. (1994). Accelerating language development through picture book reading: Replication and extension to a videotape training format. *Journal of Educational Psychology, 86,* 235–243.

Broussard, C. A. (2000). Preparing teachers to work with families: A national survey of teacher education programs. *Equity and Excellence in Education, 33*(2), 41–49.

Chrispeels, J. H., & Rivero, E. (2001). Engaging Latino families for student success: How parent education can reshape parents' sense of place in the education of their children. *Peabody Journal of Education, 76*(2), 119–169.

Compton-Lilly, C. (2003). *Reading families: The literate lives of urban children.* New York: Teachers College Press.

Cunningham, P. M. (2000). *Phonics they use: Words for reading and writing* (3rd ed.). Boston: Allyn & Bacon.

Dearing, E., Kreider, H., Simpkins, S., & Weiss, H. B. (2006). Family involvement in school and low-income children's literacy: Longitudinal associations between and within families. *Journal of Educational Psychology, 98*(4), 653–664.

Dearing, E., McCartney, K., Weiss, H. B., Krieder, H., & Simpkins, S. (2004). The promotive effects of family educational involvement for low-income children's literacy. *Journal of School Psychology, 42*(6), 445–460.

Delgado-Gaitan, C. (1994). Spanish speaking families involvement in schools. In C. L. Fagnano, & B. Z. Werber (Eds.), *School, family and community interaction: A view from the firing lines* (pp. 85–98). Boulder, CO: Westview Press.

Delgado-Gaitan, C. (2004). *Involving Latino families in schools: Raising student achievement through home–school partnerships.* Thousand Oaks, CA: Sage.

Delgado-Gaitan, C., & Allexsaht-Snider, M. (1992). Mediating school cultural knowledge for children: The parent's role. In J. H. Johnston & K. M. Borman (Eds.), *Effective schooling for economically disadvantaged students: School-based strategies for diverse student populations* (pp. 81–100). Norwood, NJ: Ablex.

Delgado-Gaitan, C., & Trueba, H. (1991). Crossing cultural borders: Education for development and relationship to family involvement outcomes. *School Effectiveness and School Improvement, 15,* 125–148.

Dickinson, D. K., & Tabors, P. O. (1991). Early literacy: Linkages between home, school, and literacy achievement at age five. *Journal of Research in Childhood Education, 6*(1), 30–45.

Edwards, P. A. (1994). Responses of teachers and African-American mothers to a book-reading intervention program. In D. K. Dickinson (Ed.), *Bridges to literacy: Children, families, and schools* (pp. 175–210). Cambridge, MA: Blackwell.

Edwards, P. A. (2009). *Tapping the potential of parents: A strategic guide to boosting student achievement through family involvement.* New York: Scholastic.

Epstein, J. L. (1986). Parents' reactions to teacher practices of parent involvement. *Elementary School Journal, 86,* 277–294.

Epstein, J. L. (1995). School/family/community partnerships: Caring for the children we share. *Phi Delta Kappan, 76,* 701–712.

Epstein, J. L. (2001). *School, family, and community partnerships.* Boulder, CO: Westview Press.

Epstein, J. L., & Sanders, M.G. (2006). Prospects for change: Preparing educators for school, family, and community partnerships. *Peabody Journal of Education, 81*(2), 81–120.

Fan, X., & Chen, M. (2001). Parental involvement and students' academic achievement: A meta-analysis. *Educational Psychology Review, 13*(1), 22.

Fantuzzo, J., Tighe, E., & Childs, S. (2000). Family involvement questionnaire: A multivariate assessment of family participation in early childhood education. *Journal of Educational Psychology, 92*(2), 367–376.

Garcia, D. C. (2004). Exploring connections between the construct of teacher efficacy and family involvement practices: Implications for urban teacher preparation. *Urban Education, 39,* 290–315.

González, N., Moll, L. C., & Amanti, C. (2005). *Funds of knowledge: Theorizing practices in households, communities, and classrooms.* Mahwah, NJ: Erlbaum.

González-DeHass, A. R., Willems, P. P., & Holbein, M. F. D. (2005). Examining the relationship between parental involvement and student motivation. *Educational Psychology Review, 17*(2), 99–123.

Graue, E. (2005). Theorizing and describing preservice teachers' images of families and schooling. *Teachers College Record, 107*(1), 157–185.

Greene, S., & Compton-Lilly, C. (2011). *Connecting home and school: Complexities and considerations in fostering parent involvement and family literacy.* New York: Teachers College Press.

Henderson, A. T., & Mapp, K. (2002). *A new wave of evidence: The impact of school, family, and community connections on student achievement.* Austin, TX: National Center for Family and Community Connections with Schools.

Hoover-Dempsey, K. V., & Sandler, H. M. (1995). Parental involvement in children's education: Why does it make a difference? *Teacher's College Record, 97,* 310–331.

Hoover-Dempsey, K. V., Walker, J. M. T., Sandler, H. M., Whetsel, D., Green, C. L., Wilkins, A. S., et al. (2005). Why do parents become involved? Research findings and implications. *Elementary School Journal, 106*(2), 105–130.

Hoover-Dempsey, K. V., & Whitaker, M. C. (2010). The parental involvement process: Implications for literacy development. In K. Dunsmore & D. Fisher (Eds.), *Bringing literacy home* (pp. 53–82). Newark, DE: International Reading Association.

Houtenville, A. J., & Conway, K. S. (2008). Parental effort, school resources, and student achievement. *Journal of Human Resources, 43*(2), 437–453.

Huntsinger, C. S., & Jose, P. E. (2009). Parental involvement in children's schooling: Different meanings in different cultures. *Early Childhood Research Quarterly, 24,* 398–410.

Ingram, M., Wolfe, R. B., & Lieberman, J. M. (2007). The role of parents in high-achieving schools serving low-income, at-risk populations. *Education and Urban Society, 39*(4), 479–497.

Jeynes, W. (2003). A meta-analysis: The effects of parental involvement on minority children's academic involvement. *Education and Urban Society, 35*(1), 202–218.

Jordan, G. E., Snow, C. E., & Porche, M. V. (2000). Project EASE: The effect of a family literacy project on kindergarten students' early literacy skills. *Reading Research Quarterly, 35,* 524–546.

Lapp, D., Fisher, D., Flood, J., & Moore, K. (2002). "I don't want to teach it wrong": An investigation of the role families believe they should play in the early literacy development of their children. *National Reading Conference Yearbook, 51,* 276–287.

Lareau, A. (1989). *Home advantage: Social class and parental intervention.* New York: Falmer Press.

Lawrence-Lightfoot, S. (1978). *Worlds apart: Relationships between families and schools.* New York: Basic Books.

Lawrence-Lightfoot, S. L. (2004). *The essential conversation: What parents and teachers can learn from each other.* New York: Random House.

McCarthey, S. J. (1997). Connecting home and school literacy practices in classrooms with diverse populations. *Journal of Literacy Research, 29,* 145–182.

Nieto, S. (1992). *Affirming diversity: The sociopolitical context of multicultural education.* New York: Longman.

Nistler, R. J., & Maiers, A. (1999). Changing parents roles in school: Effects of a 2-year study of a family literacy program in an urban first-grade classroom. *Education and Urban Society, 32,* 108–126.

Paratore, J. R., Krol-Sinclair, B., Homza, A., Lewis-Barrows, T. , Melzi, G., Sturgis, R., et al. (1995). Shifting boundaries in home/school responsibilities: Involving immigrant parents in the construction of literacy portfolios. *Research in the Teaching of English, 29,* 367–389.

Parra, E., & Henderson, R. W. (1982). Mexican-American perceptions of parent and teacher roles in child development. In J. A. Fishman & G. D. Keller (Eds.), *Bilingual education for hispanic students in the US* (pp. 289–302). New York: Teachers College Press.

Rasinski, T., & Stevenson, B. (2005). The effects of Fast Start Reading: A fluency-based home involvement reading program, on the reading achievement of beginning readers. *Reading Psychology, 26,* 109–125.

Reutzel, D. R., Fawson, P. C., & Smith, J. A. (2006). Words to Go!: Evaluating a first-grade parent involvement program for "making" words at home. *Reading Research and Instruction, 45*(2), 119–159.

Rochkind, J., Ott, A., Immerwahr, J., Doble, J., & Johnson, J. (2007). *Lessons learned: New teachers talk about their jobs, challenges, and long-range plans. A report from the National Comprehensive Center for Teacher Quality and Public Agenda.* Retrieved July 28, 2010, from *www.publicagenda.org/reports/lessons-learned-new-teachers-talk-about-their-jobs-challenges-and-long-range-plans-issue-no-2.*

Rodriguez-Brown, F. (2010). Latino culture and schooling: Reflections on family literacy with a culturally and linguistically different community. In K. Dusmore & D. Fisher (Eds.), *Bringing literacy home* (pp. 203–225). Newark, DE: International Reading Association.

Rumberger, R. W., Ghatak, R., Poulos, G., Ritter, P. L., & Dornbusch, S. M. (1990). Family influences on dropout behavior in one California high school. *Sociology of Education, 63,* 283–299.

Sheldon, S. B. (2003). Linking school–family–community partnerships in urban elementary schools to student achievement on state tests. *Urban Review, 35*(2), 145–164.

Sheldon, S. B., & Epstein, J. L. (2005). School programs of family and community involvement to support children's reading and literacy development. In J. Flood & P. Anders (Eds.), *Literacy development of students in urban schools: Research and policy* (pp. 107–138). Newark, DE: International Reading Association.

Sheldon, S. B., & Van Voorhis, V. L. (2004). Partnership programs in U.S. schools: Their development and relationship to family involvement outcomes. *School Effectiveness and School Improvement, 15,* 125–148.

Shockley, B., Michalove, B., & Allen, J. (1995). *Engaging families: Connecting home and school literacy communities.* Portsmouth, NH: Heinemann.

Smrekar, C., & Cohen-Vogel, L. (2001). The voices of parents: Rethinking the intersection of family and school. *Peabody Journal of Education, 76*(2), 75–100.

Steiner, L. M. (2008). *Effects of a school-based parent and teacher intervention to promote first-grade students' literacy achievement.* Doctoral dissertation, Boston University.

Tutwiler, S. W. (1998). Diversity among families. In M. L. Fuller & G. Olsen (Eds.), *Home–school relations: Working successfully with parents and families* (pp. 40–66). Boston: Allyn & Bacon.

Valdés, G. (1996). *Con respecto: Bridging the distances between culturally diverse families and schools.* New York: Teachers College Press.

Valdez-Menchaca, M. C., & Whitehurst, G. J. (1992). Accelerating language development through picture book reading: A systematic extension to Mexican day care. *Developmental Psychology, 28,* 1106–1114.

Whitehurst, G. J., Arnold, D. S., Epstein, J. N., Angell, A. L., Smith, M., & Fischel,

J. F. (1994). A picture book reading intervention in day care and home for children from low-income families. *Developmental Psychology, 30*(5), 679–689.

Whitehurst, G. J., Falco, F., Lonigan, C. J., Fischel, J. E., DeBaryshe, B. D., Valdez-Menchaca, M. C., et al. (1988). Accelerating language development through picture-book reading. *Developmental Psychology, 24,* 552–558.

Zevenbergen, A. A., & Whitehurst, G. J. (2006). Dialogic reading: A shared picture book intervention for preschoolers. In A. van Kleeck, S. A. Stahl, & E. B. Bauer (Eds.), *On reading books to children* (pp. 177–200). Mahwah, NJ: Erlbaum.

17

Policy Implementation

The Path from Reading Policy to Classroom Practice

Sarah L. Woulfin
Cynthia E. Coburn

Guiding Questions

- What is the impact of policy on teachers' practice? Specifically, how do teachers respond to reading policy?
- What influences how teachers respond to policy?
- What are the implications of what we know about teachers' responses to policy for literacy leaders?

Mandates, guidelines, and funding affect the work of literacy leaders. Over the last two decades, a barrage of policies that intend to alter instruction in U.S. schools have reached into the classroom in unprecedented ways. Today's policymakers and education reformers place reading instruction squarely at the center of their efforts to improve instruction and close the achievement gap. In particular, No Child Left Behind (NCLB, 2002) has dramatically raised the stakes for student performance on standardized tests in reading, placing new pressure on teachers, schools, and districts to improve achievement. Reading instruction and achievement have also been prioritized by many state- and district-level accountability policies (Coburn, Pearson, & Woulfin, 2010; Mintrop & Trujillo, 2005). In this chapter, we discuss the impact of reading policy on teachers' classroom practice.

NCLB (2002) is the latest in a long line of efforts to use policy to improve reading instruction. Throughout the 1990s, the country was in the midst of the standards movement. Encouraged by federal Goals 2000 funds, state after state enacted new state standards in different content areas including reading and language arts. These standards tended to put forth ambitious visions of teaching and learning, which were then linked with state assessments to monitor progress plus professional development to build teacher capacity (Smith & O'Day, 1990).

Since the late 1990s, two federal initiatives specifically devoted to improving reading instruction were introduced: Reading Excellence Act and, more recently, Reading First (Coburn, Pearson, & Woulfin, 2010). Reading First is distinctive in the history of educational policymaking for the degree to which the federal government and states specified appropriate instructional practice, focused on fidelity to curricular materials, and required extensive monitoring of teacher practice (U.S. Department of Education, 2002). In addition, many states and districts have conducted their own policymaking related to reading instruction. Districts across the country have adopted new reading textbooks and linked them with pacing guides, targeted professional development, and progress-monitoring assessments.

Over the course of these policies, guidance to schools and teachers became increasingly specified as it moved from outlining guiding principles, as in the case of standards, to promoting mandated curriculum linked with pacing guides, assessments, and close monitoring for fidelity. The sheer volume of policy related to reading instruction, along with the use of increasingly aggressive policy instruments makes it important to understand how instructional policy matters for school reform and teachers' instructional practice. Paying attention to the nature of reading policy, as well as how and why policy is translated into practice in schools, illuminates opportunities and challenges for improving teachers' literacy instruction and students' literacy achievement.

We begin our discussion of the relationship between reading policy and teachers' instruction by presenting a vignette[1] of a first-grade teacher in California that illustrates how teachers respond to multiple waves of reading policy (Coburn, 2001a). Next, we discuss the factors that influence teachers' responses to policy. We then provide a case example that raises issues for discussion about how literacy leaders can shape the enactment of a reading program. We close with implications for literacy leaders.

---

[1]The vignette is based on data and analyses from a doctoral dissertation (Coburn, 2001a).

CASE EXAMPLE

Sharon Robinson[2] is a longtime first-grade teacher whose career traversed a consequential span of the recent history of reading in California. She began teaching in 1964, just as early attention to phonics was gaining prominence. Thus, she experienced the basic skills approach to reading instruction that relied on sequenced skills instruction, early attention to phonics, close adherence to the textbook, reading groups, and worksheets to teach beginning reading. After teaching for 20 years in schools with colleagues and instructional materials carrying the basic skills approach, in the mid-1980s, Sharon began to come in contact with new and different approaches to reading, such as literature-based instruction. In contrast with the basic skills approach, literature-based instruction operated on the principle that, although teachers should teach the code so that children learn phonics, it was also important to move on to other elements of literacy once they did. This approach to reading taught the three cueing systems (meaning, structure, and visual), used authentic children's literature rather than textbooks, integrated reading and writing, and had a greater emphasis on whole-class instruction than the basic skills approach.

Sharon was open to incorporating new ideas into her classroom. But, she tended to use her core beliefs about teaching and learning rooted in the principles of basic skills to make sense of new ideas about literature-based instruction. In so doing, Sharon created an approach to reading instruction that blended the two together. In her classroom, rather than using heterogeneous groups as emphasized by literature-based instruction, she administered oral reading assessments and used the results to create leveled groups of students. For the majority of her reading period, she met with groups to listen to students read and respond to questions about the text, while the remainder of the class worked independently on worksheets to practice literacy skills. Sharon adopted literature-based approaches in small-group instruction that attended to comprehension and started to organize her reading instruction around thematic units, as promoted by the approach. At the same time, she implemented basic skills activities for students' independent practice of reading skills, which meant that students still spent a large portion of the day completing worksheets on isolated skills.

It is with this blended approach and in interaction with colleagues that Sharon responded to new reading policy in the late 1990s that emphasized a different, balanced approach to reading instruction. The balanced approach encouraged teachers to adopt a rigorous literature, comprehension, and language program plus explicit phonemic awareness and phonics skills instruc-

---

[2]The names in this chapter's case examples are pseudonyms.

tion with ongoing assessment to drive instruction. And, in the 1998–1999 school year, teachers at Sharon's school received a new textbook series, which we call core reading program (CRP). The state intended for this reading series to be a vehicle for moving away from literature-based instruction toward a balanced approach. Sharon evaluated the new textbook series in a series of conversations with her close colleague, Evie. They began exploring the new reading series together in a series in casual conversations, occurring before and after school and during lunch. They also began to plan lessons from the reading series with their other colleagues in first grade during their grade-level team meetings. By the end of the first month of school, Sharon and Evie had decided that the new reading series did not fit either with their conceptions of appropriate reading instruction or with the way they organized reading instruction in reading groups. They told the others on the first-grade team that CRP didn't work for reading groups ("You can't teach kids to learn to read using CRP") and halted the first-grade team's efforts to plan lessons together based on the reading series.

In coming to understand the reading series, Sharon and Evie focused on the main textbook, while paying less attention to the supplementary materials. And, to these two teachers, the textbook and its selections for student reading looked very different from the literature-based series that they had used before. They noticed that CRP's early stories were predictable texts with very few words, differing considerably from the decodable texts of the phonics readers they used that they had saved from earlier in their careers and continued to use. They also differed from the longer, more complex stories of the literature-based CRP. Based on their sense of the nature of an appropriate story to use for reading groups—a sense that was rooted in the way the principles of literature-based instruction were embedded in the previous reading program—Evie proposed and then Sharon agreed that "the stories are too easy."

The two teachers also noticed that the new program did not have "skill work" to introduce prior to the story or worksheets to use after reading the story. In fact, the skill work was increased in CRP, but it was primarily contained in supplementary texts that the two teachers did not pay attention to. But, since they didn't see the skill work where they expected to see it, Sharon and Evie expressed concern that CRP would not prepare students to do well on the standardized test.

Given differences in the kinds of stories included, the nature and quantity of skill work, and lesson structure, Sharon and Evie did not see the reading series as appropriate for reading groups. But given what they saw as its similarities to literature-based instruction (predictable texts and thematic, open-ended activities), they felt the series was appropriate for shared reading and centers. For this reason, Sharon and Evie continued to use the decodable phonics texts with their early readers and the literature-based series with their more advanced reading groups. At the same time, they began incorporating some CRP stories for shared reading and center activities. They also began to include stories from one of the supplemental reading series—the guided reading books—in their book baskets for independent reading. In this way, these first-grade teachers used a mix of instructional materials from different policy eras and layered their approaches to literacy instruction.

This response to the new reading series was enabled by the school principal. The principal's view was that it was the teacher's role to teach to the district standards. She advocated that the textbooks were one way to get there, but there were many others. She emphasized this position repeatedly in staff meetings throughout the year. For example, in one meeting she said, "There is the core curriculum and the standards, and then there is the adoption [reading series]. With the adoption, [the district] picks the materials that are closest to the standard, but no publisher can be the be-all or end-all. … There are other options. … You're supposed to teach to the standards. The adoption is one way to support it, but not the only way." Sharon and other teachers repeated this message as they discussed how to use CRP. In one meeting, for example, Sharon told her colleagues: "[The principal] has not said you have to throw everything out and just use [CRP]." In this way, Sharon felt authorized by the principal to continue her complex, blended approach to literacy that used portions of CRP plus a variety of other texts, worksheets, and activities.

TEACHERS AND READING POLICY

How do teachers respond to reading policy? When do teachers respond like Sharon by layering practices on top of their preexisting approaches, leading to more and more complex approaches to reading instruction? When do they respond by rejecting new approaches? And, when do they respond by transforming their practice? In this section, we review research that speaks to these questions. As represented in Figure 17.1, we argue that teachers' response to instructional policy is the result of the interaction between (1) individual knowledge, beliefs, and attitudes; (2) the school and district context; and (3) features of the policy itself. This chapter illuminates how individual, social, and policy factors play a role in the interactive, contextualized process of reading policy implementation.

Individual Factors Shaping Teacher Responses to Policy

Recent research provides a great deal of evidence that teachers' prior beliefs, knowledge, and practices influence how they come to understand and enact

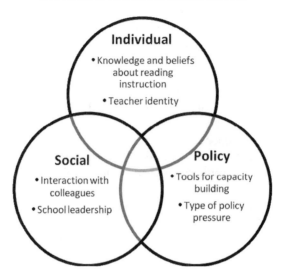

FIGURE 17.1. Factors that influence how teachers respond to reading policy.

instructional policy in their classrooms (Guthrie, 1990; Smith, 2000; Spillane, 2000; Spillane & Jennings, 1997; Coburn, 2001b, 2005a). As Spillane, Reiser, and Reimer explain: "Individuals must use their prior knowledge and experience to notice, make sense of, interpret, and react to incoming stimuli—all the while actively constructing meaning from their interactions with the environment, of which policy is part" (2002, pp. 393–394). Sharon illustrates this well. She drew on her prior experiences as a teacher to interpret and subsequently react to the particular ideas contained in the new reading series, which had been adopted and endorsed by state and district policy. For example, Sharon believed that students needed to complete worksheets to master reading skills. So, after noticing that the CRP did not include skills worksheets, she perceived a gap in this program and began assigning students supplemental worksheets to complete before and after the new program's reading selections.

Indeed, several studies during this period offer evidence that teachers' *preexisting knowledge and beliefs about reading instruction* play a major role in how they respond to new reading policies. Preexisting beliefs and practices shape how teachers come to understand the meaning and implications of reading policy. Thus, teachers with different preexisting beliefs can understand the same policy in different ways (Coburn, 2001b, 2004; Spillane et al., 2002). For example, a teacher with beliefs about the importance of explicit phonics skills instruction could interpret a new district policy asking teachers to adopt literacy centers as a message to incorporate phonics activities into centers. Yet another teacher with differing views on the role of phonics could interpret the same policy as a message to set up learning stations covering multiple elements of literacy—from phonics and fluency to comprehension and writing. These two teachers understood the district's new policy in different ways because their interpretations are shaped by preexisting beliefs about reading instruction.

In addition, prior beliefs and practice can influence change in classroom practice (Achinstein & Ogawa, 2006; Coburn, 2001b, 2004; Diamond, 2007; Spillane, 2000; Spillane et al., 2002). For example, in her study of three elementary teachers' response to changing reading policy in California from 1983 to 1999, Coburn (2004) provides evidence that teachers' responses to policy was shaped by the degree of congruence between new policy approaches and their preexisting beliefs and practices. She shows that the greater the congruence of the policy message, the more likely it was that teachers incorporated the approach into their classroom practice in some manner. Thus, teachers responded to 90% of policy messages at a high degree of congruence by creating parallel structures (e.g., a teacher adds a block of time for direct instruction of phonics skills and continues to teach phonics in a contextualized manner during small-group instruction), assimilating ideas into their preexisting practice (e.g., a teacher adopts learning centers but does not permit students to work collaboratively), or restructuring their practice in fundamental ways (e.g., a teacher learns about comprehension strategy instruction and fundamentally alters how he or she presents and discusses texts in the classroom). In contrast, teachers incorporated only 38% of messages about the content and pedagogy of reading instruction when those messages failed to match their preexisting beliefs and practices.

Additionally, the depth of teachers' knowledge shapes their policy responses in important ways (Sloan, 2006; Valencia & Wixson, 2001). For example, Sloan's study of three experienced teachers with a varied level of content knowledge in reading provides evidence that while mandated curriculum constrained the practice of the teacher with strong content knowledge, making it difficult for her to meet the diverse needs of her students, it improved the quality of instruction for the teachers with weak content knowledge.

Several studies provide evidence that *issues of identity* are also important for how teachers respond to reading policy (Achinstein & Ogawa, 2006; Kersten, 2006; Kersten & Pardo, 2007; Sloan, 2006; Spillane, 2000). Some scholars have focused on how teachers' identity as professionals—their sense of their appropriate role and what it means to be a teacher—influenced their response to reading policy. This body of work suggests that teachers resist following well-specified curricula when this requirement conflicts with their view of themselves as a professional (Achinstein & Ogawa,

2006, Kersten, 2006; Kersten & Pardo, 2007) or when they do not identify strongly with the world of schooling (Sloan, 2006). For example, the two novice teachers profiled by Achinstein and Ogawa had visions of teaching as involving autonomy, creativity, and individuality and actively resisted the mandated curriculum. Following a highly specified curriculum conflicted with their view of themselves as teachers. Both teachers rejected using the curriculum as intended and ultimately left the schools that required them to do so.

How Social and Organizational Contexts Influence Teacher Response to Policy

Individual characteristics shape teachers' responses to policy but, as shown in Figure 17.1, so do the social and organizational contexts in which they work. We discuss how two facets of these contexts—social interaction with colleagues and school leadership—matter for how teachers implement reading policy in their classroom.

First, *patterns of social interaction* influence how teachers are exposed to and learn about reading policy. There is great variability in the degree to which teachers have access to information about new policy initiatives, particularly when they are created at higher levels of the system (Coburn, 2005a; McDonnell, 2004). Teachers' connections, or social networks, with each other and those outside the school provide a powerful mechanism for learning about new ideas and approaches promoted by reading policy. They shape teachers' access to some policy messages and not others (Coburn, 2001b, 2005a; Coburn & Stein, 2006). For example, literacy leaders involved with professional organizations such as the International Reading Association may engage with different ideas and information about literacy instruction from journals, conferences, and other professional development experiences that augment their understanding of new reading policy. Those that are not members of professional associations may have little opportunity to learn about new approaches coming down the pike.

Second, literacy leaders' interactions with their colleagues influence how they come to understand the meaning and implications of a new policy. Teachers make decisions about how to respond to new policy initiatives in conversation with their colleagues. For example, Sharon, the first-grade teacher in the case example, made decisions about how to respond to the new reading series after extensive collaboration and discussion with her colleague, Evie. Their interactions influenced how Sharon came to understand the limitations, as well as affordances, of this district-mandated reading program. It is important to note that Sharon's interaction with Evie did not happen solely in the context of formal grade-level meetings. Rather, Sharon's main interpretive work happened not with the entire first-grade team, but when she sought out Evie on her own: before and after school and during lunch. Indeed, interaction in informal settings can be more influential in teachers' interpretation of new policy ideas than mandated collaboration in grade-level groups, especially if the activities in these grade-level groups have limited connections to teachers' situated needs (Coburn, 2001b).

Furthermore, how teachers come to understand the nature of instructional change required by a given policy is shaped by who they interact with (Coburn, 2001b; Booher-Jennings, 2005). For example, Booher-Jennings describes how teachers responded to high-stakes tests by rationing instructional resources—focusing on children at the margins of proficiency (the "bubble kids") rather than high- or low-performing students—in part because they felt pressure from colleagues to improve the schools' performance rating. Thus, teachers influenced each other to see rationing as the most appropriate response to the district's high-stakes accountability policy.

Research has also highlighted the role of *school leadership* in how teachers respond to reading policy. Principals influence classroom implementation by emphasizing some aspects of reading policy and not others, shaping teachers' access to some aspects of reading policy and not others (Coburn, 2001b, 2005b; Diamond, 2007; Diamond & Spillane, 2004; Spillane et al., 2002). This happens when principals craft agendas and professional development sessions that incorporate particular slices of reading policy that help advance the leader's goals and then teachers engage with those policy messages. And, at a deeper level, school leaders influence how teachers come to understand the meaning and implication of policy (Anagnostopoulos & Rutledge, 2007; Coburn 2001b, 2005b, 2006). Returning to the case example, the principal at Sharon's school played this role. Sharon's principal advanced a construction of the reading series that authorized teachers to use the reading series in a wide range of ways, or not at all, as long as they geared their instruction to the standards. This construction, in turn, framed the boundaries of possible adaptation within which Sharon, Evie, and her colleagues made sense of the new reading series.

Diamond and Spillane (2004) suggest that school leaders' choices about what to emphasize are influenced by the performance level of the school. In their 4-year study of four low-income schools in Chicago—two high performing and two under threat to probation—Diamond and Spillane found that low-performing, low-income schools tended to respond to high-stakes accountability with short-term solutions: curriculum narrowing, focus on "bubble kids," and extensive test-preparation activities—than high-performing, low-income schools. In contrast, school leaders in high-performing schools responded to high-stakes assessment by focusing attention on long-term improvement in all curricular areas (rather than just tested subjects), encouraging teachers to participate in test preparation activities just prior to the tests rather than all year long, and leading teachers to be more reflective and purposeful about instructional change efforts than schools under threat of probation. This research helps us go beyond the platitude that school leaders are important for instructional reform. It helps begin to unpack the relationship between specific actions by school leaders and teacher learning and instructional change. (See Chapter 6 for more information on the role of the principal.)

How Features of the Policy Itself Matters for Teacher Response to Reading Policy

Finally, we consider factors shaping reading policy implementation that relate to the nature of the policy itself. While implementation researchers outside of education have placed a priority on understanding the role that the design of policy plays in implementation (Matland, 1995; Mazmanian & Sabatier, 1983; Pressman & Wildavsky, 1984), the nature of the policy has received less attention in educational research. Recent policy movements have used substantively different policy strategies for influencing teacher behavior, resulting in very different policy signals. Here, we summarize what we know about how those policy strategies matter for teacher responses to reading policy.

Several studies provide evidence that the *degree of alignment* among the multiple reading initiatives that teachers experience affects implementation. These studies acknowledge the fact that teachers rarely experience a single policy initiative in isolation (Coburn, 2005a; Diamond, 2007; Kersten & Pardo, 2007). In the presence of multiple and at times conflicting reading policies, teachers tend to pick and choose which policy messages to be responsive to and which to ignore. In making these choices, teachers are more likely to respond to policy messages that are more consistent with their beliefs and prior practice. For example, Kersten (2006) documents how one experienced third-grade teacher enacted Reading First. Faced with a district curriculum guide that was not aligned with Reading First mandates, the teacher opted to be responsive to district policy when it was congruent with her prior practice. In this way, the presence of multiple and conflicting policies legitimized this teacher's lack of fidelity to some of Reading First's policy messages.

Second, there is some research on the degree to which reading initiatives include *capacity building elements* as part of their policy designs (Coburn, 2005a; Dutro, Fisk, Koch, Roop, & Wixson, 2002; McDonnell, 2004; Stein & D'Amico, 2002). These studies suggest that opportunities for teachers to learn a reform's new instructional approaches are crucial if teachers are to implement substantive changes in their classroom practice. For example, in their study of New York City District 2's comprehensive literacy policy,

Stein and D'Amico (2002) provide evidence that teachers with higher levels of participation in the district professional development offerings had
deeper enactment of the balanced literacy program. More specifically, Stein
and D'Amico show that those teachers who had participated in the district's
extensive and high-quality professional development activities for multiple
years tended to have instruction that was both aligned with the policy and
of high quality. In contrast, those with more limited experience with professional development tended to have high alignment, but low-quality implementation. That is, while the teachers incorporated the various activities
associated with the balanced literacy approach in their classroom (high
alignment), they implemented them in ways that failed to reflect the underlying pedagogical principles that knit the activities together (low quality).
The implication is that participation in high-quality professional development over an extended period of time enabled teachers to move from more
superficial to more substantive enactment of policy.[3]

In spite of the fact that Reading First (U.S. Department of Education,
2002) and many other similar policies incorporate extensive-capacity building activities, few studies deal with the issue of how those activities influenced teachers' responses. Thus, although a few state evaluations of Reading First report data on teachers' and principals' satisfaction with coaching
or professional development (Haager, Dhar, Moulton, & McMillan, 2009;
Zigmond & Bean, 2006), none look at the relationship between the levels
and quality of capacity-building activities and changes in teachers' classroom practice.

Finally, our research (Coburn, 2004, 2005a; Coburn & Woulfin, under
review) provides evidence that the *degree of voluntariness* of policy influences how teachers respond to it. We distinguish between policy that uses
normative pressure, putting forth visions of high-quality instruction and
making arguments for why teachers *should* make changes in practice (e.g.,
standards) versus those that employ regulative pressures, which require
teachers to use particular instructional methods and materials, enforcing
this vision of instruction using rules, monitoring, and sanctioning (e.g.,
mandated curricula). For example, in the case of Reading First, teachers
received normative messages about how students should practice using
comprehension strategies, and those messages were rarely monitored. At
the same time, Reading First policy delivered regulative messages about the
particular assessments, such as Dynamic Indicators of Basic Early Literacy
Skills (DIBELS), that teachers were required to administer; state and district

---

[3]This finding should be viewed with caution, however, because, as Stein and D'Amico (2002)
note, they did not have longitudinal data for their study. Thus, they cannot say with certainty
that teachers who had implementation that was aligned and high quality moved on a developmental trajectory from superficial to more substantive implementation over time.

administrators monitored the results from those assessments to ensure compliance.

In an early study, Coburn found that the vast majority of policy messages that teachers encountered were normative rather than regulative (Coburn 2004, 2005a). Importantly, teachers were less likely to reject policy messages accompanied by regulative pressure than those accompanied by normative pressure. However, at the same time, they were also less likely to incorporate them into their classroom in substantive ways than those with normative pressure. This shows that normative and regulative policy messages guide implementation in different ways and highlights how classroom practice is shaped by different types of policy signals.

Taken together, this research suggests that policy reaches into schools and shapes teachers' classroom practice in multiple ways. Researchers are beginning to pay attention to the numerous factors that influence implementation and explain the variability of policy responses. This work suggests that teachers' response to new policy is influenced by individual factors, social and organizational conditions, and the nature of the policy itself. This understanding is useful because it provides insight into the points of leverage for supporting and fostering classroom change. This knowledge can inform literacy leaders as they think strategically about how to implement new instructional approaches in schools.

READING TEAMWORK: THE CASE OF FOURTH-GRADE TEACHERS

Taking into account the research on the individual, social, and policy factors influencing how teachers respond to reading policy discussed above, consider how literacy leaders could help resolve the issues in the case example below.

CASE EXAMPLE

Lincoln Elementary is a school in West District. At the beginning of this school year, West District launched a new approach to reading instruction in which teachers were to conduct focused minilessons on reading strategies and students would engage in independent reading. Most teachers attended a district-sponsored training, and the district provided all teachers with new instructional materials related to the new approach. At Lincoln Elementary, grade-level teams meet twice a month, with the expectation that teachers will collaborate to strengthen literacy instruction. At some meetings, the literacy coach serves as a facilitator, brings resources, or gathers data from teachers. Occasionally, the principal sits in on these meetings.

There are three teachers on Lincoln's fourth-grade team. Two of these teachers, Kathleen and Mike, have each taught at Lincoln for about 10 years, whereas Theresa, the third teacher on the team, is a second-year teacher at the school. Kathleen and Mike have doubts about the new reading program. They are skeptical that students can sustain independent reading. They also believe that they should continue to use whole-class instruction. In contrast, Theresa has noticed that her students enjoy the new structure for the reading block but she has questions too. She is confused about the purpose of the program's reading lessons and has problems managing her students' independent work.

During their grade-level meetings, the fourth-grade teachers tend to discuss aspects of supplementary programs, coordinate plans for field trips and holiday celebrations, or talk about the weaknesses of particular students. When the literacy coach, Ms. Tyler, attends these meetings, she asks teachers, "How's everything going with the new program?" Kathleen and Mike frequently respond by sharing complaints about the teachers' guides or assessments and Theresa often remains silent. However, Theresa does seek out the coach—before and after school—to ask questions about materials and management. Ms. Tyler has noticed that team members rarely talk about details of their classroom practice in these meetings and have not responded to the new reading program in deep ways. As a result, the coach and the school's principal have become increasingly concerned about how to motivate this grade-level team to implement the new approach to reading. What role can literacy leaders play in supporting these teachers in improving their reading instruction? How can literacy leaders respond to new policy messages and mandates to ensure that teacher responses promote student learning?

IMPLICATIONS FOR LITERACY LEADERS

Research on reading policy suggests that a complex web of factors influence why and how teachers respond to reading policy. These studies paint a portrait of individual teachers making decisions about their practice in ways that are guided by their history, existing knowledge and practice, but also influenced by the nature and quality of their interaction with their colleagues. The broader school and district context play a role as well, shaping teachers' access to some policy ideas and not others, creating opportunities for teachers to learn, and cultivating expectations for instruction that affect how teachers respond to new approaches and mandates concerning reading instruction. Furthermore, the nature of the policy matters for implementation because different kinds of policies work in different ways to influence classroom practice. Taken together, this research has a number of important implications for literacy leaders.

First, it suggests that school literacy leaders should receive substantive professional development associated with changes in instructional policy. Principals and literacy leaders would benefit from professional development on the content of the instructional policy. Much of the professional development for school and district leaders focuses on generic leadership practices, rather than the specifics of a new instructional approach. This may leave literacy leaders ill equipped to answer teachers' questions or make schoolwide decisions that support the implementation of new instructional approaches. Content-focused professional development for literacy leaders should begin with an exploration of the nature of reading and how students learn how to read, as well as an exploration of how the new instructional approach works to foster student learning. This approach enables literacy leaders to attend to deeper features of the policy and communicate content-specific messages about the policy to teachers. Principals and coaches could then provide instructional guidance for teachers that reflects knowledge about reading instruction in addition to the policy's principles.

Second, research on policy implementation reminds us of the importance of aligning reform initiatives. The enactment of instructional reform is influenced by the consistency of policy messages. It is challenging—and even downright frustrating—for teachers to cope with contradictory demands from policy and programs. Therefore, school leaders play an important role in making sure that initiatives are pointing in the same direction so that teachers can make sense of policy and work toward changing instruction. For this reason, literacy leaders should attend to the alignment of initiatives in their schools and consider how to chart a clearer path for instructional reform.

This research also suggests that before introducing a new reading policy, literacy leaders should evaluate and reflect on teachers' preexisting beliefs and practices. This approach will likely help leaders present policy in a way that is congruent with teachers' preexisting beliefs and practices. Familiarity with teachers' current ideas and approaches to reading instruction enables coaches to scaffold teachers' learning related to a new policy and help teachers make sense of the policy. For example, if literacy leaders are aware that most teachers in a district are highly reliant on a CRP, they could introduce a new reading policy by presenting how the new approach aligns with the CRP that teachers already feel is effective and useful. For this approach to work, it would be important for literacy leaders to have an in-depth understanding of what teachers think about the existing reading program, as well as how they are teaching reading in their classrooms. This approach could strengthen leaders' delivery of policy's ideas and expectations and, in turn, clarify teachers' understanding of what is expected by a policy or reform initiative.

Finally, this review of the research suggests that literacy leaders may gain leverage by using teachers' formal and informal interaction with their colleagues as a resource to promote teachers' understanding of a policy. To that end, leaders should consider how to structure teacher meetings so that policies are engaged with and talked about. When teachers are given opportunities to collectively interpret a new reading policy, it helps demystify the policy so it can be enacted in classrooms. For example, working together, teachers and the school's literacy coach could reflect upon a new reading language arts framework in their grade-level team meetings and analyze how the new framework differs from the current content and pedagogy of their literacy instruction. Furthermore, leaders can begin to identify and tap into teachers' informal networks. Teachers make sense of policy messages while interacting with their colleagues and professional associates in a variety of settings, not just grade-level meetings. Teachers' informal networks provide opportunities for deep, highly situated professional learning about reading policy and practice.

The implementation of reading policy is challenging. Research has begun to reveal factors that impact teachers' responses to policy. The implications of this research highlight the responsibility of literacy leaders to actively engage teachers on reading policy and provide them opportunities for substantive interaction with colleagues. Schoolwide systems that facilitate collaboration, such as professional learning communities and "open door" norms to deprivatize classroom practice, encourage teachers to respond to policy in significant, yet situated, ways. Working together to engage with reading policy, educators are better able to enact instructional reform to improve educational outcomes.

ENGAGEMENT ACTIVITIES

1. Think about the situation at Lincoln Elementary and discuss with your peers: If you were a literacy leader at Lincoln Elementary, how might you work with the fourth-grade team to support their learning in the direction of the curriculum? Why? What could help these teachers attend to the policy, learn about the deeper aspects of the new reading program, and share features of their instruction?

2. Draw a timeline of the approaches to literacy instruction that you and your school have encountered over the past several years.

3. How have your beliefs about reading instruction affected your responses to reading policy?

4. At your school site, how has teacher collaboration influenced the adoption of reading practices, methods, or materials?

5. Interview a school leader (e.g., a literacy coach, principal, teacher leader, or special educator) about the reading policies guiding reading instruction at a specific school. In what ways is reading instruction influenced by local, state, or national reading policy?

REFERENCES

Achinstein, B., & Ogawa, R. T. (2006). (In)fidelity: What the resistance of new teachers reveals about professional principles and prescriptive educational policies. *Harvard Educational Review, 76*(1), 30–63.

Anagnostopoulos, D., & Rutledge, S. A. (2007). Making sense of school sanctioning policies in urban high schools. *Teachers College Record, 109*(5), 1261–1302.

Booher-Jennings, J. (2005). Below the bubble: "Educational triage" and the Texas accountability system. *American Educational Research Journal, 42*(2), 231–268.

Coburn, C. E. (2001a). *Making sense of reading: Logics of reading in the institutional environment and the classroom.* Unpublished doctoral dissertation, Stanford University, California.

Coburn, C. E. (2001b). Collective sensemaking about reading: How teachers mediate reading policy in their professional communities. *Educational Evaluation and Policy Analysis, 23*(2), 145–170.

Coburn, C. E. (2004). Beyond decoupling: Rethinking the relationship between the institutional environment and the classroom. *Sociology of Education, 77*(3), 211–244.

Coburn, C. E. (2005a). The role of nonsystem actors in the relationship between policy and practice: The case of reading instruction in California. *Educational Evaluation and Policy Analysis, 27*(1), 23–52.

Coburn, C. E. (2005b). Shaping teacher sensemaking: School leaders and the enactment of reading policy. *Educational Policy, 19*(3), 476–509.

Coburn, C. E. (2006). Framing the problem of reading instruction: Using frame analysis to uncover the microprocesses of policy implementation. *American Educational Research Journal, 43*(3), 343–379.

Coburn, C. E., Pearson, P. D., & Woulfin, S. (2010). *Reading policy in an era of accountability.* In M. Kamil, P. D. Pearson, E. Moje, & P. Afflerbach (Eds.), *Handbook of reading research Volume IV.* Mahwah, NJ: Erlbaum.

Coburn, C. E., & Stein, M. K. (2006). Communities of practice theory and the role of teacher professional community in policy implementation. In M. I. Honig (Ed.), *Confronting complexity: Defining the field of education policy implementation.* Albany: State University of New York Press.

Coburn, C. E., & Woulfin, S. L. (under review). Reading coaches and the relationship between policy and practice in Reading First.

Diamond, J. B. (2007). Where the rubber meets the road: Rethinking the connection between high-stakes testing policy and classroom instruction. *Sociology of Education, 80*(4), 285–313.

Diamond, J. B., & Spillane, J. P. (2004). High-stakes accountability in urban elementary schools: Challenging or reproducing inequality? *Teachers College Record, 106*(6), 1145–1176.

Dutro, E., Fisk, M. C., Koch, R., Roop, L. J., & Wixson, K. K. (2002). When state policies meet local district contexts: Standards-based professional development as a means to individual agency and collective ownership. *Teachers College Record, 104*(4), 787–811.

Guthrie, J. (1990). [Special Issue]. *Educational evaluation and policy analysis, 12*(3), 233–353.

Haager, D., Dhar, R., Moulton, M., & McMillan, S. (2009). *The California Reading First year 7 evaluation report.* Morgan Hill, CA: Educational Data Systems.

Kersten, J. (2006). Hybridization, resistance, and compliance: Negotiating policies to support literacy achievement. *New Educator, 2*(2), 103–121.

Kersten, J., & Pardo, L. (2007). Finessing and hybridizing: Innovative literacy practices in Reading First classrooms. *Reading Teacher, 61*(2), 146–154.

Matland, R. E. (1995). Synthesizing the implementation literature: The ambiguity–conflict model of policy implementation. *Journal of Public Administration and Theory, 5*(2), 145–174.

Mazmanian, D., & Sabatier, P. A. (1983). *Implementation and public policy.* Glenview, IL: Scott, Foresman.

McDonnell, L. M. (2004). *Politics, persuasion, and educational testing.* Cambridge, MA: Harvard University Press.

Mintrop, H., & Trujillo, T. M. (2005). Corrective action in low performing schools: Lessons for NCLB implementation from first-generation accountability systems. *Education Policy Analysis Archives, 13*(48). Retrieved April 26, 2011, from *epaa.asu.edu/epaa/v13n48.*

No Child Left Behind (NCLB) Act of 2001, Pub. L. No. 107-110, § 115, Stat. 1425 (2002).

Pressman, J. L., & Wildavsky, A. (1984). *Implementation.* Berkeley: University of California Press.

Sloan, K. (2006). Teacher identity and agency in school worlds: Beyond an all-good/all-bad discourse on accountability-explicit curriculum policies. *Curriculum Inquiry, 36*(2), 119–152.

Smith, M. S. (2000). Balancing old and new: An experienced middle school teacher's learning in the context of mathematics instructional reform. *Elementary School Journal, 100*(4), 351–375.

Smith, M. S., & O'Day, J. (1990). Systemic school reform. *Journal of Education Policy, 5*(5), 233–267.

Spillane, J. P. (2000). Constructing ambitious pedagogy in the fifth grade: The mathematics and literacy divide. *Elementary School Journal, 100*(4), 307–330.

Spillane, J. P., & Jennings, N. E. (1997). Aligned instructional policy and ambitious pedagogy: Exploring instructional reform from the classroom perspective. *Teachers College Record, 98*(3), 449–481.

Spillane, J. P., Reiser, B. J., & Reimer, T. (2002). Policy implementation and cognition: Reframing and refocusing implementation research. *Review of Educational Research, 72*(3), 387–431.

Stein, M. K., & D'Amico, L. (2002). Inquiry at the crossroads of policy and learning: A study of a district-wide literacy initiative. *Teachers College Record, 104*(7), 1313–1344.

United States Department of Education. (2002). *Guidance for the Reading First Program.* Retrieved November 10, 2007, from *www.ed.gov/programs/readingfirst/guidance.pdf#search=%22reading%20first%20guidance%22.*

Valencia, S. W., & Wixson, K. K. (2001). Inside English/language arts standards: What's in a grade? *Reading Research Quarterly, 36*(2), 202–211.

Zigmond, N., & Bean, R. (2006). *External evaluation of Reading First in Pennsylvania: Annual report, project year 3: 2005–2006.* Pittsburgh, PA: University of Pittsburgh.

18

Schools as Places of Learning
The Powerful Role of Literacy Leaders

RITA M. BEAN
ALLISON SWAN DAGEN

Guiding Questions

- What evidence does research provide about the effectiveness of job-embedded experiences on teacher learning?

- In what ways can literacy leaders contribute to the establishment of schools as places of learning? How do these learning communities function and in what ways can they function effectively in schools?

- How can literacy leaders assess their schools' readiness for collaboration and what steps can be taken to develop an action plan for collaborative learning?

Although this is the final chapter of this book, it is also only the beginning for our readers who in their role as literacy leaders can put into practice what they have learned from the book's authors. Our message is clear—literacy leadership should be shared by many, and it functions most effectively in schools that promote, nurture, and develop a culture of collaboration. In this chapter, we start by presenting a brief case example highlighting a principal's experience implementing a new initiative. We discuss research related to the importance of professional development for enhancing teacher learning and then focus on the concept that effective schools develop collaborative learning communities. We close by providing an assessment tool and action plan that can help literacy leaders establish a collaborative culture emphasizing teacher learning as a key to student learning and achievement.

In the case below, we describe a situation that illustrates the challenges faced by one principal in a school that is just beginning a new initiative and some of his thoughts about the professional development needed to address these challenges. Specifically, Mr. Sanchez's top priority is helping teachers gain the knowledge they need to work within this new framework. At the same time, he understands that helping teachers understand the rationale for the initiative and getting them to "buy in" to the new framework are also keys to successful implementation. After reading the case, think about how you might address this situation; what are some possible options that Mr. Sanchez might consider?

CASE EXAMPLE

Mr. Sanchez knew that this school year would test him as a principal. Last year, his first year on the job at this school, he had attempted to support the faculty as they began to work within the newly proposed Response to Intervention framework for the school. This initiative resulted in some changes at the school. First, a literacy coach, also new to the school, was hired to assist teachers in making decisions about grouping, instructional materials, and approaches. Second, teachers were required to meet more often in grade-level teams to talk about assessment results and to use those results to make instructional decisions. Third, teachers were now asked to teach not only the students in their room but to then be responsible for a specific group of students during the intervention time (e.g., teach students identified as needing supplemental instruction). At the end of the year, he had asked teachers for comments about the framework, their reactions to it, successes, and challenges. In many ways, he was pleased. Most of the teachers indicated that they appreciated the attention to students and now had a better sense of what students knew, did not know, and how they could help them. However, they also raised four major concerns, or challenges. First, teachers at all grade levels indicated that they needed more information about various instructional approaches that could be used to differentiate instruction and how to manage the classroom when students were working in small groups. Second, teachers were somewhat negative about the data meetings, complaining that they were not very meaningful; often there were distractions and a few teachers tended to "control" the conversation. Third, although teachers indicated that they respected and valued the literacy coach, she "wasn't there when they needed her" and "was away from the building too often." Finally, at one grade level, three of the five teachers seemed unwilling (or unable?) to buy into the framework; they were negative in the meetings and often refused covertly to modify instruction as suggested. Mr. Sanchez realized that all of these issues needed to be addressed.

He thought of several options: Perhaps working with staff to improve their ability to work collaboratively would help; perhaps there was a need to address specific school goals, especially for literacy learning. He wasn't sure that teachers were all "on the same page." He also wondered whether he should hire a second literacy coach or was there another alternative? And what about bringing in an outside consultant to build teacher knowledge? He had read Jim Collins's book, *Good to Great* (2001), in which Collins proposes that in order for organizations to be great, they need to have "the right people on the bus, the wrong people off the bus, and the right people in the right seats" (p. 13). He wondered how he might handle the few "negative" teachers in the building: Should he assign one or more of them to a different grade level?

What are your thoughts about how Mr. Sanchez might address these issues? Do you agree with the options that he is proposing? Are there others?

WHAT WE KNOW ABOUT PROFESSIONAL DEVELOPMENT

Throughout the text, we emphasize the importance of teaching for improving student learning. In fact, as highlighted in the research, quality teaching is the single most important variable contributing to student learning (Darling-Hammond et al., 2009; Hanushek, 1992; Rivkin, Hanushek, & Kain, 2005). American citizens also recognize the importance of teacher quality; in a Gallup Poll (Bushaw & Lopez, 2010), improving teacher quality was identified as the top national education priority and respondents agreed that current and prospective teachers should be provided with professional development (PD) to help them do their jobs effectively. Research findings (Desimone, Porter, Garet, Yoon, & Birman, 2002; Garet, Porter, Desimone, Birman, & Yoon, 2001; Yoon, Duncan, Lee, Scarloss, & Shapley, 2007) also indicate the importance of PD as a means of improving teacher learning—and hence, quality teaching. So, what do we know about effective PD for teachers that will best help literacy leaders as they strive to improve instruction in the schools? How can schools contribute to the professional growth of teachers?

Status of Professional Development

Individual teachers often seek sources of learning, such as graduate work, personal reading of professional books, and attendance at workshops, and these activities are important for the professional growth of these individuals. Moreover, schools may, in fact, work with individual teachers to develop a targeted PD plan for that teacher. Although such a plan is essential, it is not sufficient (Hirsh, 2010). The focus in this book is on the collective PD offered in schools to build school capacity as a means of improving literacy instruction and student learning. Such efforts require team and schoolwide professional learning where teachers develop collective responsibility for ensuring "that all students have access to the best teaching in a grade level, subject matter, or entire school ... teachers can tap the internal expertise among their colleagues" (Hirsch, p. 5). For more information about various forms of PD, see Bean and Morewood (2011). According to Little (2001), in her study of schools involved in large-scale reform initiatives, she found "the most supportive learning environments for students" (p. 24) in schools where professional development was valued and supported, and conversely, when professional development was not an integral part of the school reform effort, found impoverished learning conditions for students. As stated by Bean, Swan, and Morris (2002) in their study of a PD effort, educators must recognize that for PD to be effective, the effort must be one that highlights transformation rather than tinkering.

Wei, Darling-Hammond, and Adamson (2010) conducted a large-scale study in which they summarized information from the schools and staffing surveys conducted by the federal government and compared those findings with data from other studies. They found that teachers valued ongoing PD and learning; that is, they found it to be useful for improving their instructional practices. Further, when such PD was of greater duration and intensity, teachers valued it even more. Researchers concluded from a number of studies that between 30 and 100 hours of PD annually was needed in order to have an impact on student learning. Yet, such a great number of hours is not the norm for most schools. Another reported finding was that two-thirds of the responding teachers indicated that they had some structured opportunities for collaborative planning in schools, which translated into 2.7 hours per week. However, less than half of the teachers who responded indicated that such work culminated in cooperative efforts that were effective. Wei et al. indicate that more information is needed about how collaborative time is used in schools, and that schools need support in how to guide such collaborative efforts. As reported by Wei et al., educators in other countries had much more opportunity to collaborate and plan together, "15 to 25 hours per week outside the classroom," (p. 23) than did teachers in the United States. Yet, according to the authors, 94% of the teachers in the United States indicated that collaborative work with colleagues would improve student achievement. Many teachers also indicated that they sought assistance from their peers as a means of improving their classroom practices.

The National Staff Development Council's (Learning Forward, 2010) new definition of PD provides important information to those involved and interested in developing, implementing, and evaluating PD in schools. They define PD as "a comprehensive, sustained, and intensive approach to improving teachers' and principals' effectiveness in raising student achievement" (p. 16). Below we summarize the essential elements of effective PD, using the following sources: American Education Research Association (AERA), 2005; Desimone, 2009; Learning Forward, 2010. Effective PD must:

- Focus on content
- Focus on student learning by analyzing student, teacher, and school needs
- Provide opportunity for collective responsibility with all involved in supporting effective teaching
- Occur on a regular basis and over time, providing for a cycle of improvement
- Provide for active learning that is appropriate for adults
- Provide support through coaching or other forms of support

What is obvious in this list of six essential elements is that PD must be authentic and focused on the goals and needs of students, teachers, and the school—content is important. Further, PD must be based on teacher inquiry and take place in a culture that embraces collaboration among a community of learners. For example, as suggested by Little (2001), learning occurs both "in and from practice" (p. 37). In other words, teachers can use student work samples and their own practices to think about or reflect on their practices: What is working, what is not working, why, and how can we improve what we are doing? Such inquiry can only occur when teachers work together to make decisions about curriculum, assessment, and instruction.

The chapters of this book provide information that can assist literacy leaders in thinking about the content of PD, the means of delivering that content, and the importance of developing a climate in which personnel feel valued and are willing to participate in discussions about how to improve student learning.

But again, the individual efforts of coaches, principals, and teacher leaders are effective only when they occur in a context that is receptive to these efforts to promote teacher learning. In the following section, we address the topic of schools as places where teachers work as members of a learning community (LC) and provide ideas about how schools can establish them. In this section, we also include comments from principals and literacy coaches who have used such a model of PD as a means of developing teacher learning. Their voices make clear the importance of sustained, collaborative efforts in which the contributions of each staff member is valued and respected.

SCHOOLS AS PLACES OF LEARNING

Although there is much written about the importance of schools as LCs, there is less clarity about what this means and less research about what it takes to make such efforts meaningful for teachers and students. In this text, we define LCs broadly: these are initiatives by schools for all staff members to work collaboratively as learners to achieve a common goal, that of improving student learning. As such, staff members are provided with the time, resources, and PD they need to function as members of that community. In other words, we believe that there are many different ways of organizing the school so that it functions effectively as a community or organization of learning and that an individual school must decide the specific journey it will take, and that journey will be dependent on the expertise, knowledge, and needs of the staff as well as those of students. Below, we discuss research and literature that helps to provide a foundation for those interested in LCs. The five essential characteristics of professional learning communities (PLCs) as identified by Vescio, Ross, and Adams (2008) provide some critical insights to school personnel involved in such efforts. These include (1) development of shared values and norms, (2) focus on student learning, (3) reflective dialogue among teachers, (4) making teaching public; and (5) collaboration among educators at the school. We expand on these in the implications section below.

Vescio et al. (2008) provides evidence, reviewing 11 published studies that support the view that when schools function as PLCs, there is a positive impact on teacher practices and student learning. They concluded that PLCs provide schools with a new and different way to think about PD for teachers that is based on an authentic need to know and where, through collaborative inquiry, teachers can explore ideas that will enable them to improve their own teaching and positively affect the learning of students they teach.

Likewise, Saunders, Goldenberg, and Gallimore (2009) studied two groups of schools. In the experimental schools, grade-level teams, led by a grade-level leader, were provided with time to meet as groups and given explicit protocols to address student learning. During the first 2 years, only principals were trained to facilitate the meetings that were led by the grade-level leader; however, after those 2 years, there was limited implementation and little gain in student achievement. This result was linked to many factors, including competing demands for principals' time and uncertainty of principals about how to lead the work. During the third year, the implementation approach changed: there was more on-site support, including additional meetings of principals with project advisors as a group and individually. Project advisors also attended the monthly grade-level meetings and provided a published manual of protocols. Moreover, there were institutes held for the principal and leadership teams. At the end of the 5-year period, Saunders et al. found that in schools where grade-level teams focused on improving student learning, there were significant effects on student learning. The findings indicate the need for (1) time for learning and transfer to practice, and (2) specific ideas and protocols that provide guidance about how to collaborate effectively.

But changing schools in ways that promote collaboration and the development of a community of learners is not easy. Wood (2007) describes her qualitative research study in which she analyzes one district's attempt, over a 2½-year period, to institute LCs in its schools as a means of improving achievement of students. The district was struggling with issues related to an achievement gap between middle class and poor children, increasing diversity, which necessitated understanding the need for culturally responsive instruction, and meeting accountability demands of state and federal governments. The superintendent decided to institute "a learning community structure designed to foreground, critique, build, and enhance practitioner expertise" (p. 701) as an alternative to traditional PD practices. Although there were many successes, with teachers in these LCs learning to analyze student work for decision making and critiquing their instructional practices, there were also many challenges. Wood describes the fragile nature of such a change initiative, especially early on, and concludes that there must be district support and leadership for such an initiative (e.g., maintaining a consistent message, giving autonomy and authority to participants, providing the necessary time and resources). Wood also highlights some of the difficulties faced by the district in this effort. One of these seemed to be the overemphasis on the *process* of community building rather than to inquiry aimed at improving instructional practices. In other words, leaders were taught how to facilitate the development of LCs through the use of various protocols, but less time was spent on why such communities might be important for improving student learning. Wood suggests that protocols must "become the tools for rather than the content of meetings" (p. 734). Another challenge faced by coaches and others was addressing the problems that occur when attempting to change the culture of the school and the resistance that seeks to maintain the status quo.

Implications for Practice

We summarize the evidence about LCs and their effectiveness and identify the following as important in establishing schools as places of learning:

- Communities of practice can be effective; however, there is the danger that too much time might be spent on process, which might lessen the effectiveness of such initiatives. In other words, helping teachers understand how to work together and build community is important, but at the same time such a focus should be accompanied by work-related opportunities, where teachers talk about their students, their practices, and assignments, and how working with others can facilitate student learning. Teachers value the opportunity to learn more about the subject they teach and how to teach that subject to students. As Fullan and Hargreaves (1996) indicate, interactions with others in schools must be authentic, not contrived.

• Instituting LCs takes time, commitment, and perseverance. The movement is neither a silver bullet nor a quick fix. Leadership for such effort should begin at the district level, if possible, and other initiatives or programs must be ones that are consistent with the LC effort—and indeed, facilitate the development of an LC. Teachers, unaccustomed to working in such an environment, must be helped to understand *why* such an initiative is important for student learning. And those who serve in a coaching or facilitator role must be provided with the staff development they need to understand their roles and responsibilities (e.g., facilitating inquiry, problem solving, assisting with data analysis).

• The principal is an essential member of the team. Principals must understand and support the initiative; moreover, they must work alongside teachers as a member of the community. Principals support the initiative by providing time, modifying schedules so that teachers can meet, recognizing and acknowledging others as leaders in the building, and providing the necessary resources (e.g., data, materials). Schools have generated various solutions for identifying time to meet: some have early release days for students, even 1 day a week; others hire substitutes who cover classes while teachers meet; and principals have developed schedules so that classes at a specific grade level are free at the same time, while their students are taught by special subject teachers (Bean & Morewood, 2011). In Carroll's (2007) study of coaching in Reading First, coaches indicated that they were successful only when the principal understood their role and responsibilities and supported them in their efforts. In Boxes 18.1–18.3, we share the voices of four principals whose schools exhibit characteristics of positive high-quality learning communities.

• There is no one approach to establishing a school as a place of learning. School personnel may use a variety of activities and resources that promote collaboration among its staff, although those activities must be ongoing and provide teachers with opportunities for in-depth learning related to improving their instructional practices. In Appendix 18.1, we provide a description of various activities that leaders may use to facilitate the development of an LC and provide examples of some additional resources.

BOX 18.1: Justin Aglio

Describe your school's approach to creating a collaborative learning community.

At Propel Montour Charter School (K–8), our goal for professional development is to create a sustainable learning environment that promotes leadership opportunities. Teachers receive ongoing embedded support in literacy and other components of a comprehensive reading program. Teachers are provided with *30 days* of professional development each school year. Teachers are also encouraged to observe other classrooms; they also attend and present at local, regional, and national conferences. Teachers, coaches, and administrators also use a digital Web-based collaboration site for ongoing support. Additionally, intense coaching is provided at all levels—central office to principals and coaches, principals to teachers, teachers to teachers, teachers to students, and students to students.

Our foundation for professional development is developed around (1) professional growth plans, (2) professional learning communities, and (3) powerful practices. Each teacher, working closely with the principal, creates a professional growth plan (PGP) focusing on student learning. These PGPs are personalized to the needs and learning styles of the teachers and include a goal, strategies, or objectives, a timeline and resources needed and an action plan for demonstrating progress.

Professional learning communities (PLCs) are composed of collaborative teams of teachers and administrators. Teams are developed specifically to meet the learning needs of teachers. Members work collaboratively to create an action plan with common goals, action steps, and measurable outcomes. Common goals are established by team members through data-informed problem solving and decision making. PLCs meet monthly to discuss action steps and record feedback to share their progress with other teams.

Finally, Propel has worked intensively to identify a set of six powerful practices (*www.propelschools.org/www/propelschools/site/hosting/temp/powerful_practices.htm*). This framework provides teachers with a common schoolwide language. Once a month, teachers meet as a staff to celebrate and showcase three powerful practices that they currently apply in their classrooms. For example, at a recent showcase, two teachers (science, resource teacher) working with the seventh and eighth grade modeled how they differentiate instruction using a co-teaching model. They provided specific instructional methods including flexible grouping, learning centers, and project-based learning, all with an intense focus on the learning needs of the students.

(continued)

Justin Aglio (*jaglio@propelschools.org*) is a principal at the Propel Montour Charter School. This K–8 charter school, one of six Propel schools, was established in 2007 and is located in Allegheny County, Pennsylvania, just outside of Pittsburgh. The school's 400 students come from multiple school districts and their demographics are: 64% poverty, 43% minority, and 12% special needs. The Propel schools have recently been awarded a $3.4 million grant from the Department of Education that will be used to expand and open five additional Propel schools.

BOX 18.2: Jane Wildesen

Describe what you do, as principal, to promote a learning community in your school.

Developing or transforming a school into a place where all teachers embrace the notion of a learning community is a challenge—yet I believe one that a school's principal must assume. To create this type of environment, the first thing that comes to my mind is that every person is treated with the utmost respect. As the school leader of Southern Middle School, I always try to put my faculty and staff in professional situations that will bring out one's positive side. I recognize the talents or strengths in the teachers, and then include them in leadership tasks outside of the classroom where they can be the most successful, such as an instructional leader, professional development, grant writing, or professional collaboration with peers. I never ask a staff member to do anything that I wouldn't be willing to do myself.

Also, I think it is important to provide opportunities for teachers to work together—in and out of school. For example, at the beginning of each school year, 1 of our 4 staff development days starts off at a location outside of the school setting. We start the day with team building exercises, reconnecting with each other, and laughter! In the afternoon, as a group, we reconnect with nature by rafting, climbing, mountain biking, and rappelling! In school, our master schedule has been developed for our faculty to have common grade-level team planning times in which teachers have opportunities to collaborate by developing formative assessments, analyzing students' results, and crafting a plan to modify instruction.

Finally, I know that in order for our students to be successful academically, all stakeholders have to value education and have a voice in the process. At Southern Middle School, faculty and staff serve as members on our school improvement plan. I feel that each member of the school has to be empowered to make instructional decisions. Each teacher, instructional assistant, secretary, and administrator has to choose one of the school's comprehensive instruction plan's focus areas: needs assessment, strategies, or evaluation. Once members choose their focus group, they work together to develop how the instructional plan can be incorporated in the classrooms. For instance, when we didn't make Adequate Yearly Progress (AYP), I didn't want it to be an eighth-grade special education problem, I wanted the school to pull together and increase reading success—schoolwide. Every teacher, assistant, secretary, assistant principal, and principal is expected to reinforce a monthly skill with our students. Now when students are referred to my office for a class disruption, I'll discuss how they are doing in school and then I will ask them about what it means to "infer," which is this month's skill.

As a school leader, I hope teachers view the learning, collaboration, and leadership opportunities at Southern Middle School as being very empowering, whether the responsibilities they assume are formal or informal.

Jane Wildesen (*jwildesen@GA.K12.MD.US*) is the principal at Southern Middle School located in Garrett County, Maryland. The school serves 539 students in grades 6–8. The school demographics are: 49% poverty and 38% special education. Recently, the school partnered with an Adventure Sports Center to infuse experiential education and outdoor recreation enrichment at Southern Middle School. The underlying goal of this program is to reconnect children with nature by increasing their environmental awareness and outdoor recreation experiences such as rafting, climbing, biking, and hiking. By implementing this incentive program at the middle school, we have significantly decreased the overall number of office referrals, detentions, and suspensions, and have increased students' attendance.

BOX 18.3. Holly M. Kleppner

Describe an example of how your school has functioned as a learning community.

At Musselman High School, collaboration and communication among staff members is key to the instructional development and success of our students. Even if our master schedule does not allow regular collaboration time for our teachers, it is important that teachers find a common ground from which to discuss their instructional practices. Our teachers have always been creative in finding this time, but after seeing the benefits of student success because of scheduled collaboration, our school made the decision to create a professional learning community (PLC) focusing on the needs of incoming freshmen students.

For several years, it has been noted that our freshmen seem to be thrown into the high school experience where responsibility and expectations are much greater than anticipated. Teachers from the core areas of math, science, English, and social studies agreed to work together to create a framework for a collaborative learning environment for all freshmen students. The goal of PLC was to determine a strategic plan for a successful transition of our

(*continued*)

freshmen—from middle to high school—and give them the extra support they need for a successful start to their high school career.

For 2 years these teachers and I participated in an ongoing, long-term PLC. Studying research and book study meetings were the focus of the group's work. As a group we first read *Getting Started: Reculturing Schools to Become Professional Learning Communities* by Eaker, DuFour, and DuFour (2002). In addition to a small handful of release days where we met as a group, the teachers communicated their ideas by texting and e-mailing each other and by meeting over *working lunches*.

The plan for the incoming freshmen class of 2011 included action plans for common note-taking skills, homework policies, and classroom management expectations. Next year we will continue to meet and also invite other teachers to participate in this group. Additionally, beginning with the next academic year, daily collaboration time has been built into the master schedule for all teachers involved, with additional planning time for English and social studies teachers and math and science teachers to work together.

Holly M. Kleppner (*hkleppne@access.k12.wv.us*) is the assistant principal at Musselman High School located in Berkeley County, West Virginia. The school serves 1,600 students in grades 9–12. The school's student population is at the 33% poverty rate. Musselman is unique in that every freshman takes algebra I or higher with an added support class if needed. Also, a young adult fiction class is offered as an elective for freshmen who are below grade level in reading.

ACTION PLANNING:
DEVELOPING A PROFESSIONAL
DEVELOPMENT PLAN THAT WORKS

Before moving forward with any plan for PD, it is important to use some sort of needs assessment that informs future direction and activities. Bean and Morewood (2011) developed an inventory that faculty can complete and use as a basis for discussion (Figure 18.1) about PD in a school. This rating instrument focuses on five focus areas: content, collaboration, time, active learning, and application and feedback. Although our focus in this chapter has been on the importance of collaboration as a means of developing teacher learning, each of the other focus areas is an important aspect of building an LC: the importance of a long-term commitment (time); a respect for the adult learner and active engagement in the learning process; ongoing support for teachers through coaching, resources, and so on; and a focus on content (what do teachers need to know and be able to do in a specific content area). By taking an introspective look at the existing PD practices

FIGURE 18.1. Rubric to assess professional development program to promote school literacy learning. From Bean and Morewood (2011). Copyright The Guilford Press. Reprinted with permission of The Guilford Press.

Rating Scale: To what extent is there evidence that the school addresses each of the items in the rubric?

3	Great extent
2	Some extent
1	Little extent
0	Not present

Content

Score	Description
	School has a coherent set of literacy goals and standards across grade levels that can be used as a framework to guide PD. Standards for literacy performance at each grade level have been identified (e.g., what should students know and be able to do?).
	Curriculum and instructional practices are evidence based.
	Curriculum and instructional practices set high expectations for all students.
	Curriculum and instructional practices meet students' needs.
	Multiple sources of data are used to make decisions about curriculum and instructional practices.
	PD opportunities enable teachers to gain in-depth understanding of the theory and research underlying practices (why something is important).

_____ or _____/ 18 =_____%

Collaboration and Sense of Community in the School

Score	Description
	Teachers have decision-making role in what and how they learn.
	There is shared leadership among administrators and teachers when deciding what is necessary to achieve the goals set by the school.
	Teachers in the school are given opportunities to work together, interact, network, learn from each other in a collegial manner (in PLCs, grade-level meetings, study groups, professional development schools, etc.).
	There is a focus on the value of parents and their role as members of the community.
	Teachers are recognized for the work that they do.
	Teachers recognize the importance of ongoing professional learning.
	Teachers share leadership in planning and implementation of schoolwide PD.

_____ or _____/ 21 =_____%

(continued)

FIGURE 18.1. (*continued*)

Duration and Amount of Time

Score	Description
	PD programs are ongoing and give teachers opportunities to develop in-depth understanding of the content to be learned.
	Teachers have ample contact hours related to the professional development topic.

_____ or _____/ 6 =_____%

Active Learning

Score	Description
	School makes use of new technologies (e.g. blogs, wikis, podcasts, webinars, on-line course work, etc.) in helping teachers achieve their professional goals.
	Teachers use information from their classrooms and students in their professional development work, (e.g., they use data, review student work samples, do lesson study).
	Activities are differentiated according to teacher needs and styles of learning.
	Teachers have opportunities to participate in inquiry-based activities that require critical thinking, application, and reflection.
	Teachers have opportunities to practice what they are learning with their peers or in small groups.

_____ or _____/ 15 =_____%

Application and Feedback Opportunities

Score	Description
	Teachers have opportunities to apply what they are learning in their classrooms.
	Teachers interact and reflect with their peers about their experiences in a risk-free environment.
	Feedback is geared toward supporting and guiding teacher practices (it is not evaluative).
	Teachers are recognized for what they know and do.
	Teachers have opportunities to self-evaluate and reflect on their work (video, etc.)
	There are adequate personnel at the school to provide effective PD (literacy coaches, outside facilitators, university faculty. . . .)

_____ or _____/ 18 =_____%

in a school, literacy leaders and decision makers can craft a plan of action for change. Figure 18.2 provides a protocol that school leaders can use in discussions with staff members to talk about what they think needs to be done to build a culture of learners in the school, who will do what, resources needed, and a timeline.

CONCLUSION

Ensuring quality learning of students—and teachers—requires an all-school effort that is based on collaboration and shared leadership as a means of fostering collective responsibility among school personnel. Although PD in the past has been the source of criticism and seen as ineffective, results of

FIGURE 18.2. Action plan for developing a professional development program for improving school literacy learning. From Bean and Morewood (2011). Copyright The Guilford Press. Reprinted with permission of The Guilford Press.

	Score N %	Strength	Need	What should we do? In what order?	Who should do what? What Resources Needed?	When should we accomplish our goal?
Content						
Collaboration and Sense of Community in the School						
Duration and Amount of Time						
Active Learning						
Application and Feedback Opportunities						

research have helped educators understand the importance of job-embedded PD that builds school capacity and enables educators to provide the best education for all the students they serve. The greatest resource in schools is its educators; as such, they need opportunities to think, reflect, and learn as a means of helping them become effective professionals. Such learning opportunities should be focused on the ultimate goal of schooling, that of improving student learning. And such learning opportunities should occur in an environment that respects and values the contributions of each educator in the school. When school personnel recognize that professional learning is an integral part of every teaching day, they take the first step on the journey to becoming an LC.

ENGAGEMENT ACTIVITIES

1. Discuss the case example in this chapter with others. Decide what steps you might consider to address the challenge faced by Mr. Sanchez.

2. Think about a school with which you are familiar. What constraints exist in that school that would create challenges to creating an LC? What conditions exist that would facilitate the creation of an LC? In what ways has that school established the time for collaborative conversations and PD?

3. Think about the PD model/plan currently in place in your school district. Using Figure 18.1, survey a small group of colleagues and work through the five elements (content, collaboration, time, active learning, and application and feedback). Using the results and Figure 18.2, create an action plan focusing on one to two areas identified as the greatest needs at your school. Brainstorm possible solutions and ideas to overcome any obstacles to PD.

4. Read and compare. Read one of the sections below and compare the information provided in that chapter with the information in this chapter. Discuss similarities and differences.
    a. How similar are the views of the authors of Chapter 6 (Principals as Literacy Leaders) to those expressed in this chapter? Any differences?
    b. Read the section about PD in Chapter 15 (Technology in the Literacy Program, pp. 305–310). How similar are the views of those authors about professional development to the views expressed in this chapter? Any differences?

APPENDIX 18.1. ACTIVITIES FOR DEVELOPING LEARNING COMMUNITIES IN SCHOOLS

Below we provide examples of various activities that are effective in promoting collaborative work in schools. For each of the suggested activities, we provide a brief description and several resources that might be helpful to those interested in implementing them.

Study Groups

Over the last two decades, teacher study groups have become an emerging best practice for teacher PD. The purpose of teacher study groups is to provide a learning experience that is guided by teacher inquiry, choice, and ownership. At their core, "study groups read articles and books together and discuss the implications of the text's ideas" (Lambert, 2002, p. 38). When teachers have the opportunity to discuss, debate, and analyze facets of their teaching practices and beliefs—they grow in a variety of ways. Teachers who participate in teacher study groups voluntarily spend time together aimed at professional learning, share quality reading (fiction and nonfiction) with colleagues, model lifelong reading pleasure, explore their own literacy, gain experience and confidence with book discussion, and may transfer this new learning to the classroom.

Walpole and Beauchat (2008) discuss criteria for instituting study groups; they indicate that participants should have an opportunity to choose the subject or topic for study; that opportunities for making connections to classroom practice are essential, and that participation should be voluntary if the group meets after school hours. Allen (2006) describes how she successfully started a teacher study group at her school, in her first year as literacy leader. Her practical tips for a successful meeting include maintain a 1-hour time limit, meet in a relaxed environment, establish a consistent format, end on time, and embrace the "discovery through inquiry" (p. 55) model for teacher participants. Possible resources include:

> International Reading Association Essential Reading Collection (*www.reading.org/General/Publications/Books/EssentialReadings.aspx*)
> *Becoming a Literacy Leader* (Allen)

Teams of Learners (Grade Level, Academic Departments)

One of the most common and important means of building communities of learners is that of forming specific teams of teachers who have something in common: teaching the same grade or subject, or teaching the same students. Generally these teams are facilitated by one of the teacher leaders on the team or a literacy or instructional coach. The leader of the team must understand how to facilitate a group meeting, be an active listener, and encourage participation by all members. Leaders must also know how to help teams problem solve and address issues related to decision making. Leading a group takes much skill and patience. Kaner, Lind, Toldi, Fisk, and Berger (1996) talk about the fact that any group goes through a "groan zone" as it moves from divergent to convergent thinking! Leaders must recognize this time of potential conflict or they will become discouraged with what they see as the group's inability to work together effectively. Possible resources include:

> *The Reading Specialist: Leadership for the Classroom, School, and Community* (Bean, 2010)
>
> *Schools as Professional Learning Communities: Collaborative Activities and Strategies for Professional Development* (Roberts & Pruitt, 2003)
>
> *Revisiting Professional Learning Communities at Work: New Insights for Improving Schools* (DuFour, DuFour, & Eaker, 2008)

The following websites provide ideas for protocols that can be used by leaders to help groups learn to work more effectively:

> National Staff Development Council (*www.learningforward.com*)
>
> Harmony Education Center (*www.harmonyschool.org/nsrf/default.html*)

Curriculum Development

Teachers at specific grade levels, those who teach a specific subject (e.g., 10th-grade literature), or those at a specific school can meet to set learning goals and to develop or select curriculum and evaluative tools to measure accomplishment of the goals. These are often temporary committees or teams that have a specific goal to achieve and are terminated when they achieve those goals. These task-oriented groups give teachers an opportunity to work together on an authentic task and to increase their learning as they address a particular issue or task. Possible resources include:

> *The Curriculum Mapping Planner: Templates, Tools, and Resources for Effective Professional Development* (Jacobs & Johnson, 2009)
>
> Common Core State Standards for English Language Arts and Literacy in History/Social, Science and Technical Subjects (2010)

Lesson Study

Stigler and Hiebert (1999) describe the notion of lesson study as a process for collaborative work by teachers to systematically study and improve their daily work. Essentially, a topic or instructional issue of importance is selected; teachers as a group plan a lesson and then one teacher volunteers to teach that lesson. Others can watch or the lesson can be videotaped. Teachers as a group discuss the lesson and its effect on student learning; the lesson is then revised and taught again, generally to another class. And the process begins again. (See *www.tc.edu/centers/ lessonstudy/lessonstudy.html* for additional information.) Variations to this concept can be made; for example, teachers might *select* rather than develop a specific lesson from the core reading program and then go through the described process. Such an approach allows teachers to reflect on the appropriateness of the lesson for the many students in the classroom who have different skills and needs. Another approach is to ask teachers to discuss the assignments they give to students as a means of facilitating learning. The following are examples of what three secondary social studies teachers might ask their students to do after reading a political cartoon: write a paragraph explaining the message of the cartoon; write a letter to the editor indicating their reaction to the political cartoon; or work with a partner to draw a cartoon that takes a view different from the one expressed in the original cartoon. Each of these assignments presents a different type of learning challenge for students. By sharing and comparing assignments, teachers can get a better sense of the variation in their expectations for students and discuss ways to improve the quality of those assignments. A possible resource includes:

> *Creating High-Quality Classroom Assignments* (Matsurmara, 2005).

Analyzing and Reflecting on Data

Although data analysis has become a common activity in many schools, too often once data are analyzed, little is done to modify or change instruction in the classrooms. Part of the problem lies in the process of looking at student data in a vacuum without analyzing other aspects of how the school functions. In other words, looking across student data, a teacher can determine an area of need for her third-grade students (e.g., student writing lacks organization); however, without resources in place (e.g., opportunities to develop his or her own background about the topic or access to a co-teacher or literacy coach to model lessons), teachers may be left wondering what to do with this information. Mokhtari, Rosemary, and Edwards (2007) address this dilemma and present a framework that literacy leaders can use in their schools called the Data Analysis Framework for Instructional Decision Making. The tool focuses on student performance data but also analyzes data on PD (e.g., How does the school literacy coach function?) and classroom instruction data (e.g., teacher lesson plans, student grouping) to provide an overall view for decision making. (See Chapters 11 and 14 for possible resources and recommendations on how to analyze student data and plan for instruction.)

Classroom Observations or Walkthroughs

One of the most useful ways of promoting a sense of community is to make teaching public. In other words, teachers observe one another to share their approaches to teaching and to learn from each other. Too often in a school, there is great variability in how teachers are implementing a particular innovation or approach (e.g., guided reading, discussion groups). By participating in peer observations, teachers can become familiar with how others view and implement these approaches and develop guidelines for how the approach can be implemented schoolwide to promote consistency for students. City, Elmore, Fiarman, and Teitel (2009) discuss a new form of professional learning known as instructional rounds networks. They contend that in most schools, individual teachers have a set way of teaching, and that what is needed in schools is shared practices. They promote instructional rounds as a means for school personnel to learn from each other, using a four-step process: "identifying a problem of practice, observing, debriefing, and focusing on the next level of work" (p. 6). Such rounds can help teachers develop a common language: What do we mean by active learning? Effective classroom management? And what is the evidence that we would consider for identifying such aspects in the classroom? In some schools, the peer observation process may be one that is developed collaboratively by the principal and the leadership team. In such cases, the purpose for the observations as well as the procedures for debriefing or giving feedback are developed.

Joyce and Showers (2002), in their recent work on peer coaching, no longer include the feedback component because too often such feedback was evaluative. In their description of peer coaching, they define the coach as the teacher who is teaching, and at the completion of the lesson, the observing teacher talks briefly with the other teacher about the lesson and then is expected to apply what has been learned in his or her own classroom. School leaders might also develop a protocol that could be used for the debriefing session with questions that can help guide the conversation. Classroom observations can be made by individual teachers or a small group of teachers. Likewise, groups of teachers may visit classrooms when there are no students present and look for indications in the physical environment that promote student learning. Possible resources include:

> *Using Classroom Walkthroughs to Improve Instruction* (Protheroe, 2009)
> *Instructional Rounds in Education: A Network Approach to Improving Teaching and Learning* (City et al., 2009)

Partnerships with External Resources

In the new definition of PD, Learning Forward, 2010 (formerly the National Staff Development Council) indicates that PD may be supported by external assistance. They acknowledge that educators within the school know best their needs and, at the same time, know when they can benefit from external guidance. In other words, goals must be set by the school, but there is acknowledgment that external resources may be important. A key component to these high-quality partnerships is shared collaboration and commitment for ongoing support. Some find that these partnerships are rewarding given that these associations sometimes take place outside of school or that teacher participation is more voluntary in nature. An example of high-quality school-based working partnership is the West Virginia University's (WVU) PK–20 Collaborative (*benedumcollaborative.wvu.edu*). This partnership, which began in the 1990s and was housed in WVU's College of Education and Human Resources, focuses on collaborating to improve student learning by promoting simultaneous renewal for all stakeholders (e.g., university, faculty, public school teacher, and administrators). University faculty essentially become members of the school teams working in a variety of capacities (e.g., Collaborative Faculty in Residence, action research mentor, professional development provider, and school liaison). Teachers from participating elementary, middle, and high schools work in varying roles with WVU (e.g., adjunct and clinical instructors). These boundary-spanning opportunities (Sandholtz & Finan, 1990; Stevens, 1999) allow stakeholders to experience different perspectives as they walk in each other's shoes. This partnership strengthens a deeper understanding of PK–20 education that is developed and maintained as a part of the ongoing PD for all who engage in this collaborative work.

Collaboration through Technology

Another sort of activity that can enhance collaboration with peers is engaging with electronic resources found on the Internet. Many professional organizations have created high-quality materials available at little or no cost to educators. The International Reading Association, National Council of Teachers of English, Public Broadcasting System, and Reading Rockets have all developed opportunities for teacher or groups of teachers to use technology resources (e.g., webinars, lesson plans, podcasts, list serves, and online courses) for ongoing teacher PD (see Chapter 15 for additional discussion on the use of technology for PD). Possible resources include:

> International Reading Association (*www.reading.org*)
> National Council of Teachers of Reading (*www.ncte.org*)
> Public Broadcasting System (*www.pbs.org*)
> Reading Rockets (*www.readingrockets.org*)

REFERENCES

Allen, J. (2006). *Becoming a literacy leader.* Portland, ME: Stenhouse.

American Education Research Association (AERA) (2005). *Research points. Teaching teachers: Professional development to improve student achievement* (Vol. 3, Issue 1). [Brochure]. Washington, DC: Author. Retrieved December 4, 2008, from *www.aera.net.*

Bean, R. M. (2010). *The reading specialist: Leadership for the classroom, school, and community* (2nd ed.). New York: Guilford Press.

Bean, R. M., & Morewood, A. L. (2011). Best practices in professional development for improving literacy instruction in schools. In L. M. Morrow & L. B. Gambrel (Eds.), *Best practices in literacy instruction* (4th ed., pp. 455–478), New York: Guilford Press.

Bean, R. M., Swan, A., & Morris, G. (2002). *Tinkering or transforming: A new paradigm for professional development for teachers of beginning reading.* (ERIC Document No. ED465983). Paper presented at Annual Meeting of the American Educational Research Association Meeting (New Orleans, 2002).

Bushaw, W. J., & Lopez, S. J. (2010, September). A time for change: The 42nd annual Phi Delta Kappa gallup poll of the public's attitudes toward the public schools. *Kappan*, 9–26.

Carroll, K. (2007). *Conversations with coaches: Their roles in Pennsylvania Reading First schools.* Unpublished doctoral dissertation, University of Pittsburgh.

City, E. A., Elmore, R. F., Fiarman, S. E., & Teitel, L. (2009). *Instructional rounds in education: A network approach to improving teaching and learning.* Cambridge, MA: Harvard Education Press.

Common Core State Standards for English Language Arts and Literacy in History/Social, Science and Technical Subjects. (2010). Retrieved January 14, 2011, from *www.corestandards.org/the-standards/english-language-arts-standards.*

Darling-Hammond, L., Chung Wei, R., Andree, A., Richardson, N., & Orphanos, S. (2009). *Professional learning in the learning profession: A status report on teacher development in the United States and abroad.* Palo Alto, CA: Stanford University.

Desimone, L. M. (2009). Improving impact studies of teachers' professional development: Toward better conceptualizations and measures. *Educational Researcher, 38*(3), pp. 181–199.

Desimone, L. M., Porter, A. C., Garet, M. Yoon, S. K., & Birman, B. F. (2002). Effects of professional development on teachers' instruction: Results from a three-year longitudinal study. *Educational Evaluation and Policy Analysis, 24*(2), 81–112.

DuFour, R., DuFour, R. B., & Eaker, R. (2008). *Revisiting professional learning communities at work: New insights for improving schools.* Bloomington, IL: Solution Tree.

Eaker, R., DuFour, R., & DuFour, R. (2002). *Getting started: Reculturing schools to become professional learning communities.* Bloomington, IN: Solution Tree Press.

Fullan, M., & Hargreaves, A. (1996). *What's worth fighting for in your school?* New York: Teachers College Press.

Garet, M. S., Porter, A. C., Desimone, L., Birman, B. F., & Yoon, S. K. (2001). What makes professional development effective? Results from a national sample of teachers. *American Educational Research Journal, 38*(4), 915–945.

Hanushek, E. A. (1992). The trade-off between child quantity and quality. *Journal of Political Economy, 100*(91), 84–117. Retrieved January 10, 2011, from *www.jstor.org.*

Hirsh, S. (2010, Fall). Teacher evaluation: An opportunity to leverage learning at all levels. *Learning System*, pp. 1, 4–5.

Jacobs, H. H., & Johnson, A. (2009). *The curriculum mapping planner: Templates, tools, and resources for effective professional development.* Alexandria, VA: Association for Supervision and Curriculum Development.

Joyce, B., & Showers, B. (2002). *Student achievement through staff development* (3rd ed.). Alexandria, VA: Association for Supervision and Curriculum Development.

Kaner, S., Lind, L., Toldi, C., Fisk, S., & Berger, D. (1996). *Facilitator's guide to participatory decision-making.* Philadelphia: New Society.

Lambert, L. (2002). A framework for shared leadership. *Educational Leadership, 59*(8), 37–40.

Learning Forward. (2010, December). Key points in Learning Forward's definition of professional development. *Journal of Staff Development, 31*(6), 16–17.

Little, J. W. (2001). Professional development in pursuit of school reform. In A. Lieberman & L. Miller (Eds.), *Teachers caught in the action: Professional development that matters* (pp. 23–44). New York: Teachers College Press.

Matsumara, L. (2005). *Creating high-quality classroom assignments.* Lanham, MD: Scarecrow Education.

Mokhtari, K., Rosemary, C., & Edwards, P. (2007). Making instructional decisions based on data: What, how, and why? *Reading Teacher, 61*(4), pp. 354–359.

Protheroe, N. (March/April 2009). Using classroom walkthroughs to improve instruction. *Principal, 88*(4), 30–34.

Rivkin, S. G., Hanushek, E. A., & Kain, J. F. (2005). Teachers, schools and academic achievement. *Econometrica, 73*(2), 417–458.

Roberts, S. M., & Pruitt, E. Z. (2003). *Schools as professional learning communities: Collaborative activities and strategies for professional development.* Thousand Oaks, CA: Corwin Press.

Saunders, W. M., Goldenberg, C. N., & Gallimore, R. (2009). Classroom learning: A prospective, quasi-experimental study of Title I schools. *American Education Research Journal, 46*(4), 1006–1033.

Sandholtz, J., & Finan, E. (1990). Blurring the boundaries to promote school/university partnerships. *Journal of Teacher Education, 49*(1), 13–25.

Stevens, D. D. (1999). The ideal, real, and surreal in school–university partnerships: Reflections of a boundary spanner. *Teaching and Teacher Education, 15,* 287–299.

Stigler, J. W., & Hiebert, J. (1999). *The teaching gap: Best ideas from the world's teachers for improving education in the classroom.* New York: Free Press.

Vescio, V., Ross, D., & Adams, A. (2008). A review of research on the impact of professional learning communities on teaching practice and student learning. *Teaching and Teacher Education, 24,* 80–91.

Walpole, S., & Beauchat, K. A. (2008). *Facilitating teacher study groups.* Denver, CO: Literacy Coaching Clearinghouse. Retrieved January 20, 2009, from *www.literacycoachingonline.org.*

Wei, R. C., Darling-Hammond, L., & Adamson, F. (2010). *Professional development in the United States: Trends and challenges.* Dallas: National Staff Development Council.

Wood, D. (2007). Teachers' learning communities: Catalyst for change or a new infrastructure for the status quo? *Teachers College Record, 109*(3), 699–739.

Yoon, K. S., Duncan, T., Lee, S. W., Scarloss, B., & Shapley, K. (2007). *Reviewing the evidence on how teacher professional development affects students' achievement* (Issues & Answers Report, REL 2007-NO. 033). Washington, DC: U.S. Department of Education, Institute of Education Sciences, National Center for Education Evaluation and Regional Assistance, Regional Educational Laboratory Southwest. Retrieved January 10, 2011, from *ies.ed.gov/ncess/edlabs*.

Index

Page numbers followed by an *f* or a *t* indicate figures or tables.